W9-BRI-952

THE PRINCETON REVIEW

ANATOMY COLORING WORKBOOK

BOOKS IN THE PRINCETON REVIEW SERIES

Cracking the ACT
Cracking the ACT with Sample Tests on CD-ROM
Cracking the CLEP (College-Level Examination Program)
Cracking the GED
Cracking the GMAT
Cracking the GMAT with Sample Tests on Computer Disk
Cracking the GRE
Cracking the GRE with Sample Tests on Computer Disk
Cracking the GRE Biology Subject Test
Cracking the GRE Literature in English Subject Test
Cracking the GRE Psychology Subject Test
Cracking the LSAT
Cracking the LSAT with Sample Tests on Computer Disk
Cracking the LSAT with Sample Tests on CD-ROM
Cracking the MAT (Miller Analogies Test)
Cracking the NCLEX-RN with Sample Tests on Computer Disk
Cracking the NCLEX-RN with Sample Tests on CD-ROM
Cracking the NTE with Audio CD-ROM
Cracking the SAT and PSAT
Cracking the SAT and PSAT with Sample Tests on Computer Disk
Cracking the SAT and PSAT with Sample Tests on CD-ROM
Cracking the SAT II: Biology Subject Test
Cracking the SAT II: Chemistry Subject Test
Cracking the SAT II: English Subject Tests
Cracking the SAT II: French Subject Test
Cracking the SAT II: History Subject Tests
Cracking the SAT II: Math Subject Tests
Cracking the SAT II: Physics Subject Test
Cracking the SAT II: Spanish Subject Test
Cracking the TOEFL with Audiocassette

Cracking the AP: Biology
Cracking the AP: Calculus
Cracking the AP: Chemistry
Cracking the AP: English Literature
Cracking the AP: U.S. History Exam

Flowers & Silver MCAT
Flowers Annotated MCAT
Flowers Annotated MCATs with Sample Tests on Computer Disk
Flowers Annotated MCATs with Sample Tests on CD-ROM

Culturescope Grade School Edition
Culturescope High School Edition
Culturescope College Edition

LSAT/GRE Analytic Workout
SAT Math Workout
SAT Verbal Workout

All U Can Eat
Don't Be a Chump!
How to Survive Without Your Parents' Money
Speak Now!
Trashproof Resumes

Biology Smart
Grammar Smart
Math Smart
Reading Smart
Study Smart
Word Smart: Building an Educated Vocabulary
Word Smart II: How to Build a More Educated Vocabulary
Word Smart Executive
Word Smart Genius
Writing Smart

American History Smart Junior
Astronomy Smart Junior
Geography Smart Junior
Grammar Smart Junior
Math Smart Junior
Word Smart Junior
Writing Smart Junior

Business School Companion
College Companion
Law School Companion
Medical School Companion

Student Advantage Guide to College Admissions
Student Advantage Guide to the Best 310 Colleges
Student Advantage Guide to America's Top Internships
Student Advantage Guide to Business Schools
Student Advantage Guide to Law Schools
Student Advantage Guide to Medical Schools
Student Advantage Guide to Paying for College
Student Advantage Guide to Summer
Student Advantage Guide to the Best Graduate Programs: Engineering
Student Advantage Guide to the Best Graduate Programs: Humanaties
    and Social Sciences
Student Advantage Guide to the Best Graduate Programs: Physical
    and Biological Sciences
Student Advantage Guide to Visiting College Campuses
Student Advantage Guide: Help Yourself
Student Advantage Guide: The Complete Book of Colleges
Student Advantage Guide: The Internship Bible
Hillel Guide to Jewish Life on Campus
International Students' Guide to the United States
The Princeton Review Guide to Your Career

Also available on cassette from Living Language
Grammar Smart
Word Smart
Word Smart II

THE PRINCETON REVIEW

ANATOMY COLORING WORKBOOK

by I. Edward Alcamo, Ph.D.
State University of New York

Illustrations by John Bergdahl

Random House, Inc.
New York 1997
http://www.randomhouse.com

Princeton Review Publishing, L.L.C.
2315 Broadway
New York, NY 10024
E-mail: info@review.com

Copyright © 1997 by Princeton Review Publishing, L.L.C.

All rights reserved under International and Pan-American Copyright Conventions. Published in the United States by Random House, Inc., New York, and simultaneously in Canada by Random House of Canada Limited, Toronto.

ISBN: 0-679-77849-7

Editor: Celeste Sollod
Designer: Kirsten Ulve
Production Editor: Bruno Blumenfeld
Manufactured in the United States of America on partially recycled paper

9 8 7 6 5

DEDICATION

To Barbara Dunleavy,
my colleague, coworker, and friend all these years

ACKNOWLEDGMENTS

A number of talented people contributed their expertise to this project and I am pleased to extend my gratitude to them. Evan Schnittman conceived the project and took on various roles as supervising editor, drill sergeant, taskmaster, and make-it-happen person. Meher Khambata coordinated the production phase with skill and efficiency. John Bergdahl used his considerable talents to create the artwork that is the body of this book, and Kirsten Ulve and Bruno Blumenfeld led a hardworking production crew. It's great to work with people who know how to get the job done.

My children Michael Christopher, Elizabeth Ann, and Patricia Joy continue to add meaning to my life and share their love with me. Michael is a corporate attorney in New York City; Elizabeth is completing her doctorate in biochemical genetics at MIT; and Patricia is enjoying a successful career as a businesswoman. Since my dear wife passed away some years ago, we four have struck a bond of friendship that I never believed a parent could enjoy with his children. We continue to strengthen that bond as each day goes by. My love for them is deep and enduring.

I am also deeply indebted to Barbara Dunleavy. Though not an anatomist, Barbara managed to understand my scientific gibberish and prepare the text manuscript. Barbara's vocabulary does not include the word "mistake," nor does she know the meaning of the word "late." When confronted with a seemingly impossible schedule, she responds with a smile and a confident "No problem." I have now done a dozen books with Barbara, and each time I've marveled at her work ethic and talent. In all those cases, I've dedicated the book to someone else. But not this time. "Barbara, thanks for all the years of hard work and devotion. It gives me great pleasure to dedicate this book to you."

PREFACE

I hear, and I forget
I see, and I remember
I do, and I understand.

Classroom learning can be a drag. You sit there while the instructor drones on about seemingly useless information. You watch the clock and plan the upcoming weekend's activities or dream about last weekend's. You think, "Will this class ever end?"

Sound familiar? All too often, education has come down to a collection of facts and processes communicated from instructor to student. But it doesn't have to be that way. Learning can be enjoyable, informative, and rewarding. And that's what the Anatomy Coloring Workbook is all about!

The Anatomy Coloring Workbook engages you in the learning process. No longer are you a passive recipient of information. With this book, you become an active learner and contributor. No longer is the author the "sage on the stage." Rather, he is the "guide on the side." Together with the author, you enter an ongoing dialogue and discover the principles, processes, and relationships of human anatomy.

In this book, you will put your senses to work—you will see, touch, feel, and experience human anatomy as you learn. The traditional textbook points out the important features of a diagram, then moves on quickly. Here we usher you through the diagram and ask you to color the structures as you locate and identify them. Instantly, you begin to see the fruits of your work—a strikingly colored diagram begins to emerge.

What does coloring accomplish? Coloring gives you immediate feedback because you can see how the structures relate to one another. Coloring gives you gratification because you have something to show for your time and energy. And coloring gives you satisfaction because you have prepared a valuable learning tool. Indeed, when it comes time to study for an exam, you have an amazing review guide not found in any book. It is your creation.

And we haven't left anything out. The Anatomy Coloring Workbook conforms to the standard textbooks of anatomy and physiology used in health and allied health curricula. Whether your instructor uses the text by Smith, Jones, or anyone else, the anatomy will apply. Even the sequence of topics conforms to the standard texts. You should know, however, that each plate stands alone, so there is tremendous flexibility in the sequence. If you'd like to start with the digestive system instead of the cell, it's fine with us.

Will you need a book like this for your course in anatomy? We think so, because anatomy and physiology courses have worked their way into so many different curricula. If you're studying premed or nursing, you'll have to take "A and P." The same holds true if you are preparing for a career in health administration, medical technology, dental hygiene, psychology, art, fitness education, or nutrition. And high school students will find an understanding of anatomy very helpful in their biology classes.

Which brings up another point. You may be preparing for board exams, professional school admissions exams, licensing exams, alternative college-credit exams, and so forth. Indeed there are many self-directed courses of study now being offered. What better way to learn on your own than by using a valuable study tool you have prepared yourself?

Coloring is a great way of fixing an important concept in your mind. You pay close attention to the topic at hand, select matching and contrasting colors, and spend a reasonably extended period of time on the job. Your mind follows your hand, as your understanding of the concept solidifies. All your senses are at work. The knowledge you develop is not about to disappear, as it does when you look at a labeled diagram.

Coloring also fosters cooperative learning. You and your colleagues can work together to figure out innovative ways of using colors to identify important structures. Instructors can encourage inventiveness in students. And parents have a learning activity they can enjoy together with their children.

In most textbooks, the writing is "star" and the diagrams take second place. We've reversed that approach and made the diagram the central focus of the learning process. When you were a child, you learned by coloring in a coloring book. Here we've created diagrams of human anatomy in a more adult mode while retaining the coloring theme. Once again in your life, you are being asked to learn by coloring. We think you'll find that it's still the best way to learn.

Now it's your turn. I would enjoy hearing from you and knowing how well this book is working for you. Next year, we'll be doing a new edition and your input will be very helpful. Please let me know if the book is lacking or inaccurate in any way. I can be reached at:

Department of Biology
State University of New York
Farmingdale, NY 11735

If you prefer to telephone, my number is (516) 420-2423. My E-mail address is alcamoie@snyfarva.cc.farmingdale.edu.
Please accept my best wishes for a successful experience in anatomy. And try to remember this strikingly simple thought: "Education is like soup. What you put into it is what you get out of it."

Yours sincerely,
E. Alcamo

SOME COLORING TIPS

This book contains 126 coloring plates, each consisting of text and directions on the left side and one or more easy-to-follow diagrams on the right side. As the text proceeds, the author takes you to a structure and asks that you locate and color it. As you become more involved in the diagram, you begin to see relationships and you realize that human anatomy can be learned quite easily.

To get the most out of this book, you should have between ten and twenty different colored pencils or felt-tipped pens (be careful of the pens, however, because they can be difficult to control and they may deposit too much ink). You should have some lighter and some darker colors to begin, and you can add to your collection as you go along. Try not to be intimidated by the diagram—just dive in and begin reading and coloring ("life is hard yard-by-yard; inch-by-inch it's a cinch"). You'll soon see the rewards of your work.

We've tried to simplify matters by leaving most choices up to you. There are no unusual symbols for you to remember, and many diagrams use arrows or brackets to point out parts or processes. The text will advise you of these as you move along. Also, we use capital or small letters on occasion when there is a logical reason to do so. In the end, we hope you will use the coloring process to construct your unique image of the human body.

TABLE OF CONTENTS

CHAPTER ONE

INTRODUCTION to ANATOMY

ANATOMICAL TERMINOLOGY

Anatomy is a broad field in which the structure of the body and its parts are studied. Anatomy can be macroscopic (visible structures) or microscopic (invisible structures). It can be regional, in which all structures of a body region are studied, or systemic, in which systems are studied. In this book we follow the systemic approach.

Anatomy has certain terminology essential to the discipline. In this plate we study terms having to do with body directions, cavities, and planes.

> This plate contains several diagrams. We examine body directions using a standing figure, body cavities using a sectioned view, and planes by making various cuts through the human brain. As you read about the terminology in the following paragraphs, color the titles in the titles list, then color the structure, bracket, or arrow in the plate. We will make certain recommendations as you proceed. Begin by coloring the main title Anatomical Terminology.

Anatomy is the study of body structures and their relationships to one another. Much of the terminology of anatomy is derived from Greek and Latin roots. An important anatomical concept is the **anatomical position (A)**. The figure of the body in the anatomical position should be colored with a pale or light color. The individual is standing with the legs together, feet flat on the floor, hands at the sides, and the arms facing forward. The descriptions in all plates of this book are given with the assumption that the body is in the anatomical position, unless otherwise noted. The anatomical right is at the visual left, and the anatomical left is at the visual right.

The **midline of the body (B)** is indicated by an arrow, which may be colored in a dark, bold color. The directional term **lateral (C)** means farther away from the midline, while the term **medial (D)** means closest to the midline. In the diagram, the arms are in the lateral position, while the nose is in the medial position.

The terms **proximal (E)** and **distal (F)** refer to structures relative to one another. Proximal indicates the direction toward the attachment of a limb to the trunk, while distal refers to the region farther away. Thus, the thigh is proximal to the foot, while the foot is distal to the thigh.

The **caudal (G)** and **cranial (H)** regions of the body are indicated on the plate. The box and bracket may be colored. Caudal refers to an area near the umbilical region, while cranial is at the head. Note the indication of superior, toward the head, and inferior, toward the feet. Also, note the posterior position, toward the back, and anterior position, close to the belly. The **dorsal surface (I)** of the palm is indicated, and the **palmar surface (J)** is also seen. At the feet, there is a **dorsal surface (I)** and a **plantar surface (K)**. The term ventral is sometimes used as an equivalent to anterior, while the term dorsal is used as an equivalent to posterior.

> We now examine the main body cavities and focus on the appropriate diagram in the plate. Continue reading the following text, and color the correct titles as they occur in the list. Then color the cavities in the section of the body. Medium colors are recommended here.

Many of the body organs are suspended in internal chambers known as cavities. The cavities provide cushions against shocks and allow body organs to assume various sizes and shapes.

The **dorsal cavity (L)**, is outlined by a bracket. It includes the **cranial cavity (L_1)** and the **spinal cavity (L_2)**, which houses the spinal cord. As the plate indicates, the cavities are continuous with one another.

The **ventral cavity (M)** is also indicated by a bracket. It contains the **thoracic cavity (M_1)**, which contains the lungs, major blood vessels, and other structures, and the **pericardial cavity (M_2),** which encloses the heart. These two cavities are separated from the abdominal cavity by the **diaphragm (a)**. This dome-shaped muscle is used in breathing.

Inferior to the diaphragm is the **abdominal cavity (M_3)**, where the stomach, liver, spleen, and intestines are found. The lower portion of the abdominal cavity is set apart as the **pelvic cavity (M_4)**, where the female reproductive organs, urinary bladder, and male ducts may be found. The pelvic and abdominal cavities are considered together as the **abdominopelvic cavity (M_5)**.

> In the final portion of this plate, we consider three planes used for sectioning a body organ or tissue. These slices through the three-dimensional object provide views of the organs from different perspectives. Many sectional diagrams are presented in this book.

A plane is an imaginary flat surface passing through the body or an organ, such as the brain as shown. One light color should be used to color the plane and shaded area, and a second light color should be used for the remaining area of each diagram. A **transverse plane (N_1)** is at right angles to the long axis of the organ. It divides the organ into superior and inferior sections, as shown. A **frontal plane (N_2)** extends from side to side and divides the organ into anterior and posterior portions, and a **sagittal plane (N_3)** divides the organ into left and right halves.

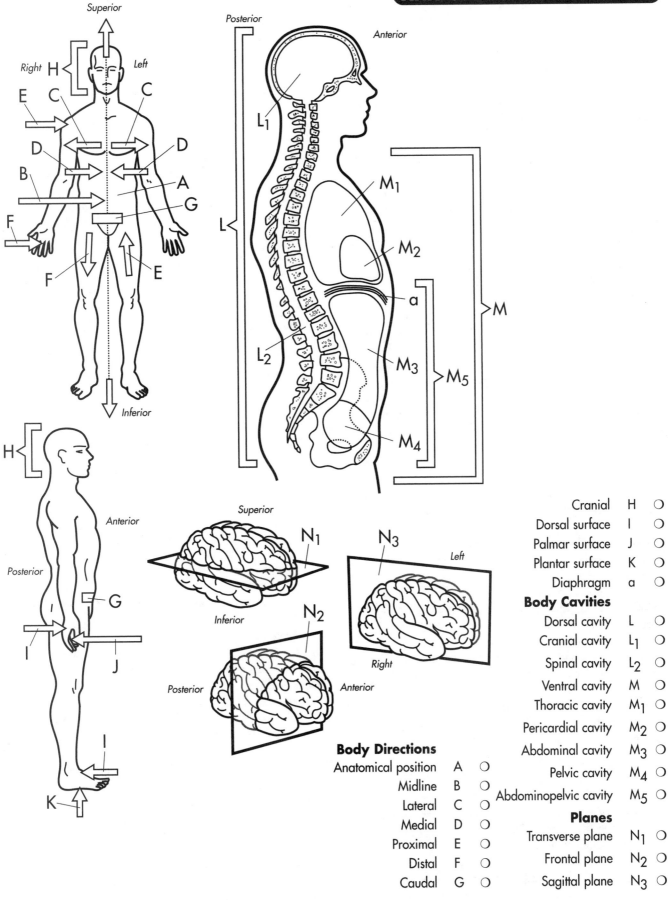

Body Directions

Anatomical position	A	○
Midline	B	○
Lateral	C	○
Medial	D	○
Proximal	E	○
Distal	F	○
Caudal	G	○

Cranial	H	○
Dorsal surface	I	○
Palmar surface	J	○
Plantar surface	K	○
Diaphragm	a	○

Body Cavities

Dorsal cavity	L	○
Cranial cavity	L_1	○
Spinal cavity	L_2	○
Ventral cavity	M	○
Thoracic cavity	M_1	○
Pericardial cavity	M_2	○
Abdominal cavity	M_3	○
Pelvic cavity	M_4	○
Abdominopelvic cavity	M_5	○

Planes

Transverse plane	N_1	○
Frontal plane	N_2	○
Sagittal plane	N_3	○

the CELL

The basic structure of all body systems, organs, and tissues is the cell. Muscles contract because their cells contract, and nerves transmit impulses when their nerve cells are sparked into action. The liver produces its important enzymes in its cells, and endocrine glands manufacture their hormones in endocrine cells.

> This plate examines some of the features of the "typical" cell as they relate to anatomy. The study of the cell prepares us for more detailed study of anatomical structures in the plates ahead.

This plate consists of a single diagram of a section of a cell. Under the light microscope the cell seems relatively simple, but the electron microscope reveals a wealth of structures that contribute to its activities. As you read about the structures in the following paragraphs, color their titles, then color the structures in the plate. Light colors are recommended because the structures tend to be small and their details should not be obscured.

A variety of cells exist in the human body, including the long, spindly muscle cell; the round red blood cell; the flagellated, motile sperm cell; and the oil-filled fat cell. It is impossible to locate a "typical" cell, but a composite cell is presented in this plate.

The cell is enclosed by a **cell membrane (A)**, which is composed of phospholipids and proteins. Various biochemical mechanisms permit small nutrients to pass across the membrane to the cell interior. A light color is recommended in the plate.

Within the cell membrane is the cytosol, also known as the **cytoplasm (B)**. This fluid portion of the cell distributes materials and is the center of metabolic activities. Enzymes and other proteins used by the body are produced within the cytosol.

The cytosol contains an internal protein framework called the **cytoskeleton (C)**, whose fibers are seen throughout the cytoplasm. Coloring over the fibers with a selected color will help highlight their presence. Microfilaments within the cytoskeleton provide the mechanism for contraction in muscles cells, and microtubules within the cytoskeleton function in replication.

Extending from the cell are a series of projections called **microvilli (D)**. These fingerlike projections are found in cells of the digestive tract, in which absorption takes place into the cells. Longer hairlike extensions called **cilia (E)** are found on the cells of the respiratory tract, where they trap dust particles and move the sticky mucus along to remove it from the respiratory surface.

> We now move to some of the submicroscopic structures within the cell and continue to relate them to functions of the cell. Continue coloring, as above, the titles in the list and the structures in the plate. Light colors are recommended, and "spots" of color may by used at times.

Within the cytoplasm, the cell contains a **centrosome (F)**. The centrosome contains two bodies called **centrioles (F_1)**. As the plate indicates, centrioles occur at right angles to one another and are composed of microtubules. They act during the movement of chromosomes when the cell divides.

Ribosomes (G) are seen at numerous locations within the cells. These ultramicroscopic bodies are the "workbenches" of the cells, where proteins are synthesized from amino acids. Ribosomes are especially important in cells that synthesize a lot of proteins such as pancreatic cells, muscle cells, and epidermal cells.

An important membranous organelle of the cytoplasm is the **mitochondrion (H)**. Membranes in the mitochondrion form chambers where the enzymes for energy production are located. High energy cells, such as muscle cells and sperm cells, contain many mitochondria, while fewer are found in cells that serve a protective function, such as epithelial cells.

The center of genetic activity of the cell is the **nucleus (I)**. With the exception of red blood cells and sex cells, all body cells have 46 chromosomes in the nucleus. A body of RNA called the **nucleolus (I_1)** is found in the nucleus suspended in the fluidlike **nucleoplasm (I_2)**. Genes within the nucleus specify the message for synthesizing proteins unique for the operation of different cells. For example, pancreatic cells produce insulin, while thyroid cells secrete thyroxin, both of which are proteins.

> We complete the plate by examining the last few cellular structures important to the activity of the cells. These structures are involved in protein synthesis, and the titles should be colored as they are encountered in the reading. Continue using light colors, as the structures are relatively small.

The internal network of membranes within the cytoplasm is the **endoplasmic reticulum (J)**, also called the ER. These membranes, seen in cross section, may or may not contain ribosomes. Where much protein synthesis is taking place, the ribosomes are associated with the ER and they form **rough ER (J_1)**. Where the endoplasmic reticulum has few or no ribosomes, it is known as **smooth ER (J_2)**. After the protein has been manufactured, it is generally stored in a series of flattened membranes called the **Golgi body (K)**. Products to be secreted, such as oil from the sebaceous glands, are also packaged in droplets here.

The cell maintains and stores digestive enzymes in an organelle called a **lysosome (L)**. Enzymes in the lysosome help break down large organic molecules into smaller ones useful to the cell in protein synthesis and metabolism. Enzymes are also stored in **peroxisomes (M)**. Toxic compounds are commonly neutralized by the peroxisome enzymes, which are abundant in liver cells.

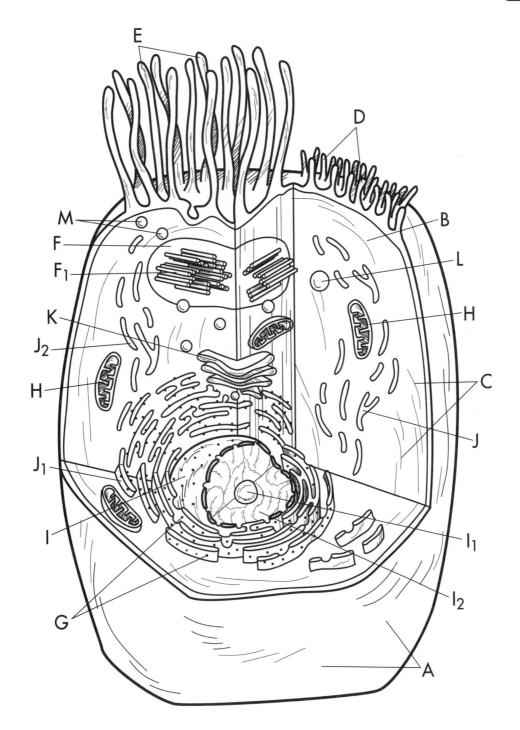

E

D

M

F

F₁

B

L

K

H

J₂

H

C

J

J₁

I

I₁

I₂

G

A

Cell membrane	A	○		Centrioles	F₁	○		Endoplasmic reticulum	J	○
Cytosol (Cytoplasm)	B	○		Ribosomes	G	○		Rough ER	J₁	○
Cytoskeleton	C	○		Mitochondrion	H	○		Smooth ER	J₂	○
Microvilli	D	○		Nucleus	I	○		Golgi body	K	○
Cilia	E	○		Nucleolus	I₁	○		Lysosome	L	○
Centrosome	F	○		Nucleoplasm	I₂	○		Peroxisome	M	○

EPITHELIAL TISSUES

Although there are trillions of cells in the body, there are only hundreds of different types of cells. The various cell types work together to form a tissue. A tissue is a collection of cells and their products organized to perform a certain function. The tissues then organize with one another to form the body organs.

Four types of tissue exist in the body. In this plate, we study the epithelial tissues, which are involved in support and protection for the body. In the next plate, the connective, muscle, and neural tissues are the topics of discussion. These tissues have more specialized functions.

Begin your work on the plate by coloring the main title Epithelial Tissues. Here, we present eight different types of epithelial tissues and point out their functions in the body. These tissues occur often in the organs, which are a collection of various types of tissues. As you read about the epithelial tissues in the following paragraphs, color the title, then color the appropriate diagram. If you wish, a dark spot of color may be used for the nucleus of the cells, but the cells themselves should be colored in a light color to preserve their structural detail.

Epithelial tissues protect the exposed portions of the body's organs and safeguard them from abrasion and injury. They are found at the surfaces of body organs. As such, they also control the passage of materials from the outside environment to the specialized body cells below, and many epithelial tissues contain sensory nerve fibers. The glands are special types of epithelial tissue as well.

The epithelial tissues are attached to a **basement membrane (A)**, which is shown in all eight diagrams. The same medium color should be used in each case. Closest to the epithelium, the basement membrane is called basal lamina, while further away it is called reticular lamina. These divisions are not shown in the plate but are offered for your information.

The first type of epithelial tissue we consider is simple **squamous epithelium (B)**. This single layer of flat cells lines the blood vessels, air sacs of the lung, and portions of the kidney. The nucleus is at the center of the cells, as the diagram shows. In the heart, it is called endothelium, while in the abdominal cavities it is called mesothelium.

The second type of epithelial tissue is **simple cuboidal epithelium (C)**. This single layer of cube-shaped cells is found in the kidney tubules and many excretory ducts of the glands. It secretes various substances and is used for protection.

Simple columnar epithelium (D) is the third type. This is a single layer of tall, cylindrical cells with the nuclei occurring at the base of the cells. The gastrointestinal tract contains this epithelium from the stomach to the anus. It is also found in the ducts of many glands.

The previous three types of epithelium all consisted of a single layer of cells. In the following epithelial tissues, we see layers or stratification of cells. Continue your coloring as before, and note the variations that occur within the diverse types of epithelium.

The next type of epithelium we consider is **pseudostratified columnar epithelium (E)**. In this tissue all the cells have contact with the basement membrane, so that layers do not truly occur. However, the tissue resembles layers seen in section, and the term pseudostratified is employed. The epithelium has cilia at its surfaces, indicated by the brush border in the diagram. A separate color may be used to indicate its presence. The nasal cavity, windpipe, and bronchi possess this epithelium.

True stratification is seen in **stratified squamous epithelium (F)**. This epithelium occurs where stress is severe such as in the lining of the mouth, esophagus, and at the terminal surface of the tongue. Protection is the main function of this epithelium.

Tall cells in layers constitute **stratified columnar epithelium (G)**. Found in portions of the pharynx and some excretory ducts, this type of epithelium is rare. It functions as a protective device.

Stratified cuboidal epithelium (H) consists of a layer of cube-shaped cells. This epithelium is also rare. It is found along the ducts of sweat glands in the skin and in certain ducts of the mammary glands. Like the other epithelial tissues, its function is to protect the underlying cells and tissues.

The final type of epithelium we consider is **transitional epithelium (I)**. As the plate shows, this type of epithelium contains a variety of cells ranging from squamous to cuboidal to columnar cells. The urinary bladder contains this type of epithelium at its surface. The epithelium stretches to permit distension of the urinary bladder when it fills with urine. After the urine is discharged, the transitional epithelium contracts and assumes a compacted appearance. Its distended appearance is shown here.

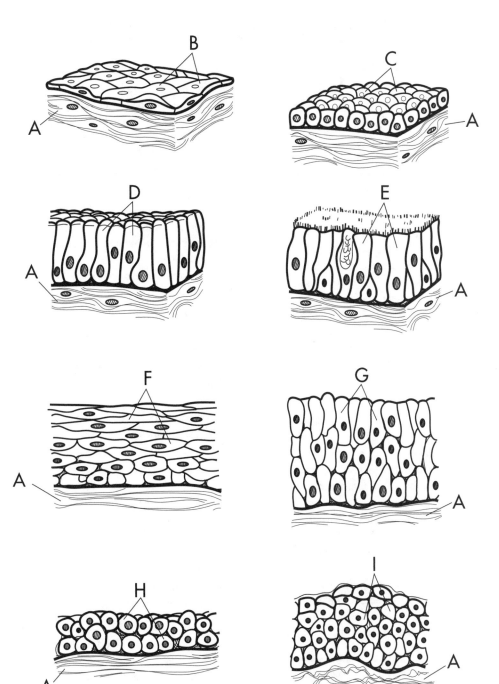

Basement membrane   A   ○

Simple squamous epithelium   B   ○

Simple cuboidal epithelium   C   ○

Simple columnar epithelium   D   ○

Pseudostratified columnar epithelium   E   ○

Stratified squamous epithelium   F   ○

Stratified columnar epithelium   G   ○

Stratified cuboidal epithelium   H   ○

Transitional epithelium   I   ○

CONNECTIVE, MUSCLE, and NEURAL TISSUES

The cells of the body are organized into functional collections called tissues. Of the hundreds of tissues, anatomists recognize four main types according to their structure and function. Epithelial tissues cover the body surfaces and are the topic of the previous plate. Connective, muscle, and nervous tissues are the topics of this plate.

This plate contains a representative view of some of the fibers and cells of the connective tissue. It also focuses briefly on some of the muscle and neural tissues to provide a comparison of all three types. As you read about the tissues in the following paragraphs, color the titles of the tissue components, then locate and color them in the plates. Because the first diagram is "busy," a series of light colors would be best. Begin by coloring the main title Connective, Muscle, and Neural Tissues.

Connective tissue is the most abundant and widely distributed tissue of the body. It includes bone, blood, cartilage, fat, and other tissue types that support, protect, and insulate the organs.

Connective tissue is composed of cells, fibers, and ground substance. The fibers and ground substance make up the noncellular matrix of the tissue. In the plate, **elastic fibers (A)** can be seen. These fibers form a network within the tissue as their fibers join one another. **Reticular fibers (B)** are thin fibers similar to the elastic fibers. They form a network (reticulum) around the muscle cells and provide support to the blood vessel walls.

The third fibers seen are **collagen fibers (C)**, composed mainly of the protein collagen. These protein fibers occur in different types and are tough, yet flexible. Lying parallel to one another, they provide great strength in the bone, tendon, and ligaments.

Next we examine the typical cells found in connective tissue. Remember that the diagram is not of one connective tissue, but a composite of several connective tissues intended to show variation among the fibers and cells. The next paragraphs discuss the cells of the connective tissues.

Various kinds of connective tissue contain **mesenchymal cells (D)**. These cells respond to the presence of pathogens by differentiating into other cells that produce antimicrobial substances. The mesenchymal cells also change into **fibroblasts (F)**, which assist the healing of wounds. Adipose connective tissue contains many **fat cells (E)**. These cells contain large droplets of oil or fat, and the nucleus is pushed over to one side, as the diagram shows.

One of the connective tissue cells that produces pigment is the melanocyte (G). Its brown pigment melanin colors the skin and the hair fibers. The **plasma cell (H)** is a cell that responds to pathogens by producing antibodies. **Mast cells (I)** are small, mobile cells containing granules, shown in the plate. Following injury the granules are released to dilate blood vessels to increase blood flow to the injured area.

Macrophages are involved in defense of the body tissues. The **wandering macrophage (J)** moves about through the tissues phagocytizing on bacteria and other pathogens. **Sessile macrophages (K)** remain in a localized area of the tissue. Also involved in defense is the **lymphocyte (L)**. This white blood cell is stimulated by foreign substances, whereupon it reverts to antibody-producing plasma cells. The diagram also shows several **red blood cells (M)** within a blood vessel.

In the next section, we briefly survey muscle tissues. These tissues permit movement in the body, and, as indicated, they occur in three types. Continue reading below, and color the types as you encounter them in the text.

Muscle tissue (N) consists of muscle cells bound together end to end to form long muscle fibers. A muscle fiber often contains several nuclei because it is composed of several cells. Three types of muscle tissue are recognized. The first type is **striated muscle (N_1)**, which is under voluntary control. The cells of this muscle tissue contain **nuclei (N_4)**, and they have bands known as **striations (N_5)**. The striations can be colored in darker tones. They represent areas where the cellular microfilaments overlap.

The second type of muscle tissue is **cardiac muscle (N_2)**, not under voluntary control. Note that these cells also have **nuclei (N_4)** and striations. Where striated muscle is found in the moving parts of the body such as the limbs, cardiac muscle is found only in the heart.

The final type of muscle tissue is **smooth muscle (N_3)**. This tissue contains cells with many **nuclei (N_4)**, but there are no striations. This is because there are fewer microfilaments in smooth muscle tissue. The muscle is found in the linings of the visceral organs such as the stomach and urinary bladder and in the linings of the blood vessels, where it provides support. The muscle is involuntary.

The last tissue considered in this plate is neural tissue. Neural tissue contains supportive cells called neuroglia and the impulse-transmitting cells called nerve cells or neurons. They are surveyed in the final paragraph.

The **nerve cell (O)** is uniquely adapted to generate and transmit impulses. It contains a **cell body (O_1)**, where the cytoplasm, nucleus, organelles, and other cell structures reside. It also contains a long extension called an **axon (O_2)**, which ends in numerous fibers. Nerve impulses travel down the axon away from the cell body. To reach the cell body, impulses arrive by means of treelike branches called **dendrites (O_3)**. Dendrites receive impulses from other nerve cells, transport them to the cell body for an appropriate interpretation, and continue them down the neural pathway.

Connective Tissue

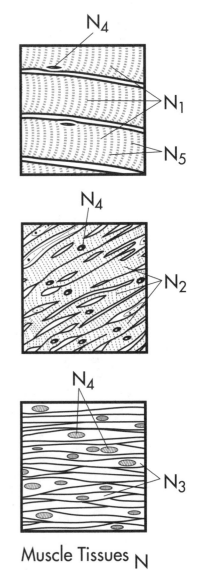

Muscle Tissues N

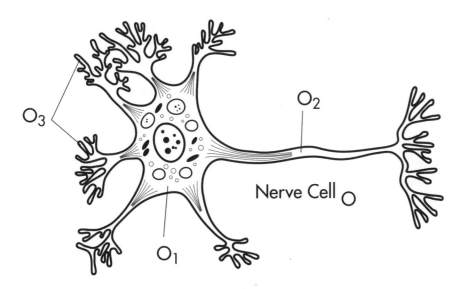

Nerve Cell O

Elastic fibers	A	○	Mast cell	I	○	Smooth muscle	N₃	○
Reticular fibers	B	○	Wandering macrophage	J	○	Nucleus	N₄	○
Collagen fibers	C	○	Sessile macrophage	K	○	Striations	N₅	○
Mesenchymal cell	D	○	Lymphocyte	L	○	Nerve cell	O	○
Fat cells	E	○	Red blood cells	M	○	Cell body	O₁	○
Fibroblast	F	○	Muscle tissue	N	○	Axon	O₂	○
Melanocyte	G	○	Striated muscle	N₁	○	Dendrites	O₃	○
Plasma cell	H	○	Cardiac muscle	N₂	○			

TYPES of EXOCRINE GLANDS

Many epithelial tissues are specialized to form glands. A gland is a series of cells specialized to synthesize and give off a product known as a secretion. The gland may be endocrine if the secretion is distributed directly into a blood vessel, or exocrine if the secretion enters a duct for delivery to a particular part of the body. Endocrine glands are called ductless glands and are the topic of the endocrine system discussed later in this book. Exocrine glands are far more numerous and are called ducted glands because of the tubes that direct the secretions away from the glands. Mucous, sweat, oil, and salivary glands are among the exocrine glands.

The exocrine glands are classified into structural and functional types, as we examine in this plate. Various functions are associated with the glands, as the plate will indicate.

Looking over the plate, note the structural and functional types of exocrine glands. In all cases there are ducts leading from the gland to the site where the secretion is delivered. As you read about the exocrine glands in the paragraphs that follow, color the appropriate titles and the glands in the plate. Begin your work by coloring the main title Types of Exocrine Glands.

There are several structural types of exocrine glands, including unicellular and multicellular glands. Here we concentrate on the diverse structures of the multicellular glands derived from the epithelium. These multicellular glands are subdivided as simple exocrine glands and compound exocrine glands.

Simple exocrine glands (A) include the **tubular glands (A$_1$)**. A light color may be used to highlight the cells of this gland. Intestinal glands secreting digestive juices are simple glands, as shown in the plate. **Coiled simple glands (A$_2$)** are typified by sweat glands. The cells occur in a coiled tube. A branched **simple exocrine gland (A$_3$)** has a single unbranched duct, even though the gland cells exist in branches. Mucous glands of the tongue and esophagus as well as the gastric glands of the stomach are of this type.

Simple alveolar glands (A$_4$) occur in flasklike sacs. They are not found in adults but are stages in the development of branched simple glands. **Branched alveolar glands (A$_5$)** have numerous sacs leading to the one major duct. The sebaceous (oil) glands are branched alveolar glands.

We now move our attention to the compound exocrine glands. These glands have branched ducts that come together to lead to the body surface. Three kinds of glands are recognized here. As before, color the gland cells to indicate their presence, and note their shape as distinctive structural types.

Various types of **compound exocrine glands (B)** are found in the body. For example, the **tubular compound gland (B$_1$)** is found in the testes of the male and the mucous glands of the mouth. It has many tubelike branches leading to the one major duct.

The **alveolar compound gland (B$_2$)** has numerous sacs distributed among its branches. The mammary glands are compound alveolar glands, which are known as acinar glands.

The final compound glands we consider are the **tubuloalveolar glands (B$_3$)**. A combination of tubes and saclike structures are found here. The salivary glands are examples of tubuloalveolar glands.

Glands derived from the epithelial tissue are also classified according to the way in which they function. Accordingly, there are three types of glands. To study these glands, continue your reading below and refer to the titles and types and diagrams of glands under functional types. Color the appropriate titles as you proceed.

The functional classification of exocrine glands is based on whether the secretion is a product of the gland cells or the secretory material includes the gland cells themselves. One type of gland is the **holocrine gland (C)**, and the bracket may be colored to indicate its presence. In this gland, we note a **discharged cell (C$_1$)**, which is a cell that has died and is being discharged with its contents as the secretion. The **developing cells (C$_2$)** are also seen. They will later become filled with secretions and discharged. Other developing cells of the gland may be colored in the same color as the bracket to distinguish them from the discharged cell. The sebaceous (oil) glands are holocrine glands.

The second functional type of exocrine gland is the **merocrine gland (D)**, indicated by the bracket. The merocrine gland discharges a secretion into a nearby duct. Spots of color should be used to indicate the **secretion (D$_1$)**. The **secretory cell (D$_2$)** lines the duct. The salivary glands are merocrine glands.

The final type of gland is the **apocrine gland (E)**, which is indicated by a bracket to be colored. In this gland, a **cell part (E$_1$)** pinches off from the **parent cell (E$_2$)**. The cell part, which is a small mass of cytoplasm, moves toward the duct. The secretory product is enclosed within the cell part and is emitted from the gland in this way. The mammary glands are apocrine glands.

Structural Types ★

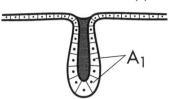

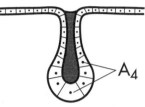

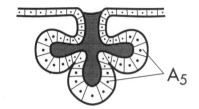

A₁

A₂

A₃

Simple Exocrine Glands A

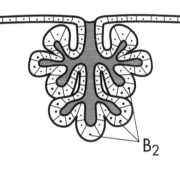

A₄

A₅

Compound Exocrine Glands B

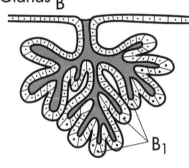

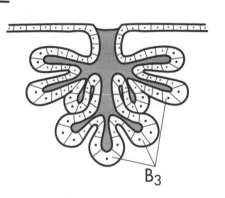

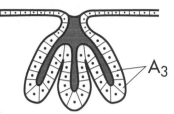

B₁

B₂

B₃

Functional Types ★

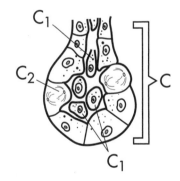

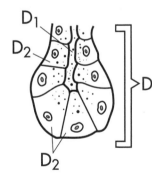

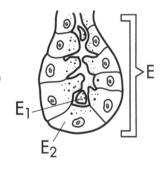

C₁

C₂

C

C₁

D₁

D₂

D

D₂

E

E₁

E₂

Simple exocrine glands	A	○	Tubular compound gland	B₁	○	Secretion	D₁	○
Tubular	A₁	○	Alveolar compound gland	B₂	○	Secretory cell	D₂	○
Coiled	A₂	○	Tubuloalveolar glands	B₃	○	Apocrine gland	E	○
Branched	A₃	○	Holocrine gland	C	○	Cell part	E₁	○
Simple alveolar glands	A₄	○	Discharged cell	C₁	○	Parent cell	E₂	○
Branched alveolar glands	A₅	○	Developing cell	C₂	○			
Compound exocrine glands	B	○	Merocrine gland	D	○			

the INTEGUMENTARY SYSTEM

the INTEGUMENT (SKIN) and DERIVATIVES

The integumentary system is composed of the integument (the skin) and its derivatives, including the hairs, sweat glands, and oil glands. As the largest body organ, the skin provides protection to the body and performs other functions noted in this plate.

Begin your work by coloring the main title The Integument (Skin) and Derivatives. In looking over the plate, you will note a section of the skin, including the hairs, glands, and other structures within it. One portion of the skin has been shown in detail to explore its layers. As you begin your study of the integumentary system, prepare to use light and pale colors, because many tissues are detailed, and it is good to preserve their important points of interest. Color the titles as you read them below, then color the structures in the plate.

On a structural basis, the skin is composed of three parts. At its surface is the **epidermis (A),** which is outlined by a bracket. The next deep layer contains connective tissue and is called the **dermis (B)**. Then comes a subcutaneous layer called the **hypodermis (C)**.

Returning to the epidermis, we note the detailed view and identify five layers of tissue. The most superficial layer is the **stratum corneum (A_1)**. This is a layer of flat, dead cells filled with the protein keratin. The layer protects against heat, pathogenic microorganisms, chemicals, and light. Then comes the **stratum lucidum (A_2)**. Clear, flat cells with a prekeratin substance called eleidin are found here. The layer is found primarily in the palms of the hands and soles of the feet.

The next lower layer of the epidermis is the **stratum granulosum (A_3),** which contains flattened cells containing the substance keratohyalin. Later, this material will become keratin. The next deeper layer is a very large layer called the **stratum spinosum (A_4)**. Keratin is produced in many of these cells.

The deepest layer is the **stratum basale (A_5)**. It is a single layer of cuboidal and columnar cells that undergo mitosis and become the cells of the more superficial layers. The layer is also called the stratum germinativum.

We now focus on the dermis and note some of the important structures within this layer. Different tissues will be found within this layer, and their presence designates the skin as an organ. Among the functions performed by tissues in this layer are protection, excretion, sensation, and immunity to disease. Continue your coloring as you read below.

The dermis contains many fibers of collagen together with various kinds of cells. The most superficial region of dermis is the papillary region with fingerlike projections in the epidermis. The remainder of the dermis is the dermal layer.

Within the dermal layer are a number of **sebaceous glands (D)**. These oil glands are generally connected to hair follicles, as the plate indicates. Their secretion is an oily substance called sebum. Other glands in the dermis are the **sweat glands (E)**, also called sudoriferous glands. These glands deliver their watery secretions (sweat) to **sweat gland ducts (E_1),** which lead to **sweat gland pores (E_2)**. A spot of color may be used for the pores. Sweat performs excretory functions by delivering metabolic waste products to the skin surface for removal. It also helps regulate body temperature.

We now focus on a tissue within the dermis, the hair. Hair provides protection and decreases heat loss. Its color is primarily due to the pigment melanin. As you read about the hair fibers below, locate and color their parts in the plate.

Hairs are epidermal growths distributed in varying amounts and textures throughout the body. The **hairs** in the plate (F) should be colored at the surface. The superficial part of the hair is the **shaft (F_1)**, projecting above the body surface. The portion penetrating into the dermis is the **root (F_2)**. The root of the hair is covered by the **root sheath (F_3)**, which is a continuation of the epidermis, as the plate indicates. At the base of the hair follicle is the enlarged **hair bulb (F_4)**. An indentation called the **papilla (F_5)** contains connective tissues and blood vessels to provide nourishment to the hair.

At the side of the hair follicle is a specialized smooth muscle called the **arrector pilius (F_6)**. This muscle contracts during stress and pulls the hair to the upright position. It can be seen in both hair fibers in the plate.

The plate closes with a brief look at the nerve receptors in the dermis and structures within the hypodermis. Complete your coloring as you read the paragraph below.

Many types of nerve receptors are located within the dermis. The plate on touch receptors treats them in detail, but we mention two receptors here. The first is the **Pacinian corpuscle (G_1)**. This nerve receptor detects vibrations and heavy touch sensations and sends impulses off to the brain. **Meissner's corpuscles (G_2)** detect light touch sensations and dispatch impulses for interpretation.

In the hypodermis, the plate shows a number of nerves, as well as the blood supply of the integumentary system. An **artery (H)** carries blood to the skin, while a **vein (I)** carries blood away. Red and blue colors may be used, respectively. Much **fat tissue (J)** is found in the hypodermis to provide cushioning to the skin. The underlying muscles and skin are below the hypodermis.

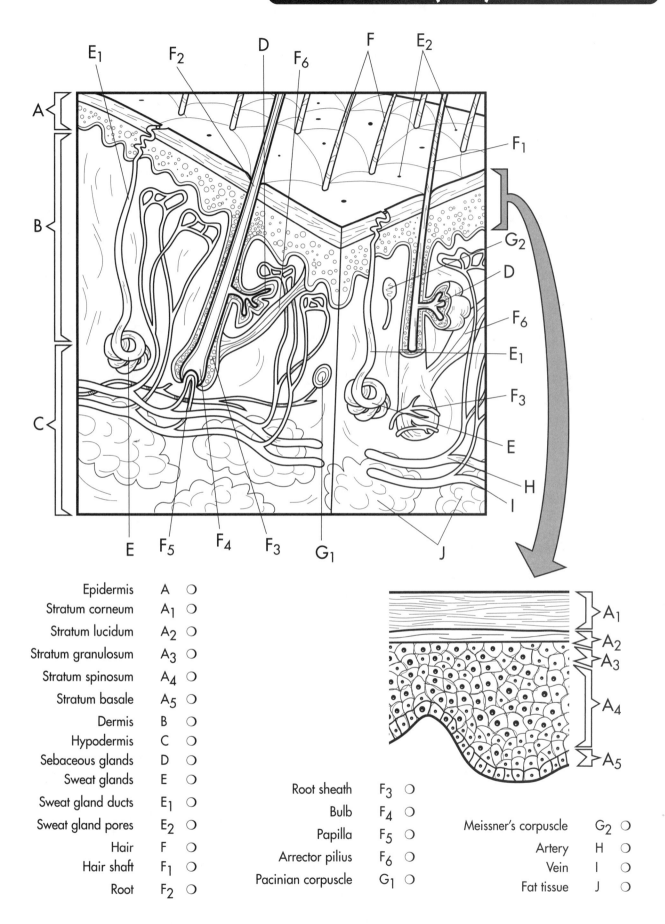

Epidermis	A	○
Stratum corneum	A_1	○
Stratum lucidum	A_2	○
Stratum granulosum	A_3	○
Stratum spinosum	A_4	○
Stratum basale	A_5	○
Dermis	B	○
Hypodermis	C	○
Sebaceous glands	D	○
Sweat glands	E	○
Sweat gland ducts	E_1	○
Sweat gland pores	E_2	○
Hair	F	○
Hair shaft	F_1	○
Root	F_2	○

Root sheath	F_3	○
Bulb	F_4	○
Papilla	F_5	○
Arrector pilius	F_6	○
Pacinian corpuscle	G_1	○

Meissner's corpuscle	G_2	○
Artery	H	○
Vein	I	○
Fat tissue	J	○

CHAPTER THREE:

the SKELETAL SYSTEM

the SKELETON

The human skeleton consists of 206 bones differing in size, shape, weight, and in some cases, composition. This diversity is related to the structural and mechanical functions of the skeleton, which include supporting the body, protecting the body cavities, acting as levers for muscle activity, and providing a site for blood cell development.

The skeleton is divided into two major parts: The axial skeleton is composed of the skull, vertebral column, sternum, and ribs; and the appendicular skeleton is composed of the upper and lower extremities and the supporting girdles. This plate will discuss the skeleton with the bones in place as a preview of the following plates, which feature the bones in detail. We also note the five different types of bones found in the skeleton.

> Looking over the plate, you will note that it contains a view of the skeleton in the anatomical position with the palms facing outward. An anterior view is presented. We also call out several of the bones to indicate the various types that are present. As you read about the skeleton, color the appropriate titles and the bones in the plate. There may be some overlapping, and pale colors are suggested for these areas. Begin by coloring the main title The Skeleton.

The first structure of the axial skeleton is the skull. This structure houses the brain and is the location of many sensory organs. The two main features of the skull are the **cranium (A)** and the **face (B)**. The skull contains 22 bones, many of which are paired; the face contains 14 bones, which are discussed in a future plate. The only bone not attached directly to the other bones of the skull is the lower jaw bone, the **mandible (C)**.

The skull and upper torso of the body are supported by another portion of the axial skeleton, the **vertebral column (G)**. There are 31 bones in this column, which extends along the dorsal aspect of the body and connects to the thoracic cage. At its ventral aspect, the thoracic cage has a three-part bone called the **sternum (E_1)** and a set of 12 **ribs (E_2)** connecting the sternum to the vertebral column.

> Having examined the axial skeleton, we now move to the appendicular skeleton and preview some of its essential bones. As you encounter the bones in the reading, locate their titles in the titles list and color the titles and bones in the plate. Two brackets demarcate the main sections.

At the upper portion of the body, the upper extremity is composed of the pectoral girdle and arm bones. The **pectoral girdle (D)** is outlined by the bracket, which should be colored. It contains two bones: The collar bone or **clavicle (D_1)** at the anterior aspect, and a flat, triangular bone called the **scapula (D_2)** at the posterior portion of the body.

Articulating with the pectoral girdle is the upper arm bone called the **humerus (F_1)**. The two lower arm bones articulating with the humerus are the **radius (F_2)** and the **ulna (F_3)**. The wrist bones are the **carpals (F_4)**, while the hand bones are **metacarpals (F_5)** and the finger bones are **phalanges (F_6)**.

At the lower portion of the body is the **pelvic girdle (H)**, indicated by the bracket. This bone appears single, but it is composed of three fused bones called the ilium, ischium, and pubis. Articulating with the pelvic girdle is the lower extremity. It consists of the thigh bone, the **femur (I_1)**, the knee cap called the **patella (I_2)**, and two lower leg bones, the **tibia (I_3)** and the **fibula (I_4)**. The ankle contains the **tarsals (I_5)**, and the foot bones are **metatarsals (I_6)**. The toes contain **phalanges (I_7)**. This completes the appendicular skeleton.

> The plate concludes with a discussion of the five different types of bones making up the skeleton. Here you are referred to the detailed views off to the side, and bold colors may be used for these bones.

Bones are classified according to their function in the body such as support, protection, or movement. They are also classified by their shape, which gives an indication of the mechanical function of the bone. An example of a **flat bone (J)** is a bone of the skull. These bones are thin and are used as protective devices. The scapula and ribs are other flat bones. An **irregular bone (K)** is typified by the vertebra. Many extensions to which muscles often attach are found on these bones. The vertebra shown is part of the vertebral column.

A **sesamoid bone (L)** is illustrated by the patella. These small bones are usually embedded in tendons and are used to protect the integrity of the tendon. A **long bone (M)** is used for movement. In the leg, for example, the femur acts as an attachment point for the muscles, and as they contract, they cause the bone to move.

The last bone we consider is the **short bone (N)**. These bones have similar dimensions but an irregular shape. They are found in the wrists and ankles as carpals and tarsals, respectively. Short bones unite with numerous other bones in their area and provide a variety of movements at that body part.

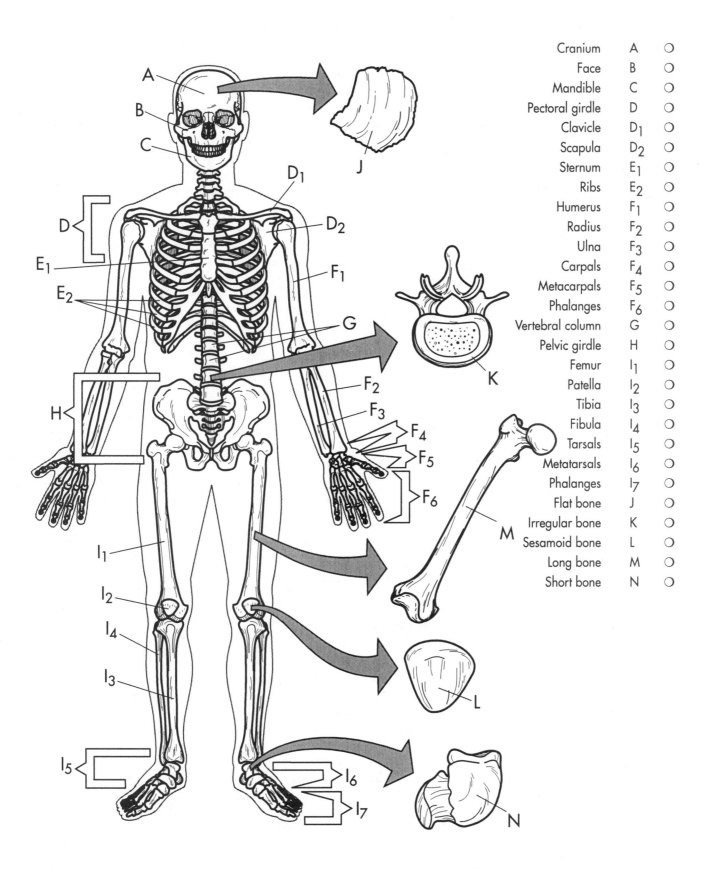

Cranium	A	○
Face	B	○
Mandible	C	○
Pectoral girdle	D	○
Clavicle	D_1	○
Scapula	D_2	○
Sternum	E_1	○
Ribs	E_2	○
Humerus	F_1	○
Radius	F_2	○
Ulna	F_3	○
Carpals	F_4	○
Metacarpals	F_5	○
Phalanges	F_6	○
Vertebral column	G	○
Pelvic girdle	H	○
Femur	I_1	○
Patella	I_2	○
Tibia	I_3	○
Fibula	I_4	○
Tarsals	I_5	○
Metatarsals	I_6	○
Phalanges	I_7	○
Flat bone	J	○
Irregular bone	K	○
Sesamoid bone	L	○
Long bone	M	○
Short bone	N	○

ANATOMY of a LONG BONE

Bones come in many sizes and shapes. Certain bones such as those in the joints of the skull are extremely small and varied in shape. By contrast, the femur (the thigh bone) is almost two feet in length in some people.

The shape of a bone is consistent with its functions. The femur, for instance, withstands great weight and pressure as it provides support for the body and attachment points for many skeletal muscles. Moreover, the hollow cylindrical design of the femur provides maximum strength with minimum weight.

The long bones of the body are considerably longer than they are wide. All bones of the limbs, with the exception of the patella and wrist and ankle bones, are considered long bones. A long bone has a shaft and two structurally-complex ends. Most long bones contain compact bone, but there is also a considerable amount of spongy bone in the interior. In this plate, we shall examine the anatomy of the long bone and point out some of the physiological processes related to the bone's structure.

Begin the plate by coloring the main title Anatomy of a Long Bone. Then look over the plate, and as you read below, color the titles and brackets pointing out areas of the long bone. Dark colors may be used for these brackets.

The **diaphysis (A)** is the shaft or long, main portion of the bone. It consists of a thick cylinder of compact bone enclosing a large, central cavity called the medullary or marrow cavity. The expanded ends of the bone are called epiphyses (singular, epiphysis). The **proximal epiphysis (B)** is the end of the bone close to the central axis of the body. The **distal epiphysis (C)** is the end of the bone farthest from the body's central axis. The epiphyses articulate with other bones to form joints. The **metaphysis (D)** is the region where the diaphysis joins the epiphysis and is the site of the **epiphyseal plate (D_1)**, which is pointed out by an arrow on the plate. The epiphyseal plate is a layer of hyaline cartilage where the diaphysis lengthens during the development of the long bone. A metaphysis exists at both ends of the bone.

Continue the plate by studying the parts and structures of the long bone. As you come upon the structures in the reading, color their titles and the structures in all views of the long bone. Use lighter colors for the structures and darker colors for arrows pointing to processes and areas. This will allow you to see the structures where they join and the important areas of the bone.

Where the epiphysis forms a joint with another bone, the epiphysis is covered with a thin layer of hyaline cartilage called the **articular cartilage (E)**. The articular cartilage absorbs shocks at the joint and reduces the friction where bones come together to form a joint. The **periosteum (F)** surrounds the diaphysis only. It is a membrane composed of an outer fibrous area and inner fibrous layer. The outer fibrous layer contains dense connective tissue with blood vessels, nerves, and lymph vessels. Its inner layer, the osteogenic layer, contains blood vessels and bone cells. The periosteum is the main center for the growth and development of bone. Its vessels supply nutrition to the bone. It is also a point where ligaments and tendons attach. The periosteum is bound to the bone by a set of connective tissue fibers called **Sharpey's fibers (G)**. **Nutrient arteries (H)** enter the periosteum bringing proteins, minerals, carbohydrates, and other essential materials for bone growth.

Now color the titles for the compact bone and spongy bone, then locate the areas of compact bone and spongy bone in the plate. As your read about these two types of bone below, color in the appropriate areas in three places on the plate. Light colors such as pale tans and grays should be used so you can see the textures of the bone.

The tightly packed tissue of the diaphysis wall is **compact bone (I)**. This bone resists bending and is solid and strong. Compact bone is dense and appears smooth and homogenous. **Spongy bone (J)** is found primarily in the epiphyses. Spongy bone contains numerous branching, bony plates with irregular interconnected spaces. The spaces reduce the weight of the bone while maintaining strength. The plates are called **trabeculae (J_1)**. The spaces between the trabeculae contain red or yellow bone marrow.

Complete the plate by exploring the medullary cavity, endosteum, and bone marrow. Prepare to color these structures as you read about them in the following paragraph. You may wish to use a red for the marrow and a lighter color for the medullary cavity.

The **medullary cavity (K)** is the central marrow cavity of the long bone. The cavity is continuous with the spaces of spongy bone at the epiphyses. The **endosteum (L)** is the membrane lining the medullary cavity. It contains cells related to bone development and breakdown. The space within the medullary cavity is filled with a specialized type of soft connective tissue called **bone marrow (M)**. The marrow consists primarily of blood cells and adipose cells. The marrow is yellow in the bone of adults. In young individuals, the marrow may be red because it is more involved in blood cell production.

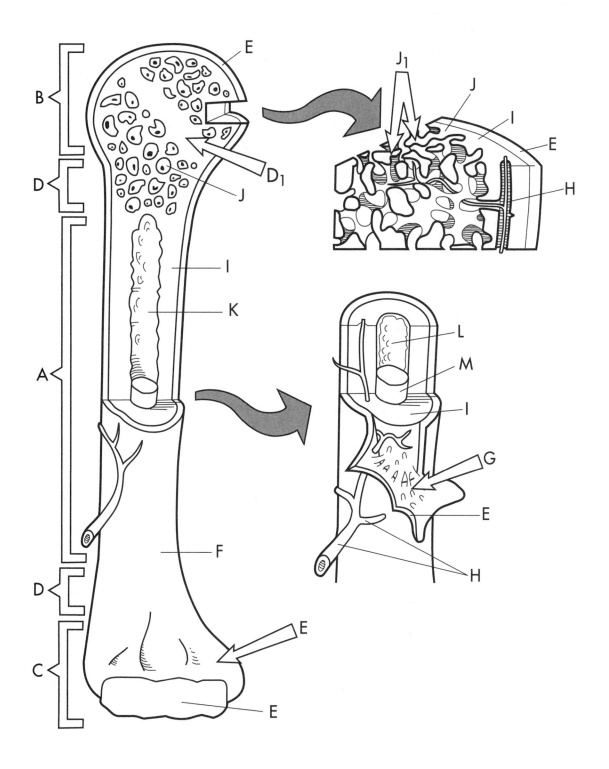

Diaphysis	A	○		Articular cartilage	E	○		Spongy bone	J	○
Proximal epiphysis	B	○		Periosteum	F	○		Trabeculae	J_1	○
Distal epiphysis	C	○		Sharpey's fibers	G	○		Medullary cavity	K	○
Metaphysis	D	○		Nutrient arteries	H	○		Endosteum	L	○
Epiphyseal plate	D_1	○		Compact bone	I	○		Marrow	M	○

the SKULL— EXTERNAL SURFACE VIEW I

There are 22 bones making up the skull. The skull rests on the atlas of the vertebral column and surrounds the cranial cavity. Several smaller cavities called sinuses are also located within the skull, as are cavities housing the hearing and equilibrium structures. A number of foramena and fissures in the skull are the openings through which blood vessels and nerves pass into and out of the cranial cavity.

The skull is subdivided into cranial bones, which form the cranial cavity and enclose the brain, and the facial bones, which form the face. The facial bones also support passageways to respiratory and digestive systems, while providing attachments for the muscles of facial expressions. Moreover, the sense organs for taste, smell, touch, hearing, and equilibrium are protected and supported by the cranial facial bones.

The skull will be the subject matter of this plate and the two plates that follow. It will be examined according to its external surface in this and the following plate, and according to its internal surface in the third.

The structures and processes of the skull are found on this plate and the two that follow. Accordingly, you should try to use the same colors when completing the three plates. The letters associated with the skull structures are the same on all three plates to help you locate them and relate them to one another in various views. There will be seven views of the skull in the three plates. Light colors (such as pale shades of tan, gray, and yellow) should be used for the main bones, and care should be taken to avoid obscuring the arrows pointing to important processes of the bones. Begin the plate by coloring the title The Skull–External Surface View I. Then read the following paragraphs and, as you encounter the bone or process, color the plate in both the lateral and interior views. Separate directions will be given for each of the following plates.

The **occipital bone (A)** is a large bone forming much of the base of the cranium. This bone articulates in the anterior position with two bones: the parietal bone and the temporal bone. The **parietal bone (B)** is one of two paired bones that are large and curved and form most of the superior and lateral aspects of the skull. These bones form much of the cranial vault. A low ridge of each parietal bone is the **superior temporal line (B$_1$)**. This is the attachment site for the temporalis, one of the muscles involved in closing the mouth. The temporalis also attaches at the **inferior temporal line (B$_2$)**.

The dome-shaped bone at the forehead is the **frontal bone (C)**. This bone forms portions of the orbits of the eyes. The smooth portions of the bone between the orbits is known as the **glabella (C$_2$)**. The margin of the orbit contains a foramen called the **supraorbital foramen (C$_1$)**. This opening allows the supraorbital artery and nerve to pass into the region of the forehead.

The **temporal bones (D)** are inferior to the parietal bones and form portions of the lateral part of the skull as portions of the cranial floor. The temporal bone is the site of the **zygomatic process (D$_1$)**, which meets the **temporal process (J$_1$)** and helps form the **zygomatic arch (D$_1$, J$_1$)**. The bracket should be colored. This is the projection of the cheek, often called the cheekbone. The temporal bone also encloses the **external auditory meatus (D$_2$)**, also

called the ear canal. Sound enters this opening and strikes the eardrum within. The mastoid region of the temporal bone contains the prominent **mastoid process (D$_3$)**. This is an attachment site for several neck muscles. Another prominent feature is the long, needle-like **styloid process (D$_4$)**. Several neck muscles attach here also. A ligament that secures the hyoid bone in the neck also attaches here.

You have now examined some of the bones of the cranial vault. We shall continue with some of the smaller but equally important bones. Continue as before, coloring the title of the bone or structure as you encounter it in the text, then color in the plate. When you encounter the bones of the eye orbit, use light colors because there are several small bones here. A complete picture of the skull will emerge as you color.

One of the most important bones of the cranial floor is the **sphenoid bone (E)**. This bone is somewhat shaped like a bat or a butterfly. It has a central body and several processes, which will be seen in a later plate. In the lateral and anterior views of the skull, the sphenoid bone can be seen at the skull surface, although it is not prominent. (It will be clearly seen in the internal view.) Another irregular bone forming part of the orbital wall is the **ethmoid bone (F)**. It is a deeply situated bone seen best in interior view, although portions can be seen at the lateral and anterior views shown here within the orbit of the eye.

The **maxilla (G)** is the upper jawbone composed of two bones (maxillae) fused to one another in the medial aspect. The maxilla carries the upper teeth and forms much of the hard palette, the bony roof of the mouth. A prominent process of the maxilla is the **infraorbital foramen (G$_1$)**. This is the site where the infraorbital artery and nerve enter the facial area.

There are two **nasal bones (H)** that articulate with the frontal bone at the midline. At the lateral surfaces, the nasal bones articulate with the maxillae on either side. The **vomer bone (I)** is seen best in the internal surface of the skull. It has its base on the floor of the nasal cavity, and it forms the inferior portion of the nasal septum, as seen in the interior view on page 27. The portion of the vomer bone in this plate is thin. It separates the right and left nasal cavities. The **zygomatic bone (J)** is the cheekbone. Its **temporal process (J$_1$)** articulates with the zygomatic process of the temporal bone to form the prominent features of the cheeks, as we noted previously. Its **zygomatical facial foramen (J$_2$)** allows nerves to pass through. The zygomatic bone also forms a portion of the orbit of the eye and is seen clearly in the anterior and lateral views. Another bone of the orbit is the **lacrimal bone (K)**. This is the smallest bone of the skull and is difficult to see in these views.

The u-shaped **mandible (N)** forms the lower jawbone. It is the site of the **mental foramen (N$_1$)**, through which nerves pass from the chin and lips on their way to the brain. The main portion of the mandible is the **body (N$_2$)**, and the ascending portion is the **ramus of the mandible (N$_3$)**. The **condylar process (N$_4$)** is where the mandible articulates with the temporal bone. The **coronoid process (N$_5$)** is the site of the temporalis muscle, which also attaches to the parietal bones.

Where the skull bones meet, they form joints known as sutures. Dense fibrous connective tissue binds the bones together at these joints. One of the major sutures is the **squamosal suture (M)**. This suture occurs where the temporal and parietal bones articulate. A second suture is the **lambdoidal suture (O)**. This suture occurs at the junction of the occipital and parietal bones. A third suture seen in the anterior view is the **coronal suture (Q)**. This is the junction between the parietal bones at the top of the head. A minor suture known as the **occipital mastoidal suture (R)** lies at the junction of the occipital bone in the region of the mastoid process of the temporal bone. Tiny irregular bones called Wormian bones often occur in the sutures of the cranium. Their number varies, and they may not be present at all.

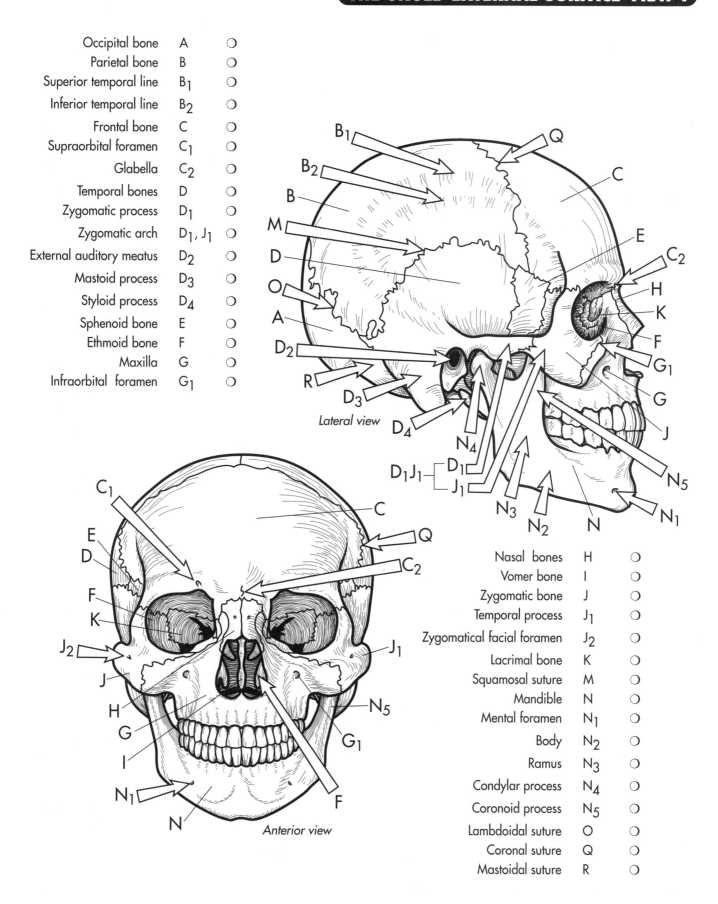

Occipital bone — A ○
Parietal bone — B ○
Superior temporal line — B_1 ○
Inferior temporal line — B_2 ○
Frontal bone — C ○
Supraorbital foramen — C_1 ○
Glabella — C_2 ○
Temporal bones — D ○
Zygomatic process — D_1 ○
Zygomatic arch — D_1, J_1 ○
External auditory meatus — D_2 ○
Mastoid process — D_3 ○
Styloid process — D_4 ○
Sphenoid bone — E ○
Ethmoid bone — F ○
Maxilla — G ○
Infraorbital foramen — G_1 ○

Lateral view

Anterior view

Nasal bones — H ○
Vomer bone — I ○
Zygomatic bone — J ○
Temporal process — J_1 ○
Zygomatical facial foramen — J_2 ○
Lacrimal bone — K ○
Squamosal suture — M ○
Mandible — N ○
Mental foramen — N_1 ○
Body — N_2 ○
Ramus — N_3 ○
Condylar process — N_4 ○
Coronoid process — N_5 ○
Lambdoidal suture — O ○
Coronal suture — Q ○
Mastoidal suture — R ○

the SKULL—EXTERNAL SURFACE VIEW II

The 22 bones of the human skull are grouped into the bones of the cranium (enclosing the brain), and the bones of the facial skeleton (making up the face). The cranial bones are the frontal, occipital, sphenoid, ethmoid, parietal (two bones), and temporal (two bones). The facial bones include the maxillae (two bones), zygomatic (two bones), nasal (two bones), lacrimal (two bones), palatine (two bones), inferior nasal conchae (two bones), vomer, and mandible. An examination of these bones began in the previous plate and continues in this plate. Here, the posterior, superior, and inferior views of the external surface of the skull are presented. In the previous plate, we began studies on the external surface. In this plate we will continue with views of the posterior, superior, and inferior views. If possible, you should use the same colors for the bones and processes as you used in the previous plate and will use in the following plate. The letters and designations for these bones and structures are identical in all three plates, so you can see the relationships and draw comparisons.

> Begin this plate by coloring the main title The Skull—External Surface View II. Then note that the plate contains three views of the skull's external surface. As you locate the bones and processes in the following paragraphs, color them in all three views and try to get a sense of the three-dimensional structure of the skull. Lighter colors should be used for the main bones, and bolder colors can be used for the arrows pointing to the processes and landmarks.

On the posterior, lateral, and inferior surfaces of the cranium is the **occipital bone (A)**. A small portion may be seen in the superior view and a large portion in the inferior view. In the inferior view, the **occipital condyles (A_1)** are seen. These processes articulate with the atlas, the first vertebra of the vertebral column. At the midline of the occipital bone is the external **occipital protuberance (A_2)**. This is an attachment point for muscles, which stabilize the skull over the vertebral column. Ligaments also attach here. The **foramen magnum (A_3)** can be clearly seen as the large opening in the occipital bone through which the spinal cord passes on its way to the vertebral canal. At the **lateral foramen (A_4)**, the internal jugular vein passes and drains blood from the brain area. The **condyloid fossa (A_5)** is an attachment site for muscles.

The large bones at the superior and lateral portions of the cranial vault are the paired **parietal bones (B)**. The parietal bones articulate at an immovable joint called the **sagittal suture (P)**. In the superior view, the **frontal bone (C)** can be observed. The frontal bone articulates with the parietal bones at the **coronal suture (Q)**.

> Continue the plate with an examination of the **temporal bone (D)**. Some of the processes are noted in the paragraph below, and the arrows pointing to them should be colored as you proceed. Darker blues, greens, and purples can be used for the arrows, but lighter colors should be used for the main bones.

The two temporal bones form the inferior lateral aspects of the cranium and part of the cranial floor. An important process of the lateral bone is the **zygomatic process (D_1)**. It articulates with the temporal process of the zygomatic bone to form the arch of the cheek. The **external auditory meatus (D_2)** opens to the eardrum and, behind the eardrum, the middle ear. The opening is part of the external ear. Posterior and inferior to the external auditory meatus is the **mastoid process (D_3)**. This rounded projection of the temporal bone is the point of attachment for several neck muscles. From the under surface of the temporal bone, the needlelike **styloid process (D_4)** projects. Tongue and neck muscles attach here. The **stylomastoid foramen (D_5)** is the opening through which the facial nerve passes to control activities of the facial muscles. Where the mandible articulates with the bone, the latter has a process called the **mandibular fossa (D_6)**. The **carotid foramen (D_7)** is the opening through which the internal carotid artery passes carrying blood to the brain. The **sphenoid bone (E)** and **foramen ovale (E_1)** are also visible.

> In the final section of this plate, some of the smaller bones of the skull are visible in posterior, superior, and inferior views. As you color these bones, use the same colors you used in the previous plate and will use in the following plate.

The **maxilla (G)** is formed from two maxillae and is the upper jawbone. It articulates with every facial bone except the mandible. With the **palatine bones (L)**, the maxillae form the hard palate. The **nasal bones (H)** are seen briefly in the superior view. The **vomer bone (I)** can be seen in the inferior view, and the **zygomatic bone (J)** is seen at the region of the cheek. In the inferior view, the palatine bone is observed at the roof of the mouth. It joins the maxillae to form the hard palate. An opening in the palatine bone is the **occipitomastoidal foramen (L_1)**. Nerves and blood vessels to the brain pass through this opening. The **mandible (N)** is also called the lower jawbone. It is seen in the posterior view only.

The final areas that we shall mention are immovable joints called sutures. The first is the **squamosal suture (M)**. This suture lies at the junction of the temporal and parietal bones and is seen in the posterior view. The second suture is a minor suture known as the **occipitomastoidal suture (R)**. It lies at the junction of the occipital bone in the region of the mastoid process of the temporal bone. This suture is prominently seen in the lateral view in the previous plate.

Occipital bone	A	○
Occipital condyles	A₁	○
External occipital protuberance	A₂	○
Foramen magnum	A₃	○
Lateral foramen	A₄	○
Condyloid fossa	A₅	○
Parietal bones	B	○

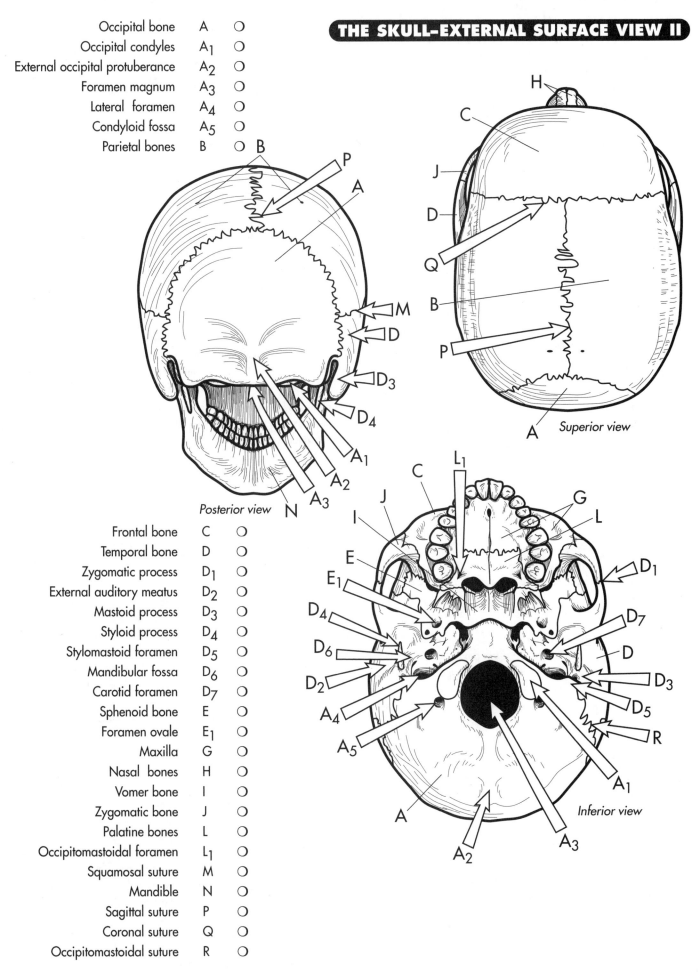

Superior view

Posterior view

Frontal bone	C	○
Temporal bone	D	○
Zygomatic process	D₁	○
External auditory meatus	D₂	○
Mastoid process	D₃	○
Styloid process	D₄	○
Stylomastoid foramen	D₅	○
Mandibular fossa	D₆	○
Carotid foramen	D₇	○
Sphenoid bone	E	○
Foramen ovale	E₁	○
Maxilla	G	○
Nasal bones	H	○
Vomer bone	I	○
Zygomatic bone	J	○
Palatine bones	L	○
Occipitomastoidal foramen	L₁	○
Squamosal suture	M	○
Mandible	N	○
Sagittal suture	P	○
Coronal suture	Q	○
Occipitomastoidal suture	R	○

Inferior view

the SKULL—INTERNAL SURFACE

The human skull is a complex structure with an architectural design that reflects the many functions it performs. For example, it is involved in speech, vision, balance, breathing, and hearing. In addition, the skull protects the most elaborate portion of the nervous system, the brain. The 22 bones of the human skull constitute the cranium and facial skeleton. The tiny ear bones of the middle ear cavity sometimes are considered skull bones, but since they are involved in hearing, we consider them with the plate on the ear. Most skull bones are flat bones, with the notable exception of the mandible. The discussion of the skull bones began with the plate on page 23 and continues with this plate. Where the external anatomy was considered previously, the internal surfaces of the skull are examined here. The same letters and numbers are used here as in the two previous plates; therefore, you should try to use the same colors that you used in those plates. Try to work with all three plates to visualize the skull as a three-dimensional object with structures viewed from various aspects.

This plate contains a superior view of the skull floor and a sagittal section of the skull. Begin your coloring with the main title The Skull—Internal Surface. When you color the skull bones, try to use light colors as before and avoid obscuring the arrows pointing to the processes. Darker colors such as reds and blues can be used for the arrows.

The superior view and the sagittal sections of the skull both show the **occipital bone (A)**. The plate shows how the bone forms a substantial portion of the skull's base. The large hole in the base is the **foramen magnum (A_3)**. The **jugular foramen (A_4)** allows passage of the internal jugular vein, which drains blood from the brain. The hypoglossal nerves pass through the bone at the **hypoglossal foramen (A_6)**. The posterior **cranial fossa (A_7)** supports the cerebellum of the brain. A narrow structure called the **basioccipital band (A_8)** is where the occipital bone joins with the sphenoid bone.

Adjacent to the occipital bone is the **parietal bone (B)**, which is prominent in the sagittal section. The **lambdoidal suture (O)** is the point of articulation between this bone and the occipital. The **frontal bone (C)** is also seen in the superior view. Within the bone, an outpocket known as the **frontal sinus (C_3)** provides an area for air conditioning and cushioning. The **squamosal suture (M)** marks the boundary between **temporal bone (D)** and the parietal bones. The **styloid process (D_4)** extends inferiorly at the mastoid area of the temporal bone and is a point of attachment for neck muscles. The **internal acoustic meatus (D_8)** is the opening for blood vessels that supply and drain the inner ear.

Continue the plate with an examination of the sphenoid and ethmoid bones. These two bones are not seen prominently on the external surface, but the superior and sagittal views of the skull show them clearly. Numerous openings occur in these bones through which nerves pass from the brain to the floor of the skull. Continue using the same colors as used in the previous two plates, and be careful to avoid obscuring the openings. Color the arrows prominently, but continue to use lighter colors for the bones.

A major bone in the floor of the cranium is the **sphenoid bone (E)**. The **foramen ovale (E_1)** in this bone is a site of nerve passages. Other sites of passage are the **foramen rotundum (E_3)**, **foramen spinosum (E_4)**, and the **foramen lacerum (E_6)**. The sphenoid bone contains a saddlelike depression called the **sella turcica (E_2)**. This important location is the site of the pituitary gland. It is apparent in both superior and sagittal views. The **sphenoidal sinus (E_5)** can be seen in the sagittal section of the skull. It is another region for air conditioning in the body. The sphenoid bone vaguely resembles a butterfly or bat. Projecting laterally in the bone are the two **greater wings (E_7)**. Part of the wings form the dorsal walls of the orbits and the external wall of the skull. The **lesser wings (E_8)** form a portion of the medial walls of the orbits and a portion of the cranial floor. The pterygoid process is not in the plate, but it projects to the inferior aspect and forms part of the wall of the nasopharynx. It also anchors part of the pterygoid muscles.

The plate should be completed by noting the position and relationships of the last few bones of the internal surface of the skull. Continue using the same colors for these bones as you have used for the other plates and note their position on the internal skull surface.

The **ethmoid bone (F)** is a complex bone found between the sphenoid bone and nasal bones. It is the most deeply situated bone of the skull and, therefore, is difficult to see in sections of the skull. The ethmoid bone forms much of the bony area between the orbit and nasal cavity. At the superior surface of the ethmoid bone, there are two **cribriform plates (F_2)**, which support portions of the anterior surface of the brain. Foramina in the plates permit passages of the olfactory nerves, which function in smell. Between the cribriform plates is a triangular projection called the **crista galli (F_1)**. The outer covering of the brain, the dura mater, attaches to the crista galli and helps secure the brain in the cranial cavity. Projecting in the inferior aspect of the ethmoid bone is the **perpendicular plate (F_3)**, which forms the superior part of the nasal septum. The **maxilla (G)** is visible in the sagittal section, and it articulates with the **palatine bone (L)**. The short stubby **nasal bone (H)** forms the bridge of the nose and attaches to the cartilages that form most of the skeleton of the external nose. The nasal bone also articulates with the frontal bones, the maxillary bones, and the perpendicular plate of the ethmoid bone.

The **vomer bone (I)** is a slender, plow-shaped bone located within the nasal cavity, where it forms part of the nasal septum. The strongest facial bone is the **mandible (N)**. Its upright branches called rami meet the body at the mandibular angle, and its body forms the chin. These portions are encountered in the external view of the skull. The **squamosal suture (M)** and **lambdoidal suture (O)** are also seen in this plate.

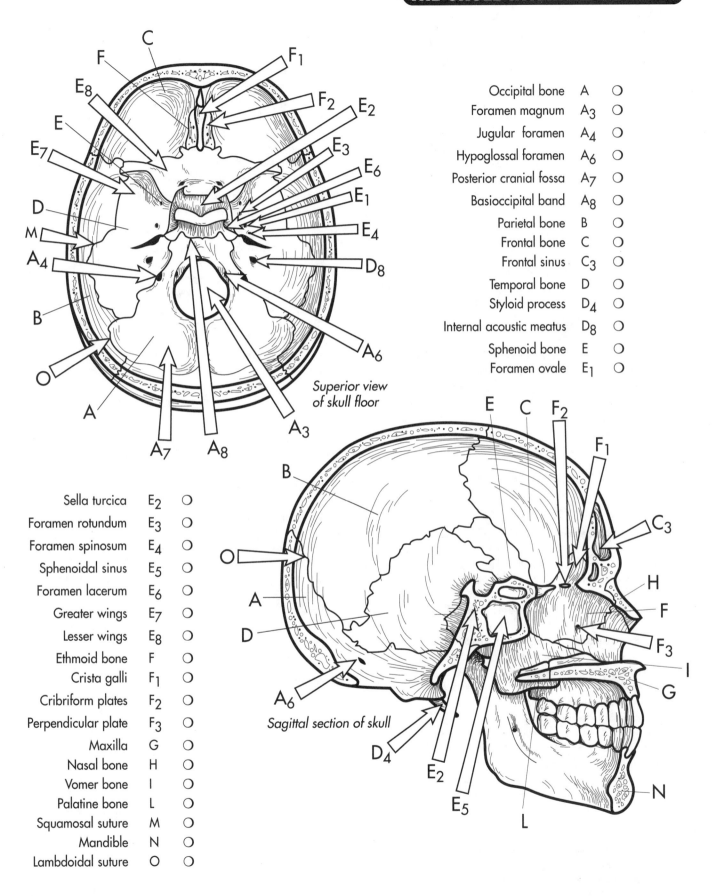

Superior view
of skull floor

Occipital bone	A	○
Foramen magnum	A₃	○
Jugular foramen	A₄	○
Hypoglossal foramen	A₆	○
Posterior cranial fossa	A₇	○
Basioccipital band	A₈	○
Parietal bone	B	○
Frontal bone	C	○
Frontal sinus	C₃	○
Temporal bone	D	○
Styloid process	D₄	○
Internal acoustic meatus	D₈	○
Sphenoid bone	E	○
Foramen ovale	E₁	○

Sella turcica	E₂	○
Foramen rotundum	E₃	○
Foramen spinosum	E₄	○
Sphenoidal sinus	E₅	○
Foramen lacerum	E₆	○
Greater wings	E₇	○
Lesser wings	E₈	○
Ethmoid bone	F	○
Crista galli	F₁	○
Cribriform plates	F₂	○
Perpendicular plate	F₃	○
Maxilla	G	○
Nasal bone	H	○
Vomer bone	I	○
Palatine bone	L	○
Squamosal suture	M	○
Mandible	N	○
Lambdoidal suture	O	○

Sagittal section of skull

the THORACIC CAGE and HYOID BONE

The chest cavity of the human body is known as the thorax. Surrounding this cavity is the skeleton of the chest, called the thoracic cage. The thoracic cage is formed in the dorsal aspect by the thoracic vertebrae, in the lateral aspect by the ribs, and in the anterior aspect by the sternum and costal cartilages, which bind the ribs to the sternum.

The thoracic cage has the basic shape of a cone, with its narrow dimension in the superior aspect and its broad dimension in the inferior aspect. The cage protects the important organs of the thoracic cavity such as the heart and lungs; it provides support for the pectoral girdles and upper limbs; it is an attachment point for many muscles of the chest, back, and shoulders; and it functions in breathing as the intercostal spaces between the ribs lift when inhaling and depress when exhaling.

> Start by coloring the main title The Thoracic Cage and Hyoid Bone. Then note that the plate contains views of the thoracic cage from the anterior and posterior aspects. In the first two sections of the plate, Sternum and Rib, you should color the structures and bones in both the anterior and posterior views as you read about them. The section Rib Articulation is discussed later, and your coloring on this section can be delayed for the time being. Now color the main title Sternum and begin your study of the sternum. As you encounter the bones and processes of the sternum, color them in on the plate. Use lighter colors for the bones (especially the ribs) because the thoracic cage is somewhat complex, and try not to obscure the markings.

The sternum is the breastbone of the body. It lies in the anterior midline of the thorax and is seen only in the anterior view. The sternum has the outline of a dagger and consists of three bones fused together. These bones are designated A, B, and C in the plate, and the bracket indicating the sternum should be colored with a dark color.

The superior portion of the sternum is the **manubrium (A)**, the widest portion of the sternum. It contains a **jugular notch (A_1)**, which is a shallow indentation where the left common carotid artery emerges from the aorta The **clavicular notch (A_2)** is the point where the clavicles articulate with the sternum. Below the clavicular notch is an articular facet for the costal cartilage of the first rib.

The second bone of the sternum is the middle and largest portion, the **body (B)**. The body develops from four separate segments, indicated by a number of transverse ridges on the anterior surface. The costal cartilages from ribs three through seven attach to the body. The second rib articulates where the body meets the manubrium, a distinctive anatomical landmark called the **sternal angle (B_1)**.

The smallest portion of the sternum at the inferior aspect is the **xiphoid process (C)**. It is an attachment site for two important muscles, the diaphragm and the rectus abdominis. The xiphoid process varies considerably in size and shape among adults.

> Continue your work on the plate by coloring the title **Rib (D)**. Then, color all the ribs of the anterior and posterior view using the same light color you used on the thoracic cage. Be careful, however, not to color the costal cartilages yet. When you have finished, read about the ribs below, and complete the anterior and posterior views of the thoracic cage.

The ribs are curved, elongated bones originating at the thoracic vertebrae and terminating in the anterior wall of the thoracic cage. They are divided into different groups depending upon their structure: the first seven pairs of ribs are the **true ribs (D_1)**, the brackets for these ribs should be colored in the anterior and posterior views. The true ribs are called this because they are connected directly to the sternum by **costal cartilages (E)**. The costal cartilages of the true ribs should be colored now. The second set of ribs are the **false ribs (D_2)**. The false ribs do not attach directly to the sternum and are ribs eight through twelve. The bracket encompassing these ribs should be colored now. The false ribs are further subdivided into vertebrochondral ribs and floating ribs. The **vertebrochondral ribs (D_3)** are ribs eight, nine, and ten. These ribs fuse together by costal cartilages before reaching the sternum. Ribs eleven and twelve are called **floating ribs (D_4)** because they have no connection to the sternum. Note in the posterior view how the ribs are attached to the **vertebrae (F)**. The vertebrae may be colored at this point to complete the anterior and posterior views of the thoracic cage.

> The third section of this plate shows the rib and its articulation. Begin the section by coloring the title Rib Articulation. Then notice in the plate that two views are shown: a superior view and a lateral view. In the superior view, color the thoracic **vertebra (F)** using a light color. Try to use the same color that you used in the anterior and posterior views. Then, in the lateral view, color the two thoracic vertebrae. Now color the **rib (D)** using the same light color you used above. Try to avoid obscuring the details of its processes. Then read about the rib and its articulation below, and color the arrows leading to the processes as you encounter them.

The "typical" rib is difficult to define because variations occur in the 12 pairs of ribs. However, ribs three through nine have distinguishing features in common. The rib has a **concave angle (D_5)**, which occurs along the body, or **shaft (D_6)** of the rib. The rib originates at a **demifacet (D_7)** of the thoracic vertebra. Articulating with the demifacet is the head, or **capitulum (D_8)** of the rib. The **neck of the rib (D_9)** follows the capitulum. Lateral from the capitulum is a projection called the **tubercle (D_{10})**. A portion of the tubercle contains the facet that articulates at the transverse process of the vertebra. These two articulations are seen in the lateral view, which also illustrates how the rib articulates at the point where two thoracic vertebrae meet. The facet of the capitulum fits into two demifacets of two adjoining vertebrae, while the articular portion of the tubercle articulates with a facet of the transverse process.

The spaces between the ribs are known as intercostal spaces. Blood vessels, nerves, and intercostal muscles occupy these spaces. The muscles contract and permit expansion of the thoracic cavity during inhalation, then relax and permit depression of the cavity during exhalation.

> Now complete the plate by examining the hyoid bone. Color its title, then color the bone in a light color and its processes in darker colors as you continue your reading.

The **hyoid bone (G)** is unique because it does not articulate with any other bone. The hyoid bone is located in the neck tissues. Ligaments and tendons suspend it from the styloid process of the temporal bone. Its features include the **body (G_1)**, the **greater horns (G_2)**, and the **lesser horns (G_3)** The horns are also called cornua. Many neck and pharyngeal muscles attach to the bone.

Manubrium A ○
Jugular notch A₁ ○
Clavicular notch A₂ ○
Body B ○
Sternal angle B₁ ○
Xiphoid process C ○
Rib D ○
True ribs D₁ ○
False ribs D₂ ○
Vertebrochondral ribs D₃ ○
Floating ribs D₄ ○
Concave angle D₅ ○
Shaft D₆ ○
Demifacet D₇ ○
Capitulum D₈ ○
Neck D₉ ○

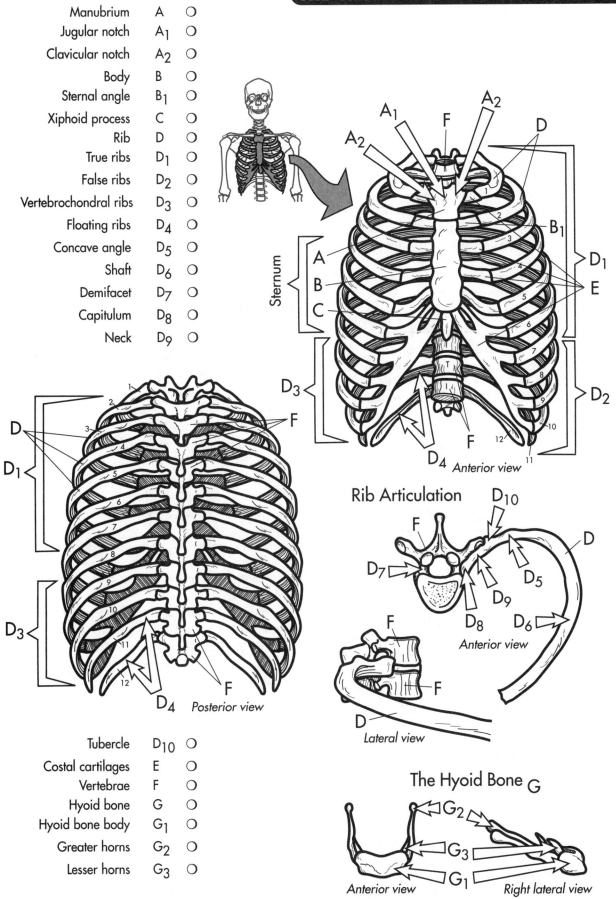

Sternum

A₁ F A₂ D

A₂ B₁ D₁ E

A B C

D₃ D₄ F D₂

Anterior view

D D₁ D₃ D₄ F *Posterior view*

Rib Articulation

D₁₀ F D D₇ D₅ D₉ D₈ D₆ *Anterior view*

F F D *Lateral view*

Tubercle D₁₀ ○
Costal cartilages E ○
Vertebrae F ○
Hyoid bone G ○
Hyoid bone body G₁ ○
Greater horns G₂ ○
Lesser horns G₃ ○

The Hyoid Bone G

G₂ G₃ G₁
Anterior view *Right lateral view*

29

the VERTEBRAL COLUMN

In the human adult, the vertebral column (also called the spinal column) consists of 26 bones. The bones of the vertebral column include 24 vertebrae, the sacrum, and the coccyx. The vertebral column is a strong, flexible series of bones that bends in the anterior, posterior, and lateral aspects. The bones also allow the column to rotate. The vertebral column encloses and protects the spinal cord. It also supports the head and is the attachment point for the ribs and muscles of the back. A series of openings between the vertebrae are known as intervertebral foramina. These are the openings through which the nerves pass from the spinal cord to other parts of the body. The vertebral column begins at the skull and anchors in the pelvis, where it transmits the weight of the trunk to the lower limbs.

You may begin your work on this plate by coloring the main title The Vertebral Column. Then examine the position of the column in the plate relative to the remainder of the body and color the title the Vertebral Column In Place. As you read about the divisions and curvatures of the vertebral column, color in the appropriate titles and the brackets that apply. Use darker colors such as deep blues, purples, and greens for the brackets. You may also color in the vertebrae of the five divisions as you encounter them. Light colors are suggested because of the proximity of the vertebrae.

The 26 bones of the vertebral column are distributed in **five divisions (A)**. In the neck region are the seven **cervical vertebrae (A_1)**. The chest region contains 12 **thoracic vertebrae (A_2)**. The lower back is supported by the five vertebrae of the **lumbar division (A_3)**. The **sacral division (A_4)** is composed of the sacrum. The sacrum originates as a group of five vertebrae that fuse to one another to form a single large bone. The final division is the **coccygeal division (A_5)**, which consists of the coccyx. The coccyx, also called the tailbone, was originally three to five small vertebrae that fused. This fusion is usually complete by the adult years.

The vertebral column displays **four curvatures (B)**. Seen from the lateral aspect are the **cervical curvature (B_1)**, which is a secondary curve appearing several months after birth. The **thoracic curvature (B_2)** is a primary curve appearing late in the development of the fetus. The **lumbar curvature (B_3)** is a secondary curve and the **sacral curvature (B_4)** is a primary curve. The cervical and lumbar curvatures are convex in the posterior aspect, while the cervical and thoracic curvatures are concave in the posterior aspect. The curvatures help maintain balance when standing, and they absorb shocks during running and walking. Moreover, they increase the strength of the vertebral column and help protect the column from fracture.

Continue your work on the plate by examining the superior and lateral views of a typical vertebra. The main focus of this section will be the **processes of the vertebra (C)**. The title should be colored in the title list and plate. As you encounter the processes in the following paragraphs, color them in both the superior and lateral views. A light color should be used for the vertebrae to avoid obscuring the landmarks pointed out by the arrows. A single light color such as tan or gray can be used for the entire vertebra in both superior and lateral views.

A considerable variation occurs in the cervical, thoracic, lumbar, sacral, and coccygeal vertebrae. Unique characteristics as well as variations in shape and size occur. All vertebrae, however, have certain basic similarities, which you will observe in this section. The typical structure of a vertebra includes two basic portions: at the anterior end is the body, also known as the **centrum (C_1)** of the vertebra. The body is generally cylindrical in shape and is rough on its superior and inferior surfaces, as the plate shows. These are the places where the body articulates with the disks between it and the next vertebra. Small arteries and veins pass through the body. The second basic structure is the **vertebral arch (C_2)**. This region is encircled in the views of the vertebra. The vertebral arch has a **floor (C_3)** at the posterior aspect of the body. Its walls are called **pedicles (C_4)**. The roof of the vertebral arch is formed by the articulation of two **laminae (C_5)**. The neural arch encloses an extremely important opening called the **vertebral foramen (C_6)**. This is the vertebral canal that contains the spinal cord. The canal is formed by the foramina of adjacent vertebrae. Connective tissues and blood vessels also pass through the vertebral foramen.

From the vertebral arch, several processes arise. Projecting posteriorly and inferiorly from the laminae there is a single **spinous process (C_7)**, also known as the spine of the vertebra. This is an attachment point for muscles. Where the lamina and pedicle join, a process extends laterally to each side of the vertebra. This is the **transverse process (C_8)**. It is also an attachment point for muscles. The **superior articular process (C_9)** is one of the several processes that form joints with other vertebrae above and below. The superior articular process articulates with two inferior processes of the vertebra immediately superior. The surface of the articular process is called a facet. In the plates immediately following, some of the details of the various vertebrae are explored and the differences become apparent as they relate to the functions of the vertebra.

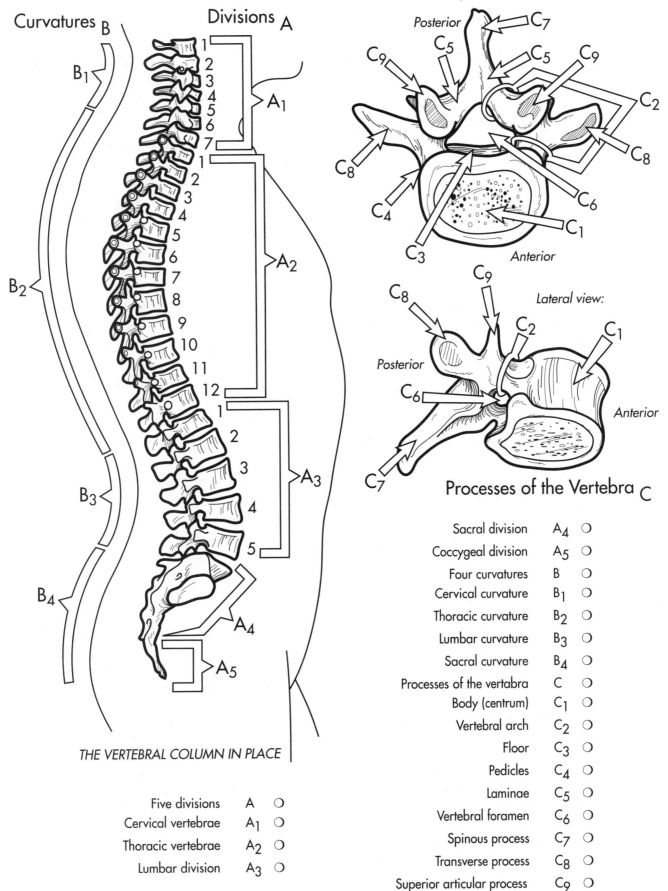

Curvatures B

Divisions A

Superior view:

Posterior

C_7
C_5
C_9
C_5
C_9
C_2
C_8
C_8
C_4
C_6
C_1
C_3

Anterior

B_1

A_1

B_2

A_2

C_9

C_8

Lateral view:

Posterior

C_2
C_1

C_6

Anterior

B_3

A_3

C_7

Processes of the Vertebra C

B_4

A_4

A_5

THE VERTEBRAL COLUMN IN PLACE

Sacral division	A_4	○
Coccygeal division	A_5	○
Four curvatures	B	○
Cervical curvature	B_1	○
Thoracic curvature	B_2	○
Lumbar curvature	B_3	○
Sacral curvature	B_4	○
Processes of the vertabra	C	○
Body (centrum)	C_1	○
Vertebral arch	C_2	○
Floor	C_3	○
Pedicles	C_4	○
Laminae	C_5	○
Vertebral foramen	C_6	○
Spinous process	C_7	○
Transverse process	C_8	○
Superior articular process	C_9	○

Five divisions	A	○
Cervical vertebrae	A_1	○
Thoracic vertebrae	A_2	○
Lumbar division	A_3	○

the CERVICAL and THORACIC VERTEBRAE

The cervical and thoracic vertebra have specific modifications reflecting the specific functions and movements they allow. The first two divisions of the vertebral column are the cervical vertebrae and the thoracic vertebrae, the topics of this plate.

> Note that in this plate two of the regions of the vertebral column are shown: the cervical vertebrae and the thoracic vertebrae. Color in the main title The Cervical and Thoracic Vertebrae, then look over the plate. Three of the diagrams refer to the cervical vertebrae and two refer to the thoracic vertebrae. Color in the main titles The Atlas and The Axis. You should select different light colors (orange, yellow, gray) for these vertebrae and be careful not to obscure the processes described. When you come to the processes, color in their titles and the arrows that point to them. Initially, we shall be concerned with the first two cervical vertebrae because they differ considerably from the other five cervical vertebrae.

The first cervical vertebra is the **atlas (A)**, so-named because it supports the head. Like the other cervical vertebrae, the atlas has a relatively large **vertebral foramen (A_1)**. Like the other cervical vertebrae it also has two other openings: the **transverse foramen (A_2)** on the left side and a second transverse foramen on the right side. Both are rimmed by a **transverse process (A_3)**. The vertebral foramen is outlined by a ring of bone consisting of the **anterior arch (A_4)** and the **posterior arch (A_5)**. A large **lateral mass (A_6)** lies where the arches meet. Note that there is no body or spinous process on the atlas. From the superior view, note a large **superior articular facet (A_7)**. This concave area is where the atlas articulates with the occipital condyle of the occipital bone of the skull. The articulation permits flexion at the joint. Inferior articular facets articulate with the axis but are not shown in this superior view. Another important process is the **articular surface for the dens (A_8)**. This is where the atlas articulates with the peglike dens from the axis.

The **axis (B)** has many of the same processes as the atlas, but they are modified. The **vertebral foramen (B_1)** is smaller, and the **transverse foramina (B_2)** are present. These foramina are surrounded by the **transverse process (B_3)**. The peglike process, the **dens (B_4)**, also called the odontoid process, is essential for articulation with the atlas. It projects up through the vertebral foramen to meet the atlas. In doing so, it provides a pivot on which the atlas and head rotate from side to side together. The **superior**

articular facet (B_5) is in a slightly different location than in the atlas, and the **lamina (B_6)** is more prominent. In addition, the axis has a spinous process split into two parts. For this reason it is called the **bifed spinous process (B_7)**.

> The remaining cervical vertebrae are similar to one another and display processes common to all. In the plate choose a light color (a pale blue, for example) and color in the title **Typical Cervical Vertebra (C)** and the figure of the vertebra. As before, this is a superior view. As you read about the vertebra, color in the arrows, indicating the processes, with dark colors.

In the remaining cervical vertebrae, the **vertebral foramen (C_1)** and the **transverse foramina (C_2)** are apparent. The vertebral foramen is triangular. The **transverse process (C_3)** surrounds the transverse foramen and serves as a site for muscle attachment. In these vertebrae, the body, or **centrum (C_4)**, is oval and broader from side to side than in the anterior-posterior aspect. The **superior articular facets (C_5)** are present, and the **pedicle (C_6)** forms part of the vertebral arch. The **lamina (C_7)** terminates in the **spinous process (C_8)**, which is short and split and, therefore, bifed.

> Continue and complete the plate by examining the figure of a **typical thoracic vertebra (D)**. The vertebra is shown in the superior and right lateral views. Color the main title Typical Thoracic Vertebra, then continue reading below. As you encounter the processes of the vertebra, color in the title and the arrow pointing to that process. Use a fourth light color for the two vertebrae since they are different from the cervical vertebrae.

A thoracic vertebra has a distinctive heart-shaped **body (D_1)** as opposed to the oval shape in the lumbar vertebrae. It is clearly larger than the body of a cervical vertebra. Note also that the vertebral foramen is smaller than that in the cervical vertebra (also smaller than that in the thoracic vertebrae), reflecting the smaller diameter of the spinal cord. Moreover, the transverse foramina have become much reduced in size and cannot be seen in the diagram. The **spinous process (D_2)** of the thoracic vertebra is longer and more slender than in the cervical region. The thoracic vertebrae articulate with the ribs. The second through eighth thoracic vertebrae, therefore, have points of articulation on each side. These points are called the **superior demifacet (D_3)** and the **inferior demifacet (D_4)**. The **transverse process (D_5)** is relatively thick in the thoracic vertebra. It contains a facet at which a rib articulates. The facet is called a **transverse costal facet (D_6)**. The rib, therefore, contacts the thoracic vertebra at both a demifacet and a transverse costal facet. The thoracic vertebra also has a superior **articular facet (D_7)** and a **prominent lamina (D_8)** terminating in the spinous process.

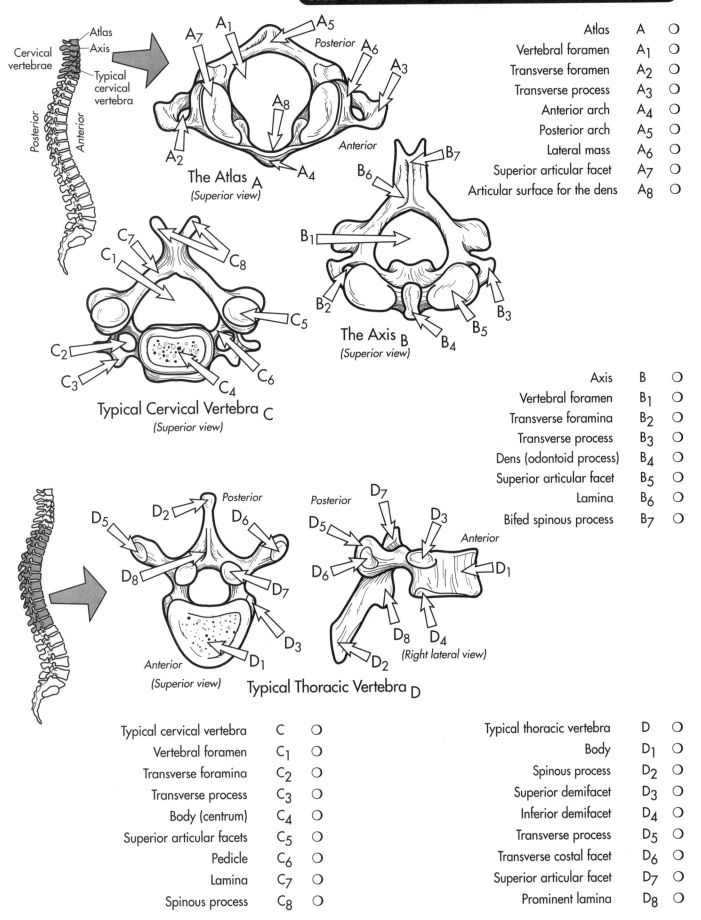

Cervical vertebrae

Atlas
Axis
Typical cervical vertebra

Posterior
Anterior

The Atlas A
(Superior view)

The Axis B
(Superior view)

Typical Cervical Vertebra C
(Superior view)

Typical Thoracic Vertebra D

Posterior
Anterior
(Superior view)

(Right lateral view)

Atlas	A	○
Vertebral foramen	A_1	○
Transverse foramen	A_2	○
Transverse process	A_3	○
Anterior arch	A_4	○
Posterior arch	A_5	○
Lateral mass	A_6	○
Superior articular facet	A_7	○
Articular surface for the dens	A_8	○

Axis	B	○
Vertebral foramen	B_1	○
Transverse foramina	B_2	○
Transverse process	B_3	○
Dens (odontoid process)	B_4	○
Superior articular facet	B_5	○
Lamina	B_6	○
Bifed spinous process	B_7	○

Typical cervical vertebra	C	○
Vertebral foramen	C_1	○
Transverse foramina	C_2	○
Transverse process	C_3	○
Body (centrum)	C_4	○
Superior articular facets	C_5	○
Pedicle	C_6	○
Lamina	C_7	○
Spinous process	C_8	○

Typical thoracic vertebra	D	○
Body	D_1	○
Spinous process	D_2	○
Superior demifacet	D_3	○
Inferior demifacet	D_4	○
Transverse process	D_5	○
Transverse costal facet	D_6	○
Superior articular facet	D_7	○
Prominent lamina	D_8	○

the LUMBAR and SACRAL VERTEBRAE

At the lower part of the body, the lumbar vertebrae support a major portion of the body's weight. They are large vertebrae with heavy bodies. In addition, the lumbar vertebrae permit flexibility of the body trunk. The sacrum at the inferior aspect of the vertebral column is so-named because ancient cultures considered it sacred to the gods. The sacrum connects the vertebral column to the pelvic girdle. The bone is substantial in size because forces generated at the lower limbs and trunk converge upon this triangular bone. This plate examines the lumbar and sacral portions of the vertebral column.

> Begin your study of the lumbar and sacral vertebrae by examining the relative positions of these structures to the vertebral column to the left of the plate. Then color the main title The Lumbar and Sacral Vertebrae. Now color the title Typical Lumbar Vertebra and examine the superior view on the left and the right lateral view on the right. As you read about the typical lumbar vertebra below, color the titles of the structures and processes as you encounter them, then color the arrow pointing to the area mentioned. The superior and right lateral views should be examined together and the structures should be colored in both views. The lumbar vertebrae should both be colored in a light shade such as gray.

There are five lumbar vertebrae. They are the largest and strongest vertebrae of the vertebral column, and they are responsible for supporting most of the body weight. In a **typical lumbar vertebra (A)**, the **body (A$_1$)** is thicker than in the other vertebra, and it is generally wider from side to side than in the anterior-posterior dimension. The body is oval, rather than heart-shaped as in the thoracic vertebrae. The **vertebral foramen (A$_2$)** is larger than in thoracic vertebrae and has a characteristic triangular shape. The **transverse processes (A$_3$)** are attachment points for the great muscles of the back. The processes are slender and project in the dorsal and lateral aspects. The **spinous process (A$_4$)** is thick and projects dorsally. It is a broad process adapted for the attachment of large muscles of the back. Other projections of the lumbar vertebrae are also short and thick. The **superior articular facets (A$_5$)** extend in the medial aspect, while the **inferior articular facets (A$_6$)** extend laterally. You may compare the location of these facets in the lumbar vertebra with those on the cervical vertebra. The inferior facets articulate with the vertebra below them in the vertebral column. The pedicles contain two indentations called the **superior vertebral notch (A$_7$)** and the **inferior vertebral notch (A$_8$)**. These indentations contain blood vessels and connective tissues.

> The plate should be continued by coloring the title Articulated Lumbar Vertebrae. This is a view of three vertebrae in place showing how they articulate with one another. As you read about these vertebrae, color in the plate as the directions specify.

Three lumbar vertebrae are shown in the plate. The first **vertebra (A)** should be colored with the same light color used for the typical lumbar vertebra. When you have finished coloring this vertebra, note its structures and processes and color the arrows pointing to them using the same colors as you used previously for these processes. This will give you an idea of how the vertebra and its processes appear in position. When your coloring is complete, select a different light color and color in the **superior vertebra (B)**. Then select a third color and color in the **inferior vertebra (C)**. Between two adjacent vertebrae is the **intervertebral disk (D)**. Each disk has an outer fibrous ring consisting of fibrocartilage and an inner soft elastic structure. The disks form joints between the vertebrae and permit movements of the vertebral column. They also absorb shocks. When compressed they may become flat and broad and they may bulge from the spaces between vertebrae. Two intervertebral disks are shown in the plate. The final area noted is the **intervertebral foramen (E)**. The intervertebral foramen is a space lying between adjoining vertebrae. This opening is where the spinal nerve emerges from the spinal cord. There are 31 pairs of spinal nerves that emerge in this manner.

> The final portion of this plate to be colored is the sacrum and coccyx. Color in the main title The Sacrum and Coccyx, and examine the sacrum in both anterior and posterior views. Color the **sacrum (F)** in a separate light color (an orange, for example) to avoid obscuring its processes, then color the **coccyx (G)** in a different light color to distinguish it from the sacrum. As you encounter the processes in the following paragraphs, color in the arrows in the plate.

Five sacral vertebrae fuse to form the triangular sacrum. Fusion begins in the normal individual between the ages of 16 and 18, and it is normally completed by the age of 25. Positioned at the posterior aspect of the pelvic cavity, the sacrum is medial to the two pelvic bones where it provides a strong foundation for the pelvic girdle. The **base of the sacrum (F$_1$)** is at the superior surface of the sacrum and is the broadest part. It has **articular processes and facets (F$_{11}$)** where the fifth lumbar vertebra articulates.

Within the substance of the sacrum is the **sacral canal (F$_2$)**, also called the vertebral canal. The sacral canal is the location of nerves and membranes that line the vertebral canal in the spinal cord and continue in the sacral canal. The canal is seen in the posterior view only. When the sacral vertebra fuse, their spinous processes form a **median sacral crest (F$_3$)**, seen in the posterior view. The laminae of the fifth sacral vertebra fail to meet one another and create an inferior entry to the sacral canal called the **sacral hiatus (F$_5$)**. Articular processes of this fifth sacral vertebra form the **sacral cornua (F$_4$)**. The cornua are connected to the coccyx by ligaments. The sacral hiatus is covered with connective tissue to restrict entry to the vertebral (sacral) canal. The intervertebral foramina of the sacrum are the sacral foramina. A **sacral foramen (F$_6$)** is visible in both anterior and posterior views.

The large smooth surface at the superior aspect of the sacrum is the **ala (F$_7$)**. This winglike structure extends laterally from the **lateral sacral crest (F$_8$)**. This crest and the median sacral crest are attachment points for muscles of the hip and lower back. Close to the ala on the posterior surface is the **sacral tuberosity (F$_9$)**, which is a depression where ligaments attach. These ligaments also secure the sacrum to the pelvic bone to form the sacroiliac joint. The caudal portion of the sacrum is the **narrow apex (F$_{10}$)**. The apex of the male sacrum is longer and narrower than that of the female.

In most instances, four **coccygeal vertebrae** form the coccyx. In the plate, these vertebrae are designated **G$_1$** to **G$_4$** and should be colored now using light colors. Muscles that constrict the opening to the anus are attached to the coccyx, and several ligaments also attach here. The **coccygeal cornua (G$_5$)** are the laminae of the first coccygeal vertebra. The coccygeal cornua meet the sacral cornua and are held to it by ligaments. The first pair of **transverse processes (G$_6$)** are prominent on the lateral surface and are largest in the first coccygeal vertebra.

In the superior aspect, the coccyx articulates with the sacrum. In males, it curves toward the anterior aspect, while in females it extends toward the inferior aspect. The base of the coccyx is in the superior position, and the apex is toward the inferior. Several muscles of the pelvis and hip have their origin at the coccyx.

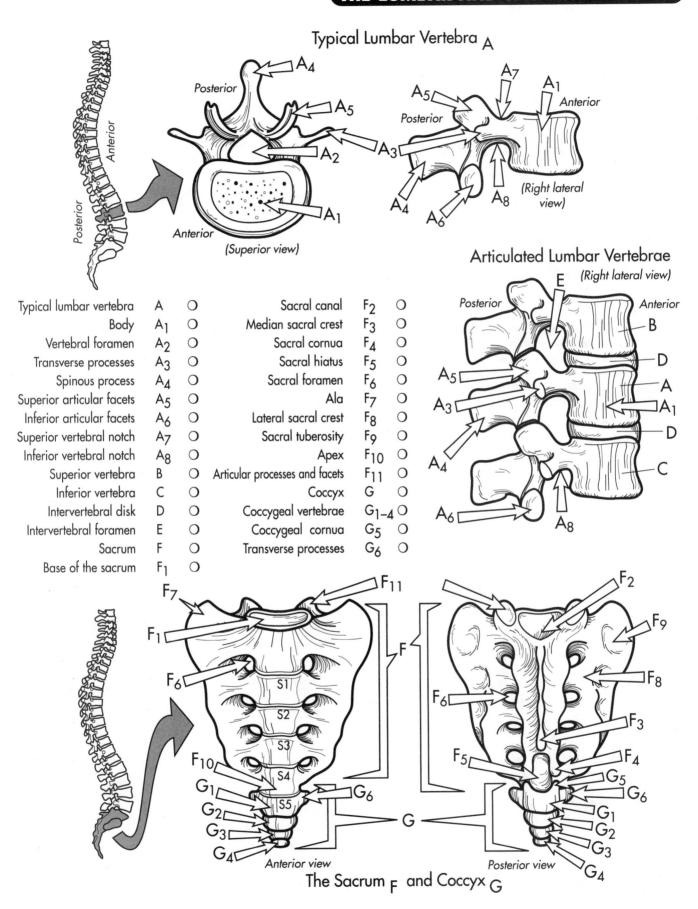

Typical Lumbar Vertebra A

Posterior

A$_4$

A$_5$

A$_7$ A$_1$ Anterior

A$_5$ Posterior

A$_2$ A$_3$

A$_4$ A$_6$ A$_8$

(Right lateral view)

Anterior

A$_1$

(Superior view)

Articulated Lumbar Vertebrae

(Right lateral view)

Posterior   Anterior

E

B

A$_5$ D

A$_3$ A

A$_1$

A$_4$ D

A$_6$ C

A$_8$

Typical lumbar vertebra	A	○	Sacral canal	F$_2$	○
Body	A$_1$	○	Median sacral crest	F$_3$	○
Vertebral foramen	A$_2$	○	Sacral cornua	F$_4$	○
Transverse processes	A$_3$	○	Sacral hiatus	F$_5$	○
Spinous process	A$_4$	○	Sacral foramen	F$_6$	○
Superior articular facets	A$_5$	○	Ala	F$_7$	○
Inferior articular facets	A$_6$	○	Lateral sacral crest	F$_8$	○
Superior vertebral notch	A$_7$	○	Sacral tuberosity	F$_9$	○
Inferior vertebral notch	A$_8$	○	Apex	F$_{10}$	○
Superior vertebra	B	○	Articular processes and facets	F$_{11}$	○
Inferior vertebra	C	○	Coccyx	G	○
Intervertebral disk	D	○	Coccygeal vertebrae	G$_{1-4}$	○
Intervertebral foramen	E	○	Coccygeal cornua	G$_5$	○
Sacrum	F	○	Transverse processes	G$_6$	○
Base of the sacrum	F$_1$	○			

F$_7$ F$_{11}$ F$_2$

F$_1$ F$_9$

F$_6$ F$_8$

S1   F

S2   F$_6$ F$_3$

S3   F$_5$ F$_4$

F$_{10}$ S4   G$_5$

G$_1$ S5   G$_6$ G$_6$

G$_2$ G   G$_1$

G$_3$ G$_2$

G$_4$ G$_3$

Anterior view   Posterior view   G$_4$

The Sacrum F and Coccyx G

the UPPER EXTREMITY/the PECTORAL GIRDLE

The appendicular skeleton consists of bones of the extremities, together with bones connecting them to the body trunk. The bones connecting the upper limb to the trunk are collectively known as the pectoral or shoulder girdle. In this plate, we study the bones of the pectoral girdle and introduce the bones of the upper extremity. Closer examination of the upper extremity bones occurs in several of the following plates.

> Begin the plate by coloring the main title The Upper Extremity/The Pectoral Girdle. Then color the title The Upper Extremity In Place. As you encounter the structures of the upper extremity in place, color the titles; then color the plate where they are located. The text has suggestions for colors to use. For the time being, do not color the Pectoral Girdle.

The pectoral girdle is made up of two bones, which make up the major portion of the shoulder. As you color the two bones, choose a light color such as tan or yellow. At the anterior end is the clavicle (A), and at the posterior aspect is the scapula (B). Although the term girdle implies a beltlike structure, the clavicle and scapula come close to but do not quite constitute a belt. Instead they are attached to the thorax and vertebral columns by the muscles covering their surfaces. Other structures close to the scapula and clavicle are the ribs (C) and the sternum (D). The pectoral girdle serves two important functions: (1) it provides a point where the upper extremity attaches to the axial skeleton, and (2) it provides attachment points for many muscles that move the upper extremity.

The bones of the upper limb attach to the scapula at the glenoid fossa (B_4), a ball-and-socket joint. Choose darker colors for the bones since their processes will not be considered here. The upper limb bones include the humerus (E) and the two bones of the forearm, the radius (F) and ulna (G). Completing the upper extremity are the eight carpal bones (H) and the bones of the hand, the metacarpals (I), and finally the bones of the fingers, the phalanges (J). When you color the phalanges, make note of the fact that there are three phalanges on each of the fingers, except for the thumb which has only two.

> Continue the plate by coloring the section entitled The Pectoral Girdle. This figure shows a closeup of the humerus (E) and the two bones of the pectoral girdle. Color in the clavicle (A) and the scapula (B) using the light colors you used previously. Then continue reading below. Watch for the arrows pointing out the landmarks and processes.

The clavicle (A) is also known as the collarbone. It is a long, slender bone. The bone can be felt along its entire course as it extends horizontally across the thorax. At its medial end, the clavicle attaches to the manubrium of the sternum,

while at its lateral end it articulates with the acromion process (B_1) of the scapula. The scapula (B) is a large, flattened, triangular bone lying on the posterio-lateral aspect of the ribcage. It overlies the second through seventh ribs and has two surfaces: one facing the ribs known as the costal surface, and the second directed posteriorly and called the dorsal surface. At its anterior aspect in the lateral end, the scapula has an enlarged projection called the acromion process (B_1), which forms the point of the shoulder. The acromion process articulates with the clavicle at the acromioclavicular joint (B_2). At the anterior aspect, the superior surface of the scapula contains the coracoid process (B_3). This is the point of attachment for the biceps muscle of the arm. We shall encounter these two important processes a bit later.

> Now color the title The Clavicle (A) both in the title list and the plate. Then focus your attention on the two views of the clavicle. The first is a view from the superior aspect, the second is an inferior view. Color both clavicles with the same light colors you used before, then continue your reading. When you encounter the processes and structures of the clavicle, the arrows may be colored in. Darker colors are recommended for the arrows.

The clavicle is S-shaped, with convex and concave curves. The junction of the two curves is the weakest point of the clavicle and is a frequent site of fractures. The broad, flat end of the bone is called the acromial end (A_1), because it articulates with the acromion process of the scapula. At the medial end of the bone, the clavicle has its sternal end (A_2), referring to its articulation with the sternum. In the inferior aspect, the clavicle has a conoid tubercle (A_3), which serves as a point of attachment for ligaments. Also on the inferior surface is the costal tuberosity (A_4), which also serves as an attachment point for ligaments.

> The final portions of the plate are detailed diagrams of the scapula. This bone is presented in three views: anterior, lateral, and posterior. As you encounter the areas, processes, or structures, you should color them in all three views using the same color. Begin by coloring in the main title The Scapula (B) in the list and in the plate, then continue reading.

As previously noted, the scapula has the shape of a broad triangle. As we have seen, the two major processes are the acromion process (B_1) and the coracoid process (B_3). These projections can be felt through the skin. Their ends meet to form a large concavity called the glenoid fossa (B_4). This cavity can be seen particularly well in the lateral view of the right scapula. A rim of cartilage is attached to the circumference of the glenoid cavity, and the head of the humerus articulates with the scapula at the cavity to form the shoulder joint.

The dorsal surface of the scapula is divided into two regions by the spine of the scapula (B_5). The area above the spine is called the supraspinous fossa (B_6). The area below (inferior to the spine) is known as the infraspinous fossa (B_7). These areas are seen in the lateral and posterior views. With the subscapular fossa (B_8), they serve as sites of attachment for numerous shoulder muscles. Each scapula has three borders and two angles. The medial border (B_9), sometimes called the vertebral border, is thin and lies close to the vertebral column. The lateral or axillary border (B_{10}) is thicker and lies closer to the humerus. The superior border (B_{11}) is at the upper edge of the scapula. It contains a notch called the scapular notch (B_{12}) where nerves pass through the upper border. Where the medial and lateral borders meet, the scapula has an inferior angle (B_{13}). The superior angle (B_{14}) lies where the medial border meets the superior border.

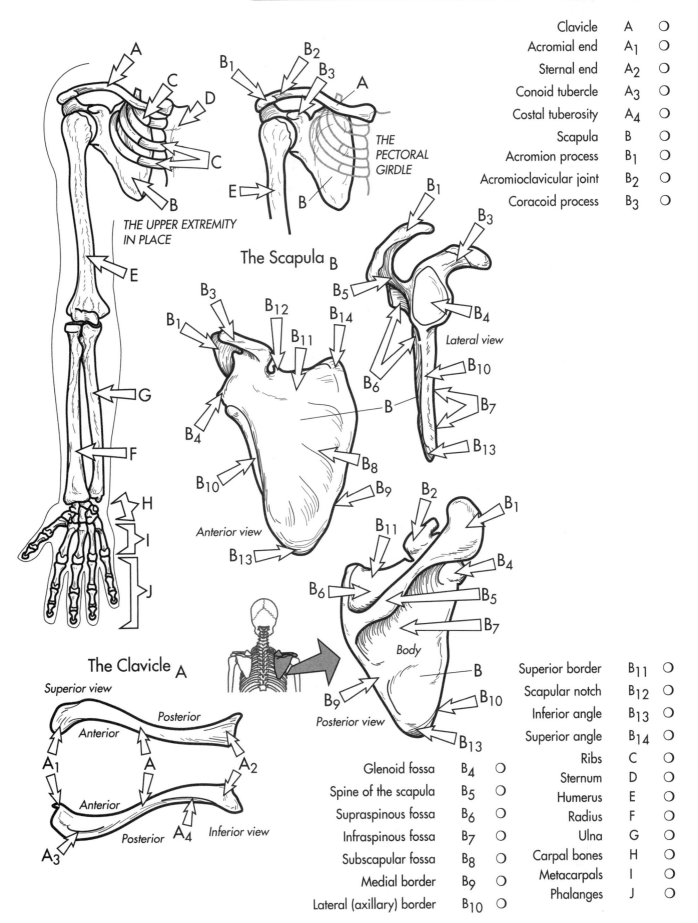

The Scapula B

THE PECTORAL GIRDLE

THE UPPER EXTREMITY IN PLACE

Lateral view

Anterior view

Posterior view

Body

The Clavicle A

Superior view

Posterior

Anterior

Anterior

Posterior

Inferior view

Clavicle	A	○
Acromial end	A$_1$	○
Sternal end	A$_2$	○
Conoid tubercle	A$_3$	○
Costal tuberosity	A$_4$	○
Scapula	B	○
Acromion process	B$_1$	○
Acromioclavicular joint	B$_2$	○
Coracoid process	B$_3$	○

Superior border	B$_{11}$	○
Scapular notch	B$_{12}$	○
Inferior angle	B$_{13}$	○
Superior angle	B$_{14}$	○
Ribs	C	○
Sternum	D	○
Humerus	E	○
Radius	F	○
Ulna	G	○
Carpal bones	H	○
Metacarpals	I	○
Phalanges	J	○

Glenoid fossa	B$_4$	○
Spine of the scapula	B$_5$	○
Supraspinous fossa	B$_6$	○
Infraspinous fossa	B$_7$	○
Subscapular fossa	B$_8$	○
Medial border	B$_9$	○
Lateral (axillary) border	B$_{10}$	○

the UPPER EXTREMITY/the HUMERUS

The humerus, also known as the upper arm bone, is the largest and longest bone of the upper extremity. It is a relatively thick bone with a large, smooth head at the proximal end, and a number of projections (processes) at the distal end. Sixty bones are found in both the upper and lower extremities.

Begin this plate by coloring the main title The Upper Extremity/The Humerus, and then color the title The Humerus In Place. Now examine this section of the plate and color in the main features of the upper limb as you encounter them in the reading below. The humerus should be colored a light color such as pale blue, but the other bones can be darker.

The **humerus (A)** is the main bone of the upper extremity. It articulates with the **scapula (B)** at the glenoid fossa. Another prominent bone in this area is the **clavicle (C)**. The nearby bones to the pectoral girdle include the **ribs (D)**, which articulate with the **sternum (E)**. Distally, the humerus articulates with the **radius (F)** and the **ulna (G)**; these are described in the next plate.

The remainder of the plate shows the important processes of the humerus. Color in the title Processes of the Humerus. The humerus in both anterior and posterior views should be colored in the same light color used previously. (A light color is recommended so that the important processes are not obscured.) As you read about the processes in the following paragraphs, locate them and color their arrows in both the anterior and posterior views. Some processes are present on the anterior aspect but not on the posterior aspect, and vice versa.

Beginning at the proximal end, the humerus features a **head (A$_1$)** that articulates at the glenoid cavity of the scapula. The head is prominent in the posterior view, and both anterior and posterior arrows should be colored at this time. On the lateral surface of the epiphysis of the humerus is the **greater tubercle (A$_2$)**. This is an attachment point for shoulder joint ligaments and is the most lateral point of the shoulder region that can be felt through the skin. The **lesser tubercle (A$_3$)** is also an attachment point for ligaments. It lies on the anterior and medial surface of the humerus. A groove called the **intertubercular groove (A$_4$)** separates the greater and lesser tubercles. The **anatomical neck (A$_5$)** is the distal limit of the articular capsule. It is the site of what once was the epiphyseal plate. The **surgical neck (A$_6$)** is a constricted portion distal to the tubercles and a common site of fractures.

Continue with the plate by focusing on the shaft and distal portion of the humerus. As you encounter the structures in the paragraphs below, color the titles and arrows that point to the appropriate processes and landmarks. Dark colors may be used for the arrows to contrast with the light color of the bone.

The **shaft of the humerus (A$_7$)** is rounded at the proximal end, but more triangular at the distal end. An important process on the shaft is the **deltoid tuberosity (A$_8$)**. This is where the deltoid muscle (the fleshy mass of the shoulder) attaches to the humerus. The tuberosity is shaped like a V. At the distal end of the bone is a depression called the **radial fossa (A$_9$)**. The head of the radius articulates here when the arm is flexed. The **coronoid fossa (A$_{10}$)** is the depression that receives the ulna's coronoid process during flexion. The **lateral epicondyle (A$_{11}$)** is an attachment site for muscles that move the forearm. The **medial epicondyle (A$_{12}$)** is a second attachment site for these muscles. The **capitulum (A$_{13}$)** is seen prominently in the anterior view. It is a "little head" that articulates with the radius. The **trochlear (A$_{14}$)** is a point of articulation with the ulna. The posterior view of the humerus shows the **olecranon fossa (A$_{15}$)**. This is a depression that receives the olecranon process of the ulna during extension of the forearm.

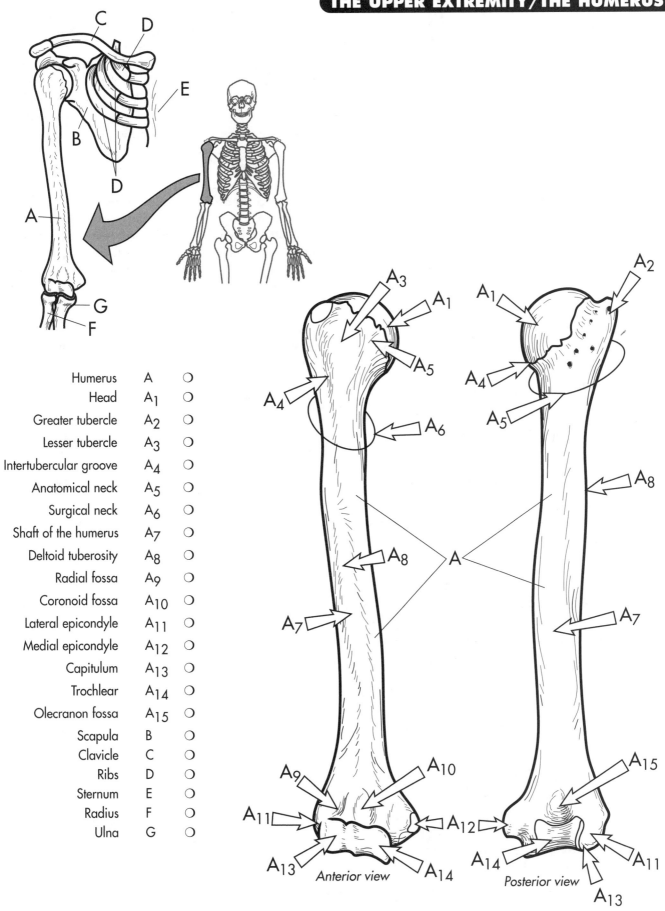

Humerus	A	○
Head	A₁	○
Greater tubercle	A₂	○
Lesser tubercle	A₃	○
Intertubercular groove	A₄	○
Anatomical neck	A₅	○
Surgical neck	A₆	○
Shaft of the humerus	A₇	○
Deltoid tuberosity	A₈	○
Radial fossa	A₉	○
Coronoid fossa	A₁₀	○
Lateral epicondyle	A₁₁	○
Medial epicondyle	A₁₂	○
Capitulum	A₁₃	○
Trochlear	A₁₄	○
Olecranon fossa	A₁₅	○
Scapula	B	○
Clavicle	C	○
Ribs	D	○
Sternum	E	○
Radius	F	○
Ulna	G	○

Anterior view

Posterior view

the UPPER EXTREMITY/the RADIUS and ULNA

The radius and ulna are two parallel long bones of the forearm. These bones can be felt along their entire length in the normal forearm. At the proximal ends, they articulate with the humerus, while at their distal ends they form joints with bones of the wrist. This plate shows the anatomical features of the radius and ulna.

Begin the plate by coloring the main title The Upper Extremity/The Radius and Ulna. Then color the radius (A) and locate the radius bone in both the anterior view and the posterior view. Color the entire radius bone in both views, using a light red, green, or blue so as to avoid obscuring the leader lines. After you have colored the radius, begin reading the paragraph below. As you encounter the fine details of the radius, color in the appropriate title and then color the arrow that points to it. Finally, read the descriptions of the radial processes.

In the anatomical position, the radius is the lateral bone of the forearm. It is narrow at its proximal end and wide at its distal end (the ulna has the opposite shape). At its most proximal point, the **head of the radius (A_1)** articulates with the capitulum of the humerus. The head has the shape of a disk. The next area encountered is the **neck of the radius (A_2)**. Distal to the neck is the **radial tuberosity (A_3)**, where a muscle attaches to permit flexion of the forearm. The **shaft (A_4)** is the long section of the radius. At the expanded portion of the radius is the **ulnar notch (A_5)**, where the ulna articulates. At the lateral margin is the **styloid process (A_6)**, the anchoring site for ligaments extending to the hand. These processes can be seen on the plate in both the anterior and posterior views.

Continue the plate by coloring the title **ulna (B)** and the entire bone in both the anterior and posterior views. Once again, a light color should be used to permit viewing of the markings. After you have completed your coloring, read the descriptions of the processes below. As you encounter each, color the title of the process or marking and the leader line pointing to it. Do this in both the anterior and posterior views using dark colors.

In the anatomical position, the ulna is medial to the radius. It is the slightly longer bone, and it forms the elbow joint with the humerus. At its most proximal end, the ulna has the **olecranon process (B_6)**. This process is the point of the elbow. On the anterior side, it has a concave depression called the **trochlear notch (B_1)**. This depression articulates with the trochlear of the humerus at the elbow joint, also known as the olecranal joint. At the inferior end of the cavity is the **coronoid process (B_2)**. This process also joins with the trochlear of the humerus during extreme flexion when the process projects into the coronoid fossa on the surface of the humerus. The **ulnar tuberosity (B_3)** serves as an attachment point for muscles, and the **radial notch (B_4)** is the point where the head of the radius articulates.

At its distal end, the shaft of the ulna narrows and ends in a disk-shaped **head (B_7)**. At the medial surface is a **short styloid process (B_5)** from which ligaments extend to the wrist. Attached to the styloid process is an **articular cartilage (B_8)** that separates the head of the ulna from the wrist bones.

At this point, color the title **interosseus membrane (C)** using a medium color to contrast with the bone and its markings. Also, color the arrows pointing to the **radial-ulnar joints (D_1 and D_2)**. Locate these structures as you read about them below, and color them in the plate.

The **interosseous membrane (C)** is a flexible membrane that connects the radius and ulna along their entire length. It is a fibrous membrane. The radius and ulna come together at two radial-ulnar joints, the **distal radial-ulnar joint (D_1)** and the **proximal radial-ulnar joint (D_2)**.

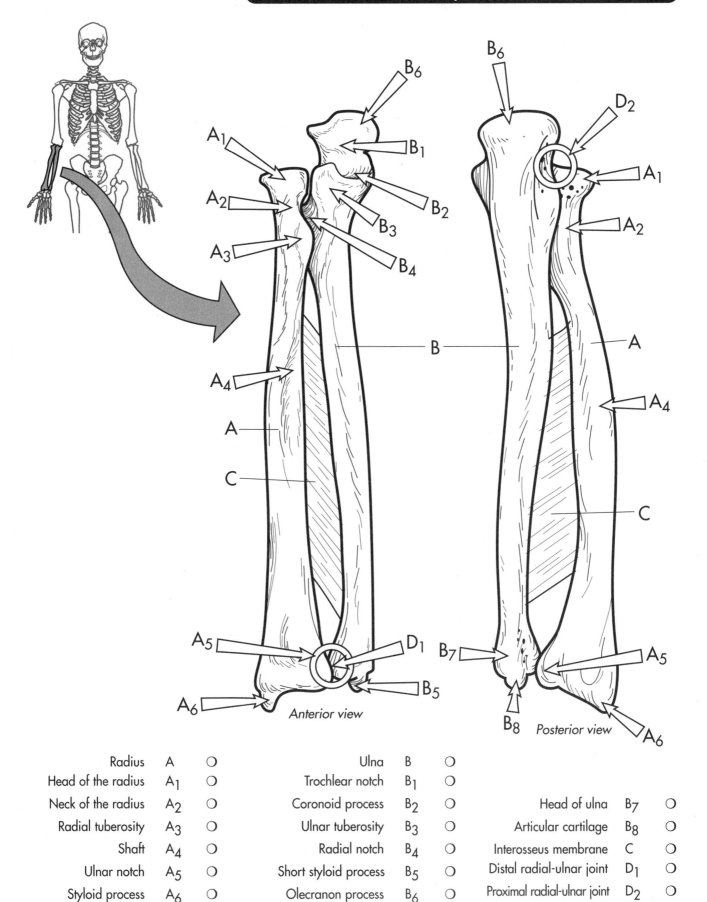

Anterior view

Posterior view

Radius	A	○		Ulna	B	○			
Head of the radius	A₁	○		Trochlear notch	B₁	○			
Neck of the radius	A₂	○		Coronoid process	B₂	○		Head of ulna	B₇	○
Radial tuberosity	A₃	○		Ulnar tuberosity	B₃	○		Articular cartilage	B₈	○
Shaft	A₄	○		Radial notch	B₄	○		Interosseus membrane	C	○
Ulnar notch	A₅	○		Short styloid process	B₅	○		Distal radial-ulnar joint	D₁	○
Styloid process	A₆	○		Olecranon process	B₆	○		Proximal radial-ulnar joint	D₂	○

the UPPER EXTREMITY/the WRIST and HAND

The 27 bones that constitute the skeletal framework of the hand are distributed among three distinct regions: the wrist with carpal bones; the palm with metacarpals; and the digits with phalanges (singular, phalanx). The plate shows the bones of the right hand in both anterior and posterior views.

> Begin coloring the plate with the main title The Upper Extremity/The Wrist and Hand. Next, color the titles **radius (A)** and **ulna (B)** using dark colors. Then color the title **carpals (C)** and color the bracket using a dark color. Now read the paragraph below and color in the titles of the bones as you encounter them using a different color for each title. Then color the bones to match the titles using dark colors to provide contrast. Color both the anterior and posterior views at the same time.

The lower forearm consists of the **radius (A)** and the **ulna (B)**. These bones articulate with the first of two rows of carpals. The **carpals (C)** consist of the proximal row of carpals and the distal row. There are four carpal bones in each row.

The **scaphoid bone (C$_1$)** is found on the lateral border of the wrist near the styloid process of the radius. Proceeding from the lateral to the medial side of the hand on the anterior surface, the next bone is the **lunate bone (C$_2$)**. This bone also articulates with the radius. Next medial to the lunate bone is the **triquetal bone (C$_3$)**. This bone is somewhat triangular in shape. The triquetal bone articulates with the cartilage separating the ulna from the carpals. The most medial of the carpal bones is the small **pisiform bone (C$_4$)**. This bone is evident from the outside body, because it projects posteriorly on the little finger side as a small, rounded elevation. The lateral bone of the distal row of carpals is the **trapezium bone (C$_5$)**. Medial to the trapezium bone is the **trapezoid bone (C$_6$)**. This bone articulates with the scaphoid bone, as does the trapezium. The trapezoid bone is shaped like a wedge. The largest bone is the **capitate bone (C$_7$)**, and the medial carpal bone in the distal row is the **hamate bone (C$_8$)**. This bone has roughly the shape of a hook.

> Now color the title **metacarpals (D)**. Continue reading about the metacarpals below, and as you encounter them in the reading, locate them in the plate and color them in. Different colors should be used where possible. Also, look for the parts of the metacarpals and color their arrows.

There are five metacarpal bones radiating from the distal row of carpals much like the spokes of a wheel. The metacarpal bones form the palm of the hand. The bones are long, and are not given names but are numbered I to V beginning with the thumb and ending with the little finger. The metacarpal bones should be colored with five different colors using the same colors for both the anterior and posterior views. Each metacarpal has three distinctive areas: **the base of the metacarpal (D$_1$)**, followed by the long **shaft of the metacarpal (D$_2$)**, and the **head of the metacarpal (D$_3$)**. The heads of the metacarpals are prominent as the proximal knuckles of the hand. They articulate with the phalanges.

> To complete the plate, color the title **phalanges (E)**. Then color the bracket outlining the phalanges. Color the titles of the three types of phalanges: **proximal (E$_1$)**, **middle (E$_2$)**, and **distal (E$_3$)**. Also color the three regions of the phalanx, the **base (E$_4$)**, the **shaft (E$_5$)**, and the **head (E$_6$)**, using the same color as for the titles. Both anterior and posterior views should be colored.

Distally, the metacarpals articulate with the finger bones, the **phalanges (E)**. Each hand has 14 phalanges. They are distinguished as **proximal phalanges (E$_1$)**, **middle phalanges (E$_2$)**, and **distal phalanges (E$_3$)**. The thumb has no middle phalanx. It has only a **proximal phalanx (E$_1$)** and a **distal phalanx (E$_3$)**. A phalanx has three distinctive areas: **base (E$_4$)**, the most proximal part of the phalanx; the **shaft (E$_5$)**; and the **head (E$_6$)**, the most distal portion of the phalanx.

Radius	A	○	Base of the metacarpal	D_1	○
Ulna	B	○	Shaft of the metacarpal	D_2	○
Carpals	C	○	Head of the metacarpal	D_3	○
Scaphoid bone	C_1	○	Phalanges	E	○
Lunate bone	C_2	○	Proximal phalanx	E_1	○
Triquetal bone	C_3	○	Middle phalanx	E_2	○
Pisiform bone	C_4	○	Distal phalanx	E_3	○
Trapezium bone	C_5	○	Base of the phalanx	E_4	○
Trapezoid bone	C_6	○	Shaft of the phalanx	E_5	○
Capitate bone	C_7	○	Head of the phalanx	E_6	○
Hamate bone	C_8	○			
Metacarpals	D	○			

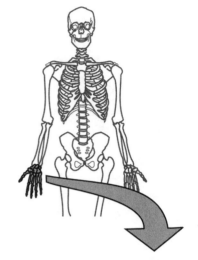

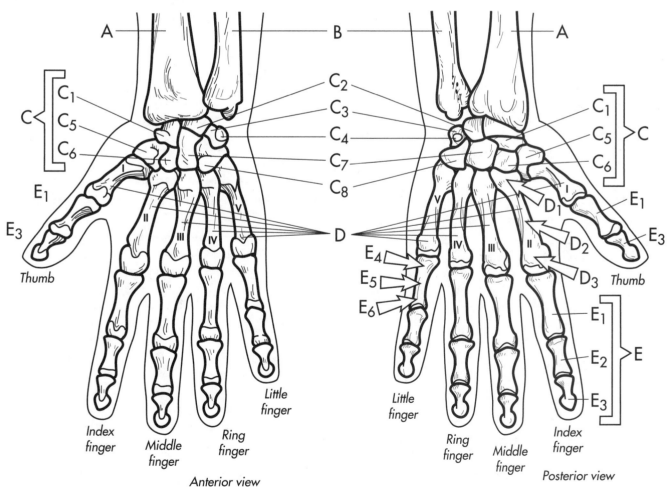

Anterior view

Posterior view

Thumb

Index finger

Middle finger

Ring finger

Little finger

Little finger

Ring finger

Middle finger

Index finger

Thumb

the LOWER EXTREMITY/the PELVIC GIRDLE

The pelvic girdle, also called the hip girdle, attaches the lower extremity to the axial skeleton. It transmits the upper body weight to the lower limbs while supporting the visceral organs of the pelvis. Because the pelvic girdle is secured to the axial skeleton by strong ligaments, movement at the hip joints is not as great as at the shoulder joint. Moreover, the sockets of the lower extremity are heavily reinforced by ligaments, also limiting the degree of freedom at the hip joint.

> The pelvic girdle encircles the body and provides an attachment point for the lower extremity. Begin the plate by coloring in the main title The Lower Extremity/The Pelvic Girdle. Then color in the title, The Lower Extremity In Place. Examine this part of the plate, and as you read about the structures of the lower extremity, color their titles and structures. Dark colors may be used for contrast since there are few processes to point out. However, you should use a light color for the pelvic bone since it will be explained in detail below.

The pelvic girdle is formed by two bones called os coxae. The coxal bones unite with one another in the anterior aspect and with the sacrum in the posterior aspect. They form a deep basinlike structure called the pelvis. With the lower extremity in place, the **pelvic bone (A)** can be seen articulating with the **sacrum (B)**. The thigh bone (known as the femur), articulates with the pelvic bone at a cuplike socket called the **acetabulum (R)**. Distally, the femur articulates with the kneecap or **patella (D)** and the large leg bone known as the **tibia (E)**. Lateral to the tibia is the smaller leg bone known as the **fibula (F)**. The ankle bones are the **tarsals (G)**, and the bones of the foot are the **metatarsals (H)**. The toe bones are the **phalanges (I)**.

> We will now examine the structure of the pelvic girdle and os coxae more closely by noting the difference between the male and female pelvis. Begin coloring this portion of plate by coloring the titles Male and Female Pelvis. Then read below and examine the differences between the two.

Differences between the male pelvis and female pelvis are clear and striking. Indeed, a trained anatomist can determine the sex of a skeleton by examining the pelvis. Each pelvis has similar **pelvic bones (A)**. The **acetabulum (R)** is visible in each pelvis. The pelvic bones articulate with the **sacrum (J)** at a joint called the **sacroiliac joint (K)**. Posterior to the sacrum is the **coccyx (L)**, the last vertebra. The **male pelvis** has a **pubic arch** less than 90° **(M)**. By contrast, the **pubic arch** of the **female pelvis** is greater than 90° **(N)**. Thus, the female pelvis is wider, shallower, and rounder than the male pelvis. This allows the female to accommodate the growing fetus, and it permits the infant to exit through the pubic bones at birth. The bones separate at a point called the **pubic symphysis (A$_1$)**. This is the point where the os coxae come together in the anterior aspect.

> Continue the plate with two lateral views of the os coxa. Begin by coloring the titles Bones of the Os Coxa and Processes of the Os Coxa. First you will examine the components of the pelvic girdle, then learn some of its important processes. The figure of the bones (the first one) should be colored in darkly so you can see their relationships, but light colors such as pale red, green, and blue should be used for the processes figure so as to avoid obscuring the arrows. Read the paragraph below as you continue and color in the titles and processes as you proceed.

After birth and during early childhood, each os coxa consists of three separate bones. These bones are the **ileum (O)**, the **ischium (P)**, and the **pubis (Q)**. By the adult years, these bones have fused firmly to one another and their boundaries cannot be distinguished. However, their names are retained for reference to different portions of the pelvic bone. Processes therefore include the names of the three bones. Each of the three bones contributes to the formation of the cuplike **acetabulum (R)** seen on the lateral surface.

We shall begin noting the processes of the os coxa and focus on those of the ileum. In the anterior aspect, the expansion of the ileum begins with the **anterior inferior iliac spine (O$_1$)**. This is an attachment point for hip, thigh, and trunk muscles. This spine is palpable through the skin. Next is the **anterior superior iliac spine (O$_2$)**, which is another muscle attachment point. Curving posteriorly is the **iliac crest (O$_3$)**. This ridge is an attachment point for ligaments and muscles of the abdomen and leg. The iliac crest extends to the **posterior superior iliac spine (O$_4$)**. The margin continues as the **posterior inferior iliac spine (O$_5$)**, which is also a muscle attachment site. Inferior to the posterior inferior iliac spine, the ileum indents deeply and forms the **greater sciatic notch (O$_6$)**. This is the place through which the sciatic nerve passes. The sciatic nerve is the longest nerve of the body and it enters the thigh.

> We shall complete the plate by focusing on the important markings and processes of the ischium and pubis. Watch for the arrows associated with the processes and color them in dark colors.

Posterior to the acetabulum is the **ischial spine (P$_1$)**. The ischial spine can be palpated by the physician through the vaginal wall and is used for determining pelvic measurements during childbirth. The lesser **sciatic notch (P$_2$)** is the site where a number of nerves and blood vessels pass to the perineum, which is the anogenital region. The inferior surface is thickened as the **ischial tuberosity (P$_3$)**. When sitting, the body's weight is placed on the ischial tuberosity, the strongest part of the pelvic girdle. The **ramus of the ischium (P$_4$)** joins the pubis in the anterior aspect. The pubis, also called the pubic bone, is the major portion of the anterior os coxa. At the lateral end is the **pubic tubercle (Q$_1$)**, which is an attachment site for the important inguinal ligament. Essentially the pubis is a V-shaped bone with a **superior ramus (Q$_2$)** and the **inferior ramus (Q$_3$)**. Between the superior and inferior rami of the pubis is the **body of the pubis (Q$_4$)**. The pubic rami and the rami of the ischium form the **obturator foramen (Q$_5$)**. Collagen fibers enclose this space, and the inner and outer surfaces of the foramen are used as attachment sites for various muscles. A few blood vessels and nerves pass through this foramen and enter the thigh. Portions of the pubis, ileum, and ischium form the **acetabulum (R)**.

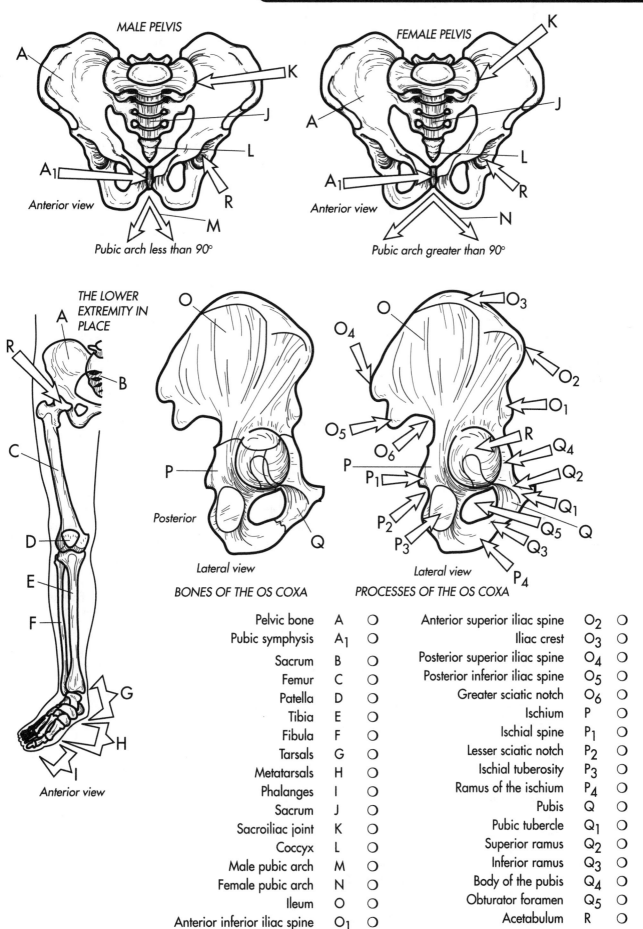

MALE PELVIS

A

K

J

L

A_1

Anterior view

R

M

Pubic arch less than 90°

FEMALE PELVIS

K

J

A

L

A_1

Anterior view

R

N

Pubic arch greater than 90°

THE LOWER EXTREMITY IN PLACE

A

R

B

C

D

E

F

G

H

I

Anterior view

O

P

Q

Posterior

Lateral view

BONES OF THE OS COXA

O

O_4

O_3

O_2

O_1

O_5

O_6

R

Q_4

Q_2

Q_1

P

P_1

P_2

P_3

Q_5

Q_3

Q

P_4

Lateral view

PROCESSES OF THE OS COXA

Pelvic bone	A	O
Pubic symphysis	A_1	O
Sacrum	B	O
Femur	C	O
Patella	D	O
Tibia	E	O
Fibula	F	O
Tarsals	G	O
Metatarsals	H	O
Phalanges	I	O
Sacrum	J	O
Sacroiliac joint	K	O
Coccyx	L	O
Male pubic arch	M	O
Female pubic arch	N	O
Ileum	O	O
Anterior inferior iliac spine	O_1	O

Anterior superior iliac spine	O_2	O
Iliac crest	O_3	O
Posterior superior iliac spine	O_4	O
Posterior inferior iliac spine	O_5	O
Greater sciatic notch	O_6	O
Ischium	P	O
Ischial spine	P_1	O
Lesser sciatic notch	P_2	O
Ischial tuberosity	P_3	O
Ramus of the ischium	P_4	O
Pubis	Q	O
Pubic tubercle	Q_1	O
Superior ramus	Q_2	O
Inferior ramus	Q_3	O
Body of the pubis	Q_4	O
Obturator foramen	Q_5	O
Acetabulum	R	O

the LOWER EXTREMITY/ the FEMUR

Each lower limb has the same number of bones as the upper limb: 60. The lower limb is divided into several regions, with the thigh extending from the hip joint to the knee. The thigh contains a single bone called the femur. Other regions, known as the leg, ankle, and foot, are considered in plates following this one.

Color in the main title The Lower Extremity/The Femur. Now color in the title The Femur In Place. Then read the paragraph below, and when you encounter the bone, color its title in the titles list and in the plate. Use a light color for the femur and darker colors for the other bones in the figure entitled The Femur In Place.

The thighbone is anatomically known as the **femur (A)**. It is the longest, heaviest, and strongest bone in the body. At the proximal end it articulates with the hipbone, technically known as the **pelvic girdle (B)**. The femur then courses medially and descends toward the knee. At the distal end, it articulates with the **patella (C)** and the **tibia (D)**. The second bone of the leg, the **fibula (E)**, is nearby but does not articulate with the femur. The femur is covered by strong and bulky muscles that permit it to endure the stress placed on the bone. The length of the femur is about one-quarter of a person's height.

Look over the list of processes associated with the femur, but do not color them yet. Instead, wait until you encounter the process in the reading below. At that point, color the arrow pointing out the process in both the anterior and posterior views. Certain processes will be present on only one of the views. You should begin by coloring the femur itself in a light color (as used above) so as not to obscure the arrows pointing out the important processes. Both the anterior and posterior views of the femur can be colored before you begin your study of its processes.

At its proximal end, the femur contains a rounded epiphysis known as the **head (A_1)**. The femur articulates with the pelvic bone at the hip joint, which is called the acetabulum. The view of the femur in place shows this articulation. A small central pit called the fovea capitis is at the center of the head. This is a point of attachment for ligaments. The head of the femur is found on a **neck (A_2)**. The neck angles to the lateral aspect and joins the **shaft (A_3)** of the femur. Fractures often occur at the neck of the femur, especially when bone degradation has taken place. The condi-

tion is often called a broken hip. Projecting laterally where the neck and shaft join is the **greater trochanter (A_4)**. This is a point of attachment for several muscles of the thigh and pelvic region. Prominently on the posterior aspect is the **lesser trochanter (A_5)**, which is also an attachment point for various muscles. On the anterior aspect of the femur is a raised area called the **intertrochanteric line (A_6)**. This region connects the greater and lesser trochanters. On the posterior surfaces is the **intertrochanteric crest (A_7)**. This ridge also connects the trochanters. A ridge below in the intertrochanteric crest is the gluteal tuberosity, a point of attachment for several thigh muscles.

At this point, you have completed a study of the proximal end of the femur. The remainder of the plate deals with structures at the distal end. Look over the remaining markings and processes of the femur and as you encounter them in the reading below, color the arrows pointing out the processes.

Continuing from the gluteal tuberosity, the posterior surface of the femur contains a vertical ridge called the **linea aspera (A_8)**. This is the site of muscles that bring about abduction of the thigh. Except for this ridge, the shaft of the femur is smooth and round. At the distal end, the femur is constructed to permit articulation with the femur. The linea aspera divides to form a flattened, triangular area called the **popliteal surface (A_9)**. This is the point of attachment of the popliteal muscle. On the medial surface is the **medial epicondyle (A_{10})** where several muscles attach. On the opposite surface is the **lateral epicondyle (A_{11})**, which is also a site of muscle attachment. Also on the medial surface is the **medial condyle (A_{12})**. This is a point of articulation with the tibia. The **lateral condyle (A_{13})** is a second point of articulation. The depressed area between the condyles on the posterior surface is the **intercondylar fossa (A_{14})**. On the anterior surface is a smooth area called the **patellar space surface (A_{15})**. This area is located between the condyles and is the point of articulation with the patella, also called the knee cap. The patella glides over this smooth surface.

Femur — A ○
Head of femur — A₁ ○
Neck of femur — A₂ ○
Shaft of femur — A₃ ○
Greater trochanter — A₄ ○
Lesser trochanter — A₅ ○
Intertrochanteric line — A₆ ○
Intertrochanteric crest — A₇ ○
Linea aspera — A₈ ○
Popliteal surface — A₉ ○

Medial epicondyle — A₁₀ ○
Lateral epicondyle — A₁₁ ○
Medial condyle — A₁₂ ○
Lateral condyle — A₁₃ ○
Intercondylar fossa — A₁₄ ○
Patellar space surface — A₁₅ ○
Pelvic girdle — B ○
Patella — C ○
Tibia — D ○
Fibula — E ○

THE FEMUR IN PLACE

Anterior view

Posterior view

Posterior view

47

the LOWER EXTREMITY/the TIBIA and FIBULA

Where the femur is the bone of the thigh, two parallel bones, the tibia and fibula, form the skeleton of the leg. The two bones articulate with each other both proximally and distally. The larger bone, the tibia, articulates with the femur in the proximal region and forms a hinge joint at the knee. Distally, it articulates with the talus bone in the ankle. The fibula is not involved in the knee joint. We shall also consider a third bone, the patella, commonly known as the kneecap.

> Begin your work on the plate by coloring the main title The Lower Extremity/The Tibia and Fibula. Then color the title The Patella In Place. After you have colored the title, begin reading the paragraph below. As you encounter the structures, color their titles and color the structure on the plate. The patella should be colored in a light tone, so that the arrows are not obscured. The humerus can be colored in a darker tone, but lighter colors should be used for the tibia and fibula.

The **patella (A)** is seen in the anterior aspect at the knee joint. Also known as the kneecap, the patella is embedded in the tendon of the quadriceps femoris muscle, which is found on the anterior aspect of the thigh. The tendon is attached to the tibia of the leg and pulls on the tibia when the leg is extended. The patella, a triangular sesamoid bone, facilitates the tendon's movement across the ankle at the knee joint when the leg is flexed. At the patella's broad superior end is the **base (A_1)**; at the inferior end is the **apex (A_2)**. Distally, the patella articulates with the **tibia (B)**. It does not articulate with the **fibula (C)**, which lies off to the lateral aspect. At its proximal end, the patella articulates at the patellar surface of the **femur (D)**. Lateral to the patella is the **lateral epicondyle of the femur (D_1)**, and medial to it is the **medial epicondyle of the femur (D_2)**. The patella provides protection to the knee joint.

> Continue the plate by coloring the title **Tibia (B)**. Also color the tibia in the anterior and posterior views using the same light color as above so that the arrows pointing to the processes are not obscured. As you read about the tibia below, color the titles of the processes as you encounter them, then color the arrows pointing to the processes themselves.

The tibia is often called the shinbone. It receives the body's weight from the femur and transmits it to the foot. With the excep-

tion of the femur, it is the strongest and largest bone of the body. At its broad, proximal end are two concave condyles: the **lateral condyle (B_1)** and the **medial condyle (B_2)**. These condyles articulate with the lateral and medial condyles of the femur at the knee joint. Between the condyles of the tibia, there is a ridge called the **intercondylar eminence (B_3)**. This ridge varies in size among individuals and separates the condyles. On the anterior surface, the tibia contains a prominent process called the **tibial tuberosity (B_4)**. This is the point of attachment for the patellar ligament. The ligament lies inferior to the apex of the patella and attaches the quadriceps femoris tendon to the tibia. Beginning at the tibial tuberosity and extending distally across the anterior surface is the **anterior crest (B_5)**. Since the shaft of the tibia is triangular, the anterior crest makes up the anterior border. No muscle covers the crest and it can be felt beneath the skin, especially when one experiences an injury to the shin. At its distal end, the medial surface of the tibia forms the **medial malleolus (B_6)**. This process articulates with the talus bone of the ankle, and its prominence can be felt on the medial surface of the ankle. On the lateral surface at the distal end, the **fibular notch (B_7)** is the point of articulation with the fibula.

> Complete your work on the plate by coloring the **fibula (C)** in a light color. Then read about the fibula and its processes below. Color in the titles of the processes as you encounter them and the arrows pointing to them in the plate. Dark colors such as deep blues, greens, and purples can be used for the arrows.

The fibula is a sticklike bone having slightly expanded ends. Both proximally and distally it articulates with lateral aspects of the tibia. The fibula does not bear any of the body's weight. Instead, it serves as the origin for several muscles. At its proximal end, the fibula contains an enlarged **head (C_1)**. Here it articulates with the lateral condyle of the tibia. At its distal end, the fibula has a projection called the **lateral malleolus (C_2)**. This expanded process is where the fibula articulates with the talus. The lateral malleolus provides lateral stability to the ankle and its bones. At its medial border, the fibula is bound to the tibia by the **interosseus membrane (E)**.

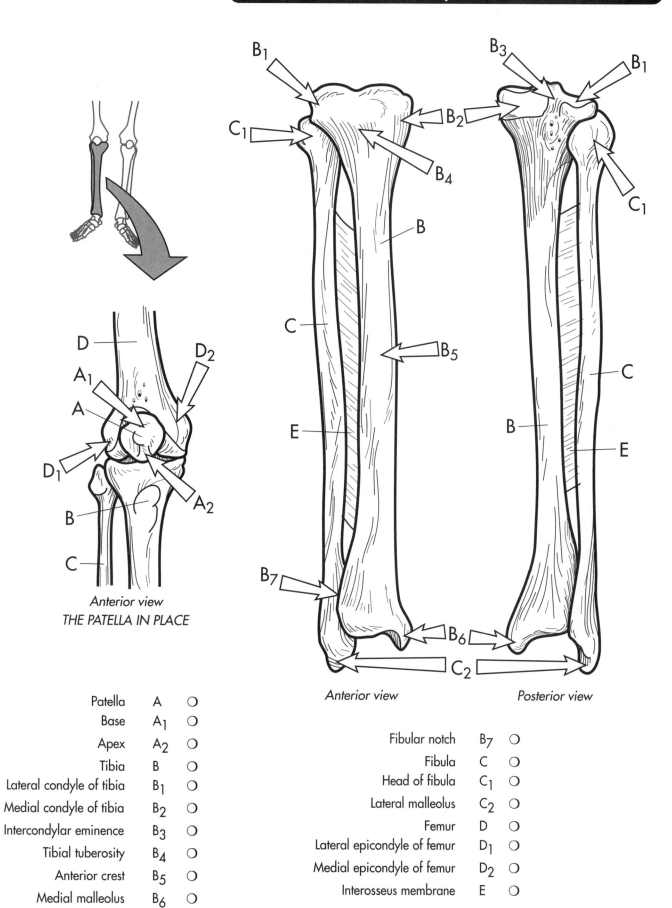

Anterior view
THE PATELLA IN PLACE

Anterior view

Posterior view

Patella	A	○
Base	A₁	○
Apex	A₂	○
Tibia	B	○
Lateral condyle of tibia	B₁	○
Medial condyle of tibia	B₂	○
Intercondylar eminence	B₃	○
Tibial tuberosity	B₄	○
Anterior crest	B₅	○
Medial malleolus	B₆	○

Fibular notch	B₇	○
Fibula	C	○
Head of fibula	C₁	○
Lateral malleolus	C₂	○
Femur	D	○
Lateral epicondyle of femur	D₁	○
Medial epicondyle of femur	D₂	○
Interosseus membrane	E	○

the LOWER EXTREMITY/the ANKLE and FOOT

The ankle and foot have two important functions in the body: they support the weight of the body, and they act as a lever to propel the body forward during walking. There are 26 bones in the ankle and foot. This number is identical to those in the hand. Bones of the ankle and foot are arranged in three distinct regions: the ankle region, called the tarsus, includes the tarsal bones; the second region is the metatarsus, which includes the metatarsal bones; and the third region includes the phalanges.

> To begin the plate, color the main title The Lower Extremity/The Ankle and Foot. Then note on the plate that the ankle and foot are being observed from a superior view. Note which side is lateral and which side is medial in this view, and notice in what direction the eye is looking, as indicated in the arrow of the skeleton. The second view of the foot is from the lateral aspect. Notice how this relates to the skeleton also. Continue your work by coloring in the main title **Tarsals (A)**. In the lateral view, there is a bracket outlining the tarsals. The bracket should be colored, but not the bones it encompasses. A bracket is also available in the superior view, and it should be colored. Now read about the tarsals below, and as you encounter them in the reading, color their titles, and using the same color, color the individual bones. Dark colors such as purples, reds, and greens are suitable.

Seven tarsal bones make up the tarsus. Most body weight is carried on the two largest and most posterior tarsals, the talus and the calcaneus. The **talus (A_1)** transmits weight from the tibia toward the toes. The talus is seen in the superior and lateral views. The talus articulates on one side at the medial malleolus of the tibia and on the other side by the lateral malleolus of the fibula. The **tibia (D)** articulates with the talus at the superior surface of the trochlear. Ligaments connect the talus to the tibia as well as with the fibula. The talus is often called the ankle bone.

The **calcaneus (A_2)** is the heel bone. It forms the heel of the foot and has the talus on its superior surface. The Achilles (calcaneal) tendon attaches the calf muscle to the posterior surface of the calcaneus. The calcaneus is the largest tarsal. It transmits most weight to the ground. The third tarsal is the **cuboid (A_3)**. The cuboid articulates with the metatarsal bones anteriorly and is the first tarsal bone of the distal row. The **navicular (A_4)** is shaped

like a boat. It lies between the proximal row of talus and calcaneus and the distal row beginning with the cuboid. The other three bones of the distal row are the **medial cuneiform (A_5)**, the **intermediate cuneiform (A_6)**, and the **lateral cuneiform (A_7)**. The lateral **cuneiform (A_7)** and the **navicular (A_4)** can be seen in the lateral view.

> The plate should be continued by coloring in the main title **Metatarsals (B)**. Then, using a dark color, color in the bracket in the lateral view and the individual tarsals in the superior view. Use dark colors except in the most lateral tarsal, be careful not to obscure the arrow pointing to sections of the tarsal. When you have completed coloring the bracket, read below and continue studying the metatarsals.

The sole of the foot is formed by five long metatarsal bones. They are identified by I to V from the medial to the lateral aspect. Each metatarsal has three areas: its **base (B_1)**, its **shaft (B_2)**, and its **head (B_3)**. Where the metatarsals articulate with the proximal phalanges, the head of the first metatarsal helps form the "ball" of the foot. The metatarsals articulate proximally with the cuboid and cuneiform bones.

> Now color in the bracket of the **phalanges (C)** in both the superior and lateral views. When the brackets have been colored, read about the phalanges below and color the different rows with three different colors as you encounter them in the reading.

The phalanges are the toes of the foot. There are 14 phalanges. The **proximal phalanges (C_1)** articulate with the metatarsals. The **middle phalanges (C_2)** occur in all the phalanges except the big toe. The **distal phalanges (C_3)** are found in all the toes, including the big toe. The big toe is known as the hallux. The phalanges of the foot resemble those of the hand in both number and arrangement.

The interlocking shape of the foot bones maintains two main arches: the **longitudinal arch (E)** consists of tarsal and metatarsal bones. It enables the foot to support the body's weight and provides leverage while walking. In addition, it absorbs shocks. The **transverse arch (F)** is also formed by tarsal and metatarsal bones. It exists from the medial to the lateral border of the foot. There is one transverse arch, and there are both medial and lateral longitudinal arches. Ligaments, interlocking shape of the bones, and the pull of some tendons help maintain these arches.

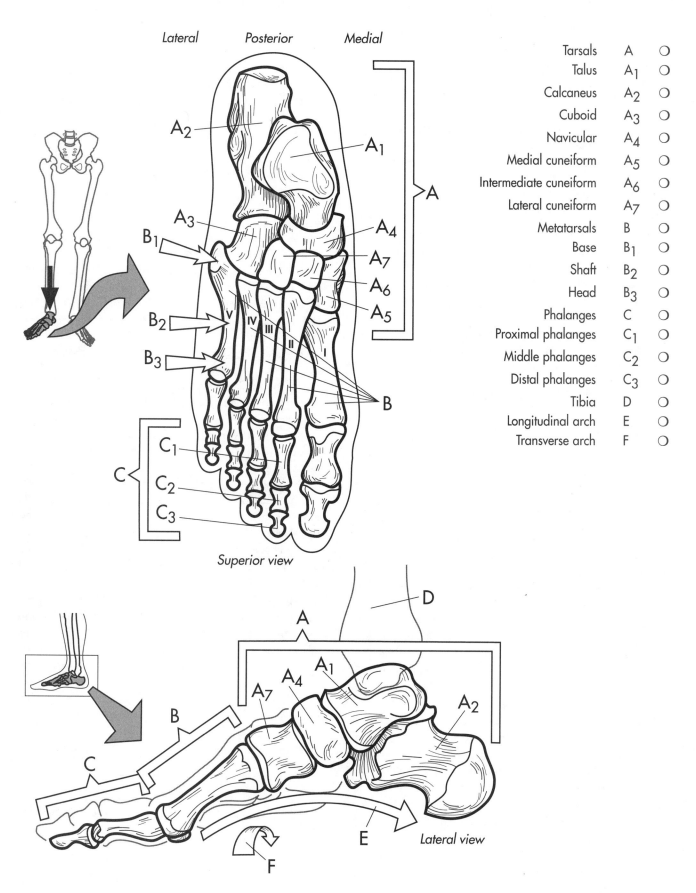

Lateral   Posterior   Medial

A₂
A₁
A₃
B₁
A₄
A₇
A₆
A₅

B₂   v IV III II I

B₃

B

C₁
C
C₂
C₃

Superior view

Tarsals	A	○
Talus	A₁	○
Calcaneus	A₂	○
Cuboid	A₃	○
Navicular	A₄	○
Medial cuneiform	A₅	○
Intermediate cuneiform	A₆	○
Lateral cuneiform	A₇	○
Metatarsals	B	○
Base	B₁	○
Shaft	B₂	○
Head	B₃	○
Phalanges	C	○
Proximal phalanges	C₁	○
Middle phalanges	C₂	○
Distal phalanges	C₃	○
Tibia	D	○
Longitudinal arch	E	○
Transverse arch	F	○

D

A

A₁
A₄
A₇
A₂

B

C

E   *Lateral view*

F

JOINTS and ARTICULATIONS

Where two or more bones come together, the site is called a joint. The term articulation is also frequently used, so we have entitled this plate Joints and Articulations, even though the two are basically the same. The joints hold the bones of the skeleton together while giving the skeleton mobility. At some parts of the body such as in the skull, the joints resist various forces placed on the skeleton, while at other parts such as the hip and shoulder, they are essential factors in movement. This plate discusses the various joints and articulations found in the body.

Joints and articulations are surveyed in this plate from two aspects: the three categories of joints, and the six types of freely movable joints (known as diarthroses). An essential feature is the arrows pointing to the area of a joint. These arrows should be colored in a bold color. You may select other colors for structures in the area depending upon whether you wish to preserve or obscure the details. Begin by coloring the main title Joints and Articulations.

There are several means of classifying joints and articulations. The structural classification is based on the material binding the bones together at the joints and whether or not a joint cavity exists. We shall use the functional classification, which is based on the amount of movement occurring at the joint.

The first category of joints is the **synarthrosis (A)**, indicated by an arrow in the detailed view of the skull. A synarthrosis is an immovable joint, found only between skull bones. The joint is filled with **fibrocartilage (A_1)**, which fuses the skull bones together at the joint.

The second joint category is the **amphiarthrosis (B)**, shown between the vertebrae of the vertebral column. The amphiarthrosis permits a slight degree of movement. The **vertebrae (B_1)** are connected by a disk of fibrocartilage known as the **intervertebral disk (B_2)**. This pad of material is composed of **fibrocartilage (B_3)**, indicated as the material in the disk. Another amphiarthrosis is found between the left and right halves of the pelvis and between the bones of the lower leg and forearm.

A freely movable joint is the **diarthrosis (C)**. Also known as a synovial joint, the diarthrosis permits a variety of motions, as the next section will show. The bones meet within a **fibrous joint capsule (C_1)**. Within the capsule is the **synovial membrane (C_2)** which produces **synovial fluid (C_3)** filling the joint cavity. Synovial fluid lubricates the joint, nourishes the cells in the area of the joint, and absorbs shocks. It is produced by cells within the synovial membrane. Within the joint, the **articular cartilages (C_4)** occur at the joining surfaces of the bones. Most of the joints of the human body are diarthroses.

In the second part of this plate, we describe six types of diarthroses. These six different joints and articulations are found throughout the body. We have indicated their presence in the plate with arrows, which should be colored in bold tones. The surrounding bones may be identified and colored if you wish. Alternately, you may select a light color for the bones to distinguish them from the surrounding background. Color the titles in the titles list, then observe and color the joint as you read the following paragraphs.

All diarthroses have a synovial cavity separating the articulating bones. However, the shapes of the articulating surfaces differ, and diarthroses are, therefore, divided into six types.

The first type of diarthrosis is the **condyloid joint (D)**. Here an oval-shaped condyle of a bone fits into a cavity formed by another bone. The plate shows carpals fitting into the cavity formed by the radius and ulna at the wrist.

The **ball-and-socket joint (E)** has a ball-like surface fitting into a cuplike depression. The two examples in the body are the shoulder and hip joints, with the hip joint displayed in the plate. Here, we present the head of the femur joining the pelvic bone at the acetabulum.

The articulating surfaces of flat bones form a **gliding joint (F)**. Back and forth movements occur, such as shown between the carpals and metacarpals in the plate.

The fourth type of joint is the **saddle joint (G)**. The surface of one bone is shaped like a saddle, and the other bone fits into it. The diagram shows a metacarpal articulating with a carpal, the carpal providing the saddle for the metacarpal. Movement in this joint is limited.

A **hinge joint (H)** is found at the elbow and knee. Here, the convex surface of one bone fits into the concave cavity of another. Movement occurs in a single plane, such as seen in the elbow joint. A hinged door displays the same movement.

The final joint we consider is the **pivot joint (I)**. In this joint a rounded projection of a bone articulates in the ring formed by another bone. In the plate, the **atlas (I_1)** provides the ring for the **axis (I_2)**, whose **odontoid process (I_3)** projects into the ring at the joint. This joint permits rotation and allows the head to move from side to side as in saying "no." A pivot joint also allows the palms to turn forward and backward.

CATEGORIES OF JOINTS

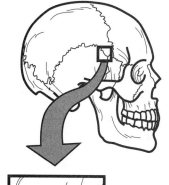

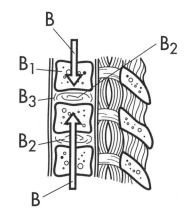

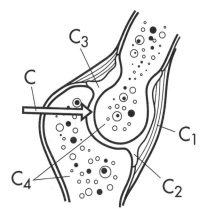

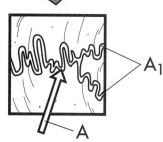

TYPES OF DIARTHROSES

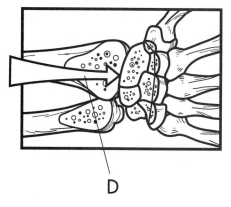

D

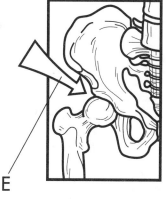

E

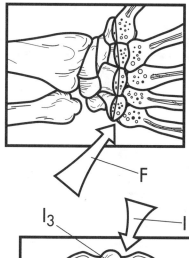

F

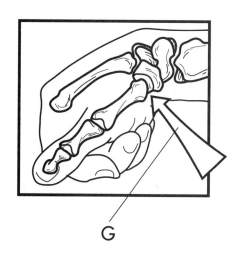

G

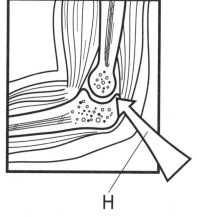

H

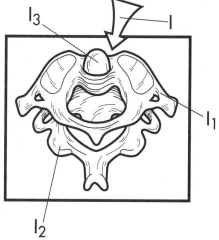

Synarthrosis	A	○	Fibrous joint capsule	C₁	○	Saddle joint	G	○
Fibrocartilage	A₁	○	Synovial membrane	C₂	○	Hinge joint	H	○
Amphiarthrosis	B	○	Synovial fluid	C₃	○	Pivot joint	I	○
Vertebrae	B₁	○	Articular cartilages	C₄	○	Atlas	I₁	○
Invertebral disk	B₂	○	Condyloid joint	D	○	Axis	I₂	○
Fibrocartilage	B₃	○	Ball-and-socket joint	E	○	Odontoid process	I₃	○
Diarthrosis	C	○	Gliding joint	F	○			

JOINT MOVEMENTS

Various types of movements occur at the joints and articulations. Certain ones are gliding movements, such as those of flat bones that glide over one another. There are also angular movements that increase or decrease angles between joints, rotational movements that permit turning at a joint, and special movements that occur at specific areas of the body and at specific joints.

In this plate, we consider many of the movements occurring at the freely movable joints known as diarthroses. These joints are described in the previous plate. Remember that movement of the joints depends on contraction of muscle fibers pulling the bone in one direction.

Looking over the plate, note that we present various parts of the body and various movements taking place. Each movement is described by an arrow and a movement of an anatomical part. These three items should be colored in the same color as you proceed. We suggest bold tones for the arrows, and light colors for the anatomical parts. We have used letters with subscript numbers to indicate that movements are related to one another. Generally, the related movements oppose one another. Begin by reading the paragraph below, and color the main title Joint Movements.

The angular movements of the joints include abduction and adduction. In **abduction (A_1)** a body part is moved away from the midline of the body. Raising the arm, as shown in the plate, typifies this movement. **Adduction (A_2)** is a movement in which a limb is brought toward the body surface. It is the opposite movement of abduction. Many muscles are abductors, while others are adductors.

Pronation and supination refer generally to movements at the wrist, and are considered special movements. **Pronation (B_1)** refers to a movement in which the palm turns down to the posterior position. **Supination (B_2)** turns the palm forward to the anterior position. Thus, to supinate the palm is to turn it forward.

Angular movements are also displayed in flexion and extension. In **flexion (C_1)**, the angle at a joint is decreased. In the plate, the arm is being flexed as the elbow joint bends and the forearm is brought up. **Extension (C_2)** is the opposing motion in which the angle at a joint is increased. In the plate, the movement at the elbow joint brings the forearm down and "extends" the forearm.

We have begun a discussion of joint movements by focusing on four angular joint movements and two special joint movements. We continue the discussion with a consideration of additional joint movements beginning with circumduction. Continue as before by coloring the titles, arrows, and figures as you continue to read.

Circumduction (D) is a joint movement in which a distal part of the body moves in a circle. In the plate, we see the pitching motion of a baseball player as an example of circumduction. Rotating the arm in space to describe a cone is also a circumduction.

Two special movements are depression and elevation. In **depression (E_1)**, structures such as the forehead muscles move in the inferior direction, while in **elevation (E_2)**, they move in the superior direction. Frowning and raising the eyebrows are shown.

Retraction and protraction also illustrate special movements in which no angles are involved. **Retraction (F_1)** is movement of a body part toward the posterior, while **protraction (F_2)** is movement in the anterior direction. Pulling the chin back illustrates retraction, while extending the chin forward illustrates protraction.

Thus far, we have noted a variety of movements possible at the body joints. We shall complete the discussion by examining rotation and a number of other special movements. Continue reading the paragraphs below and as you encounter the movements, study them in the plate by coloring them appropriately.

Rotation is a type of joint movement in which a bone turns on its own long axis. Rotation occurs at the hip and shoulder joints, but it is most obvious when the head turns left and right as when expressing "no." **Rotation (G)** occurs in the head when a projection of the axis extends into a foramen formed by the atlas, as shown in the previous plate.

One of the body's special movements is **dorsiflexion (H_1)**. This movement occurs at the foot. The ankle bones undergo flexion, and the sole elevates. When the opposite takes place, and the foot bends in the direction of the plantar surface, the movement is called **plantar flexion (H_2)**.

The final movements we consider are inversion and eversion. During **inversion (I_1)**, the foot twists to turn the sole inward. During **eversion (I_2)**, the foot twists so that the sole faces outward in the lateral direction. These and other movements illustrate the variety of movements that occur in the body.

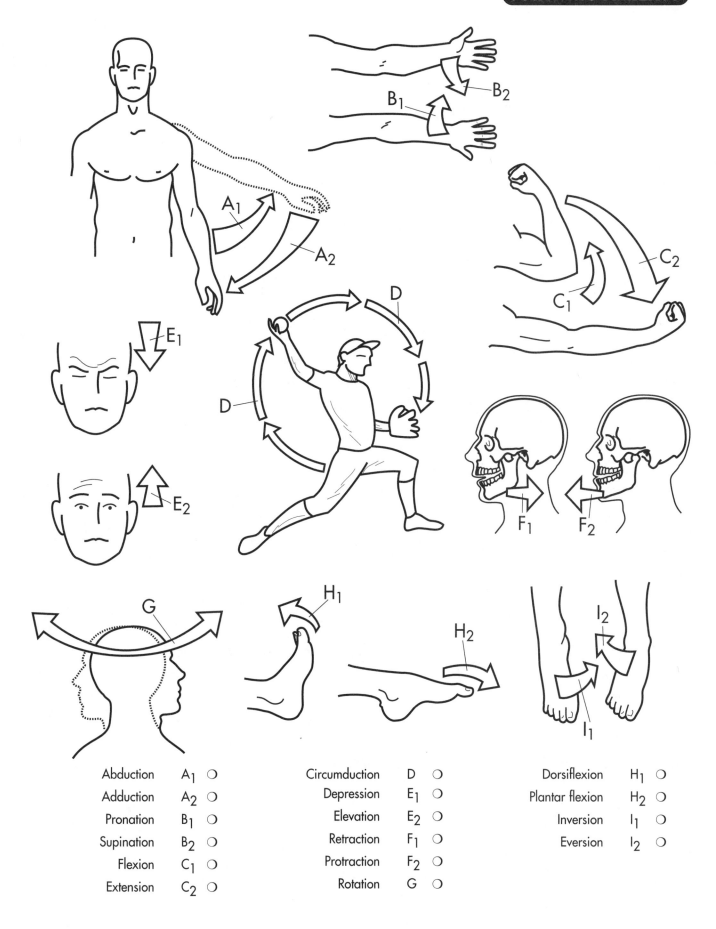

Abduction	A_1	○	Circumduction	D	○	Dorsiflexion	H_1	○
Adduction	A_2	○	Depression	E_1	○	Plantar flexion	H_2	○
Pronation	B_1	○	Elevation	E_2	○	Inversion	I_1	○
Supination	B_2	○	Retraction	F_1	○	Eversion	I_2	○
Flexion	C_1	○	Protraction	F_2	○			
Extension	C_2	○	Rotation	G	○			

the MUSCULAR SYSTEM

MUSCLES of the FACE

This will be one of several plates describing the muscles of the face, axial, and appendicular skeleton. Approximately 700 skeletal muscles have been identified based on such characteristics as location, size, shape, action, and other features. The plates will discuss major muscles of a particular area and point out some of the other muscles seen in that area. In most cases, the origin and insertion of the muscle will be described. The origin is the muscle's attachment site at a stationary bone, while the insertion is the attachment site at a movable bone (there are exceptions, however). A tendon usually makes the attachment between muscle and bone. The general trend will be to highlight the major muscles of the area using capital letters and the minor muscles seen in the area using lowercase letters. In situations where other anatomical features are visible in the plate, they have been labeled for you since the primary focus is on the muscles.

> Begin this plate by coloring in the main title Muscles of the Face. Then look over the plate and note that there are capital letters and lowercase letters. The capital letters refer to the major muscles of the area and will be discussed first. As you read about the muscles below, color their titles, then color the muscles in the plate. Use darker colors for the larger muscles and lighter colors for the smaller muscles to avoid obscuring the places where they overlap or come close to one another. Many muscles will be close to one another, so be careful to note where one muscles overlies another muscle. Also, you should color in the anterior and lateral views at the same time using the same colors. In this plate, the anterior view shows a superficial view on the visual left (the anatomical right) and a deep view of the muscles on the visual right (the anatomical left).

The major muscle covering the dome of the skull and the forehead is the **frontalis (A)**. This muscle has no bony attachments. It is attached to a sheet-like tendon called an aponeurosis. We shall name this particular aponeurosis in a moment. A second major muscle of the skull is the **occipitalis (B)**. The occipitalis is connected to the frontalis by an aponeurosis called the **galea aponeurotica (B₁)**. Thus, the latter serves as the origin for the frontalis and the insertion for the occipitalis. Both muscles move the scalp. The frontalis draws it to the anterior aspect, while the occipitalis draws it to the posterior aspect. The facial nerve innervates both muscles.

> Having begun this plate, you may continue with more of the major muscles of the face. Continue reading below, and as you encounter the muscles, color them in the appropriate position on the plate. Coloring should be done in both the anterior and right lateral views.

The muscle fibers surrounding the opening of the mouth compose a muscle called the **orbicularis oris (C)**. This muscle originates in the muscles near the mouth opening and inserts at the skin at the corner of the mouth. It protrudes the lips and compresses them against the teeth, while shaping them during speech. The facial nerve innervates the muscle. The **zygomaticus (D)** is the muscle at the angle of the mouth. It originates at the zygomatic bone and inserts in the skin at the angle of the mouth. Its function is to draw the corner of the mouth back and up. Another muscle of the mouth area is the **levator labii superioris (E)**. This muscle raises the upper lip and, like the other muscles, is innervated by the facial nerve. The **depressor labii inferioris (F)** is responsible for depressing or lowering the lower lip. It originates at the mandible and inserts at the skin at the lower lip.

The **buccinator (G)** is sometimes called the trumpeter muscle because it compresses the cheeks when forcefully blowing on a trumpet. During chewing, it moves food back across the teeth inside the cheeks. Its origins are on the maxilla and mandible, and its insertion is in the orbicularis oris. When one pouts, the skin of the chin is elevated and the lower lip protruded by the **mentalis (H)**.

The **platysma (I)** is a neck muscle originating at the upper thoracic cage. It inserts on the mandible and skin of the cheek and depresses the mandible to permit movements of the lower lip. Like the muscles discussed previously, it is innervated by the facial nerve. Further along near the angle of the mouth is the **risorius (J)**. This muscle permits one to grimace. It is a slender muscle near the zygomaticus.

> At this point you have completed an examination of many of the muscles of the skull, face, and facial expressions. The remaining major muscles will be concerned with the region of the eye. Continue reading about these muscles below, and color the titles and the muscles as you encounter them.

One of the muscles at the orbit at the eye is the **orbicularis oculi (K)**. Innervated by the facial nerve, this muscle allows one to close the eyelid, and to blink, squint, and perform other movements to protect the eye. It originates at the frontal bone and maxilla and inserts at the tissue of the eyelid. A second muscle of this region is the **corrugator supercilii (L)**. This muscle draws the eyebrow to the inferior position and wrinkles the skin of the forehead as in frowning. The final major muscle of the face is the **levator palpebrae superioris (M)**. This muscle operates when one raises the upper eyelid. It is innervated by the oculomotor nerve.

> Several other muscles can be seen in these views of the face. These muscles are not prime movers of the face, as are the above muscles. They are noted by lowercase letters, and they will be discussed in more depth in other plates. As you read about them below, color their titles and locate and color them in the diagrams. Lighter colors may be used.

The muscle that compresses the bridge of the nose and elevates the corners of the nostrils is the **nasalis (a)**. This muscle originates at the maxilla and inserts at the bridge and tip of the nose. The **masseter (b)** elevates the mandible and is innervated by the trigeminal nerve. It originates at the zygomatic arch. A major muscle of the neck is the **sternocleidomastoid (c)**. This muscle flexes and bends the neck towards the shoulder, while moving the head to the opposite side. One of the muscles of the neck is the **omohyoid (d)**. This muscle depresses the larynx and hyoid bone. The **sternohyoid (e)** performs a similar action.

The **temporalis (f)** is seen briefly in the superficial view. It is an important muscle in mastication (chewing) as it elevates the mandible when the lower jaw moves. We shall encounter it in a future plate. One of the muscles involved in moving the outer ear is the **posterior auricular (g)**. The **splenius capitis (h)** is involved in extension of the head. It helps rotate and tilt the head to one side. In the same area, the **trapezius (i)** is a major shoulder muscle, and the **levator scapulae (j)** helps in elevation of the scapula. To complete the plate, the **middle scalene (k)** is partly responsible for flexing the neck. Its origin is at the cervical vertebrae and insertion at the first two ribs.

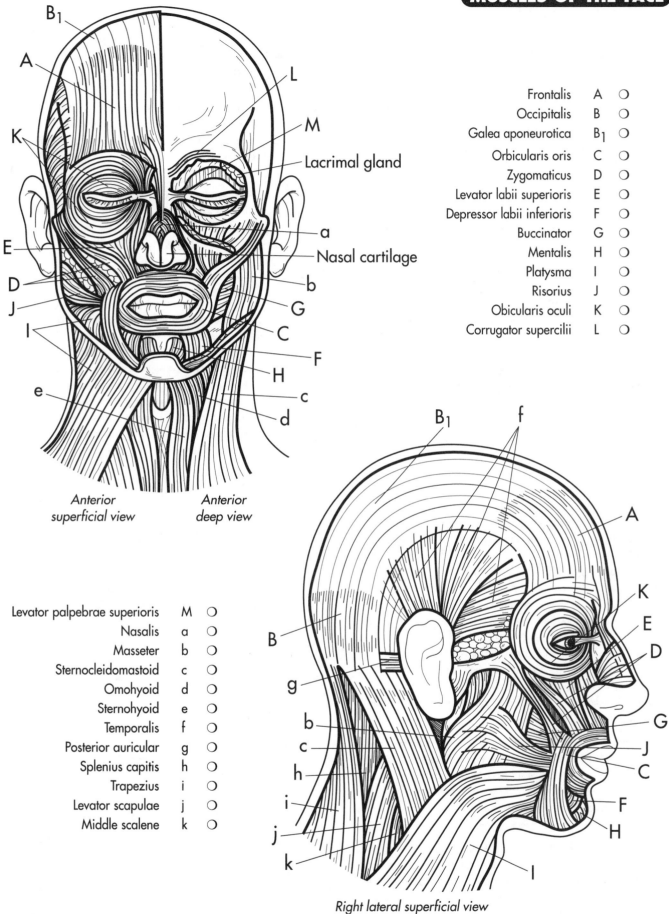

B₁

A

K

L

M

Lacrimal gland

E

a

Nasal cartilage

D

b

J

G

I

C

F

H

e

c

d

*Anterior
superficial view*

*Anterior
deep view*

Frontalis	A	○
Occipitalis	B	○
Galea aponeurotica	B₁	○
Orbicularis oris	C	○
Zygomaticus	D	○
Levator labii superioris	E	○
Depressor labii inferioris	F	○
Buccinator	G	○
Mentalis	H	○
Platysma	I	○
Risorius	J	○
Obicularis oculi	K	○
Corrugator supercilii	L	○

Levator palpebrae superioris	M	○
Nasalis	a	○
Masseter	b	○
Sternocleidomastoid	c	○
Omohyoid	d	○
Sternohyoid	e	○
Temporalis	f	○
Posterior auricular	g	○
Splenius capitis	h	○
Trapezius	i	○
Levator scapulae	j	○
Middle scalene	k	○

B₁

f

A

K

E

D

B

g

G

b

J

c

C

h

F

i

H

j

k

I

Right lateral superficial view

MUSCLES of the JAWS and TONGUE

Several muscles are involved in the process of mastication (chewing), and are important muscles of the jaw. These muscles are generally innervated by a division of the trigeminal nerve called the mandibular division. As with other muscles, each has an origin and insertion. The origin typically remains stationary, while the insertion area moves. Generally, the origin of a muscle is proximal to the insertion of the muscle. An aponeurosis, or broad tendon, sometimes serves as the origin or insertion. As in other plates, this plate will consider major muscles designated by capital letters and minor muscles in the area designated by lowercase letters. In this particular plate you should be concerned with the lateral views of the head, before going on to the muscles associated with the tongue. The directions below will lead you in this pattern.

Examine the plate to see that two major subjects are involved: the muscles of the jaws and the muscles associated with the tongue. Two views of the right lateral aspect of the body examine the jaw muscles, and a deep view of the right lateral region examines the tongue muscles. You should concern yourself with the jaw muscles at first and the two appropriate diagrams. Color the main title to orient yourself then read about the jaw muscles below. As you encounter them, color their titles, then color the muscles themselves. Be careful where the muscles encounter one another, and try to use contrasting colors to set them apart. Larger muscles are best colored with darker colors and smaller muscles with lighter colors. Note that the bones and bony structures have been labeled for you.

Four major muscles contribute to closure of the jaws and the biting and chewing actions that accompany mastication. The first of these muscles is the **masseter (A)**. This is a powerful muscle covering the lateral aspect of the ramus of the mandible. It is seen prominently in the right superficial view. The muscle originates at the zygomatic arch, and it inserts in the lateral surface of the ramus of the mandible. The muscle elevates the mandible when the jaw is closed and assists in side-to-side movement of the mandible.

The second muscle involved in mastication is the fan-shaped **temporalis (B)**. Both the lateral and deep views show how large this muscle is (a darker color can be used for coloring). Superficial aspects of the temporalis can be seen in the previous plate. The temporalis originates along the temporal lines of the parietal bone and inserts at the coronoid process of the mandible. The muscle retracts and elevates the mandible and assists in side-to-side movement. In doing so, it closes the jaw.

In addition to the muscles discussed, several other muscles may be observed in the area of the jaw in these views. Although they are not directly involved in the movement of the jaw, they have functions in the associated areas. Three such muscles are noted below.

The third important muscle is the **medial pterygoid (C)**. This muscle is seen in the deep view. This muscle protracts the mandible, elevates it, and moves it from side to side. Its origin is at the pterygoid process of the sphenoid bone and the maxilla. Its insertion is at the ramus and angle of the mandible. The final muscle we shall consider is the **lateral pterygoid (D)**. Seen only in the deep view,

the lateral pterygoid protracts the mandible, opens the mouth, and moves the mandible from side to side.

In the region of the jaw, one muscle seen in the superficial view is the **levator labii superioris (a)**. This muscle elevates the upper lip, and you can see its insertion to this area. The muscle originates at the maxilla. It is innervated by the facial nerve. In both superficial and deep views, the **buccinator (b)** can be seen. This is a cheek muscle, which draws the corner of the mouth laterally and compresses the cheek to hold food between the teeth during chewing. A third muscle is the **orbicularis oris (c)**. This multi-layered muscle surrounds the lips and has fibers moving in many different directions. This is the "kissing muscle." It protrudes the lips and closes them.

For the second portion of this plate, concentrate on the lateral view of the deep muscles of the lower portion of the face. These are the muscles associated with movements of the tongue. As you read about the major muscles in capital letters, color their titles, then color the muscles in the diagram.

Although the tongue is composed of muscle fibers, these muscles change the shape of the tongue but do not move the tongue. Instead, a number of muscles are directly involved in tongue movements. One such muscle is the **geniogollus (E)**. This muscle is shaped somewhat like a fan. It protrudes the tongue.

The second muscle promoting tongue movement is the **styloglossus (F)**. This muscle elevates the tongue and retracts it. The muscle has its origin at the styloid process of the temporal bone and its insertion at the side and undersurface of the tongue. The **palatoglossus (G)** elevates the posterior portion of the tongue and depresses the fleshy soft palette. The innervation for this muscle is the spinal accessory nerve, in comparison to the hypoglossal nerve, which innervates the first two muscles.

The fourth muscle is also innervated by the hypoglossal nerve. This is the **hyoglossus (H)**. This muscle depresses the tongue and retracts it. As the name implies, this muscle has its origin at the hyoid bone and its insertion at the tongue. The diagram shows its association with the hyoid bone.

Numerous other muscles are seen in the deep examination of the jaw area and the tongue. These muscles are designated by lowercase letters and are noted briefly below. They will be encountered in other plates as well.

Another muscle seen in the tongue area is the **inferior longitudinal (d)**. This muscle runs along the underside of the tongue. The **geniohyoid (e)** is a muscle of the floor of the oral cavity. It draws the tongue anteriorly and depresses the mandible. A similar muscle is the **mylohyoid (f)**. Its action is similar to that of the geniohyoid and as the name implies, it inserts in the hyoid bone. The **digastric (g)** has been cut in this diagram to view the muscles beneath. A posterior belly of the muscle has its origin at the mastoid process of the temporal bone (as shown in the plate) and it inserts by means of a tendon to the hyoid bone. The **middle constrictor (h)** originates at the hyoid and helps constrict the pharynx during the action of swallowing. It works with the **inferior constrictor (k)**.

A prominent muscle is the **stylohyoid (i)**. This muscle elevates the hyoid bone. It is a slender muscle at the angle of the jaw. As the diagram shows, its origin is at the styloid process and its insertion is at the hyoid bone. The facial nerve innervates it. The final muscle that we shall consider is the **stylopharyngeus (j)**. This muscle originates at the styloid process and inserts in the wall of the pharynx. Its function is to regulate activity of the pharynx, such as elevation. This activity occurs during the swallowing process.

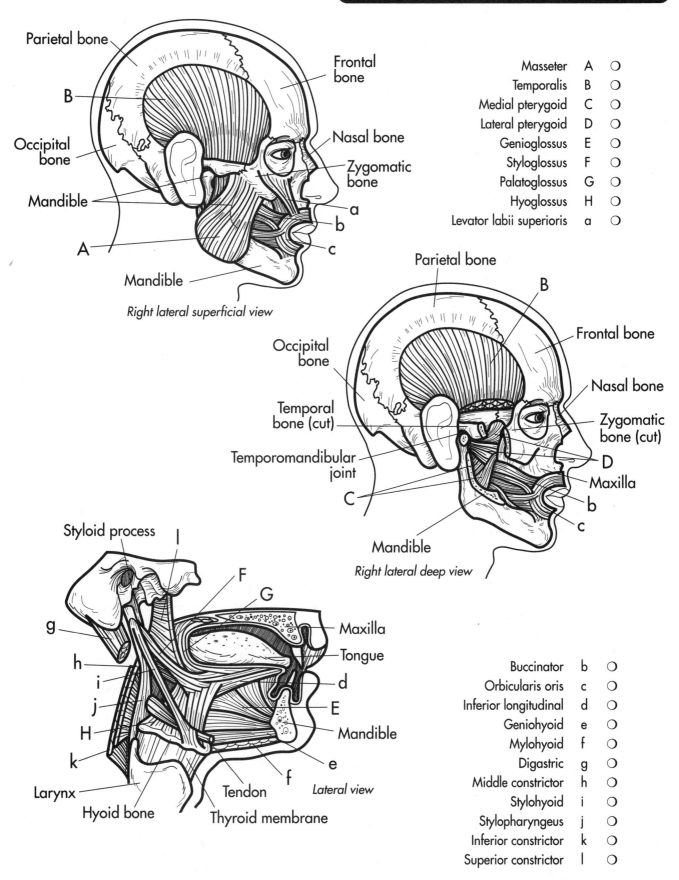

Parietal bone

Frontal bone

B

Occipital bone

Nasal bone

Zygomatic bone

Mandible

a

b

c

A

Mandible

Right lateral superficial view

Masseter	A	○
Temporalis	B	○
Medial pterygoid	C	○
Lateral pterygoid	D	○
Genioglossus	E	○
Styloglossus	F	○
Palatoglossus	G	○
Hyoglossus	H	○
Levator labii superioris	a	○

Parietal bone

B

Occipital bone

Frontal bone

Temporal bone (cut)

Nasal bone

Zygomatic bone (cut)

Temporomandibular joint

D

Maxilla

C

b

c

Mandible

Right lateral deep view

Styloid process

l

F

G

g

Maxilla

Tongue

h

i

d

j

E

H

Mandible

k

e

f

Larynx

Lateral view

Hyoid bone

Tendon

Thyroid membrane

Buccinator	b	○
Orbicularis oris	c	○
Inferior longitudinal	d	○
Geniohyoid	e	○
Mylohyoid	f	○
Digastric	g	○
Middle constrictor	h	○
Stylohyoid	i	○
Stylopharyngeus	j	○
Inferior constrictor	k	○
Superior constrictor	l	○

MUSCLES of the EYE (EXTRINSIC)

Among the different kinds of muscles in the body are extrinsic and intrinsic muscles. Intrinsic muscles are those that operate within an organ, while extrinsic muscles are superficial muscles that stabilize an organ or place it in a particular position. Muscles associated with the human eyeball are of both types. The intrinsic muscles move structures within the eyeballs, such as the lenses, while extrinsic muscles originate outside the eyeballs and insert on their outer surface, known as the sclera. This plate is concerned with the extrinsic eye muscles.

There are six extrinsic eye muscles originating on the surface of the orbit and controlling the position of the eyeball. The six muscles are sometimes called oculomotor muscles. Several are innervated by the oculomotor nerve, but others are innervated by the abducens or trochlear nerve.

To begin the plate, color the main title Muscles of the Eye (Extrinsic). Then read about the muscles below and locate them in all views shown in the plate. Color their titles and color in the muscle in the lateral view, medial view, and anterior view of the eye. The eyeball itself can be colored in using a light color such as a pale beige so as to avoid obscuring the muscles. The muscles themselves are rather large and obvious, so they can be colored in darker greens, blues, and purples. If you wish to color in the bones, use lighter colors. The individual structures of the eye and the intrinsic muscles are examined in the plate concerning the anatomy of the eye.

The first muscle we shall examine is the **superior rectus (A)**. The fibers of this muscle run parallel to the long axis of the eyeball. The muscle has its origin at a tendinous ring attached to the orbit of the eye. The muscle then inserts at the superior and central part of the eyeball, as the plate shows. The muscle is innervated by the oculomotor nerve. It rolls the eyeball in the superior direction. This permits the eye to look up.

The second important muscle is the **inferior rectus (B)**. This muscle runs below the eyeball parallel to its long axis. The muscle has its origin in the sphenoid bone in the orbit of the eye and its insertion at the inferior, medial surface of the eyeball. When this muscle acts, the eye looks down as the eyeball rolls inferiorly. The oculomotor nerve innervates this muscle.

On the lateral surface of the eyeball, the **lateral rectus (C)** is observed prominently. This muscle also originates in the orbit, but it inserts on the lateral surface of the eyeball as the diagram shows. The lateral rectus rotates the eye in the lateral direction, and this activity can be observed in the anterior view. Innervation of the lateral rectus is by the abducens nerve. The muscle opposing the lateral rectus is the **medial rectus (D)**. As another promi-nent muscle seen in the medial view, the medial rectus has its origin in the sphenoid bone in the orbit and its insertion at the medial surface of the eyeball. The muscle rotates the eye towards the medial aspect. The anterior view shows its opposition to the lateral rectus.

Continue and complete your work on the extrinsic muscles of the eye by examining the two oblique muscles. These muscles not only have activity on the eyeball of the eye, but also on its cornea. Note in the diagram the position of the optic nerve extending away from the eyeball to carry impulses away from the nervous tissue of the eyeball to the brain. Also note the position of the frontal bone and its sinus, as well as the lacrimal or tear gland. Color the titles of the important muscles below, then point them out with colors in the diagram. Darker colors are recommended.

The first of the two oblique muscles of the eye is the **superior oblique (E)**. This muscle is innervated by the trochlear nerve. Its fibers run diagonal to the long axis of the eyeball. Originating in bones of the orbit, the muscle passes through a ring of fibrocartilaginous tissue acting as a pulley. The ring of tissue is called the trochlea and is shown in the diagram in the anterior view. Note how the superior oblique then inserts on the eyeball slightly to the left of the superior rectus. When the muscle contracts, it pulls the eyeball toward the lateral aspect as designated by the circular arrow seen in the anterior view. This action also directs the cornea toward the lateral aspect. The eye rolls, looks down, and looks to the side.

Acting antagonistically to the superior oblique is the **inferior oblique (F)**. This muscle has its origin in the maxilla seen in the lateral view of the eye. It then passes under the eyeball to insert on the eyeball between the **inferior rectus (B)** and the **lateral rectus (C)**. This insertion can be seen in the anterior view of the eye and partially in the lateral view. When the muscle contracts, it pulls the eyeball in a rotary fashion and causes the eyeball to rotate toward the superior and lateral aspects. The curved arrow shows this movement. For both the superior and inferior oblique, the arrows should be colored with the same color to indicate the direction of motion. The inferior oblique is innervated by the oculomotor nerve.

Although not an extrinsic muscle of the eye the **levator palpebrae superioris (a)** is seen in the plate. This muscle inserts in the upper eyelid and raises the upper lid of the eye. It is innervated by the oculomotor nerve.

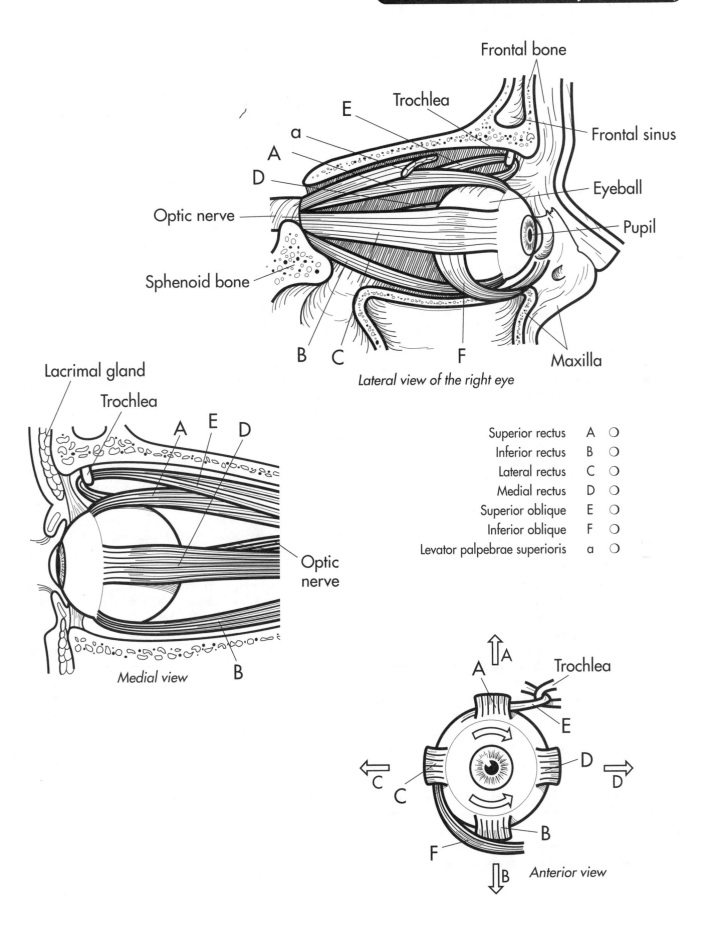

Frontal bone

Trochlea

E

a

A

D

Frontal sinus

Eyeball

Optic nerve

Pupil

Sphenoid bone

B   C

F

Maxilla

Lateral view of the right eye

Lacrimal gland

Trochlea

A   E   D

Optic nerve

B

Medial view

Superior rectus	A	○
Inferior rectus	B	○
Lateral rectus	C	○
Medial rectus	D	○
Superior oblique	E	○
Inferior oblique	F	○
Levator palpebrae superioris	a	○

A   A

Trochlea

E

C   C

D   D

F   B

B

Anterior view

MUSCLES of the NECK and ORAL CAVITY

The prime consideration of this plate will be muscles of the neck and oral cavity. Emphasis will be placed on the anterior neck muscles. These muscles overlie the larynx and are the deep throat muscles involved in movements that accompany swallowing. The muscles lie underneath the chin, and depress the mandible while tensing the floor of the mouth. Some of the muscles also move the head as well. These are the strap muscles of the neck.

To begin the plate, the main title Muscles of the Neck and Oral Cavity should be colored. As you read about the muscles below and encounter them in the text, color them in the plate. The plate has been labeled with the names of bones and other structures to orient you to the positions they occupy. Your main emphasis, however, is the appropriate muscles. The muscles of the anterior view of the neck and oral cavity are shown in both superficial and deep views and are very close to one another. Five of the muscles are also shown in the right lateral view of the deep neck muscles. Color these with dark colors, then use the same colors in the anterior view. Lighter colors such as tans and grays can then be used for the remaining muscles. Use darker colors for the arrows.

A major muscle of the anterior neck region is the **digastric (A)**. Note in the diagram that this muscle contains an anterior belly and a posterior belly united by an **intermediate tendon (A$_1$)**. A loop of **fibrous tissue (A$_2$)** unites the tendons from the two bellies. The anterior belly of the digastric originates at the lower border of the mandible, while the posterior belly has its origin at the mastoid process of the temporal bone. The function of this muscle is to open the mouth by depressing the mandible. The right lateral view of the neck area shows the digastric muscle clearly and indicates how the fibrous loop connects the tendon from the bellies. This view should be colored in at the same time the anterior view is colored.

A second muscle of this area is the **stylohyoid (B)**. As the name implies, this muscle has its origin at the styloid process at the temporal bone. It then inserts at the hyoid bone, as shown in the anterior view. The stylohyoid elevates the hyoid bone, thereby elongating the floor of the mouth. The **mylohyoid (C)** is a large muscle originating along the inner surface of the mandible. This flat, relatively triangular muscle inserts on the hyoid bone and helps depress the mandible and elevates the floor of the mouth. This helps the tongue force food into the pharynx. Another elevator, the geniohyoid, is not seen on this plate (but it is visible in the previous plate). It helps elevate the hyoid bone also. The four muscles mentioned here constitute the suprahyoid muscles, so-named because they lie above the hyoid bone.

Continue the plate by concentrating on the infrahyoid muscles. These muscles lie below the hyoid bone. They lie close to one another and may be difficult to distinguish in the diagram. Therefore, you should use light colors.

Most deep muscles of the throat help coordinate swallowing movements. The first of the infrahyoid muscles is the **omohyoid (D)**. This muscle is seen clearly in both the anterior and lateral views. The muscle has an anterior belly, which has its insertion at the hyoid bone, and a posterior belly that inserts to the superior margin of the scapula. An intermediate tendon unites the two bellies. The **sternohyoid (E)** runs parallel to the omohyoid. Like the omohyoid, the sternohyoid depresses the hyoid bone. Its origin is at the clavicle and sternum and its insertion is at the hyoid bone.

A third important infrahyoid muscle is the **sternothyroid (F)**. This muscle has its origin at the manubrium of the sternum and its insertion at the thyroid cartilage of the larynx. This muscle holds the thyroid cartilage and depresses the larynx. The **thyrohyoid (G)** acts to elevate the thyroid cartilage. Its origin is on the manubrium of the sternum and its insertion is at the thyroid cartilage of the larynx.

At this point, we have examined some of the major muscles of the floor of the oral cavity and the anterior portion of the neck. Some of the remaining muscles are intrinsic muscles since they are found so deep in the tissues. Others are strap muscles that help to move and control the actions of the head. Two of the muscles are rather prominent in the lateral view.

One of the intrinsic muscles is the **cricothyroid (H)**. This muscle is seen only in the anterior deep view. It is important because it places tension on the vocal cords. The muscle has its origin at the cricoid cartilage of the larynx and its insertion on the anterior border of the thyroid cartilage and the nearby area. The anterior view shows the **levator scapulae (I)**. This muscle is found at the side of the neck. It is a thick, straplike muscle that helps elevate and adopt the scapula when it works together with the trapezius. In the anterior view, there is a small portion of the **masseter (J)**. This powerful muscle is a prime mover in the closing of the jaw as it elevates the mandible. The muscle is seen more clearly in the plate of the facial muscles.

Two deep muscles observed in the anterior plate are the **scalene muscles (K)**. These muscles in the lateral aspect elevate the first two ribs and thereby aid in breathing. The scalene muscles originate at the transverse processes of the cervical vertebrae and insert at the first two ribs. The right lateral view prominently shows the size of the **sternocleidomastoid (L)**. This deep muscle originates at the manubrium of the sternum and medial portion of the clavicle and inserts at the mastoid process of the temporal bone, as the diagram shows. The muscle is the prime mover in flexion of the head. It can also rotate the head toward the shoulder and tilt the head. The spinal accessory nerve innervates this muscle.

The sternocleidomastoid divides the neck into two triangles for reference purposes. As the right lateral view shows, these two triangles are the posterior triangle and the anterior triangle. (Their brackets may be colored in with a dark color.) Many smaller triangles exist between these two triangles. Also seen in the neck is the **trapezius (M)**. This muscle elevates the clavicle and scapula to extend the head. It is an extremely powerful superficial muscle of the posterior region of the thorax and is seen in other plates.

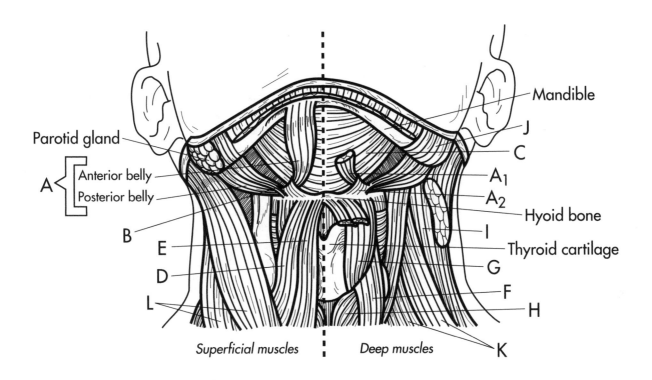

Mandible

Parotid gland

A { Anterior belly
Posterior belly }

B

E

D

L

Superficial muscles

J

C

A₁

A₂

Hyoid bone

I

Thyroid cartilage

G

F

H

K

Deep muscles

Digastric	A	○
Intermediate tendon	A₁	○
Fibrous tissue	A₂	○
Stylohyoid	B	○
Mylohyoid	C	○
Omohyoid	D	○
Sternohyoid	E	○
Sternothyroid	F	○
Thyrohyoid	G	○
Cricothyroid	H	○
Levator scapulae	I	○
Masseter	J	○
Scalene muscles	K	○
Sternocleidomastoid	L	○
Trapezius	M	○

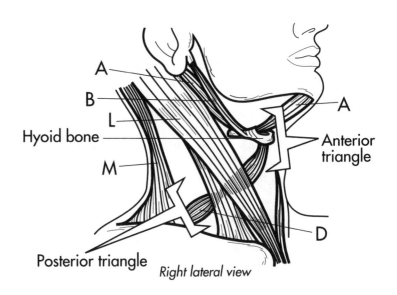

A

B

L

Hyoid bone

M

A

Anterior triangle

D

Posterior triangle

Right lateral view

MUSCLES of the LARYNX

The muscles of the larynx are intimately involved with the swallowing process and are assisted by many of the muscles seen in the previous plate. Many other muscles are surveyed in this plate. Indeed, the passage of food into the esophagus depends upon the activity of several of these muscles.

> Look over the plate and note that it consists of three parts. The first part is a deep view of the muscles close to the larynx and trachea. Then the other two parts zoom in to give lateral views of the same area. Many small muscles are involved in movements of the larynx, and they will be surveyed here. Begin by coloring the main title Muscles of the Larynx. Then begin your reading below. As you encounter the muscle, read about it and color it in the plate. When you color the muscles close to the larynx, use light colors since they are very close to one another. We have labeled the important muscles of the larynx and pharyngeal area to orient you to the correct body part. Moreover, the same labels are used for the muscles in all three parts of the plate.

The first laryngeal muscle that we shall consider is the **omohyoid (A)**. As the plate shows, this muscle is composed of several parts. It has a **superior belly (A$_1$)** followed by an **intermediate tendon (A$_2$)**, then an **inferior belly (A$_3$)**. The muscle is straplike and originates at the superior surface of the scapula and inserts on the hyoid bone. This muscle is responsible for depressing the hyoid bone in the swallowing process. A **sheath of fascia (A$_4$)** helps keep it in place. Nerves from the cervical region of the spinal cord innervate the muscle. Running parallel to the omohyoid is the **sternohyoid (B)**. This is the most medial muscle of the neck. It originates at the manubrium and clavicle and inserts to the lower margin of the hyoid bone, as shown. The sternohyoid also depresses the hyoid bone during swallowing.

The **sternothyroid muscle (C)** is another muscle running parallel. This muscle has its origin on the manubrium and its insertion on the thyroid cartilage on the larynx. It depresses the thyroid cartilage and pulls it inferiorly. The **thyrohyoid (D)** originates at the thyroid cartilage close to where the sternothyroid inserts. The thyrohyoid inserts at the hyoid bone and acts to elevate the thyroid cartilage.

> At this point, we have seen some of the major muscles located along the trachea and larynx and noted their relationships to one another and the hyoid bone. Now we shall focus on some of the deeper muscles located along the surface of the larynx. Some of these muscles will appear in the anterior view, but many will also be seen in the lateral views. Continue your reading below and color the muscles as you encounter them in the text. Lighter colors are recommended to avoid obscuring any of the muscles.

The muscles close to the laryngeal surface are the intrinsic muscles. The first of these intrinsic muscles is the **cricohyoid (E)**. Seen in both the anterior and lateral views, this muscle places tension on the vocal cords. It originates on the cricoid cartilage of the larynx and inserts on the thyroid cartilage of the larynx. Another muscle seen in this area is the **posterior cricoarytenoid (F)**. This muscle opens the space between the vocal cords to assist speech. Its origin is at the cricoid cartilage of the larynx and its insertion is at the surface of the arytenoid cartilage of the larynx. A branch of the vagus nerve innervates it. Close by is the **lateral cricoarytenoid (G)**. This muscle also regulates the space between the vocal cords. It originates at the cricoid cartilage and inserts at the arytenoid cartilage. The muscle can be seen in the right posteriolateral view.

The **arytenoid (H)** has the same name as the arytenoid cartilage of the larynx. It originates at the border of one of the arytenoid cartilages and inserts at the opposite arytenoid. The muscle thus contracts the vocal cord space. The **thyroarytenoid (I)** originates at the thyroid cartilage and inserts at the arytenoid cartilage, as the diagram shows. Its function is to regulate the size of the vocal cords.

Two other muscles seen along the surface of the larynx are the **thyroepiglottis (J)** and the **aryepiglottis (K)**. As the names indicate, these muscles control the action of the epiglottis during the swallowing process. The epiglottis can be seen in the diagram and it is recommended that it be colored to allow it to stand out. Also, the hyoid bone may be colored to distinguish it from the surrounding tissues.

> The plate will be completed with a brief examination of the constrictor muscles. These muscle constrict the pharynx and help propel food into the esophagus. As you read about the muscles, color them in the lateral view of the larynx and esophagus. Note how their location permits them to exert pressure on the pharynx and larynx areas.

There are three constrictor muscles of the pharynx. They are paired muscles whose fibers are arranged to overlap. The first muscle is the **superior constrictor (L)**. This muscle has its origin at portions of the sphenoid and mandible bones. Its fibers run in a circular fashion as the plate shows. The insertion is at the posterior median raphe of the pharynx. Close to the hyoid bone is the **middle constrictor (M)**. This muscle lies outside the superior constrictor. Its insertion is at the hyoid and insertion is at the median raphe. The **inferior constrictor (N)** is the outermost muscle. Originating at the cartilages of the larynx, it extends around to the back of the pharynx and also inserts at the posterior median raphe. Working with the other constrictors, it constricts the pharynx during the swallowing process. Branches of the vagus and glossopharyngeal control the movements of these muscles.

Three other muscles bear brief mention. These muscles all help elevate the larynx and insert at the thyroid cartilage. The first elevator is the **palatopharyngeus (O)**. This muscle originates at the soft palate. The second muscle is the **salpingopharyngeus (P)**. This muscle originates near the inferior portion of the Eustachian tube. The third muscle is the **stylopharyngeus (Q)**. This muscle has its origin at the styloid process of the temporal bone. These muscles work with other muscles to elevate the larynx when innervated by nerves from the spinal cord.

Omohyoid A ○
Superior belly A₁ ○
Intermediate tendon A₂ ○
Inferior belly A₃ ○
Sheath of fascia A₄ ○

Sternohyoid B ○
Sternothyroid C ○
Thyrohyoid D ○
Cricohyoid E ○
Posterior cricoarytenoid F ○
Lateral cricoarytenoid G ○
Arytenoid H ○
Thyroarytenoid I ○
Thyroepiglottis J ○
Aryepiglottis K ○
Superior constrictor L ○
Middle constrictor M ○
Inferior constrictor N ○
Palatopharyngeus O ○
Salpingopharyngeus P ○
Stylopharyngeus Q ○

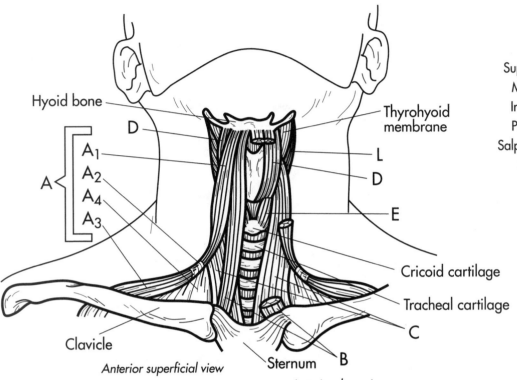

Hyoid bone

Thyrohyoid membrane

Cricoid cartilage

Tracheal cartilage

Clavicle

Sternum

Anterior superficial view

Anterior deep view

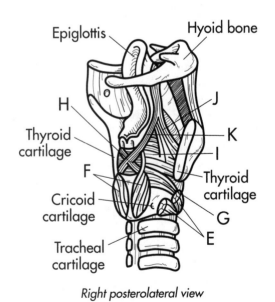

Epiglottis

Hyoid bone

Thyroid cartilage

Thyroid cartilage

Cricoid cartilage

Tracheal cartilage

Right posterolateral view

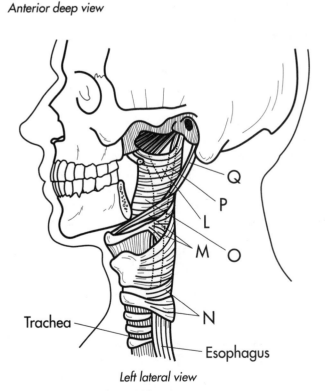

Trachea

Esophagus

Left lateral view

67

MUSCLES of the THORAX and ABDOMEN (ANTERIOR)

Many of the most prominent of the 700 skeletal muscles of the body are found on the wall of the thorax and abdomen. Like other muscles, these muscles produce movements by exerting forces upon tendons, which in turn pull on bones or skin or other structures. Many of the abdominal and thoracic muscles move the shoulder or thigh, and many permit movements of the body torso. The anterior and lateral walls of the thorax and abdomen consist of skin, fascia, and four sheetlike muscles that we shall examine presently. The muscles lend support to the body and provide protection to the thoracic and abdominal muscles beneath. Many also assist the breathing process.

In this first section, we shall examine the four major muscles of the abdominal wall. You should start the plate by coloring the main title Muscles of the Thorax and Abdomen (Anterior). As you encounter the muscles, color their titles and the muscles in the plate using darker colors for the muscles in this section. The posterior muscles will be discussed in a separate plate and will be considered only briefly here. You will note that we also consider some of the muscles of the shoulder and thigh even though they are not strictly considered muscles of the abdominal region.

A major muscle of the anterior abdominal surface is the **rectus abdominis (A)**. This muscle has its origin at the superior surface of the pubis (the pubic crest) and its insertion at the cartilages of the fifth to seventh ribs. The rectus abdominis depresses the ribs and permits flexion at the waistline. The muscle is divided at points by several **intersections of tendon (A_1)**. They are thought to be the remnants of divisions separating muscle sections during development of the embryo.

The second important muscle is the **external oblique (B)**. This muscle has actions similar to those of the rectus abdominis. The muscle is the largest and most superficial of the three lateral muscles. The fibers run downward, as the plate shows, and end at a large **aponeurosis (B_1)**. The aponeurosis of this muscle and the two following muscles meet at the midline to form a fibrous band of tissue called the **linea alba (B_2)**. The external oblique inserts at the linea alba.

The third muscle is the **internal oblique (C)**. Its fibers fan upward, running at right angles to the external oblique. The actions of this muscle are similar to those of the external oblique. The **transversus abdominis (D)** is the deepest of the four muscles. Its fibers run across the body surface in a horizontal plane. Its function is to compress the abdominal wall. This muscle and those previous to it are all innervated by nerves originating in the thoracic area of the spinal cord.

In the next section of this plate, we will mention muscles of the thoracic portion of the anterior body surface. Many of these muscles are involved in movements of the shoulder and upper arm, and many are involved in breathing. As you encounter the muscle, color its title, then locate it on the plate and color it in using lighter colors for the smaller muscles and dark ones for the larger muscles.

An important muscle of the chest region is the **pectoralis major (E)**. This muscle originates at the clavicle, sternum, and rib cartilages, then runs horizontally across the chest surface to insert at the greater tubercle of the humerus. It flexes the arm and adducts it. Although better seen in the posterior view, a small portion of the **latissimus dorsi (F)** can be seen here. It is a broad, triangular muscle of the lower back.

The **serratus anterior (G)** is also seen here briefly. This muscle originates at the ribs, as shown in the diagram, and inserts at the scapula. It is better seen on the posterior view. The **deltoid (H)** is the prominent shoulder muscle. This thick muscle forms the rounded part of the shoulder and is a prime abductor of the arm. The **pectoralis minor (I)** is a flat, thin muscle close to the pectoralis major.

The two key sets of muscles with respect to breathing are the internal and external intercostals. The **external intercostals (J)** originate at the inferior borders of the above ribs and insert at the superior borders of the ribs below them. They elevate the ribs during inspiration. The **internal intercostals (K)** originate at the superior border of one rib and insert at the inferior border of the rib above. They decrease the size of the thorax during forced expirations. Both muscle groups are innervated by intercostal nerves.

The **subclavius (L)** lies under the clavicle. It originates at the first rib and inserts at the clavicle. The **subscapularis (M)** lies beneath the scapula. Its origin is at the subscapular fossa of the scapula and its insertion is at the humerus. This muscle rotates the arm in the medial direction. The **teres major (N)** lies at the inferior angle of the scapula. It also inserts on the humerus, but its function is to extend the arm.

The remaining portions of this plate will point out some of the important muscles associated with body sections. Although the muscles themselves are not considered in depth here, it is well to understand their relationships to the abdominal and thoracic portions of the body. Some of the origins or insertions of the muscles can also be seen in relation to the abdominal or thoracic regions. Lowercase letters have been used to denote their presence; they should be colored in the plate with darker reds, greens, and blues since they are quite large.

One of the muscles of the arm is the **coracobrachialis (a)**. This muscle adducts the arm. The **biceps brachii (b)** is a main flexor of the forearm. One of its heads originates at the scapula. The **platysma (c)** is seen as a broad, sheetlike muscle at the superficial neck surface. This muscle plays a role in facial expression. The **sternocleidomastoid (d)** is a straplike muscle associated with movements of the head. The muscle has two origins seen in this plate: one origin is on the sternum and the second is on the medial portion of the clavicle. Close to the sternocleidomastoid is the **trapezius (e)**. Better seen in the posterior view, this is an important shoulder and back muscle.

In the region of the thigh is the **gluteus medius (f)**. This thick muscle is an important site for intramuscular injections; the muscle adducts and rotates the thigh. The **tensor fascia latae (g)** is a flexor of the thigh. One of the most important flexors of the thigh is the **iliopsoas (h)**. It is prominent on the anterior surface on the superficial and deep views.

The **pectineus (i)** is also seen in the anterior surface. It is a short, flat muscle that adducts and flexes the thigh. The **adductor longus (j)** is another flexor of the thigh. The **gracilis (k)** is a long and thin muscle that adducts and flexes the leg. The **sartorius (l)** is a straplike muscle of the superficial area and is one of the body's longest muscles. Finally, the **rectus femoris (m)** is a superficial thigh muscle that extends the knee and flexes the thigh at the hip joint. These and numerous other muscles of the lower appendage are studied in depth in other plates.

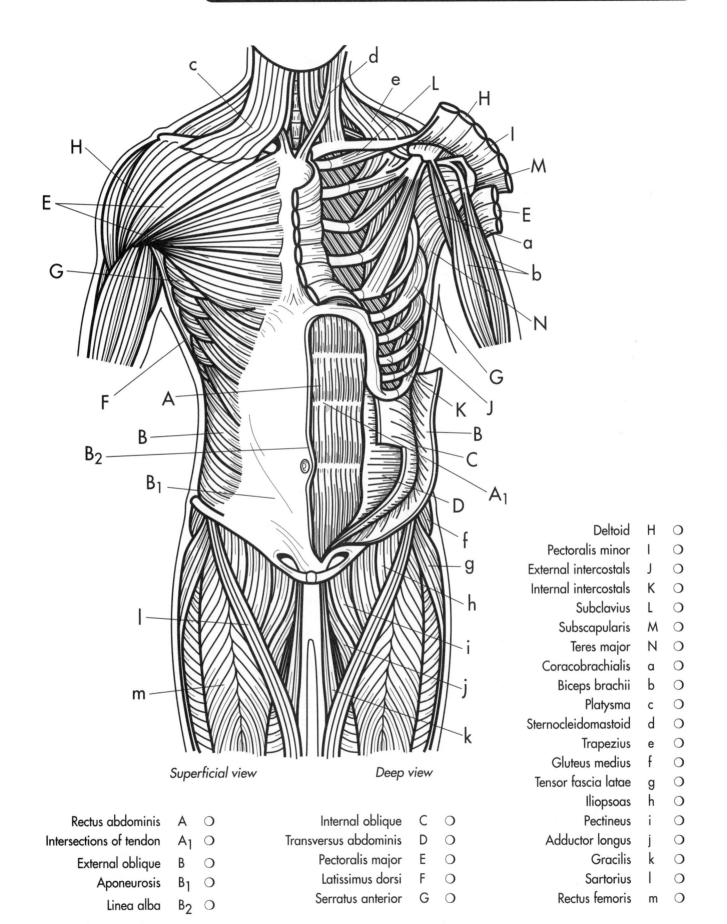

Superficial view   *Deep view*

Deltoid	H	○		
Pectoralis minor	I	○		
External intercostals	J	○		
Internal intercostals	K	○		
Subclavius	L	○		
Subscapularis	M	○		
Teres major	N	○		
Coracobrachialis	a	○		
Biceps brachii	b	○		
Platysma	c	○		
Sternocleidomastoid	d	○		
Trapezius	e	○		
Gluteus medius	f	○		
Tensor fascia latae	g	○		
Iliopsoas	h	○		
Pectineus	i	○		
Adductor longus	j	○		
Gracilis	k	○		
Sartorius	l	○		
Rectus femoris	m	○		

Rectus abdominis	A	○		Internal oblique	C	○
Intersections of tendon	A₁	○		Transversus abdominis	D	○
External oblique	B	○		Pectoralis major	E	○
Aponeurosis	B₁	○		Latissimus dorsi	F	○
Linea alba	B₂	○		Serratus anterior	G	○

MUSCLES of the THORAX and ABDOMEN (DEEP)

The anterior and lateral abdominal wall is composed of four paired muscles together with their aponeuroses and fasciae. These four muscles are partly shown in this plate on the visual right side of the figure (the anatomical left). On the figure's left side (the anatomical right) they have been removed to show the deep portions of the abdominal cavity and portions of the posterior abdominal wall. Overlying and between the ribs are several important muscles also discussed in this plate. Many of the muscles encountered in this plate are identical to those seen in the previous plate, and we have used the same letters to identify them. This will allow you to see them in the more superficial view in the previous plate and in the more deep view in this plate. As you examine this plate, you will note that the abdominal organs have been removed on the anatomical left side of the abdominal cavity and the vertebral column and posterior wall have been exposed.

Color the main title Muscles of the Thorax and Abdomen (Deep) to begin the plate, then look over the plate to orient yourself. On your visual left (the anatomical right), there is a more superficial view of the deep muscles. By contrast, on your visual right (the anatomical left), the view is of the deep muscles, and for the abdomen, this includes portions of the posterior abdominal wall. Note that some of the bony structures have been labeled to give you orientation. These bones may be colored in a gray color if you wish, but you should be careful to avoid obscuring the muscles associated with them. Read the paragraph below, and as you encounter the muscles, color their titles and color the muscles in the plate. Lighter and pale colors are recommended for this plate. You may wish to refer to the previous plate occasionally, since the same colors should be used for the same muscles in both plates.

The **rectus abdominis (A)** is a straplike muscle in the medial aspect of the body. As the diagram shows, the muscle extends from the pubis to the ribcage, and a portion has been cut to allow vision of the muscle beneath. Beneath the rectus abdominis is the second major muscle of the abdominal wall, the **external oblique (B)**. This muscle is a large and superficial muscle of the lateral aspect. Its fibers run downward, and the muscle can also be seen in the previous plate. The muscle originates at the lower ribs and inserts at the midline of the body.

The fibers of the **internal oblique (C)** run at right angles to those of the external oblique. They can be seen running in the superior and medial direction. The **aponeurosis (C$_1$)** arising from the internal oblique is apparent in the diagram and it can be observed overlying and enclosing the rectus abdominis. The **transversus abdominis (D)** is the deepest of the four muscles. The fibers of this muscle run horizontally at an angle to the external and internal oblique. The muscle originates at the fascia in the lumbar region in the dorsal aspect of the body and the cartilages of the last six ribs.

The muscle then runs around the lateral aspect and inserts at the linea alba and pubic crest.

The four muscles we have considered compose most of the interior and lateral wall of the abdominal cavity. They support and protect the abdominal organs but have no bony reinforcement of their own. However, the fibers run in alternating directions and support one another in this manner. The plate should be continued by focusing on the muscles of the deep regions of the thoracic cavity and the remainder of the plate. As you encounter these muscles in the following paragraph, color their titles, then color the muscles in the following diagram. The intercostal muscles should be colored in light colors.

A large superficial muscle of the thoracic cavity seen in the previous plate is the pectoralis major. When this muscle is removed, the flat, thin muscle directly beneath it is revealed. This muscle of the thoracic wall is the **pectoralis minor (I)**. Like other muscles of the anterior group, this muscle inserts into the pectoral girdle. The muscle is one of the extrinsic shoulder muscles because it runs from the ribs to the pectoral girdle. The pectoralis minor draws the scapula forward and downward and adjusts the position of the ribcage.

Note in the diagram that the pectoralis minor has been cut and lifted toward the medial surface to reveal the underlying rib muscles. The **external intercostals (J)** lie between the ribs and run downward from a rib to the rib below. Thus, there are eleven pairs of external intercostals. When they contract, they pull the ribs toward one another and elevate the ribcage. The **internal intercostals (K)** are deep to the external intercostals. Their fibers run at right angles to those of the external intercostals. These muscles also originate at one rib and insert at the rib below. When they contract, they draw the ribs together and thereby depress the ribcage. This action aids in forced expiration. The external and internal intercostals are antagonistic to one another. Both groups of muscles are supplied by the intercostal nerves.

The diagram will be completed with a brief look at the diaphragm. Note in the diagram on the anatomical left that the abdominal organs have been removed to reveal the diaphragm as a dome-shaped muscle, which is quite extensive. As you read about the muscle below, color it in together with its parts.

The floor of the thoracic cavity is formed by the **diaphragm (O)**. This key muscle of inspiration divides the abdominal and thoracic cavities. The diagram shows the diaphragm in the relaxed dome position. However, when it is stimulated by branches of the phrenic nerve, it contracts, moves to the inferior aspect, and becomes flat. This action increases the volume of the thoracic cavity and contributes to the process of inspiration. The muscle has its origin at the inferior border of the ribcage and sternum, and it inserts at a **central tendon (O$_1$)**. The diaphragm is also anchored by several strong **ligaments (O$_2$)**.

The final muscle we shall consider in this plate is the **quadratus lumborum (P)**. This muscle is seen on the posterior abdominal wall. It originates at the iliac crest, as shown, and inserts at the twelfth rib and transverse processes of the lumbar vertebrae. The muscle contributes to upright posture, and during forced expiration, it pulls on the twelfth rib. During a deep inspiration, it maintains the position of the twelfth rib, to prevent its elevation. Thus, it contributes to the activity and positioning of the thoracic cage.

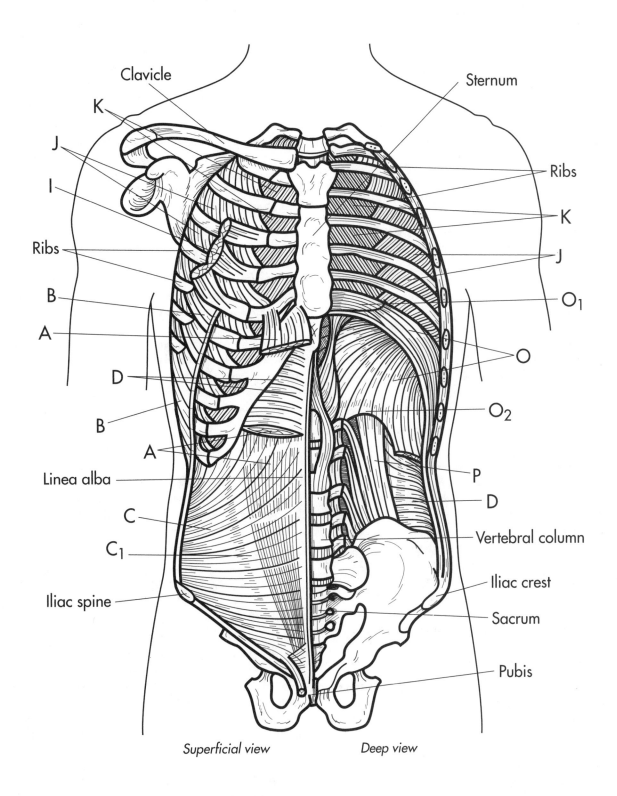

Clavicle

Sternum

K

J

I

Ribs

K

Ribs

J

B

O_1

A

O

D

O_2

B

A

Linea alba

P

C

D

C_1

Vertebral column

Iliac spine

Iliac crest

Sacrum

Pubis

Superficial view   *Deep view*

Rectus abdominis	A	○	Transversus abdominis	D	○	Diaphragm	O	○ ○
External oblique	B	○	Pectoralis minor	I	○	Central tendon	O_1	○
Internal oblique	C	○	External intercostals	J	○	Ligaments	O_2	○
Aponeurosis	C_1	○	Internal intercostals	K	○	Quadratus lumborum	P	○

MUSCLES of the THORAX and ABDOMEN (POSTERIOR)

Like the muscles on the anterior aspect, the posterior muscles of the thorax and abdomen have several functions. They provide protection and support to organs of the abdominal and thoracic cavity; they support the vertebral column; they help move the upper and lower extremities; and they are involved in movements of the head. The origin of the muscle is usually a stationary bone to which the muscle tendon attaches. At the other end, the tendon of the muscle generally attaches to a movable bone called an insertion. The fleshy portion of the muscle is known as the belly of the muscle.

A muscle bringing about a desired action is called a prime mover or agonist. Another muscle, called the antagonist, has an action opposite to that of the prime mover. For example, an agonist will flex the arm while an antagonist will extend it. The roles of individual muscles can be reversed under other circumstances. Approximately 700 muscles have been identified in the body, and this plate surveys the muscles seen in superficial and deep views of the thorax and abdomen. Many of the muscles are encountered in previous plates and in following plates. It is well to recall their names from other plates and to use this plate as a review device and to prepare for other plates. Some brief information will be given about each muscle, with more extensive discussions presented in other plates.

> Begin the plate by coloring the main title Muscles of the Thorax and Abdomen (Posterior). Then examine the plate and note that a superficial view is given on the visual left (anatomical left), and a deep view of the thoracic and abdominal walls is given on the visual right (anatomical right). As you encounter the names of the muscles below, color the titles, then color the muscles where they appear in the diagram. Note that some of the muscles have been cut to reveal the underlying muscles. If you wish you may color the muscles with the same colors used in other plates. Dark colors are generally recommended for this plate because the muscles are fairly large and separated from one another. Both superficial and deep views should be colored together.

One of the most obvious muscles of the posterior thoracic wall is the **trapezius (A)**. This flat, triangular muscle has fibers running in many different directions, as the plate shows. The fibers come together to insert along the acromion process and spine of the scapula and portion of the clavicle. Various actions are performed by this muscle including head, neck, and shoulder movements. One of the superficial prime movers of the arm is the **latissimus dorsi (B)**. This broad muscle is found along the lower back. It originates at the fascia of the spines of the thoracic and lumber vertebrae, passes laterally, then inserts in a groove of the humerus. It is one of the most important adductors of the arm.

The muscle along the posterior aspect of the scapula is the **supraspinatus (C)**. This muscle is deep to the trapezius, which has been reflected in the deep view of the thoracic area. The supraspinatus originates at the scapula, inserts at the humerus, and assists in the abduction of the arm. The **infraspinatus (D)** lies inferior to the supraspinatus. Its action is to rotate the arm in the lateral direction

as well as to adduct it. With the supraspinatus, it is one of the rotator cuff muscles, so-named because they assist in rotation and enclose portions of the shoulder capsule.

The fleshy mass of the shoulder is formed by the **deltoid (E)**. This muscle abducts the arm and is a prime mover of the arm. It originates at the clavicle and scapula and inserts at the deltoid tuberosity of the humerus. In the same region are the **rhomboideus major (F)** and the **rhomboideus minor (G)**. These muscles act to stabilize the scapula and retract it so that the shoulders become "square."

> Most of the emphasis of the early part of the plate has been on the muscles surrounding the thoracic cage and portions of the shoulder. We shall now continue this plate by examining muscles of the lower thoracic area and the posterior portion of the abdomen. As you read about the muscles below, color their titles, then color the muscles in the diagrams. Dark colors may be employed, as before.

The serratus muscles have "serrated" origins, meaning that they appear as the teeth of a saw. The muscles lie below the latissimus dorsi and pectoralis muscles, which must be reflected to show the serratus muscles. These muscles are designated the **serratus posterior superior (H)**, the **serratus anterior (I)**, and the **serratus posterior inferior (J)**. They provide support, and the serratus anterior helps stabilize the scapula.

Two main muscles of the anterior and lateral abdominal wall are briefly seen on the plate. They are the **external oblique (K)** and the **internal oblique (L)**. These large muscles are more clear on the anterior surface. They overlie one another, and their fibers run opposite to one another, thereby supplying a muscular framework to the abdominal wall. The **erector spinous (M)** is also seen.

> The remaining muscles in this plate are seen in this view, but are not portions of the thoracic or abdominal walls. They are examined extensively in other plates, but we include them here to show their relative positions. The muscles are designated with lowercase letters to indicate their treatment elsewhere. We recommend greens, blues, and reds for coloring them.

A major muscle of the neck area is the **sternocleidomastoid (a)**. This muscle is one of the prime movers of the head. As the name implies, the muscle originates at the sternum and clavicle and inserts at the mastoid process of the temporal bone. Another muscle that moves the head is the **semispinalis capitis (b)**. This muscle originates at the transverse processes of several vertebrae and inserts at the occipital bone. It extends the head, and contractions of one muscle can rotate the head to the side opposite. A large muscle of the posterior neck region is the **splenius capitis (c)**. The muscle extends the head and rotates it. The splenius capitis originates at the spinous processes of several vertebrae and inserts on the occipital bone and the mastoid process of the temporal bone.

The **levator scapulae (d)** is found in the side of the neck deep to the trapezius. This muscle elevates the scapula and flexes the neck. It originates at the transverse processes of several cervical vertebrae and inserts into a border of the scapula. The **triceps brachii (e)** is the large fleshy muscle at the posterior surface of the upper arm. The muscle is an important extensor of the forearm.

The **gluteus medius (f)** is observed in the thigh region. This thick muscle is partially covered by the gluteus maximus, as the plate shows. The muscle abducts and rotates the thigh while providing support for the pelvis. The **gluteus maximus (g)** is the most superficial gluteal muscle. It forms the mass of the buttock. Originating at the ileum, sacrum, and coccyx, the muscle inserts at the gluteal tuberosity of the femur. It is a major extensor of the thigh. This and other muscles of the area are examined in depth in the appropriate plate.

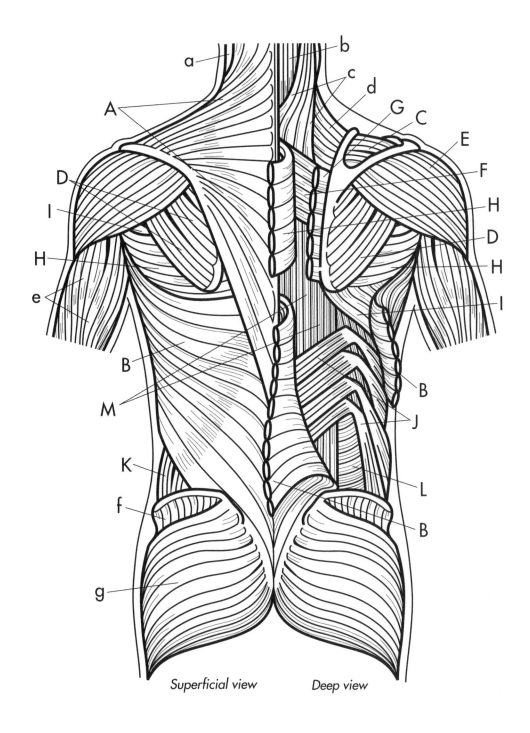

Superficial view   *Deep view*

Trapezius	A ○	Serratus posterior superior	H ○	Semispinalis capitis	b ○
Latissimus dorsi	B ○	Serratus anterior	I ○	Splenius capitis	c ○
Supraspinatus	C ○	Serratus posterior inferior	J ○	Levator scapulae	d ○
Infraspinatus	D ○	External oblique	K ○	Triceps brachii	e ○
Deltoid	E ○	Internal oblique	L ○	Gluteus medius	f ○
Rhomboideus major	F ○	Erector spinous	M ○	Gluteus maximus	g ○
Rhomboideus minor	G ○	Sternocleidomastoid	a ○		

MUSCLES of the SHOULDER

The shoulder muscles have the responsibility of moving the humerus as well as the pectoral girdle. Many of the these muscles form the coverings of the thoracic cage and contribute to movements of the humerus. The muscles involved with movement of the humerus are discussed in a separate plate, while those that move the pectoral girdle are explained here.

Begin your work on this plate by coloring the main title Muscles of the Shoulder. As you examine the plate, note that both anterior and posterior views of the shoulder area are presented. Therefore, as you encounter the muscles in the reading below, you should locate and color them in both views. In addition, you should note that different sides contain different views and that one view is deeper than the first view. This will give you insight into which muscles overlie which others. We recommend that you use dark colors since the muscles are fairly distinct from one another.

Many of the muscles of the shoulder act to stabilize the scapula so that the scapula can form an origin point for muscles moving the upper arm (or humerus). One such muscle of the shoulder is the **subclavius (A)**. As the plate shows, this muscle originates at the first rib and inserts at the clavicle. It is a small, cylindrical muscle that helps stabilize the clavicle portion of the pectoral girdle. The posterior view shows the muscle briefly.

The **pectoralis minor (B)** was mentioned in the previous plates. It can be seen clearly in this plate, with origins on the third, fourth, and fifth ribs and insertion to the coracoid process of the scapula. This muscle stabilizes the ribcage when the scapula is fixed, and it stabilizes the scapula when the ribs are fixed. At the lateral surface is the **serratus anterior (C)**. This muscle is visible on both anterior and posterior surfaces. The muscle originates at several superior ribs and inserts at the vertebral border of the scapula. It rotates the scapula and abducts it. The muscle is sometimes called the "boxer's muscle" because it is used in punching.

The posterior superficial view shows the triangular muscle called the **trapezius (D)**. A portion of this muscle at the shoulder is visible at the anterior view. Fibers of this muscle run along the posterior wall of the scapula. The muscle originates at the occipital bone, as the diagram shows, and insertion occurs along the acromion process and spine of the scapula. The muscle brings about multiple movements and stabilization of the scapula. It is innervated by the spinal accessory nerve.

We have examined some of the key muscles in the region of the shoulder, especially the scapula. You may continue the plate by reading about additional muscles of this region in the paragraph below. As the muscles occur in the reading, color their titles and the muscles in the plate.

A muscle that elevates the scapula is called the **levator scapulae (E)**. This thick straplike muscle can be seen in the anterior and posterior views running from the cervical vertebrae to the scapula. It is apparent in the posterior view. The muscle originates at the cervical vertebrae and inserts at the cervical vertebral border of the scapula. In the posterior view, it can be seen that the levator scapulae is deep to the trapezius.

There are two rhomboid muscles, both deep to the trapezius and both seen on the posterior deep view. The first muscle is the **rhomboideus major (F)**. This muscle originates at the thoracic vertebrae and inserts at the vertebral border of the scapula. It adducts the scapula. The **rhomboideus minor (G)** also originates at the thoracic vertebrae, but higher on the vertebral column. It inserts at the same location as the rhomboideus major. It also adducts the scapula. The plate illustrates the location of the **sternocleidomastoid (H)**. This can be considered a shoulder muscle since it inserts at the clavicle and helps stabilize the pectoral girdle.

A very thick muscle and a prime mover of the arm is the **deltoid (I)**. As the plate shows in the posterior view, the deltoid forms much of the muscle mass of the shoulder. The muscle originates at several points on the scapula and inserts at the deltoid tuberosity of the humerus. When it contracts, it brings about many movements of the arm including abduction, flexion, and extension. These various movements occur depending upon which fibers of the muscle undergo contraction.

There are several other muscles visible in these views. Even though they are not part of the shoulder group, they can be viewed in context with the shoulder muscle. Many of the muscles are involved in stabilization of the pectoral girdle and movement of the arm. You will note that they are designated by small letters to distinguish them from the main shoulder muscles. Since the muscles are small, a pale color is recommended.

In the plate, the **infraspinatus muscle (a)** can be seen. This muscle originates at a fossa of the scapula and inserts at the greater tubercle of the humerus. Its action is to adduct the arm. A muscle in the same region as the infraspinatus is the **teres minor (b)**. Like the infraspinatus, it adducts the arm and rotates it laterally. The **teres major (c)** may also be seen on the posterior view. This muscle extends the arm and assists in adduction. Note that the three preceding muscles are muscles of the thoracic cage functioning in arm movements rather than as protectors of the thoracic organs.

Two groups of muscles deeply involved in breathing are the **external intercostals (d)** and the **internal intercostals (e)**. These muscles are discussed extensively in the previous plates, and they may also be seen here. Note how the muscle fibers move in directions opposite to one another. The muscles originate at the above rib and insert at the below rib. When the external intercostals contract during inspiration, the ribs elevate and increase the dimensions of the thorax. When the internal intercostals contract during expiration, the dimensions of the thorax decrease, and air is forced out of the lungs.

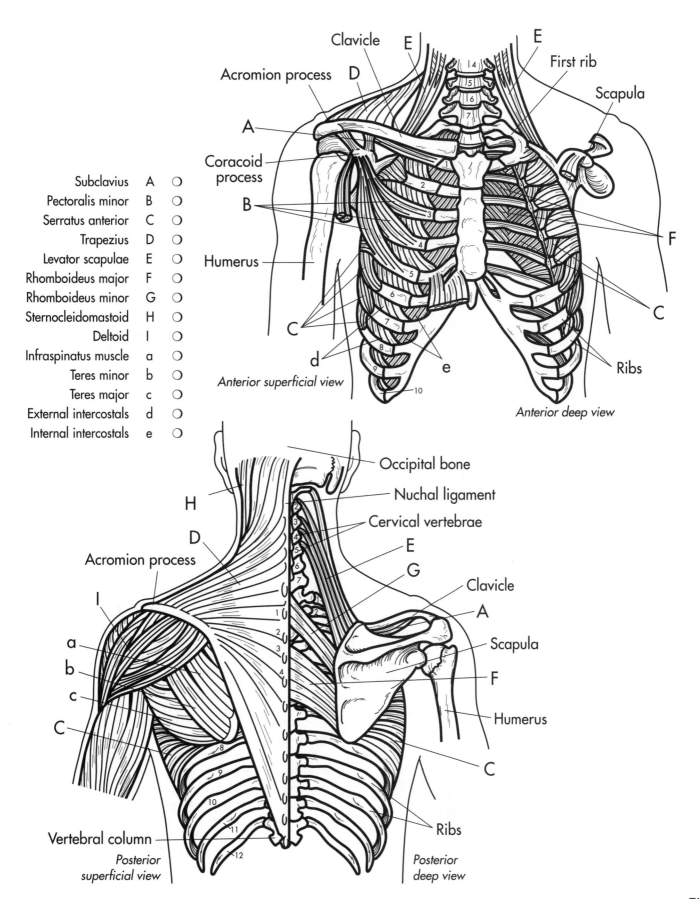

Subclavius A ○
Pectoralis minor B ○
Serratus anterior C ○
Trapezius D ○
Levator scapulae E ○
Rhomboideus major F ○
Rhomboideus minor G ○
Sternocleidomastoid H ○
Deltoid I ○
Infraspinatus muscle a ○
Teres minor b ○
Teres major c ○
External intercostals d ○
Internal intercostals e ○

Clavicle
Acromion process
Coracoid process
Humerus
E
D
A
B
C
d

First rib
Scapula
E
F
C
e
Ribs

Anterior superficial view

Anterior deep view

Occipital bone
Nuchal ligament
Cervical vertebrae
E
G
Clavicle
A
Scapula
F
Humerus
C
Ribs

H
D
Acromion process
I
a
b
c
C

Vertebral column
Posterior superficial view
Posterior deep view

MUSCLES of the VERTEBRAL COLUMN

The superficial back muscles, such as the latissimus dorsi and trapezius, overlie a series of deeper muscles known collectively as the erector spinae muscles. These muscles generally act as extensors of the spine. They work antagonistically to the flexors on the anterior aspect of the abdominal cavity.

The erector spinae muscles include numerous superficial spinal extensors arranged in three divisions: the spinalis division, the longissimus division, and the iliocostalis division. Muscles in these divisions are the major concern of this plate. We shall also encounter a number of deeper extensors of the spine.

> Start by coloring in the main title of the plate Muscles of the Vertebral Column. Then look over the plate and note that superficial muscles shown in previous plates have been removed, and the focus is on muscles close to the vertebral column. Many of the bones of the thoracic cage, vertebral column, and pelvis are showing, and they may be colored using lighter colors such as grays and tans. The main objective is to study the three divisions of muscles of the erector spinae. Dark colors can be used for these muscles, because most are separated from other muscles. Where you see smaller muscles, use lighter colors to avoid obscuring places where the muscles overlap.

Muscles of the spinalis division include the **splenius capitis (A)** and **splenius cervicis (B)**. These muscles near the neck region function together to extend the head, as in tilting the head backward. Either muscle acting alone can also rotate the head. The muscles originate at processes of the cervical vertebrae and insert at the mastoid process and occipital bone of the skull.

The iliocostalis division includes the **iliocostalis cervicis (C)**, the **iliocostalis thoracis (D)**, and the **iliocostalis lumborum (E)**. This is a lateral group of three muscles extending from the pelvis to the neck. The muscles extend the vertebral column and help maintain erect posture. They can also bend the vertebral column to one side or the other. The plate shows the approximate points of origin or insertion for each muscle. Note how the name corresponds to the general location to the muscle.

The longissimus division of the erector spinae is composed of three muscles known as the **longissimus capitis (F)**, the **longissimus cervicis (G)**, and the **longissimus thoracis (H)**. These long muscles act together to extend the vertebral column, or they may act individually to bend it laterally. As the plate shows, the muscles have their origin on the transverse processes of several vertebrae and their insertions either at the vertebrae, ribs, or skull

bones. Darker colors can be used for these muscles to distinguish them from other nearby muscles.

> We have thus far seen representatives of the three divisions of the erector spinae and have seen how these muscles can act as extensors. Continue with the plate by focusing on several additional muscles of the group. As you read about the muscles, color their titles, then color in the muscles. If you note that the muscle is distinct from the surrounding tissues, then use a dark color such as a purple, blue, or green. However, if it is close to its adjoining muscles, use a pale color.

Muscles of the spinalis division include the **spinalis capitis (I)**, the **spinalis cervicis (J)**, and the **spinalis thoracis (K)**. These extensors of the spinal column originate at the spinal processes of thoracic and lumbar vertebrae and insert at spinal processes of other thoracic vertebrae. The muscles are in the medial aspect and are innervated by spinal nerves. Also in the spinalis group are the **semispinalis capitis (L)**, the **semispinalis cervicis (M)**, and the **semispinalis thoracis (N)**. These small muscles may be difficult to see in the plate, and light colors should be used. They are extensors of the vertebral column and rotators of the head. As you have probably noted, there are generally three aspects of each muscle named, corresponding to the area where that particular muscle is found. Muscles with three subdivisions are called tripartate muscles.

> In the concluding section of this plate, we examine some of the deeper muscles of the spine, particularly those that interconnect and stabilize the vertebrae of the spinal column. For this portion, you should focus your attention at the diagrams of the vertebrae in place, shown in the posterolateral view and anterior view. Note how the muscles are important to stabilizing the vertebral column.

Among the deepest muscles of the spine is **multifidus group (O)**. These muscles originate at the transverse processes of the lumbar and thoracic vertebrae and the sacrum and insert at the spinous process of the cervical vertebrae. They help extend the vertebral column and rotate it to the side. The **rotators (P)** are another group of muscles associated with the transverse processes of all vertebrae. They are spinal column extensors and rotators.

In the posterolateral view, the **interspinales (Q)** can be seen. These muscles pass among the spinous processes of all vertebrae and help stabilize the vertebrae. The **intertransversarii (R)** may also be seen in the posterolateral view as connectors of transverse processes of vertebrae. The scalenes are lateral muscles found in the neck region. They elevate ribs one and two and assist in inspiration. The muscles originate at the cervical vertebrae and insert at the ribs. They include the **interior scalene (S)**, the **middle scalene (T)**, and the **posterior scalene (U)**.

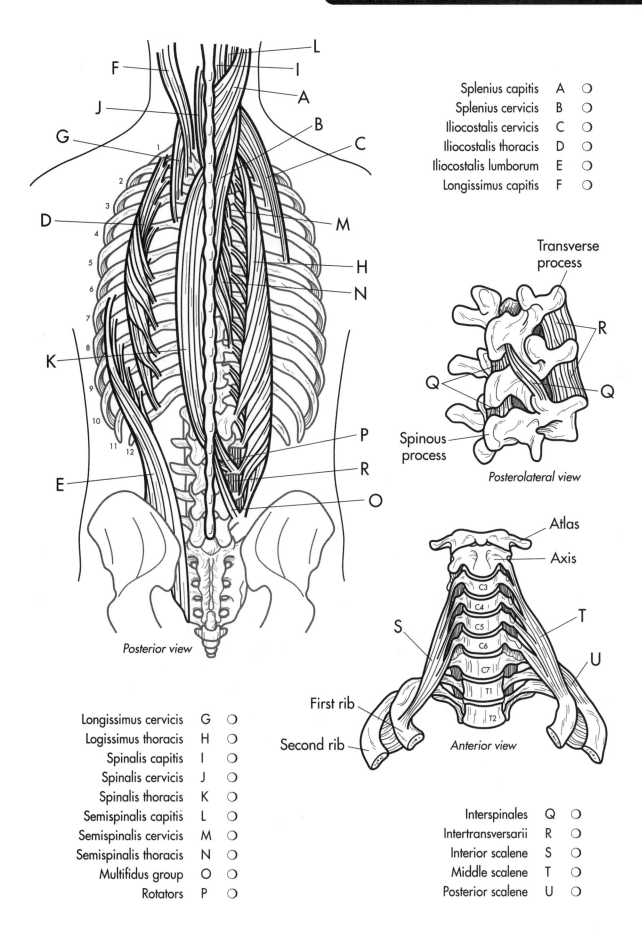

Posterior view

Splenius capitis A ○
Splenius cervicis B ○
Iliocostalis cervicis C ○
Iliocostalis thoracis D ○
Iliocostalis lumborum E ○
Longissimus capitis F ○

Transverse process

R

Q

Q

Spinous process

Posterolateral view

Atlas

Axis

C3
C4
C5
C6
C7
T1
T2

First rib

Second rib

S

T

U

Anterior view

Longissimus cervicis G ○
Logissimus thoracis H ○
Spinalis capitis I ○
Spinalis cervicis J ○
Spinalis thoracis K ○
Semispinalis capitis L ○
Semispinalis cervicis M ○
Semispinalis thoracis N ○
Multifidus group O ○
Rotators P ○

Interspinales Q ○
Intertransversarii R ○
Interior scalene S ○
Middle scalene T ○
Posterior scalene U ○

MUSCLES of the FEMALE PERINEUM

The floor of the pelvis and its associated structures are collectively known as the perineum. In the perineum, the pelvic floor extends from the sacrum and coccyx to the pubis and ischium. The muscles support the organs of the pelvic cavity and bring about flexion of the sacrum and coccyx. They also control the movement of materials through the urethra and anus. In this plate you examine the muscles of the female perineum. Many of the muscles are identical to those in the male perineum in the following plate, and the same letters are used. You may, therefore, see the relationships of the muscles of the pelvic floor in the male and female. You will note that structures other than muscles have been labeled to orient you to the correct area.

> Start by looking over the plate and noting that a superficial view is presented to your visual left (the anatomical right), and a deep view is presented at your visual right (the anatomical left). The openings at the urethra, vagina, and anus have been labeled to provide orientation. Note that the muscles are close to one another, and lighter colors should be employed in this plate. Color the main title Muscles of the Female Perineum.

Muscles of the pelvic floor are collectively referred to as the pelvic diaphragm. Openings at the anus and urethra pierce the pelvic diaphragm in the male and female, and the opening at the vagina pierces the pelvic diaphragm in the female. Two paired muscles form a major portion of the pelvic floor. They are the levator ani and the coccygeus.

The levator ani is subdivided into two parts. The first part is the **pubococcygeus (A)**. This muscle is seen in the deep view in the plate. It originates at the pubis and inserts in structures of the pelvic region and the inner surface of the coccyx. The muscle supports the pelvic floor. The second portion of the levator ani is the **iliococcygeus (B)**. Its origin is the spine of the ischium and its insertion is at the coccyx. The muscle also supports the pelvic floor and elevates it slightly.

The second major muscle is the **coccygeus (C)**. Its origin is at the spine of the ischium, and its insertion is at the borders of the sacrum. The muscle flexes the coccyx and supports and slightly elevates the pelvic floor.

> The levator ani and coccygeus form a region of the pelvic diaphragm known as the anal triangle. A second triangle is the urogenital triangle. We shall continue with the plate by examining the muscles of this region. As before, the muscles are small, so they should be colored carefully using pale colors.

An important muscle of the urogenital triangle is the **ischiocavernosus (D)**. This muscle maintains erection of the penis in the male and the clitoris in the female. The muscle originates at the ischium and inserts at the base of the penis or clitoris. Another muscle of this area is the **bulbocavernosus (E)**. The action of this muscle is similar to that of the ischiocavernosus.

The muscle responsible for stabilizing the central tendon of the perineum is the **superficial transverse perineus (F)**. It originates at the ischium and inserts at the central tendon. The tendon is located at the midline between the anus and vagina in the female. The **deep transverse perineus (G)** has the same origin and insertion. It also stabilizes the central tendon and assists the expulsion of urine in the female.

Surrounding the urethral meatus is the **urethral sphincter (H)**. This circular muscle decreases the opening of the urethra and helps expel the last drops of urine in the female. The **external anal sphincter (I)** surrounds the opening of the anus and closes the anal opening. It originates at a tendon close to the coccyx and inserts at the central tendon of the perineum.

> The plate review is completed by noting a few last structures of the perineum. The first two structures are large and can be colored in dark colors. The last structure is small by comparison.

The view of the perineum shows a portion of the **gluteus maximus (J)**. This large, superficial muscle forms a major portion of the buttock mass. Its large fibers are the site of intramuscular injection in the buttock area. This muscle is encountered in a study of the muscles innervating the thigh. A large ligament known as the **sacrotuberous ligament (K)** is seen in the deep view of the perineum below the gluteus maximus. This ligament extends from the sacrum to the ischial tuberosity and helps support the muscles of the perineum.

The last muscle we shall consider is the **obturator internus (L)**. This muscle surrounds the obturator foramen within the pelvic bone. The muscle helps stabilize the hip joint and contributes to lateral rotation of the thigh.

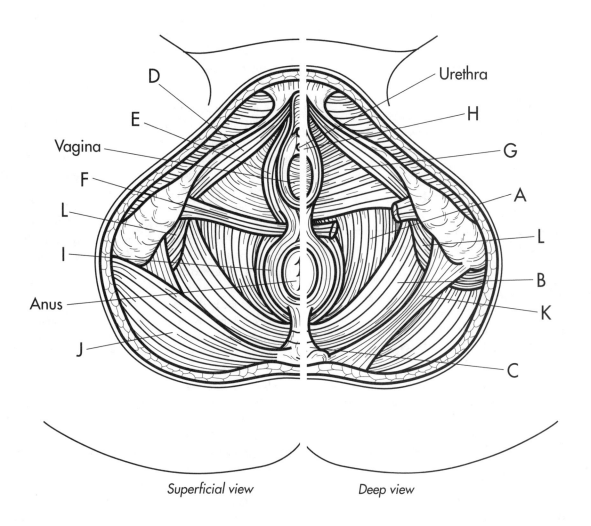

D

E

Vagina

F

L

I

Anus

J

Urethra

H

G

A

L

B

K

C

Superficial view   *Deep view*

Pubococcygeus	A	○
Iliococcygeus	B	○
Coccygeus	C	○
Ischiocavernosus	D	○
Bulbocavernosus	E	○
Superficial transverse perineus	F	○
Deep transverse perineus	G	○
Urethral sphincter	H	○
External anal sphincter	I	○
Gluteus maximus	J	○
Sacrotuberous ligament	K	○
Obturator internus	L	○

MUSCLES of the MALE PERINEUM

The floor of the pelvis is often referred to as the pelvic diaphragm. It is a funnel-shaped structure composed of muscles and fasciae covering the internal and external surfaces. The pelvic floor together with other structures constitutes an area called the perineum. The muscles allow flexion of the sacrum and coccyx, control movements of materials through the anus and urethra, and support the pelvic organs.

Drawing an imaginary line between the ischial tuberosities creates two triangles, an anterior triangle and a posterior triangle. The anterior triangle is also called the urogenital triangle, while the posterior triangle is also known as the anal triangle. Most of the region of the anal triangle is formed by the pelvic diaphragm.

The muscles seen in the male perineum are similar to those observed in the female perineum in the previous plate. For that reason, the same letters are used to point out the muscles. You may wish to compare the two plates to see the muscle relationships. You will also see some obvious differences in the male perineum in this plate.

Start your work on the plate by coloring the main title Muscles of the Male Perineum. Then look over the plate and note that a single view is shown. Therefore, the muscles shown on the left side carry over to the right side of the plate, and the muscles should be colored in the same color on each side. The muscles are fairly distinctive, so we recommend darker colors. We have labeled some of the structures other than muscles for your orientation. As you encounter the muscles in your reading, color the titles and then color the muscles in the plate.

The two important muscles of the pelvic diaphragm in the anal (posterior) triangle are the levator ani and coccygeus. The levator ani contains two parts, the pubococcygeus and the iliococcygeus. The **pubococcygeus (A)** originates at the pubis bone and inserts partly at the coccyx. It elevates the pelvic floor slightly and provides support to various organs. The fibers of this muscle form a sling around the prostate gland and the urethra, then meet in the medial region. The second muscle of the levator ani is the **iliococcygeus (B)**. This muscle originates at the spine of the ischium and the pubis. It inserts at the coccyx and median raphe. Its actions are similar to those of the pubococcygeus. The pudendal nerve innervates both parts of the levator ani.

The next muscle we consider is the **coccygeus (C)**. This small triangular muscle is posterior to the levator ani. It forms the pos-terior region of the pelvic diaphragm. The muscle is seen on the visual left of the diagram when the gluteus maximus is removed.

The final muscle of the anal triangle is the **external anal sphincter (I)**. This muscle closes the anal opening and originates at a tendon associated with the coccyx. The attachment can be seen in the diagram.

We continue studying the male perineum by focusing on the urogenital triangle. As before, darker colors can be used for the muscles since they are separate from one another.

A major muscle of the urogenital triangle is the **ischiocavernosus (D)**. The muscle originates at the ramus of the ischium, as the plate indicates. It inserts at the corpus cavernosum of the penis and helps maintain the erection of the penis in the male.

Also in the urogenital triangle is the **superficial transverse perineus (F)**. In the diagram, this muscle can be seen originating at the ramus of the ischium. It passes toward the medial line and inserts at the **central tendon (N)**. The muscle stabilizes the central tendon. A related muscle in that area is the **deep transverse perineus (G)**. Also originating at the ramus of the ischium, this muscle inserts at the median raphe and helps stabilize the central tendon. The central tendon of the perineum is one of the stronger tendons of the body.

Originating at the central tendon is the **bulbospongiosus (M)**. This muscle passes anteriorly into the corpus cavernosa of the penis and encloses the base of the penis. It is also found in the female as a deep muscle. The bulbospongiosus assists in penile and clitoral erection. The pudendal nerve innervates it.

Also seen in the plate is the **sacrotuberous ligament (K)**. This ligament extends from the sacrum to the ischial tuberosity and helps stabilize the sacrum. The **gluteus maximus (J)** is a large superficial muscle of the posterior pelvis. Its thick coarse fibers are the site of intramuscular injections. As the plate shows, this muscle covers the ischial tuberosity when an individual is standing. The **obturator internus (L)** is briefly seen in the diagram. It encloses the obturator foramen in the pelvic bone and helps stabilize the hip joint. The **deep transverse perineus (G)** is also visible.

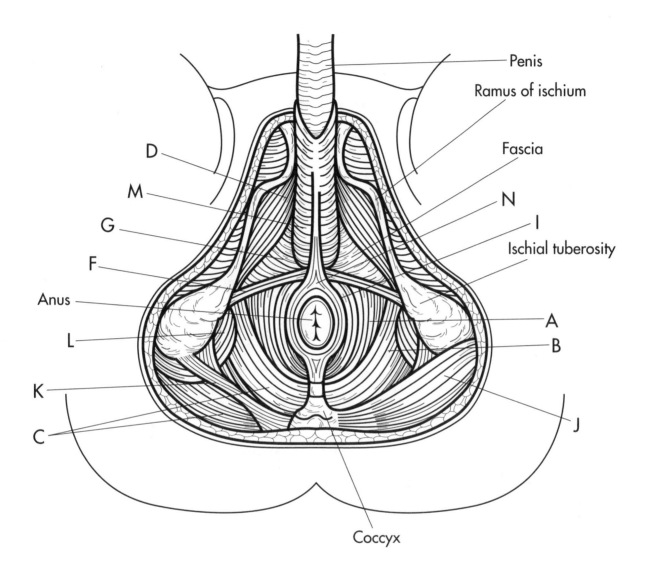

Penis

Ramus of ischium

Fascia

D

M

N

G

I

F

Ischial tuberosity

Anus

L

A

B

K

J

C

Coccyx

Pubococcygeus	A	○
Iliococcygeus	B	○
Coccygeus	C	○
Ischiocavernosus	D	○
Superficial transverse perineus	F	○
Deep transverse perineus	G	○
External anal sphincter	I	○
Gluteus maximus	J	○
Sacrotuberous ligament	K	○
Obturator internus	L	○
Bulbospongiosus	M	○
Central tendon	N	○

MUSCLES of the LATERAL THORAX

Having studied the three prime movers of the arm, we now move on to the remaining six muscles of the lateral thorax that insert on the humerus and move the arm. These muscles are smaller than the previous ones and should be colored with lighter shades of color.

Nine muscles of the body originate at the lateral thorax then cross the shoulder joint and insert on the humerus to move the arm. All these muscles originate at the pectoral girdle, and two of the muscles originate on the axial skeleton as well. These two muscles are known as axial muscles. They include the pectoralis major and the latissimus dorsi. The other seven muscles arise solely from the scapula and are referred to as scapular muscles. The scapular muscles contribute to the strength and stability of the shoulder joint. They do so by joining the scapula to the humerus.

In this plate, we shall examine the nine important muscles that originate at the lateral thorax and move the arm. Anterior and posterior views of the muscles are presented, and in the posterior view, there are both superficial and deep views.

You may begin with the plate by coloring in the main title Muscles of the Lateral Thorax. Then look over the plate and notice that the muscles are exposed in anterior and posterior views. Many of these muscles were featured on pages 74 and 75 on the shoulder muscles, and you may relate that plate to this one. Also, many muscles are designated by lowercase letters. These are not part of the nine muscles that move the arm, but they are presented here to show their relationships to one another and the nine key muscles. As you read about the muscles in the upcoming paragraphs, color their titles, then locate the muscles in both anterior and posterior views. If the muscle is a larger one, we recommend darker colors; if it is smaller, then we recommend lighter colors so you can seen the points where the muscles overlap or run parallel. The bones may be colored in using light and pale colors. Many of the bones and their processes have been labeled so you can relate them to their muscles.

Of the nine muscles to be considered, three are prime movers of the humerus (arm). The first of these three is the **pectoralis major (A)**. This is an axial muscle, originating at the cartilages of the second to sixth ribs and the body of the sternum and portion of the clavicle. These origins may be seen on the plate. The muscle then inserts at the greater tubercle of the humerus. The muscle helps flex the arm, lifting it anteriorly, in the sagittal plane.

The **latissimus dorsi (B)** acts antagonistically to the pectoralis major. It extends the arm. The latissimus dorsi originates at the thoracic and lumbar vertebrae and inserts at the lesser tubercle of the humerus. The third prime mover of the arm is the **deltoid (C)**. This large muscle forms the fleshy mass of the shoulder and is clear in the posterior view. Like the latissimus dorsi, the deltoid is a very large muscle and should be colored in a dark color. This muscle abducts the arm. It is a scapular muscle, originating at the clavicle and acromion process of the scapula and inserting in the deltoid tuberosity of the humerus.

The remaining six muscles of arm movement rotate the arm. One example is the **subscapularis (D)**. It is a rotator cuff muscle whose tendon blends with the capsule of the shoulder joint to reinforce the shoulder joint capsule. The muscle originates at the scapula and inserts at the lesser tubercle of the humerus.

Close to the subscapularis is the **supraspinatus (E)**. This deep muscle is seen in the posterior view. It is also a scapular muscle and part of the rotator cuff muscle group. Close to it is the **infraspinatus (F)**. Also seen best in the posterior view, this muscle originates at the scapula and inserts at the greater tubercle of the humerus. It permits lateral rotation of the humerus.

The **teres major (G)** is visible in the anterior view, but it is best seen in the posterior superficial view. It originates at the scapula and inserts in the intertubercular groove of the humerus. It adducts and rotates the arm. The **teres minor (H)** is visible in the posterior view.

Another adductor and flexor of the humerus is the **coracobrachialis (I)**. It has its origin at the coracoid process of the scapula and its insertion along the shaft of the humerus, as the posterior view shows.

The remaining muscles in these views are associated with the shoulder and arm, but they are not considered in the movements of the arm. We have labeled them with lowercase letters in the plate to point them out to you. Full discussions are presented elsewhere, but brief mentions are made here to indicate their relative positions. We suggest that lighter colors be used because these muscles are not to be confused with prime movers of the arm.

Note in the plate the placement and location of the **brachialis (a)**. This muscle is a flexor of the forearm. The **biceps brachii (b)** has been cut in the diagram to show the muscles below. Note here that the muscle has two heads: the short head originates at the coracoid process, while the long head originates at a tuberosity further off on the scapula.

Along the posterior surface of the humerus, the **triceps brachii (c)** can be seen. This muscle is an extensor of the forearm. Along the thoracic wall, the **serratus anterior (d)** can be seen in the anterior view. Its purpose is to hold the scapula against the wall of the chest and to rotate it.

The **levator scapula (e)** is seen in the posterior view. This straplike muscle elevates and stabilizes the scapula. The **subclavius (f)** does likewise as it extends from a rib to the clavicle. The **pectoralis minor (g)** inserts on the scapula and draws the scapula forward. You can see how this action is performed by noting the position of the muscle in the anterior view.

The two muscles acting together to retract the scapula and "square" the shoulders are the **rhomboideus minor (h)** and the **rhomboideus major (i)**. Also visible in the plate are the **external intercostals (j)** and beneath them, the **internal intercostals (k)**. As noted in other plates, these muscles are responsible for raising and lowering the thoracic cage during inspiration and expiration.

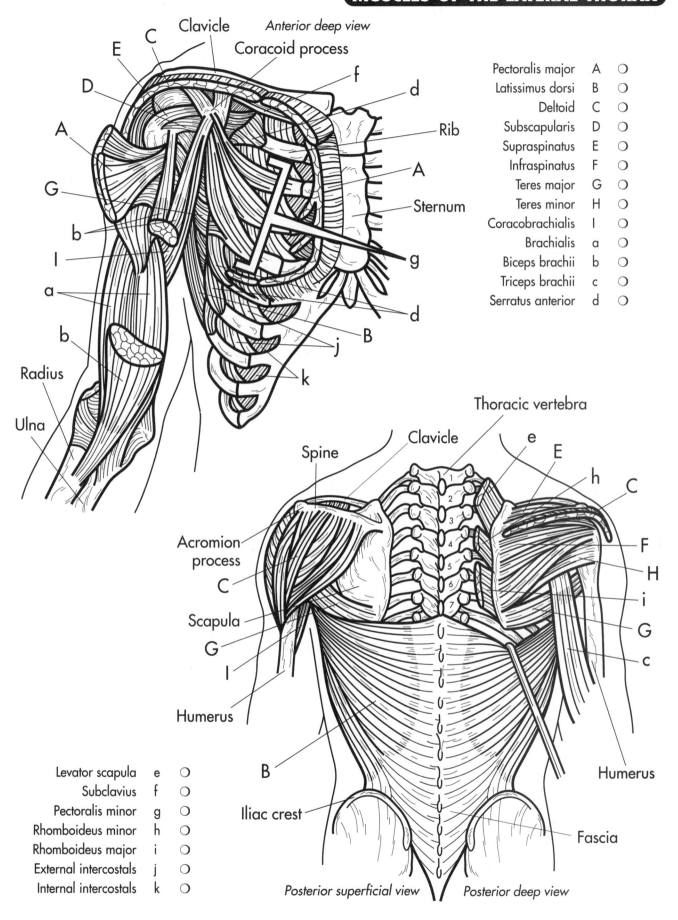

Anterior deep view

Clavicle
Coracoid process
E
C
D
f
d
Rib
A
A
G
Sternum
b
I
g
a
d
b
B
Radius
j
Ulna
k

Pectoralis major   A   ○
Latissimus dorsi   B   ○
Deltoid   C   ○
Subscapularis   D   ○
Supraspinatus   E   ○
Infraspinatus   F   ○
Teres major   G   ○
Teres minor   H   ○
Coracobrachialis   I   ○
Brachialis   a   ○
Biceps brachii   b   ○
Triceps brachii   c   ○
Serratus anterior   d   ○

Thoracic vertebra
Spine
Clavicle
e
E
h
C
Acromion process
F
C
H
i
Scapula
G
G
c
I
Humerus
Humerus
B
Iliac crest
Fascia

Levator scapula   e   ○
Subclavius   f   ○
Pectoralis minor   g   ○
Rhomboideus minor   h   ○
Rhomboideus major   i   ○
External intercostals   j   ○
Internal intercostals   k   ○

Posterior superficial view   Posterior deep view

MUSCLES of the UPPER ARM

Several muscles of the upper arm (the "arm") cross the elbow joint to insert on the radius and the ulna (the "forearm"). The actions brought about by these muscles are flexion and extension, since the elbow joint is a hinge joint. For this reason, the muscles of the upper arm are divided into flexors and extensors. In this plate, we shall examine three flexors and two extensors. Muscles that allow pronation and supination of the radius and ulna are considered with muscles that move the forearm.

A small number of muscles are examined in this plate, because antagonistic muscles provide most flexion and extension of the forearm. Begin the plate by coloring the main title Muscles of the Upper Arm. Then note that views are presented of the anterior right arm and the posterior right arm. The muscles are closely associated with the humerus because they originate here before inserting on the forearm bones. Dark colors such as reds, greens, and blues are suggested so that the muscles may be clearly distinguished from one another. The same color should be used in the views of the arm and the forearm. Also note that a transverse section has been made through the arm so that you can see the muscles associated with the humerus. These are the flexors and extensors of the forearm. When you read about the muscle, color its title, then color the muscle in all views shown in this plate.

The first flexor that we shall consider is the **biceps brachii (A)**. As the name biceps implies, this muscle has two heads. Both heads are clearly seen in the anterior view of the arm. One head, the **long head (A_1)**, originates at the tubercle superior to the glenoid cavity. The **short head (A_2)** originates at the coracoid process of the scapula. The biceps brachii inserts by a large tendon into the radial tuberosity, as the anterior view shows. The muscle's action is to flex the elbow joint and to supinate the forearm. The two heads of the muscle are shown in the transverse section and should be colored.

The second important flexor is the **brachialis (B)**. The brachialis lies deep to the biceps brachii, as the transverse section indicates. Portions of it can be seen in both the anterior view of the arm and anterior view of the forearm. The brachialis is a prime mover of the forearm and encourages flexion. It originates at the humerus and inserts at the coronoid process of the ulna. The musculocutaneous nerve innervates it.

The third flexor that we examine is the **brachioradialis (C)**. This muscle is best seen in the anterior view of the forearm. The muscle originates at the distal portion of the humerus and runs along the lateral forearm to insert at the styloid process of the radius. The long tendon leading to this insertion can be seen in the anterior view of the forearm. The brachioradialis flexes the forearm weakly and is used primarily when the elbow joint is already flexed by one of its prime movers. In the transverse section of the arm, the brachioradialis is not present, because the muscle is found primarily in the forearm.

Having studied the flexors of the forearm, we now move to the extensors. These muscles are located primarily in the posterior aspect of the arm and partly in the forearm. They include one very large and bulky muscle and one much smaller muscle. Dark colors are suggested for these muscles to set them off from the other muscles in the area.

When an individual does pushups, the extension of the forearm is brought about by the **triceps brachii (D)**. This very large muscle has three heads (as the word triceps implies). We suggest you use three different variations of a color to color the three heads of the triceps brachii. As seen in the posterior view, the **long head (D_1)** originates near the glenoid cavity and inserts at the olecranon process of the ulna. The second head is the **lateral head (D_2)**. This head is shown originating from the surface of the humerus and inserting at the olecranon process. The **medial head (D_3)** is in the medial aspect. It originates at the surface of the humerus and inserts at the olecranon process. A common tendon brings together all three heads. The three heads are seen prominently in the transverse section of the arm. The bracket enclosing all three should be colored in a dark color on the plate.

The second important flexor operating at the elbow joint is the **anconeus (E)**. This small muscle is seen at the elbow in the posterior view. It is a short muscle close to the distal end of the triceps. Its origin is at the lateral epicondyle of the humerus and its insertion is at the olecranon process of the ulna. The anconeus works with the triceps brachii, and like the triceps brachii, it is innervated by the radial nerve. It is not present in the transverse section of the arm, because it occurs further down, closer to the forearm.

Two other muscles are seen in this plate. The first is the **deltoid (a)**. This is the large, fleshy muscle of the shoulder that has been cut to reveal the underlying muscles operating in movement of the forearm. The second muscle is the **teres major (b)**. This muscle adducts the humerus. As the posterior view shows, it has its origin at the scapula and its insertion at the humerus.

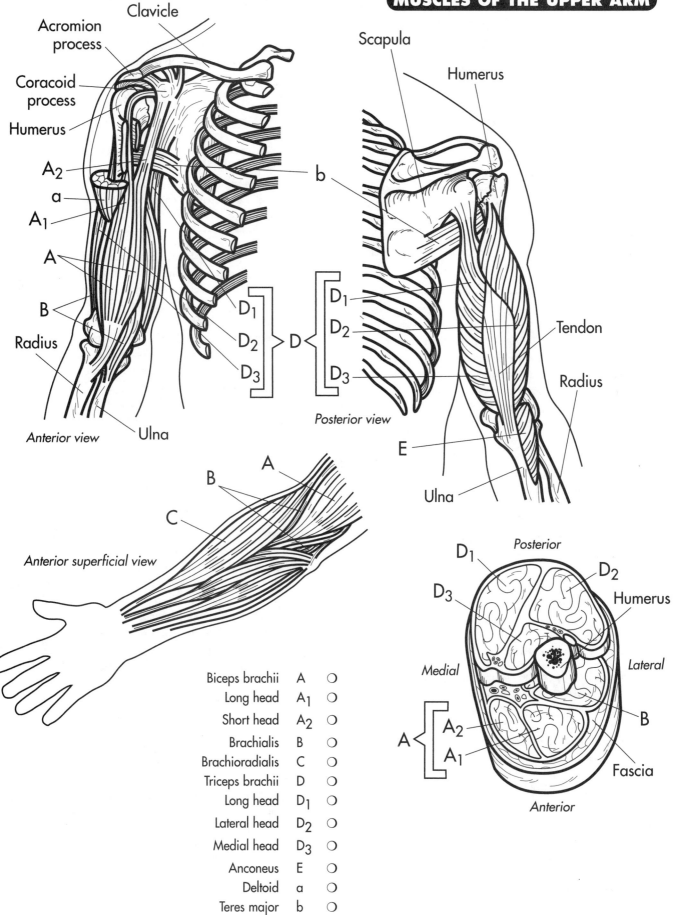

Acromion process
Clavicle
Coracoid process
Humerus
A₂
a
A₁
A
B
Radius
Ulna
Anterior view
D₁
D₂
D₃
D

Scapula
Humerus
b
D₁
D₂
D₃
Tendon
Radius
E
Ulna
Posterior view

A
B
C
Anterior superficial view

Posterior
D₁
D₂
D₃
Humerus
Medial
Lateral
A
A₂
A₁
B
Fascia
Anterior

Biceps brachii   A   ○
Long head   A₁   ○
Short head   A₂   ○
Brachialis   B   ○
Brachioradialis   C   ○
Triceps brachii   D   ○
Long head   D₁   ○
Lateral head   D₂   ○
Medial head   D₃   ○
Anconeus   E   ○
Deltoid   a   ○
Teres major   b   ○

MUSCLES of the LOWER ARM

Muscles of the lower arm (the "forearm") are responsible for moving the wrist and hand. The muscles are divided into two major groups, the anterior flexor muscles and the posterior extensor muscles. Most of these muscles have their origins on the humerus and their insertions at the wrist and hand. The flexors insert at the carpals, metacarpals, and phalanges, while the extensors have their insertions at the metacarpals and phalanges. The anterior and posterior muscles are further subdivided into superficial and deep muscles. This will be the pattern in this plate. In addition to the flexors and extensors, there are muscles acting as pronators and supinators, both of which are in this plate.

Start your work on the plate by coloring the main title Muscles of the Lower Arm. Then, as you look over the plate, make note of the four views of the right hand given in the plate. Two views are of the anterior surface, the superficial and deep views, while two views are of the posterior surface, the superficial and deep views. Notice that there are many tendons in the hand. The tendons have been labeled for your information. Although the hand performs many movements, it has relatively few muscles. Instead most hand muscles are located in the forearm, and their operation occurs by means of long tendons. Also notice how tendons in the wrist area are surrounded by sheaths. In the anterior view, the fibrous sheath of tissue is called the flexor retinaculum, while in the posterior view, the fibrous band of tissue is called the extensor retinaculum. It is a good idea to color the tendons in a light gray so as to avoid obscuring the muscles below. When you encounter the muscles in your reading, color their titles, then color them in any of the four views in which they appear. Darker colors are suggested for the large muscles, and lighter colors for the small muscles. If you wish to color the bones, then do so with a pale shade.

In the anterior compartment of forearm muscles, one of the superficial flexors is the **flexor carpi radialis (A)**. The muscle originates at the humerus and inserts by a tendon in the metacarpals. Its action is to flex the wrist and adduct the palm of the hand. Adjacent to this muscle is the **palmaris longis (B)**. Also seen in the anterior superficial view, this muscle inserts at an aponeurosis in the center of the palm and flexes the wrist.

A third superficial muscle is the **flexor carpi ulnaris (C)**. Originating at the humerus and ulna and inserting in several metacarpals, this muscle flexes and adducts the wrist. The fourth superficial muscle is the **flexor digitorum superficialis (D)**. It originates at the humerus, ulna, and radius and inserts into the middle phalanges of the fingers. The muscle flexes the wrist and the middle phalanges.

There are two deep muscles of the forearm that attach to the wrist and hand region. The first is the **flexor digitorum profundus (E)**. This muscle is seen in the anterior deep view in the plate. It originates at the

interosseous membrane and inserts by long tendons into the distal phalanges. The second deep muscle is the **flexor pollicis longus (F)**. This is another flexor of the fingers. It can be seen in the plate as its tendon passes underneath the flexor retinaculum then moves to the left to finally come to rest in the distal thumb phalanx.

The second major set of muscles are the extensors of the posterior compartment. As before, they are subdivided as superficial and deep muscles. As you encounter the muscles in your reading, color their titles, then color the muscles in the plate. As before, watch for long tendons associated with the muscles. These tendons attach to the bones, and when the muscles contract, the tendons pull on the bones to perform the action of extension.

Among the superficial muscles of the posterior region is the **extensor carpi radialis longus (G)**. This muscle has its origin at the humerus and its insertion at the second metacarpal. It extends and adducts the wrist. Also in this area is the **extensor carpi radialis brevis (H)**. This muscle inserts at the third metacarpal.

The **extensor digitorum (I)** has a long tendon connecting the muscle to the distal and middle phalanges, as the plate indicates. Originating at the humerus, this muscle passes across the forearm and extends the phalanges. A smaller extensor muscle also connected to a phalanx is the **extensor digiti minimi (J)**. The final superficial muscle is the **extensor carpi ulnaris (K)**. The muscle extends and adducts the wrist.

There are several deep muscles of the posterior compartment. The first is the **abductor pollicis longus (L)**. The muscle extends the thumb and adducts the wrist. A second deep muscle is the **extensor pollicis brevis (M)**. Arising from the surface of the radius and inserting at the base of the proximal phalanx of the thumb, this muscle extends the thumb. Its tendon can be seen in the plate. Another thumb extender is the **extensor pollicis longus (N)**. The tendon of this muscle inserts at the distal phalanx of the thumb. The final muscle in this group, the **extensor indicis (O)**, inserts at the index finger to extends it.

A prominent muscle of the forearm area is the **brachioradialis (P)**. This muscle forms a large portion of the fleshy area of the forearm. Its primary function is to flex the forearm.

The **supinator (Q)** is seen in the anterior deep view. It originates at the lateral epicondyle of the humerus and inserts at the proximal end of the radius to supinate the forearm. Two pronator muscles are significant. The first is the **pronator quadratus (R)**. This deep muscle originates at the ulna and inserts at the surface of the radius. It pronates the forearm and acts antagonistically to the supinator. The second pronator of the forearm is the **pronator teres (S)**. The muscle originates at the medial epicondyle of the humerus and coronoid process of the ulna. It inserts into the shaft of the radius. It is also antagonistic to the supinator.

Several other muscles may be seen close to the forearm. They are designated by lowercase letters, and they include the **biceps brachii (a)**, the **brachialis (b)**, the **triceps brachii (c)**, and the **anconeus (d)**. These muscles are considered in detail in the previous plate. They are presented here so you can see their relationships to muscles of the forearm, wrist, and hand.

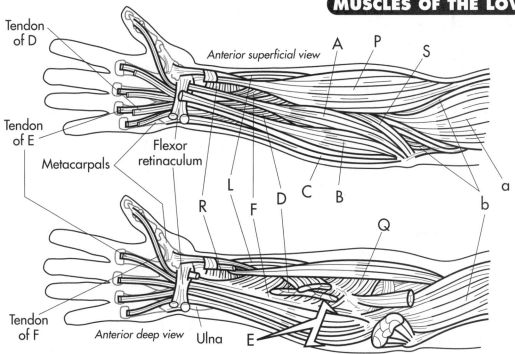

Tendon of D

Anterior superficial view

A   P   S

Tendon of E

Metacarpals

Flexor retinaculum

L   R   F   D   C   B   a   b

Tendon of F

Q

Anterior deep view   Ulna   E

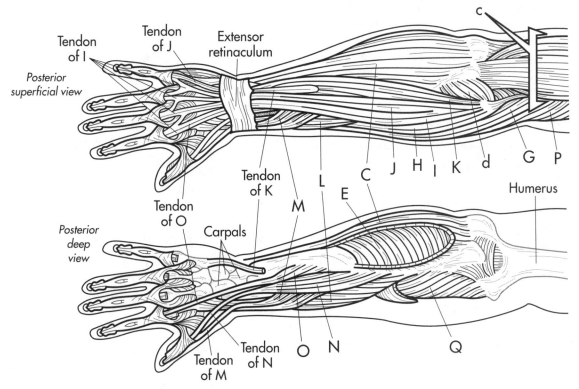

Tendon of I

Tendon of J

Extensor retinaculum

Posterior superficial view

c

J   H   I   K   d   G   P

Tendon of K

Tendon of O

Carpals

M   L   C   E

Posterior deep view

Humerus

O   N   Q

Tendon of N

Tendon of M

Flexor carpi radialis	A ○	Extensor digitorum	I ○	Supinator	Q ○
Palmaris longis	B ○	Extensor digiti minimi	J ○	Pronator quadratus	R ○
Flexor carpi ulnaris	C ○	Extensor carpi ulnaris	K ○	Pronator teres	S ○
Flexor digitorum superficialis	D ○	Abductor pollicis longus	L ○	Biceps brachii	a ○
Flexor digitorum profundus	E ○	Extensor pollicis brevis	M ○	Brachialis	b ○
Flexor pollicis longus	F ○	Extensor pollicis longus	N ○	Triceps brachii	c ○
Extensor carpi radialis longus	G ○	Extensor indicis	O ○	Anconeus	d ○
Extensor carpi radialis brevis	H ○	Brachioradialis	P ○		

MUSCLES of the THIGH (ANTERIOR)

The muscles of the thigh and lower leg are very powerful. They contribute to locomotion, stability, and posture maintenance. The muscles are generally difficult to differentiate based on their action, and classification is difficult. In this plate, we examine muscles on the anterior surface of the right thigh. The posterior views are presented on the following plate. We also show three frontal views at various levels of the anterior thigh, as well as a transverse section through the thigh muscles.

Begin your work on this plate by coloring the main title Muscles of the Thigh (Anterior). Four views of the right thigh are presented in the plate: two superficial views from the anterior aspect, one deep view, and one transverse section through the thigh muscles. When you color the plate, you should locate the muscles in all four diagrams and color them using the same colors. If you spot a large muscle (for example, D and E), use a darker color, but if the muscle is small in the diagram, a lighter color is best. Darker colors can be preserved for the last three muscles (O, P, and Q), because they are only seen in the transverse section. As you read about the muscles, color their titles and color them in the diagram.

One of the long thick muscles of the anterior surface is the **psoas major (A)**. Seen in the anterior view, this muscle originates at the lumbar vertebrae and inserts at the lesser trochanter of the femur. It flexes and rotates the thigh. The **iliacus (B)** runs alongside and is seen in both superficial views. This muscle also flexes the thigh. The combination of psoas major and iliacus is referred to together as the iliopsoas.

Along the lateral aspect of the thigh, we see the **tensor fasciae latae (C)**. A dark color may be used for this muscle since it is clear. The muscle originates at the iliac crest, inserts at the tibia, and brings about flexion and abduction of the thigh. The straplike muscle running superficially along the surface of the thigh is the **sartorius (D)**. The sartorius is the body's longest muscle, crossing both the hip joint and knee joint. It originates at the iliac spine and inserts at the medial portion of the tibia. The muscle comes into action when we cross the legs as a tailor might ("sartorius" means tailor's muscle).

We have examined some of the prime movers of the thigh and some of the most important flexors. We continue in the next section with additional muscles of the anterior aspect, and we encounter some of the important extensors. Continue your coloring as before and notice that the next few muscles form part of the fleshy anterior aspect of the thigh and area above the knee. As you encounter the muscles color their titles, then color the muscles.

The anterior compartment of the thigh contains four muscles considered together as the quadriceps femoris. The four muscles come together at the quadriceps tendon, which inserts into the patella and continues as the patellar ligament, which inserts into the tibial tuberosity. These structures have been labeled for you on the plate.

The first quadriceps muscle is the **rectus femoris (E)**. This large muscle runs in the midline of the thigh after it originates at the iliac spine. It extends the knee joint and flexes the thigh at the hip. The femoral nerve innervates it and the other quadriceps muscles. The second muscle of the group is the **vastus lateralis (F)**. Seen clearly in the anterior superficial view, this muscle originates at the greater trochanter of the femur and extends the knee. It and the rectus femoris are very large and obvious in the transverse section. The third muscle is the **vastus medialis (G)**. This muscle is an extensor of the knee joint. The final muscle is the **vastus intermedius (H)**. Also seen in the transverse section and superficial view, this muscle is an extensor of the knee originating at the shaft of the femur.

We now proceed to muscles that bring about adduction. These muscles are found in the medial aspect of the thigh and are deep muscles. You should, therefore, concentrate on this area of the plate and on the transverse section, in which they are also seen. Darker colors may be used where the muscles are large and separated from the others.

The adductor group of muscles consists of five muscles, all innervated by the obturator nerve. The first of these muscles is the **adductor magnus (I)**. The large size of this muscle is seen in the transverse section. Arising at the pelvic bone, the muscle inserts in the femur and adducts the thigh. The **adductor longus (J)** is a smaller muscle toward the medial aspect, while the **adductor brevis (K)** is a short muscle that also adducts the thigh.

A slender muscle adducting the thigh and also flexing the leg is the **gracilis (L)**. This muscle runs along the medial aspect of the thigh, as the transverse section and deep view illustrate. The **pectineus (M)** is a flat muscle seen in the first superficial view and cut in the deeper view. The muscle originates at the tubercle of the pubis and inserts at the femur.

Examination of the plate ends with a brief mention of some of the posterior muscles and other small muscles of the thigh and leg. The posterior muscles may be colored using a dark color, since they will be seen only in the transverse section. A light color should be used for the first muscle we encounter, because it is a small one.

One of the important rotators of the thigh is the **obturator externus (N)**. Seen in the anterior deep view, this muscle originates at the obturator membrane and inserts at the greater trochanter of the femur. The transverse section shows the position of some of the posterior muscles of the leg. These muscles extend the thigh, and they flex the lower leg. The muscles include the **biceps femoris (O)**, the **semitendinosus (P)**, and the **semimembranosus (Q)**. They are considered in the following plate.

At the upper edge of the leg close to the pelvic bone are three muscles. The **gluteus medius (a)** lies at the medial aspect of the leg. It abducts the thigh and rotates it. The **quadratus lumborum (b)** can be seen in the superficial view originating at the ilium and inserting at the last rib. This muscle holds the rib in place during deep inspiration. The **psoas minor (c)** is another flexor of the thigh.

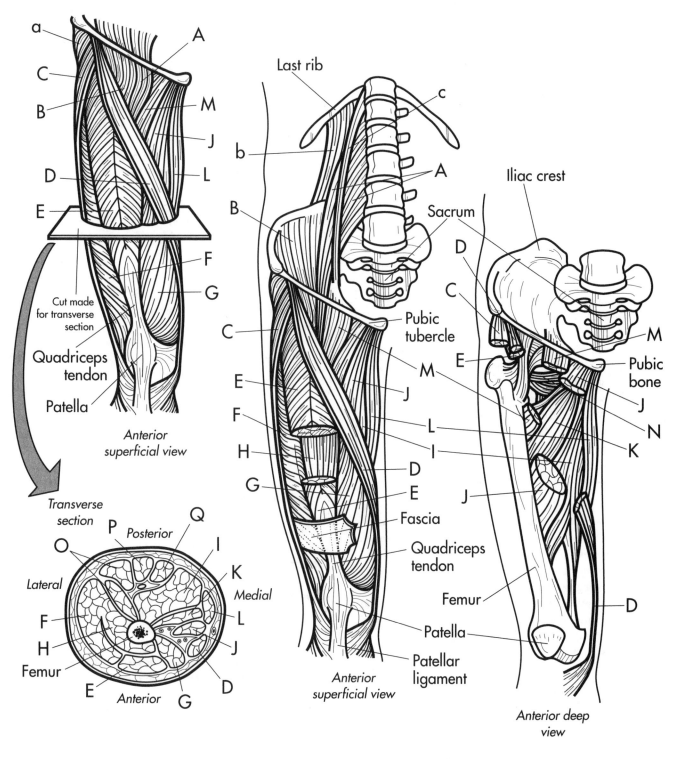

Last rib

Iliac crest

Sacrum

Pubic tubercle

Pubic bone

Fascia

Quadriceps tendon

Femur

Patella

Patellar ligament

Quadriceps tendon

Patella

Cut made for transverse section

Anterior superficial view

Transverse section

Posterior

Lateral

Medial

Anterior

Femur

Anterior superficial view

Anterior deep view

Psoas major	A	○	Vastus intermedius	H	○	Biceps femoris	O	○
Iliacus	B	○	Adductor magnus	I	○	Semitendinosus	P	○
Tensor fasciae latae	C	○	Adductor longus	J	○	Semimembranosus	Q	○
Sartorius	D	○	Adductor brevis	K	○	Gluteus medius	a	○
Rectus femoris	E	○	Gracilis	L	○	Quadratus lumborum	b	○
Vastus lateralis	F	○	Pectineus	M	○	Psoas minor	c	○
Vastus medialis	G	○	Obturator externus	N	○			

MUSCLES of the THIGH (POSTERIOR)

A number of important muscles originate at the surface of the pelvis and insert on the femur to bring about movement of the thigh. Other muscles originate either at the pelvis or femur and insert at the lower leg to bring about movements of this area of the body. In general terms, the muscles located along the posterior surface of the thigh are flexors. They are the main subject of this plate. The muscles involved in foot movements are explored in the next plate.

> Look over the plate and note the three views of the right thigh. The first view is the most superficial view. Then comes another superficial view (but of a deeper area), and finally a deep view. Now color the main title Muscles of the Thigh (Posterior). When you color the muscles you should choose darker colors for the superficial muscles because they are large, and lighter colors for the deep muscles because they are smaller and many overlay one another. As you read about the muscle, locate it and color it in all three views wherever possible. Of course, a muscle may be a superficial one and not appear in the deep view, or vice versa.

The flexors of the leg include the three muscles of the hamstring group. They are fleshy muscles along the posterior surface and are clearly seen in the most superficial view. The first hamstring muscle is the **semitendinosus (A)**. This muscle flexes the knee and can also extend the thigh at the hip. The sciatic nerve innervates it and the other two hamstring muscles.

The second member of this group is the **semimembranosus (B)**. It lies deep to the semitendinosus. It also flexes the leg at the knee joint and extends the thigh at the hip joint. The third hamstring is the **biceps femoris (G)**. This is a very large muscle observed in the posterior superficial views. As the name (biceps) implies, it has two heads. Its long head originates at the ischial tuberosity, its short head at the femur. The muscle joins a large tendon passing downward and inserting into the fibula and tibia. The muscle is a prime mover of thigh extension and an important flexor of the knee joint.

> The next group of muscles are distributed among several diagrams. Some are considered in the previous plate, as well. As you encounter the muscle, locate it in the three diagrams if possible and color it there.

The **sartorius (C)** is best seen on the anterior aspect, but a portion is visible from the posterior view in this plate. The straplike sartorius runs obliquely across the anterior surface of the thigh towards the knee. A small portion of the **gracilis (D)** is also seen. This is a long, thin muscle in the most superficial view. It forms part of the medial surface of the thigh. It adducts the thigh and flexes the leg, particularly during the act of walking.

The gluteal muscles cover the lateral surface of the ilium. One of these, the **gluteus maximus (E)** is the largest and most posterior of the muscles. As the superficial view shows, it originates at the iliac crest, then extends laterally as a massive muscle across the fleshy portion of the buttock and thigh. The muscle inserts on the femur and is a major extensor of the thigh. It is an antagonist of the iliopsoas muscle.

At the deeper level is the **adductor magnus (F)**. This muscle is triangular, as the deep view illustrates. Its origin at the ischium can be seen and its insertion along the shaft of the femur is clear in the deep view. The **vastus lateralis (H)** forms a portion of the lateral aspect of the thigh as the superficial view indicates. This muscle extends the knee. It is one of the quadriceps femoris muscles discussed in the previous plate.

> Continue with an exploration of some of the smaller muscles of the thigh and leg. These muscles help stabilize the hip joint and contribute to lateral and other movements of the thigh and leg. Most will be seen in the deeper views of the thigh, so you should concentrate in this area. Lighter colors such as pale blues, greens, and reds are recommended.

The posterior superficial view and the deep view show the **obturator internus (I)**. This muscle rotates the thigh laterally and helps keep the hip joint in place while the thigh and leg are moving. It inserts at the femur. The **quadratus femoris (J)** is a short muscle originating at the ischial tuberosity and inserting on the femur. Its function is to assist lateral motion and stabilize the hip joint.

There are two gemellus muscles. The **superior gemellus (K)** is a small muscle that contributes to hip joint stability. Below it is the **inferior gemellus (L)**, which has the same function. Both muscles originate at the ischial tuberosity and insert at the femur. The **obturator externus (M)** is close to the obturator internus. The obturator externus is a flat triangular muscle surrounding the hip joint and giving it stability.

In the same region is the gluteus minimus. This is the smallest and deepest of the gluteus muscles. It is seen in the deep view originating on the external surface of the ilium and inserting on the greater trochanter of the femur. The gluteus minimus helps abduct the thigh, especially during walking. The **gluteus medius (O)** has been cut in the deep view to show the muscle underneath it. This muscle originates at the iliac crest and inserts at the greater trochanter of the femur. Its action is similar to that of the gluteus minimus, that is, it abducts the thigh and rotates it toward the medial direction.

Two other muscles seen briefly in this plate are the **gastrocnemius (a)** and the **plantaris (b)**. We use lowercase letters to indicate they are not thigh muscles. The muscles have their origins at the femur and their insertions at the Achilles (calcaneal) tendon. Their position permits them to move the foot. These muscles are considered more extensively in the next plate.

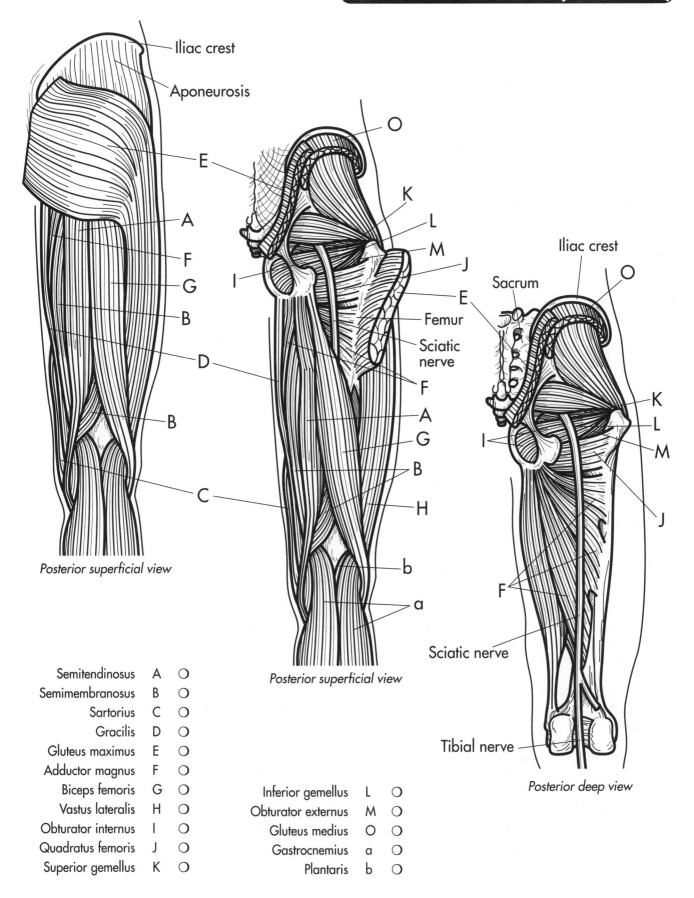

Iliac crest

Aponeurosis

E

A

F

G

B

D

B

C

Posterior superficial view

O

K

L

M

J

I

E

Femur

Sciatic nerve

F

A

G

B

H

b

a

Posterior superficial view

Iliac crest

O

Sacrum

K

L

M

I

J

F

Sciatic nerve

Tibial nerve

Posterior deep view

Semitendinosus	A	○
Semimembranosus	B	○
Sartorius	C	○
Gracilis	D	○
Gluteus maximus	E	○
Adductor magnus	F	○
Biceps femoris	G	○
Vastus lateralis	H	○
Obturator internus	I	○
Quadratus femoris	J	○
Superior gemellus	K	○

Inferior gemellus	L	○
Obturator externus	M	○
Gluteus medius	O	○
Gastrocnemius	a	○
Plantaris	b	○

MUSCLES of the LOWER LEG (ANTERIOR and LATERAL)

Muscles of the lower leg are primarily involved in movement of the ankle and toes. These muscles are separated into three compartments: the anterior compartment, the lateral compartment, and the posterior compartment. Muscles of the anterior and lateral compartments are concerned with movement of the toes, while muscles of the posterior compartment move the ankle. This plate examines the anterior and lateral muscles, while the next plate explores the posterior muscles. The muscles of the anterior and lateral compartments are extensors and flexors of the toes. As in the hand, tendons are important aspects of the anatomy, because these extensive protein fibers connect the muscles to the toes.

Start your work on this plate by coloring the main title Muscles of the Lower Leg (Anterior and Lateral). Then look over the plate and note that it contains two views. A superficial view of the anterior aspect of the right leg and a lateral superficial view of the same leg are given. The muscles we study are rather large, and as you encounter them in the reading, you may color their titles and locations in the plate. Darker colors such as reds, purples, and blues may be used in this plate. Grays and pale shades should be used to color in the tendons. Work with both views as you encounter the muscles in the reading.

In the anterior compartment of the leg, there are four important extensors of the toes. The first is the **tibialis anterior (A)**. This prominent muscle originates at the upper region of the tibia and inserts by a considerable tendon at the medial cuneiform and first metatarsal. When innervated by the peroneal nerve, it permits dorsiflexion of the foot and helps maintain the arch of the foot.

The next muscle is the **extensor hallucis longus (B)**. This muscle is difficult to see in the plate. It inserts at the distal phalanx of the great toe and extends the great toe. It also dorsiflexes the foot. The peroneal nerve innervates it and many of the following muscles. The **extensor digitorum longus (C)** also extends the great toe and encourages dorsiflexion. It can be seen on the anterior and lateral surface of the leg. This muscle is an important extensor of the toes. The fourth extensor of the anterior compartment is the **peroneus tertius (D)**. It is a small muscle originating at the fibula and inserting at the fifth metatarsal to bring about dorsiflexion and eversion of the foot.

Having examined the anterior compartment, we now move to the lateral compartment and note the position and action of two muscles in the lateral aspect. These muscles may also be seen in the anterior aspect, and you should locate them in both views. Continue your coloring as before, and consider using darker colors for these muscles.

The lateral compartment contains the **peroneus longus (E)**. This prominent muscle of the lateral part of the leg everts and flexes the foot, while supporting the longitudinal arch. It originates at the tibia and head of the fibula and inserts at the base of the first metatarsal by a long tendon. The muscle overlies the fibula.

The second lateral muscle is the **peroneus brevis (F)**. This smaller muscle is deep to the peroneus longus. Its action is similar. The peroneal nerve innervates both muscles.

At this point, you should note in the diagram how the long tendons from the muscles discussed extend down through the ankle area and are held in place by two wrappings. The superior band of tendons is the superior extensor retinaculum. The inferior band of tendon is the inferior extensor retinaculum. These bands of tissue secure the muscle tendons in place as they cross the ankle and prevent the tendons from bulging out. They have been labeled in the diagram and may be colored in a light color if you wish.

In views of the anterior and lateral aspects of the lower leg, some of the posterior muscles may be observed. They are mentioned here briefly and are considered in more detail in the next plate.

The lateral view of the lower leg displays the **gastrocnemius (G)**. This muscle adducts the foot and flexes the leg. It is innervated by the tibial nerve and is attached to the calcaneus (tarsal) by the Achilles tendon, more correctly called the **calcaneal tendon (G$_1$)**. The **soleus (H)** muscle can also be seen in the anterior and lateral view. This is a calf muscle whose action is similar to that of the gastrocnemius. It also inserts at the calcaneus by the calcaneal nerve.

At the superior end of the lower leg, the **plantaris (I)** may be seen. It is a small muscle that assists in flexion of the knee and plantar flexion of the foot. A long tendon connects it to the calcaneus.

Two deep muscles are the **flexor digitorum longus (J)** and the **extensor digitorum brevis (K)**. The first is a long narrow muscle that helps invert the foot and flex the toes. Its tendon inserts at several distal phalanges. The extensor digitorum brevis originates at the calcaneus and inserts at the dorsal surfaces of several toes to bring about extension of the proximal phalanges.

At the upper edge of the diagram, three structures from the thigh may be seen. We label them in lowercase letters because they are not muscles of the lower leg. The **quadriceps femoris (a)** is a group of four muscles we discussed in the previous plate. It is just above the patella. The four muscles have a **tendon (a$_1$)** that inserts into the patella and becomes the patellar ligament to insert into the tuberosity of the tibia. The muscle is an extensor of the knee joint.

The diagram also shows the **fascia latae (b)**. This is the deep fascia of the thigh; it is not a muscle. It supports many of the muscles of the knee joint. A portion of the **biceps femoris (c)** may also be seen, especially in the lateral aspect. The tendon of this muscle passes downward to insert into the fibula and tibia.

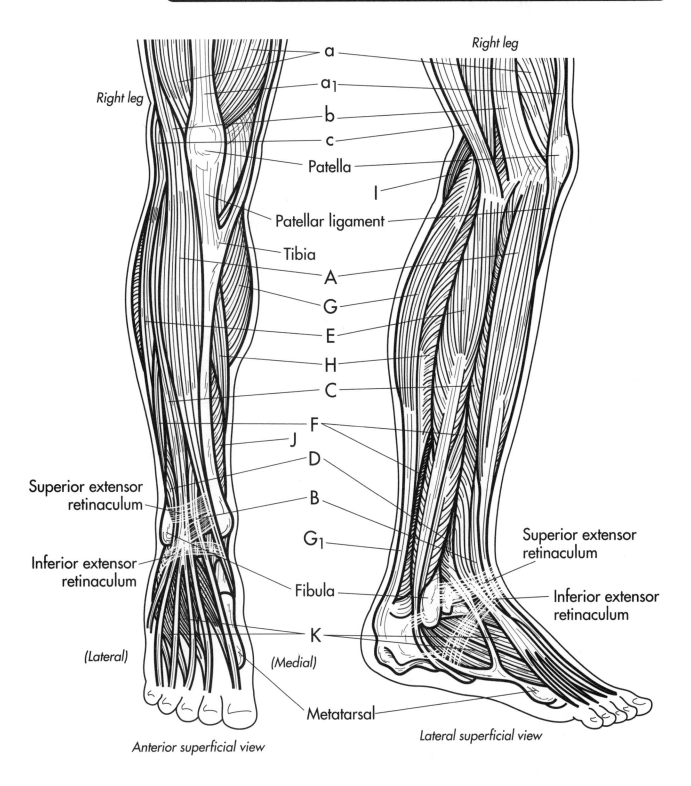

Right leg

Right leg

a

a₁

b

c

Patella

I

Patellar ligament

Tibia

A

G

E

H

C

F

J

D

B

G₁

Fibula

K

Metatarsal

Superior extensor retinaculum

Inferior extensor retinaculum

(Lateral)

(Medial)

Anterior superficial view

Superior extensor retinaculum

Inferior extensor retinaculum

Lateral superficial view

Tibialis anterior	A	○	Gastrocnemius	G	○	Quadriceps femoris	a	○
Extensor hallucis longus	B	○	Calcaneal tendon	G₁	○	Tendon	a₁	○
Extensor digitorum longus	C	○	Soleus	H	○	Fascia latae	b	○
Peroneus tertius	D	○	Plantaris	I	○	Biceps femoris	c	○
Peroneus longus	E	○	Flexor digitorum longus	J	○			
Peroneus brevis	F	○	Extensor digitorum brevis	K	○			

MUSCLES of the LOWER LEG (POSTERIOR)

The muscles of the lower leg are divided into anterior, lateral, and posterior compartments. The muscles of the anterior and lateral compartments are discussed in the previous plate and are prime movers of the toes. This plate explores the muscles of the posterior compartment of the lower leg. The muscles in this group are plantar flexors of the ankle.

There are a number of superficial and deep muscles in the posterior portion of the lower leg. The two diagrams in this plate show the two views. Some of the muscles are observed in the lateral aspect of the leg, and you might wish to refer to the previous plate to locate them. All the muscles of the posterior region are innervated by a branch of the sciatic nerve called the tibial nerve.

As you look over the plate, color in the main title Muscles of the Lower Leg (Posterior). Then note that we are presenting superficial and deep views of the right leg. The medial and lateral aspects have been noted for your orientation. Muscles of the superficial view are rather large, and dark colors may be used.

We consider now three superficial muscles of the posterior lower leg. The first is the **gastrocnemius (A)**. As the diagram clearly shows, this muscle has two bellies that form the calf muscle. The muscle originates by two heads at the lateral and medial condyles of the femur and inserts by a major tendon into the calcaneus (a tarsal). The tendon is the **calcaneal tendon (A₁)**, also called the Achilles tendon. It is the strongest tendon of the body.

The second superficial muscle is the **soleus (B)**. The muscle lies deep to the gastrocnemius. It originates at the tibia and fibula and also inserts into the calcaneus by the calcaneal tendon. Like the gastrocnemius, the soleus brings about plantar flexion at the ankle. The third superficial muscle we consider is the **plantaris (C)**. This small muscle is seen in both the superficial and deep views. It originates at the femur and inserts into the calcaneus with the two previous muscles. The plantaris assists flexion of the knee and provides plantar flexion of the ankle.

The remainder of this plate reviews the deep muscles of the lower leg in the posterior view. Like the previous muscles, these muscles are innervated by the tibial nerve. As you encounter the muscles, color their titles, then color the muscles, using darker colors if the muscle is prominent and lighter colors if the muscle is obscure. Locate the muscles in both the superficial and deep view as you proceed. Note that the superficial muscles have been cut to allow a deep view.

One of the deep muscles of the posterior compartment of the lower leg is the **popliteus (D)**. Found at the back of the knee, the popliteus is a thin triangular muscle that inserts at the tibia. It helps flex and rotate the lower leg.

A prominent muscle extending downward is the **flexor hallucis longus (E)**. This muscle originates at the shaft of the fibula, and its tendon runs through the foot to the distal phalanx of the great toe. The muscle provides plantar flexion and inversion of the foot and is a key element in use of the great toe while walking.

The **flexor digitorum longus (F)** is a long muscle originating at the tibia and inserting into the distal phalanges of the second through fifth toes. It brings about flexion of the toes and plantar flexion and inversion of the ankle. This muscle helps the toes make contact with the ground while walking. Beneath the soleus is the **tibialis posterior (G)**. This thick muscle originates at the tibia and fibula and inserts at several tarsals and metatarsals. It is one of the main muscles of inversion of the foot. It also stabilizes the arch of the foot.

Two peroneus muscles also contribute to actions of the ankle and foot. The **peroneus longus (H)** is a lateral muscle near the fibula. It inserts at a tarsal and metatarsal to help evert and plantar flex the foot. This action helps the foot remain in contact flat on the ground. The **peroneus brevis (I)** is close to the previous muscle. It is a short muscle originating at the shaft of the fibula and inserting at a metatarsal. The peroneus brevis brings about plantar flexion and eversion of the foot.

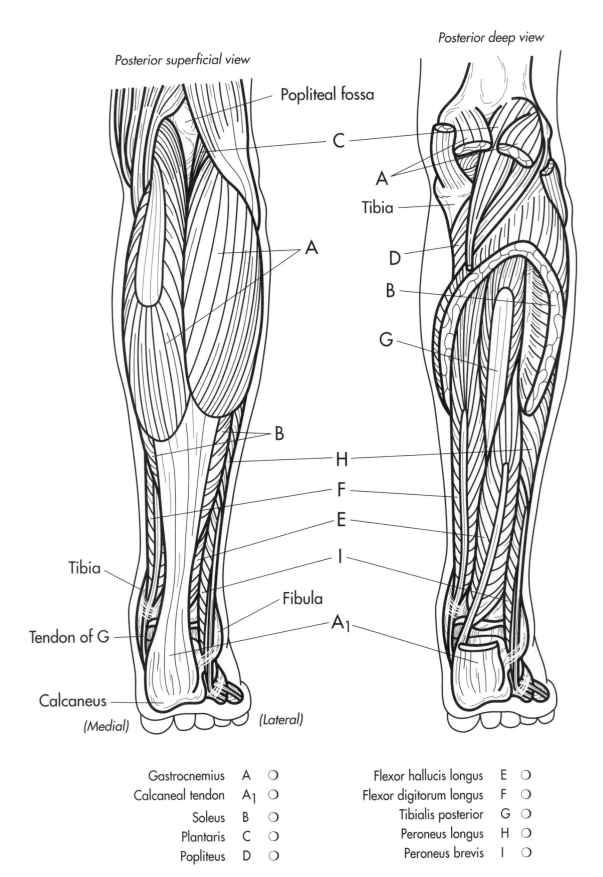

Posterior superficial view

Posterior deep view

Popliteal fossa

C

A

Tibia

D

B

G

A

B

H

F

E

I

Tibia

Fibula

A₁

Tendon of G

Calcaneus

(Medial)   (Lateral)

Gastrocnemius	A	○	Flexor hallucis longus	E	○
Calcaneal tendon	A₁	○	Flexor digitorum longus	F	○
Soleus	B	○	Tibialis posterior	G	○
Plantaris	C	○	Peroneus longus	H	○
Popliteus	D	○	Peroneus brevis	I	○

CHAPTER FIVE:

the NERVOUS SYSTEM

OVERVIEW of the NERVOUS SYSTEM

The nervous system permits the body to react and adjust to changes in the outside environment and within the body. Sensing stimuli and conveying them to the brain and spinal cord, the nervous system encourages analysis, comparisons, and coordination by the body. Messages are then conveyed by the nerves to the glands and muscles for a response.

This plate details the general pattern in the nervous system. It indicates the major divisions and subdivisions of the system and provides an introduction to the plates that follow. As the major regulatory system of the body, the nervous system is specialized to develop the correct response to environmental stimuli.

> You may begin your work on this plate by coloring the main title Overview of the Nervous System. We are showing the nervous system and several organs that detect stimuli and effect a response to the stimulus. As you encounter the parts of the nervous system in the readings, color their titles and locations in the appropriate part of the diagram. For large divisions of the nervous system, we have used brackets to set them apart. We use subscript numbers to indicate related parts of the system.

The nervous system is a single, unified network of communications. On an anatomical basis, however, it is divided into two primary portions. The first portion is the **central nervous system (A)**, or CNS. The second major portion is the **peripheral nervous system (B)**, or PNS. The brackets may be colored in bold colors.

The two key components of the CNS are the **brain (C)** and the **spinal cord (D)**. We suggest light or medium colors for these organs. The spinal cord is a continuation of the stem of the brain, so that it would be best if the two colors blend. The spinal cord begins at the location indicated by the shaded arrow.

The brain and spinal cord are the central control system of the body. The tissue of these organs receives and interprets stimuli, then dispatches impulses to glands and muscles for appropriate actions. Higher mental faculties are centered in the brain, while many automatic reflex actions depend on activity in the spinal cord. The spinal cord is also a relay station for impulses.

> We now focus on the second portion of the nervous system, the peripheral nervous system. Here we see two divisions and several subdivisions. Bold colors may be used to indicate the pathway of nerves, and the organs should be colored in light colors to preserve their detail.

The nerves associated with the brain and spinal cord make up the PNS, whose bracket you have previously colored. The PNS lies outside the brain and spinal cord and allows them to communicate with the remainder of the body.

There are two divisions of the PNS. The first is the sensory division, whose title should be colored. Nerves in this division carry impulses from the organs within the body and from the surface of the body. Nerves that carry impulses from body organs are called **visceral sensory nerves (E_1)**. We recommend you color over the visceral sensory nerve leading from the **heart (a)** to the CNS. The second aspect of the sensory division is the **somatic sensory nerves (E_2)**, which carry nerves from the body surface. The **skin senses (b)** are shown in the plate, and we recommend coloring over the nerve in a bold color.

The second division is the motor division. This division of the PNS has two subdivisions. The first is the somatic subdivision, a system of nerve fibers that carry impulses from the CNS to the skeletal muscle. A **somatic motor nerve (F_1)** is shown carrying impulses to the **skeletal muscle (c)**.

The second subdivision of the motor division is the autonomic subdivision. This is sometimes called the autonomic nervous system. It has two parts. The sympathetic carries impulses to stimulate the activity of body organs. A **sympathetic nerve (F_2)** is shown extending to the heart from the spinal cord. The second part is the parasympathetic part. We show a **parasympathetic nerve fiber (F_3)** also extending to the heart. Activity of this nerve opposes that of the sympathetic nerve and reduces the stimulation on the body organ.

> Before leaving the nervous system, we take a brief view of the tissue of the brain and note the organization of some of the nerve cells. As you continue to read below, locate the structures in the diagram and color them in with appropriate colors.

The nervous system is very rich in cells. The functional cells are called neurons, or nerve cells. In the plate, we show a small section of the brain tissue. Toward the surface is the area known as the **gray matter (G)**. Within the gray matter are the **cell bodies (I_1)** of the nerve cells. Many cell bodies are shown. Deep to the gray matter is the **white matter (H)**. White matter consists primarily of extensions from the cell bodies called **axons (I_2)**. Because these cellular extensions are enclosed in white material, the accumulation of axons causes the entire area to be white matter. A more thorough discussion of these cell parts is given in the following plates.

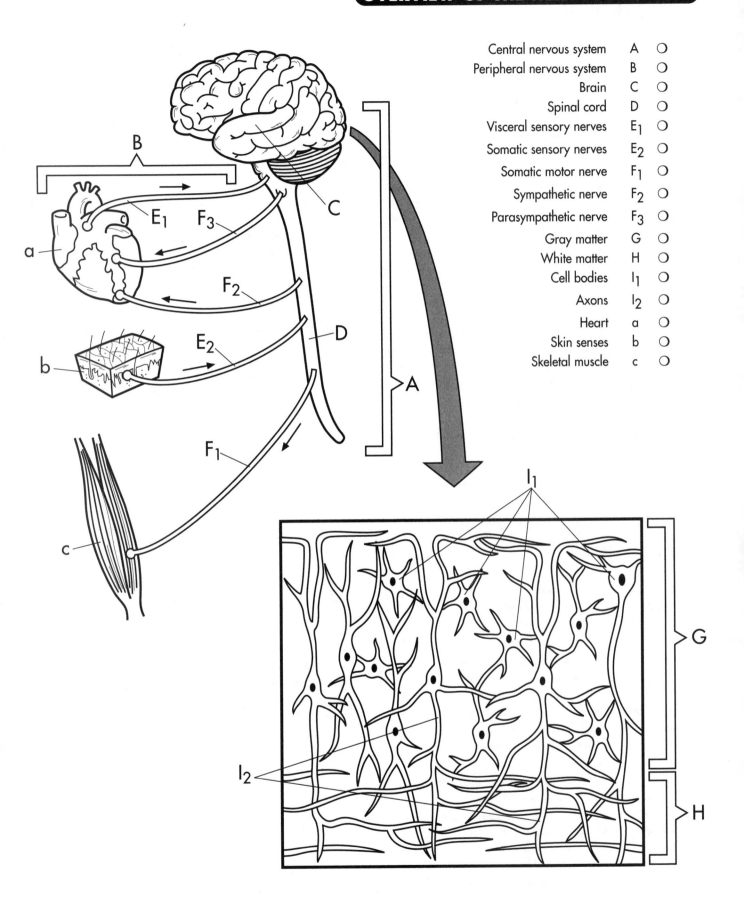

Central nervous system   A   ○
Peripheral nervous system   B   ○
Brain   C   ○
Spinal cord   D   ○
Visceral sensory nerves E_1 ○
Somatic sensory nerves E_2 ○
Somatic motor nerve F_1 ○
Sympathetic nerve F_2 ○
Parasympathetic nerve F_3 ○
Gray matter   G   ○
White matter   H   ○
Cell bodies I_1 ○
Axons I_2 ○
Heart   a   ○
Skin senses   b   ○
Skeletal muscle   c   ○

NERVE CELLS

The nervous system is composed of two basic types of cells, the neurons (nerve cells) and the neuroglia (supporting cells). Neurons are specialized to respond to stimuli and transmit impulses from one body part to another. Neuroglia protect and nurture the neurons. In this plate, we examine both types of cells. In the plate we show an expanded view of a single neuron and diagrams of various types of neurons and neuroglia cells. Since the neuron has three major parts, you should use three major colors. Arrows point to various sections of the neuron, and the arrows may be colored boldly. Begin by coloring the main title Nerve Cells. Read about the anatomy of neurons below.

Neurons are highly specialized cells of the nervous system. Each neuron has three main parts. The first part is the **cell body (A)**, the second part is the **dendrites (B)**, and the third part is the **axon (C)**.

Begin with the **cell body (A)** and color this entire structure in a light color. As does a typical cell, the cell body has a **nucleus (A_1)** and a **nucleolus (A_2)**. It has at least one **mitochondrion (A_3)** and a mass of endoplasmic reticulum known as the **Nissl body (A_4)**. Cross sections of **neurofibril (A_5)** can be seen within the cytoplasm of the cell, and a spot of color will point out their presence.

Extending to the cell body are a number of short processes called **dendrites (B)**. A single color may be used for all these processes. Dendrites conduct nerve impulses toward the cell body from the senses or from another nerve cell. The arrow shows this direction.

Having noted the first two main parts of the neuron, we now turn to the third part, the axon. This is the long extension from the body. It has many subdivisions and parts. Continue your reading, and locate the parts and arrows on the diagram as you proceed. A single light color should be used for the axon.

A nerve cell generally has an **axon (C)** extending away from the cell body to a muscle cell, gland, or adjacent nerve cell. Typically, it is a long process. The axon originates at a cone-shaped elevation of the cell body known as the **axon hillock (C_1)**, which is shown by an arrow. Immediately next is the **initial segment (C_2)** where the nerve impulse is initiated. The **axis cylinder (C_3)** contains cytoplasm known as axoplasm and is enclosed by the plasma membrane known as the **axolemma (C_4)**. The axolemma may be outlined in a bold color.

At its distal end, the axon ends in a group of small branches called **telodendria (D)**. An arrow points these out. Further along, the telodendria lead to shorter branches known as **axon terminals (E)**, and these terminate in **end bulbs (F)**. Substances released at the end bulb permit transmission of the impulse to the next receptor.

The axons of many nerves are covered with a sheath of material called the **myelin sheath (G)**. Such a nerve fiber is called a myelinated fiber. In many nerve fibers, the myelin sheath is composed of rolled layers of the plasma membrane produced by special cells called **Schwann cells (H)**, or **neurolemmocytes**. The **cytoplasm of the Schwann cell** is indicated on the plate (H_1), and the **nucleus of the cell (H_2)** may be colored.

The outer layer enclosing the rolls of plasma cell membrane is called the **neurolemma (H_3)**, or the Schwann sheath. At some points along the axon, the myelin sheath is interrupted by unsheathed areas called the **nodes of Ranvier (I)**.

Not all nerve cells are exactly as pictured. Indeed, nerve cells have been classified into four types depending upon their structure. These types are examined next. The same colors used above for the cell body, dendrites, and axons should be used here.

Depending upon their structure, neurons are classified as four types. The first are the **anaxonic neurons (*)**. These small neurons have no axons and are found in the central nervous system with unknown function. The **unipolar neurons (*)** have their cell body off to the side, and the axon and dendrite are continuous. Sensory neurons are usually of this type.

Bipolar neurons (*) have a single dendrite and axon with the cell body between and are relatively rare. **Multipolar neurons (*)** have several dendrites and a single axon with one or more branches. They are relatively common in the CNS.

We close the plate with a brief examination of the neuroglia, which support the neurons of the central nervous system. Three types of cells are pictured here and should be colored with medium colors as you read below.

In the plate, we show a section of the brain matter of the CNS with three kinds of neuroglia. The first type are the **astrocytes (J)**. These cells provide structural support to the neurons and help maintain the blood-brain barrier. The second type of neuroglia are the **oligodendrocytes (K)**. Extensions of these cells wrap themselves around axons in parts of the CNS and provide a structural framework. The final type are the **microglia (L)**, which function by phagocytosis to remove cell debris and waste.

The Neuron

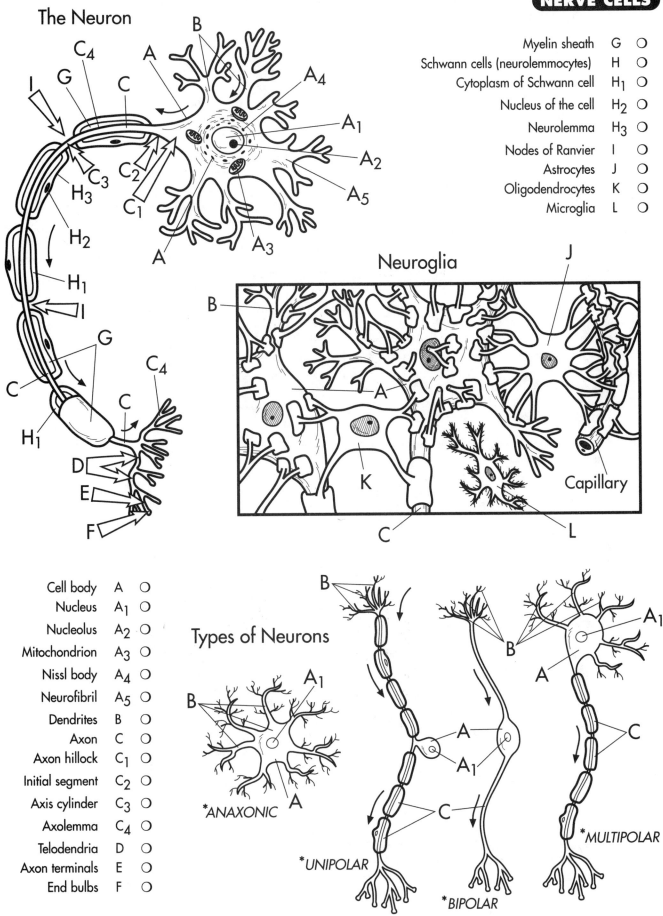

Neuroglia

Capillary

Types of Neurons

*ANAXONIC

*UNIPOLAR

*BIPOLAR

*MULTIPOLAR

Myelin sheath	G	○
Schwann cells (neurolemmocytes)	H	○
Cytoplasm of Schwann cell	H_1	○
Nucleus of the cell	H_2	○
Neurolemma	H_3	○
Nodes of Ranvier	I	○
Astrocytes	J	○
Oligodendrocytes	K	○
Microglia	L	○

Cell body	A	○
Nucleus	A_1	○
Nucleolus	A_2	○
Mitochondrion	A_3	○
Nissl body	A_4	○
Neurofibril	A_5	○
Dendrites	B	○
Axon	C	○
Axon hillock	C_1	○
Initial segment	C_2	○
Axis cylinder	C_3	○
Axolemma	C_4	○
Telodendria	D	○
Axon terminals	E	○
End bulbs	F	○

ANATOMY of the SPINAL CORD

The central nervous system consists of the brain and spinal cord. The spinal cord is a connecting link between the brain and nerves leading to various body regions, and it is involved in reflex actions. This plate covers the anatomy of the spinal cord and its coverings.

As you look over the plate, note that we use various devices in this plate including both capital and lower-case letters, subscript numbers, and subscript letters. These are used to identify subdivisions of the main structures as well as nearby organs. As you read about the spinal cord, color the titles, then locate and color the structures in the first diagram showing the spinal cord in place. Be sure to color the main title Anatomy of the Spinal Cord.

The spinal cord extends caudally from the foramen magnum of the skull for approximately 18 inches to the level of the first lumbar vertebra. At its upper end, the **spinal cord (A)** is continuous with the medulla of the brain. A single color should be used, and if possible, one that has five variations since we will color the five different sections of the spinal cord. The **cerebrum (a)** and **cerebellum (b)** of the brain may be colored, and the **occipital bone (c)** may be colored to show where the spinal cord emerges. At the lower end of the cord, we see the **sacrum (d)** and **coccyx (e)**.

The spinal cord is divided into 31 segments related to the 31 vertebrae. The first segment is the **cervical segment (A_C)**. The spinal cord and nerves arising laterally should be colored in a variation of the spinal cord color. The second segment, the **thoracic segment (A_T)** should be colored in a second variation of the color for the spinal cord. The **lumbar segment (A_L)** corresponds to the area of the five lumbar vertebrae and the **sacral segment (A_S)** to the sacral vertebrae.

The spinal cord is flattened dorsally and ventrally and has two prominent enlargements. The first is the **cervical enlargement (A_1),** indicated by an arrow to be colored boldly. The second enlargement is the **lumbar enlargement (A_2)**. At these enlargements, the spinal nerves emerge to innervate the upper and lower limbs, respectively.

Below the lumbar enlargement, the spinal cord tapers and forms an area called the **conus medullaris (A_3)**, which is in the area of the first lumbar vertebra. Extending caudally as far as the second sacral vertebra is a nonneural fiber known as the **filum terminale (A_4)**, a strand of fibrous tissue. The spinal cord extends only to the area of the first lumbar vertebra. The regions beyond

it are extensions from the inferior portion that continue and then emerge laterally as spinal nerves. Thus, there are lumbar spinal nerves, sacral spinal nerves, and coccygeal spinal nerves even though the spinal cord has ended.

We now focus on a cross section of the spinal cord to show some of its details and set the stage for upcoming plates. New colors may be used here, because we are interested in details of the spinal cord rather than the spinal cord in toto.

The plate shows a cross section through the spinal cord with the ventral aspect to the right and the dorsal aspect to the left. In the spinal cord, the cell bodies of neurons give the central portion a gray appearance; therefore, the tissue is called **gray matter (B)**. Surrounding the gray matter are the myelinated axons extending outward. This tissue is called **white matter (C)**.

Extensions from the spinal cord proceed laterally. The extension of the dorsal aspect is called the **dorsal root (C_1)**. It should be colored in the same color as the white matter since it is covered by myelin tissue. The swelling in the dorsal root is the **dorsal root ganglion (C_3)**, an area containing cell bodies outside the spinal cord. Sensory fibers exit the spinal cord through the dorsal root.

At the ventral aspect is the **ventral root (C_2)**. Motor fibers enter through here. The same color as the white matter may be used for the dorsal root. Note that the ventral and dorsal roots unite to form a single extension, the **spinal nerve (D)**. Use a spot of color to indicate its presence. Further details on these structures are given in the next plate. Note the location of the spinal cord within the vertebrae. In the diagram, two vertebrae are shown, and the spinal cord is seen within the vertebral cavity.

The neural tissues are extremely delicate and are protected against damage by a series of specialized membranes called meninges. These membranes are shown in the final portion of the plate and are listed in the titles list. Color the titles, then locate and color the membranes in the plate to complete it.

The spinal meninges provide protection, stability, and absorption against shock. They contain the blood vessels that provide oxygen and nutrients to spinal cord tissue and remove the waste products. Three meningeal layers are found at the border of the spinal cord. The first lies against the spinal cord and is the **pia mater (E)**. Blood vessels are rich here, and the pia mater is bound to the neural tissue. Superficial to the pia mater is the subarachnoid space, which contains a network of blood vessels. Then comes the second layer, the **arachnoid (F)**. This spiderlike membrane is delicate and transparent and has numerous connective strands. The outer layer is the **dura mater (G)**. This is a tough, fibrous membrane composed of dense fibers. Between the dura mater and the arachnoid is the subdural space.

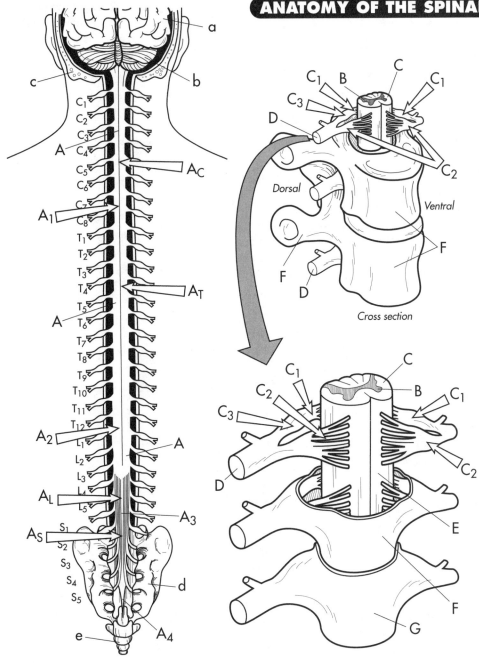

Spinal cord	A	○
Cervical enlargement	A₁	○
Lumbar enlargement	A₂	○
Conus medullaris	A₃	○
Filum terminal	A₄	○
Cervical segment	A_C	○
Thoracic segment	A_T	○
Lumbar segment	A_L	○
Sacral segment	A_S	○

Gray matter	B	○
White matter	C	○
Dorsal root	C₁	○
Ventral root	C₂	○
Dorsal root ganglion	C₃	○
Spinal nerve	D	○
Pia mater	E	○
Arachnoid	F	○
Dura mater	G	○
Cerebrum	a	○
Cerebellum	b	○
Occipital bone	c	○
Sacrum	d	○
Coccyx	e	○

DETAILS of the SPINAL CORD and NERVE

The spinal cord is located within the vertebral canal of the vertebral column. The cord is surrounded by vertebral ligaments, meninges, and cerebrospinal fluid. We examine the details of the spinal cord in this plate and study the anatomy of the spinal nerves arising from it. These nerves convey impulses to the skin and visceral organs and carry impulses from them in the direction of the spinal cord. Motor nerves accomplish the former function, sensory nerves the latter.

This plate contains two diagrams. A cross section of the spinal cord is presented in the first diagram, and details of the spinal cord are presented in the second. Each part should be considered separately as you proceed. Begin by coloring the main title Details of the Spinal Cord and Nerve, then focus on the first diagram as you read below. Many arrows are used to point out certain regions and only two colors are required. They should be light, pale yellow or tan colors.

At its central region, the spinal cord contains **gray matter (A)**, which is shaped somewhat like the letter H. A single color should be used for the entire area of gray matter within the spinal cord and extending laterally left and right. The region closer to the back of the spinal cord constitutes the **dorsal gray horn (A$_1$)**, and the arrow should be colored boldly. Toward the front of the spinal cord are the **ventral gray horns (A$_2$)**, and an arrow points to their location. Lying between the dorsal and ventral gray horns is the region called the **lateral gray horn (A$_3$)**.

The gray matter consists primarily of the cell bodies of neurons together with supporting cells. The central portion of the gray matter dividing the lateral halves is the **gray commissure (A$_4$)**, designated by an arrow. Arising from the dorsal gray horn is the **dorsal root (A$_5$)**. An enlargement called the **dorsal root ganglion (A$_6$)** is seen on both lateral halves. This is the site of nerve cell bodies. Arising from the ventral horn is the **ventral root (A$_7$)**. This root combines with the dorsal root to form the **spinal nerve (A$_8$)**.

The white matter of the **spinal cord (B)** should be colored a different light color. At the ventral aspect is a broad area called the **ventral white columns (B$_1$)**, which are designated by arrows. On the other side of the gray commissure is an area known as the **dorsal white columns (B$_2$)**. The dorsal and ventral horns divide the white matter and set off the third broad region called the **lateral white columns (B$_3$)**. A small area called the **anterior white commissure (B$_4$)** is located near the gray commissure.

At the center of the gray commissure is the **central canal (C)** of the spinal cord. This canal continues with the fourth ventricle of the brain and contains cerebrospinal fluid to nourish the tissue of the spinal cord.

We now focus briefly on the nerve cells within the spinal cord to note how they relate to the gray matter. You may use dark colors to overcolor the lines represented by the cells. Read below as you color and color the titles as you encounter them. Then locate and color the structures with the appropriate colors.

The gray matter contains the nerve tissue of the brain, while the white matter consists primarily of the myelinated axons of the cell bodies. Sensory impulses enter the brain through the axons of sensory neurons. These are the sensory axons. The cell body of the sensory neuron is located in the **dorsal root ganglion (G$_2$)**, as the plate shows. Impulses are carried away from the spinal cord by the motor neurons. The cell body of the **motor neuron (F$_2$)** is located in the gray matter, and the axons of the motor neurons, the **motor axons (F$_1$)**, extend away from the cell body and out the spinal cord.

In the second part of this plate, we focus on some of the structures of the spinal nerve. Axons travel together in the spinal nerves to and from the spinal cord. The diagram indicates their organization as they travel through the spinal nerve. Read about this concept in the following paragraphs, and color the titles and structures appropriately.

The spinal nerve begins at the junction of the dorsal and ventral root. The nerve is covered by a superficial wrapping called the **epineurium (H)**. The entire spinal nerve can be colored with a single color, beginning at the junction of the dorsal and ventral roots. Beneath the epineurium, groups of axons are bundled together to form a fascicle. The bracket enclosing the **fascicle (I)** should be colored boldly. The fascicle is covered with a wrapping called the **perineurium (J)**. The perineurium encloses several axons. Each axon is wrapped in a covering called the **endoneurium (K)**. An endoneurium exists whether the axon is myelinated or unmyelinated. The individual **axon (L)** can be indicated with a spot of color.

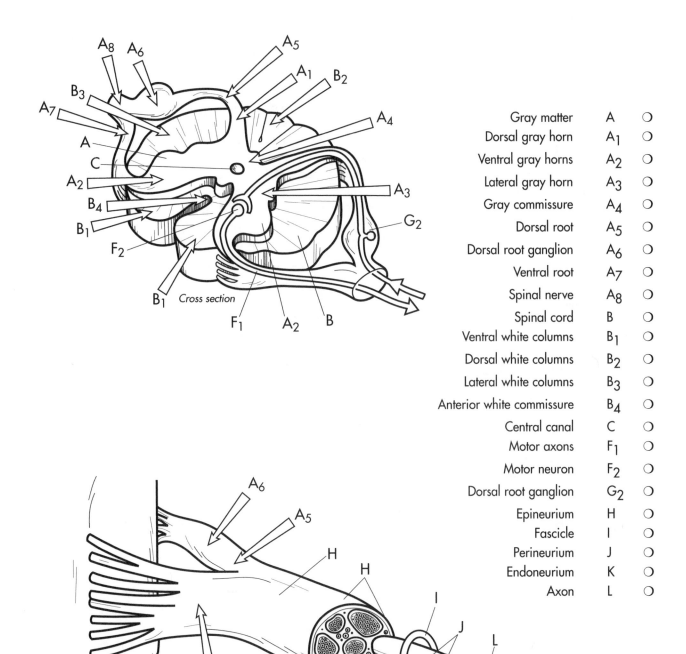

Cross section

F_1 A_2 B

SPINAL NERVE

Gray matter	A	○
Dorsal gray horn	A_1	○
Ventral gray horns	A_2	○
Lateral gray horn	A_3	○
Gray commissure	A_4	○
Dorsal root	A_5	○
Dorsal root ganglion	A_6	○
Ventral root	A_7	○
Spinal nerve	A_8	○
Spinal cord	B	○
Ventral white columns	B_1	○
Dorsal white columns	B_2	○
Lateral white columns	B_3	○
Anterior white commissure	B_4	○
Central canal	C	○
Motor axons	F_1	○
Motor neuron	F_2	○
Dorsal root ganglion	G_2	○
Epineurium	H	○
Fascicle	I	○
Perineurium	J	○
Endoneurium	K	○
Axon	L	○

the CERVICAL and BRACHIAL PLEXUSES

As seen in the previous plate, a spinal nerve is formed when the ventral root and the dorsal root of the spinal cord meet shortly after passing through the spinal column. Sensory and motor fibers come together here. A short distance later, the spinal nerve divides into several branches called rami. The dorsal ramus innervates the skin of the back, tissues, and deep muscles of the back. The meningeal ramus innervates the vertebrae, meninges, and spinal blood vessels. The ventral ramus innervates tissues of the skin, abdominal wall, limbs, pelvic area, and numerous muscles.

Before the ventral rami extend to their destinations, they form several complex networks of nerves called plexuses. In a plexus, the nerve fibers of different spinal nerves are sorted and recombined. The nerve fibers associated with a particular peripheral nerve are composed of fibers from several different rami. In this plate, we point out the four plexuses of the peripheral nerves, and study the cervical and brachial plexuses in detail.

> The plate contains a view of the spinal nerves exiting the spinal cord and a detailed diagram of nerves of the cervical and brachial areas. As you study the regions and nerves, use light colors for them in the diagram. Begin by coloring the main title The Cervical and Brachial Plexuses.

The spinal nerves use four plexuses to recombine themselves before forming the fibers of the spinal nerves. The four plexuses are indicated in the plate by brackets, which can be colored with bold colors. The plexuses are the **cervical plexus (A)**, the **brachial plexus (B)**, the **lumbar plexus (C)**, and the **sacral plexus (D)**. There is some overlap of the plexuses in the lumbar and sacral regions. The **ventral rami (E)** of nerves from thoracic vertebrae two through twelve do not form plexuses. These nerves are indicated, and you may color them at this time.

> We now focus on the cervical plexus and the nerves that arise from it. If you wish, you may color the brain, cerebellum, and spinal cord in colors of your choice to indicate their presence. Also, you may wish to color the spinal nerves exiting from the cervical vertebrae (C_1 to C_8). As you read about the nerves of the cervical plexus, use light colors to color them. The entire cervical plexus is complex and may be colored using a light color to avoid obscuring its construction.

The cervical plexus is composed of the dorsal rami of spinal nerves C_1 through C_4. The fifth cervical vertebra also makes contributions, as the plate shows. Nerves from this plexus supply the skin and muscles of the head, neck, and superior aspect of the shoulders. Branches of the plexus also connect with cranial nerves XI and XII, not shown on the plate.

Several important nerves arise from the cervical plexus. The nerves include the **ansa cervalis (A_1)**, which supplies laryngeal muscles examined in an earlier plate. Another nerve is the **lesser occipital (A_2)**, which is distributed through the skin of the scalp superior to the ear. The **transverse cervical nerve (A_3)** is distributed at the anterior aspect of the neck, and the **greater auricular nerve (A_4)** lies near the parotid glands. The **supraclavicular nerve (A_5)** supplies impulses to the superior portion of the chest and shoulder, and the **phrenic nerve (A_6)** is a major nerve to the diaphragm. Impulses supplied by motor fibers of this nerve are essential to the breathing process.

> The final focus of this plate is on the nerves of the brachial plexus, including the nerves into the arm. A posterior view of the right arm is shown in the plate, and the names of the nerves should be colored as you color in the nerves themselves. Read the following paragraphs as you study these nerves.

The brachial plexus is formed by the ventral rami of spinal nerves C_5 to C_8 and T_1. The plexus passes superior to the first rib then enters the axilla, supplying the nerve supply to the shoulder and upper limb.

As the plate shows, the brachial plexus gives rise to three trunks or cords named by their location. A light color may be used for the brachial plexus before the three cords arise. They include the **lateral cord (B_1)**, the **posterior cord (B_2)**, and the **medial cord (B_3)**. The cords give rise to other important nerves of the shoulder and arm. Among these are the **axillary nerve (B_4)**, which is distributed through the deltoid and teres minor muscles. The **musculocutaneous nerve (B_5)** supplies the biceps brachii, brachialis, and other important muscles of the shoulder and humerus area.

The **radial nerve (B_6)** supplies muscles on the posterior aspect of the arm and forearm after arising from the lateral cord. The **median nerve (B_7)** arises from both the lateral and medial cords and is distributed through flexors of the forearm. The final nerve considered is the **ulnar nerve (B_8)**. Arising in the same way as the median nerve, the ulnar nerve supplies most hand muscles as well as much of the forearm.

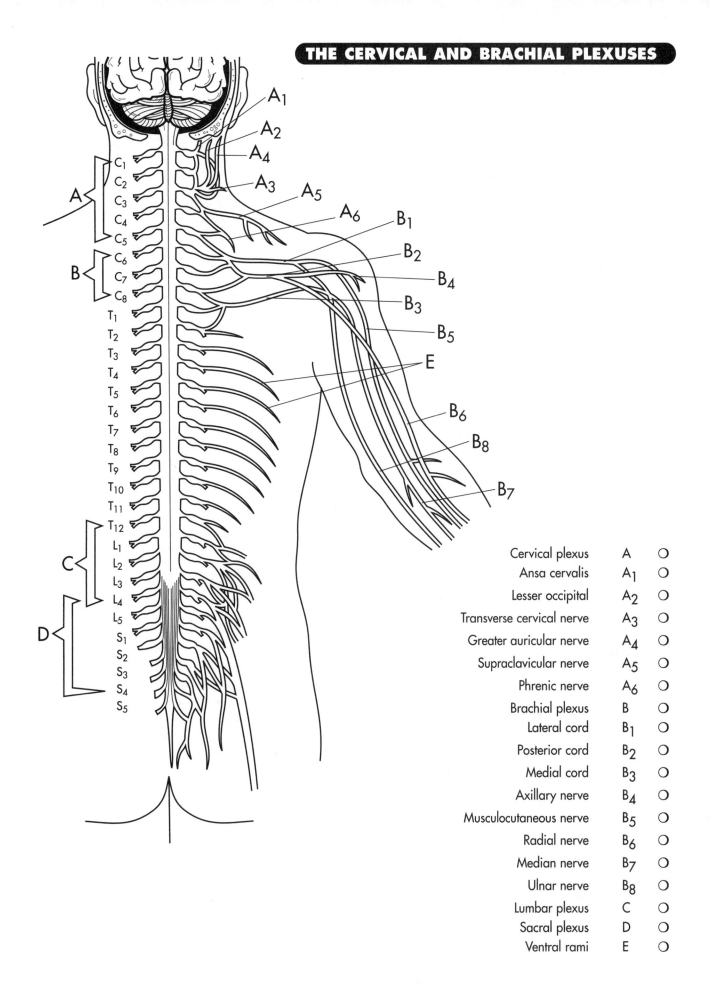

THE CERVICAL AND BRACHIAL PLEXUSES

Cervical plexus	A	○
Ansa cervalis	A₁	○
Lesser occipital	A₂	○
Transverse cervical nerve	A₃	○
Greater auricular nerve	A₄	○
Supraclavicular nerve	A₅	○
Phrenic nerve	A₆	○
Brachial plexus	B	○
Lateral cord	B₁	○
Posterior cord	B₂	○
Medial cord	B₃	○
Axillary nerve	B₄	○
Musculocutaneous nerve	B₅	○
Radial nerve	B₆	○
Median nerve	B₇	○
Ulnar nerve	B₈	○
Lumbar plexus	C	○
Sacral plexus	D	○
Ventral rami	E	○

the LUMBAR and SACRAL PLEXUSES

After leaving the spinal cord, the dorsal and ventral roots unite to form the spinal nerve. Shortly thereafter, the spinal nerves branch to form several rami, including the dorsal ramus, meningeal ramus, ramus communicantes, and ventral ramus. Before proceeding to their organs, the ventral rami come together to form networks called plexuses. Here the fibers are recombined so that the nerve fiber emerging carries impulses from several different rami.

In the previous plate, we examined the four plexuses and concentrated on the cervical and brachial plexuses and their nerves. In this plate, we continue that pattern with a focus on the lumbar and sacral plexuses and their nerves.

Begin by coloring the main title The Lumbar and Sacral Plexuses. As you look over the plate, note that we are concentrating on the lower portion of the body, with the right leg shown in the posterior view. We describe the lumbar and sacral plexuses, which may be colored using a light color to retain the visibility of the network system. As you read below, color the titles of the nerves, then locate and color them in the plate.

The lumbar and sacral plexuses are sometimes considered together as the lumbosacral plexus since there are many connections. However, we treat them separately in this plate as they arise at the posterior abdominal wall.

The lumbar plexus is formed by the ventral rami of spinal nerve 12 and **lumbar nerves 1 to 4 (A)**. The bracket outlining these vertebral areas and nerves may be colored in a dark color. There is less intermingling of fibers than seen in the brachial and cervical plexuses. The plexus supplies the anterior lateral abdominal walls as well as the genital organs and thighs.

Among the important nerves arising from the lumbar plexus is the **iliohypogastric (A_1)**. Muscles of the anterior and lateral abdominal wall receive impulses from this nerve. The **ilioinguinal (A_2)** nerve supplies the genital organs in the male and female as well as aspects of the thigh. The cremaster muscle of the male genital organs receives impulses from the **genitofemoral nerve (A_3)**. This muscle raises the testis when the outside temperature is cold to bring the testis closer to the abdominal wall. The labia of the female are also supplied by this nerve.

Various aspects of the thigh receive impulses by the **lateral femoral cutaneous nerve (A_4)**, as the plate shows. This very long nerve supplies much of the skin area. The **femoral nerve (A_5)** reaches to the flexor muscles of the thigh and extensor muscles of the lower leg. The **obturator nerve (A_6)** is distributed through the adductor muscles of the thigh and the skin over the medial surface of the thigh. The final nerve we consider is the **saphenous (A_7)**. After arising from the lumbar plexus, this nerve is distributed over the medial surface of the leg.

We now turn to the nerves of the sacral plexus. Many of these nerves reach into the leg as well as the buttocks and perineum. As you read below, color the titles, then use the same color for the nerve in the plate. Many of the nerves have names similar to the muscles they innervate.

The **sacral plexus (B)** is outlined by a bracket, which may be colored. This plexus is composed of fibers of the ventral rami exiting from the fourth and fifth lumbar vertebrae and sacral vertebrae S_1 to S_4. Note that there is some overlap with the lumbar plexus since ventral rami from both plexuses come together at one point.

The sacral plexus passes in front of the sacrum and is distributed through regions of the buttocks. Among the important nerves arising from it are the **superior gluteal nerve (B_1)** and the **inferior gluteal nerve (B_2)**. Abductors of the thigh and extensors of the thigh are innervated by these two nerves respectively.

The sacral plexus gives rise to the largest nerve in the body, the **sciatic nerve (B_3)**. As the thickest and longest nerve in the body, the sciatic nerve extends from the pelvic area to the foot. Branches of it innervate the hamstring muscles and adductor magnus. The sciatic nerve splits to form the **tibial nerve (B_4)** and the **perineal nerve (B_5)**. The tibial supplies the gastrocnemius and other muscles of the lower leg, then branches in the foot to the medial plantar nerve and lateral plantar nerve. The perineal nerve divides into superficial and deep branches supplying various areas of the lower leg, foot, and toes. The **medial sural cutaneous nerve (B_7)** arises from the tibial nerve and supplies the skin of the medial portion of the lower leg, while the **lateral sural cutaneous (B_8)** arises from the perineal nerve to supply the lateral portion of the skin.

The final nerve we consider is the **pudendal nerve (B_6)**. After arising from the sacral plexus, this nerve extends to the perineum and supplies many regions of the male and female external genital organs. Since upright walking is a critical human function, the impulses supplied by these nerves are an essential aspect of life.

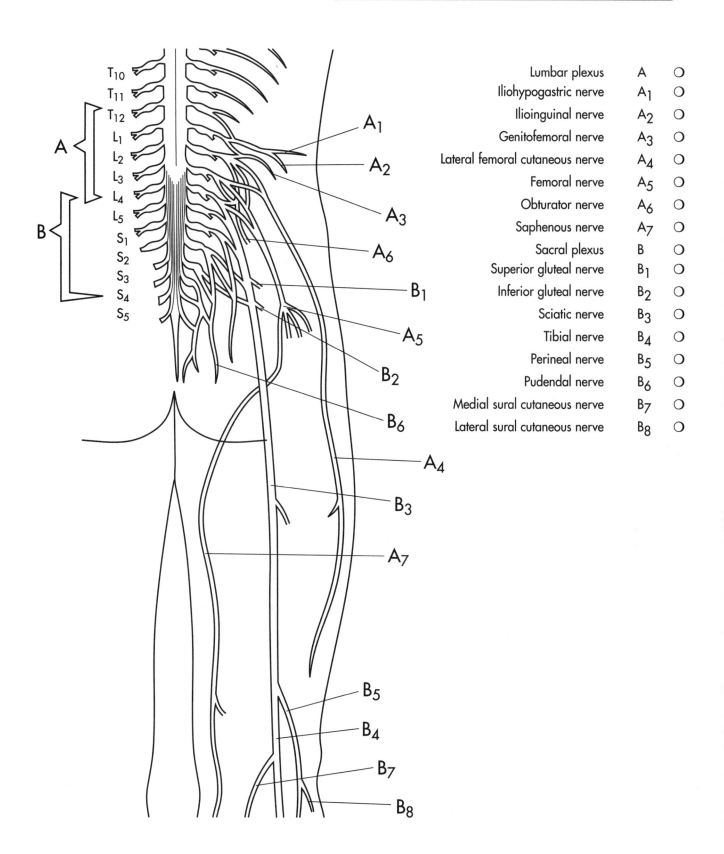

Lumbar plexus	A	○
Iliohypogastric nerve	A_1	○
Ilioinguinal nerve	A_2	○
Genitofemoral nerve	A_3	○
Lateral femoral cutaneous nerve	A_4	○
Femoral nerve	A_5	○
Obturator nerve	A_6	○
Saphenous nerve	A_7	○
Sacral plexus	B	○
Superior gluteal nerve	B_1	○
Inferior gluteal nerve	B_2	○
Sciatic nerve	B_3	○
Tibial nerve	B_4	○
Perineal nerve	B_5	○
Pudendal nerve	B_6	○
Medial sural cutaneous nerve	B_7	○
Lateral sural cutaneous nerve	B_8	○

DERMATOMES

Over the entire body surface, the skin is supplied by branches of the sensory portion of the nervous system. Neurons and their branches bear impulses from the skin area into the spinal cord and brain stem. In like matter, the skeletal muscles beneath the skin receive the signals from motor neurons of this system, which carry impulses back from the spinal cord.

Physiologists have discovered that a spinal nerve contains both sensory and motor neurons, and that a spinal nerve services a specific segment of the body. Such a segment is called a dermatome.

Thirty-one dermatomes have been identified on the skin surface as a result of a number of experimental, clinical, and surgical procedures and studies. The dermatomes correspond to 30 of the 31 spinal nerves. The spinal nerve from the first cervical vertebra has no dorsal root and does not have a dermatome. There is, however, a dermatome innervated by one of the cranial nerves.

In this plate, we denote the 31 dermatomes of the body surface. You should use five main colors with variations of four of the five colors.

Note that the plate contains anterior and posterior views of the skin surface of the body. The numerous lines denote the dermatomes. You should select five basic colors for this plate. The first color is to be used one time, but the other four colors should have varying shades and intensities for denoting the four classes of dermatomes. These correspond to dermatomes supplied by the cervical, thoracic, lumbar, and sacral nerves. Color the main title Dermatomes, then read about the dermatomes and begin your coloring.

As noted above, the area of the skin providing sensory input to a pair of spinal nerves is a dermatome. The one exception is the dermatome supplying sensory input to a **cranial nerve (A)**. Most of the skin of the face and scalp is serviced by cranial nerve V, called the trigeminal nerve. This nerve has three divisions: the ophthalmic, maxillary, and mandibular nerves, and each division innervates a separate region of the face and scalp. However, the plate shows a single area, and a single color can be used to indicate this general area supplied by cranial nerve V.

We now proceed to dermatomes that provide sensory input to the cervical nerves. Seven variations of a single color should be used here. If variations are not available, try to alter closely matching colors with light and dark colors to distinguish adjacent dermatomes.

There are eight dermatomes supplied by **cervical nerves C_2 to C_8**. (As noted previously, C_1 has no dermatome.) These dermatomes are distributed over the neck, shoulders, and portions of the upper limb, as the plate indicates. Adjacent dermatomes are known to overlap, which makes the separation between them difficult to identify.

Now proceed to the dermatomes supplying input to the thoracic nerves. Twelve variations of a single color are advised to separate the dermatomes clearly.

Twelve thoracic dermatomes are distributed over the body trunk and upper limbs in the anterior and posterior aspects. Dermatomes as these are valuable assets to physicians, because a complaint of pain and loss of sensation in the skin gives a clue to the spinal nerve affected. A physician's awareness of **thoracic dermatomes (T_{1-12})** is an essential part of medical care. Another reason for understanding the dermatomes is that pain is often "referred" to a specific cutaneous area. This derives from the fact that both cutaneous and visceral areas are served by the spinal cord. For example, kidney pain may be referred to dermatomes T_{10} or T_{11}. Thus, by noting pain in the dermatome, the physician may help identify problems in the deeper visceral organs.

We complete the plate by noting the dermatomes serviced by the lumbar and sacral nerves. Fewer variations of colors are needed here since there are only five lumbar and five sacral dermatomes. As you read the following paragraphs, color the dermatomes in both anterior and posterior aspect.

When a single dorsal nerve root has been injured, an increase in the sensitivity of the dermatome occurs. Also, when the function of the dorsal nerve root has been interrupted, a decrease of sensitivity is observed. A pen scratch to detect pain sensation demonstrates this diminished sensitivity. The site of injury to the dorsal root can thus be identified. Also, since there is some overlap of dermatomes, an injury to a spinal nerve may result in loss of sensation to more than one dermatome.

You should complete your work by observing the position of dermatomes supplied by L_1 to L_5. These dermatomes are found primarily on the anterior aspect of the legs. Dermatomes supplied by nerves S_1 to S_5 are located on the posterior side of the legs and the buttocks. The soles of the feet supply sensory input to a sacral nerve.

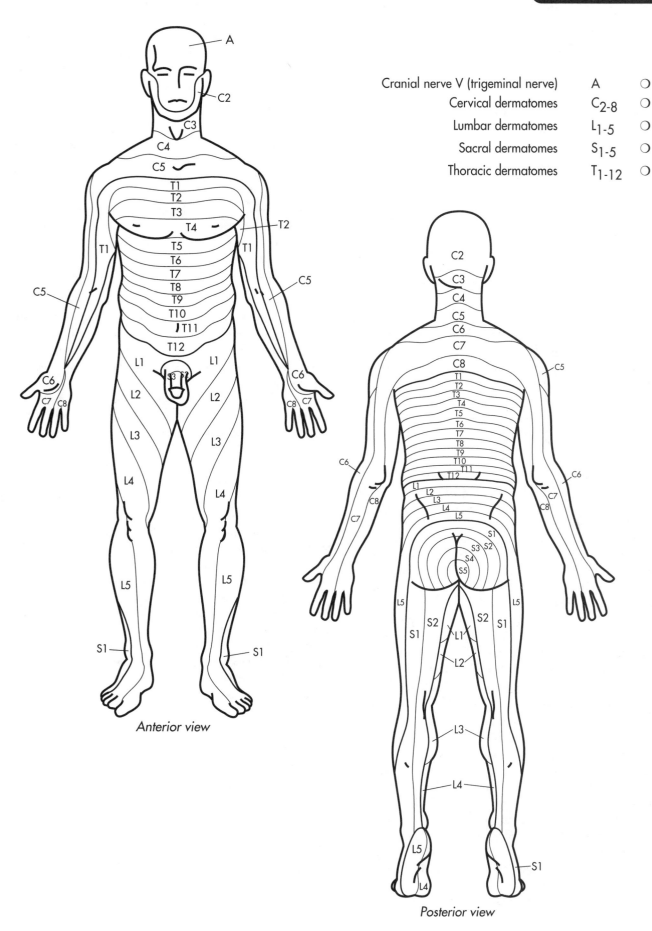

Cranial nerve V (trigeminal nerve)	A	○
Cervical dermatomes	C_{2-8}	○
Lumbar dermatomes	L_{1-5}	○
Sacral dermatomes	S_{1-5}	○
Thoracic dermatomes	T_{1-12}	○

Anterior view

Posterior view

OVERVIEW of the BRAIN

The brain is the center of human behavior. It embodies memory, understanding, and a number of higher order functions. In the following plates we examine some of the details of the anatomy of the brain, but to set the stage, we present an overview of the brain in this plate.

This plate presents three views of the brain to provide an overall orientation to this organ. We see the brain in place in the skull; we observe a sagittal section of the brain, also in the skull; and we observe the floor of the brain from below. Our objective in this plate is to point out the major portions of the brain as a prelude to the discussions ahead. Darker colors may be used for the various parts, or you may choose lighter shades to avoid obscuring the folds and details of the brain. As you read about the brain below, color the titles then locate the structures in all three views and color them in the appropriate diagram.

We learn about our environment by means of signals received in the brain. Our responses consist of signals allowing us to conduct responsive activities such as talking and moving. The brain is thus the center of nervous activity in the body and is an exceedingly complex organ with many components.

By far, the largest part of the human brain is the **cerebrum (A)**. All conscious processes occur in the cerebrum seen in whole, sectioned, and inferior views. The surface of the cerebrum is greatly folded with upward folds called gyri and downward grooves called sulci. Fissures divide the cerebrum into two hemispheres, as the view from below indicates.

The second major part of the brain is the **diencephalon (B)**, indicated by a bracket. This portion of the brain surrounds an enlarged space called the third ventricle, which is discussed in a future plate. The diencephalon consists of the **thalamus (B_1)**, the **hypothalamus (B_2)**, and the **epithalamus (B_3)**. The thalamus contains paired masses of gray matter organized into bodies called nuclei. It is a relay station for sensory impulses to the cerebral cortex. The hypothalamus is inferior to the thalamus and composed of a dozen or more nuclei. Homeostasis is regulated in this region, and receptors receive impulses from numerous senses and visceral areas of the body. Hormones stored in the posterior pituitary gland are produced in the hypothalamus. The epithalamus lies at the roof of the third ventricle.

The second largest portion of the human brain is the **cerebellum (C)**. Seen in all three diagrams, the cerebellum is located under the occipital bones posterior and inferior to the cerebrum. It has two hemispheres and small surface folds. The cerebellum helps coordinate and control movements initiated by the cerebrum.

The last region we survey is the **brain stem (D)**, which is outlined by a bracket. The bracket may be colored in a bold color. The brain stem is continuous with the **spinal cord (E)** and variations of the same color should be used for it and the brain stem. One of the important parts of the brain stem is the **midbrain (D_1)**. The midbrain has fibers that carry sensory impulses from the spinal cord to the thalamus and motor impulses from the cerebral cortex back to the spinal cord.

We now move to the two remaining regions of the brain and examine them briefly. Because these regions are discussed in more depth in other plates, our review is limited to the general functions performed. Continue your coloring as before, indicating the important structures and their location. You may wish to select variations of the same color to indicate where one area of a structure begins and another ends.

Also in the brain stem is the **pons (D_2)**. The pons is a bridge-like structure containing many fibers carrying signals between various regions of the brain. For example, signals from the spinal cord extend to the superior brain regions, while others passing through the pons are concerned with the coordination of voluntary movements.

The actual portion of the brain continuous with the spinal cord is the **medulla oblongata (D_3)**. This structure contains the gray matter carrying signals from the spinal cord and other parts of the brain.

Certain nuclei in the medulla coordinate activities by integrating signals from sensory neurons and sending responses on to the cerebellum or thalamus. Other signals are sent out to various visceral organs. The cardiac center is a mass of neurons located in the medulla for the regulation of the heart rate, and other vasomotor centers regulate the diameters of blood vessels. The depth and rate of breathing are regulated in the respiratory center, also in the medulla.

Various other structures may be seen in the plate, and you should identify and color them in. For example, the **pituitary gland (F)** is seen together with the **corpus callosum (G)** and the **olfactory bulbs (H)**. The corpus callosum is a mass of fibers carrying signals between the two cerebral hemispheres, while the olfactory bulb is associated with the sense of smell. Various **cranial nerves (I)** may be seen at the base of the brain.

Cerebrum	A	○
Diencephalon	B	○
Thalamus	B_1	○
Hypothalamus	B_2	○
Epithalamus	B_3	○
Cerebellum	C	○
Brain stem	D	○
Midbrain	D_1	○
Pons	D_2	○

Medulla oblongata	D_3	○
Spinal cord	E	○
Pituitary gland	F	○
Corpus callosum	G	○
Olfactory bulbs	H	○
Cranial nerves	I	○

the MENINGES

The meninges supply protection and support for the brain tissues and carry many important vessels between them. They cushion the brain during violent contact with the surrounding bones. They also interface with the cerebrospinal fluid, a type of plasmalike fluid that supplies nutrients and oxygen to the brain and spinal cord tissues and removes their metabolic waste products.

The cranial meninges are continuous with the meninges of the spinal cord examined in an earlier plate but with several distinguishing features. In this plate, we examine the unique features and relate them to functions performed by each meninx.

Begin by coloring the main title The Meninges. Then, as you look over the plate, note the closeup views of the meninges and their details. As you read about the three meninges below, color their titles, then locate and color the structures in any of the diagrams where they are found. Light colors are recommended since many of the structures are detailed. Also, watch for arrows pointing out specific regions. These arrows may be colored with darker colors such as greens, blues, and reds.

We begin with the outer layer of the head, and note the position of the **scalp (A)**. A medium color may be used here. A medium color may also be used to highlight the **skull bone (B)**, since we are merely showing its position.

The outermost cranial meninx is the **dura mater (C)**. This covering layer is actually two layers, an **outer layer (C₁)**, also called the endosteal layer (since it is fused to the periosteum of the cranial bones), and an **inner layer (C₂)**. As the diagram shows, the outer and inner layers separate to form a gap containing tissue fluids and blood vessels. One of the large vessels is the large vein known as the **dural sinus (C₃)**. Veins leading from the brain tissue open into this and other sinuses, which then lead to the jugular vein extending through the neck. At certain points, the inner dura mater extends into the fissure dividing the right and left hemispheres of the cerebrum. This extension or fold of tissue is the **falx cerebri (C₄)**. Other extensions are found near the cerebella and near the floor of the brain. Beneath the dura mater is a small space called the **subdural space (D)**, which separates it from the next layer.

We now concentrate on the second meninx and note some of its details. This second layer tends to be the most complex of the layers because cerebrospinal fluid absorption takes place here. Many blood vessels are found here, and the exchange between the circulatory system and the cerebrospinal fluid occurs here.

The middle layer of the meninges is the **arachnoid (E)**. It is a delicate connective tissue so named because of its spiderlike appearance. Beneath the arachnoid is a substantial area called the **subarachnoid space (F)**. Within this space are a number of fibers separating the space into compartments. The fibers are called the **arachnoid trabeculae (E₁)**. The detailed diagrams show their structure. The space between the trabeculae is filled with cerebrospinal fluid. The fluid will return to the venous circulation as we shall see momentarily.

Between the trabeculae in the subarachnoid space are a series of **blood vessels (F₁)**. These vessels supply the brain tissues with oxygen and nutrients and remove waste products. The arachnoid layer itself has no blood vessels.

Extending into the dural sinus are a number of fingerlike extensions of the arachnoid called arachnoid villi. An **arachnoid villus (E₂)** is indicated in the plate and drawn in detail. The cerebrospinal fluid percolating through the subarachnoid space enters the arachnoid villus, then passes down into the blood vessel, which leads it away from the brain tissue. This is the second method by which fluid leaves the brain.

We finish with the plate by paying brief attention to the third meninx. This innermost layer is attached to the brain. As you read about the layer, locate it in the diagram and color it with a light color.

The last of the meninges is the **pia mater (G)**. This layer adheres to the surface of the brain and follows its contours as the brain folds in at the gyri and forms its fissures called sulci. Astrocytes anchor the pia mater to the brain tissue. There are many blood vessels within the pia mater and the major cerebral blood vessels lie on top of it within the subarachnoid space below the arachnoid.

Beneath the pia mater is the **cerebral cortex (H)**. This brain tissue may be colored in the diagram to complete the plate. A light color is recommended since it is detailed, and it is best to avoid obscuring its details.

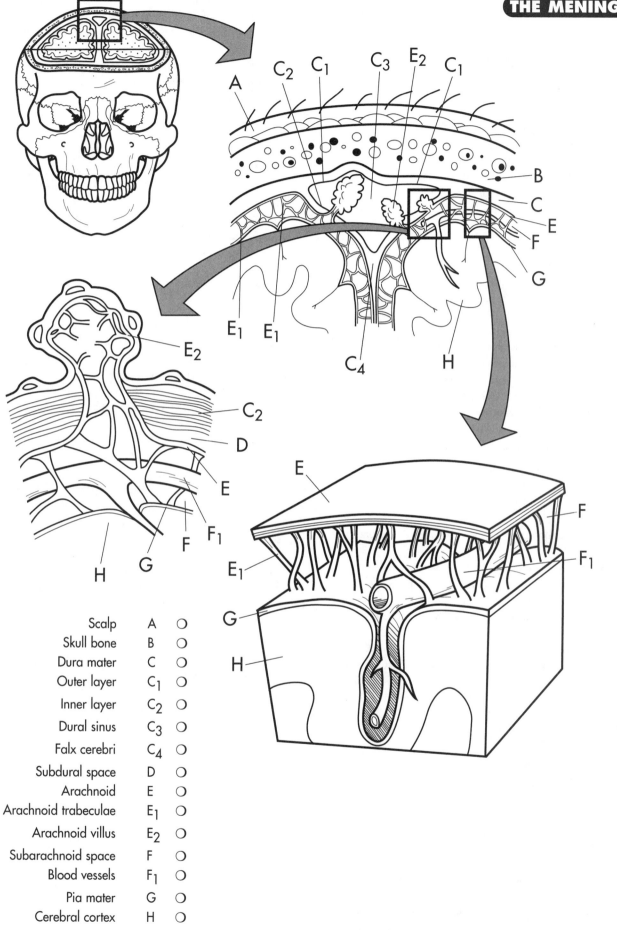

Scalp	A	○
Skull bone	B	○
Dura mater	C	○
Outer layer	C_1	○
Inner layer	C_2	○
Dural sinus	C_3	○
Falx cerebri	C_4	○
Subdural space	D	○
Arachnoid	E	○
Arachnoid trabeculae	E_1	○
Arachnoid villus	E_2	○
Subarachnoid space	F	○
Blood vessels	F_1	○
Pia mater	G	○
Cerebral cortex	H	○

VENTRICLES of the BRAIN

Protection and nourishment for the spinal cord and brain and the removal of metabolic waste products are the services provided by the cerebrospinal fluid (CSF). This fluid circulates continuously between the subarachnoid space, as discussed in the previous plate, and cavities within the brain and spinal cord. Within the brain, the cavities are called ventricles. They are the major topic of this plate.

Within this plate, we provide three views of the brain: a lateral view from the right side, an anterior view, and a frontal section. The purpose is to show the cavities of the brain from different angles so you can develop a perspective on their location. Because there is one large, continuous cavity you should color it using a pale or tan shade. Then, the arrows pointing to various portions of the main cavity should be colored. Begin by coloring the main title Ventricles of the Brain. Then watch for many overlapping areas that require lighter colors to preserve their detail.

The ventricles of the brain arise from expansion of the neural tube of the embryo. They are continuous with each other and with the central canal of the spinal cord. CSF fills the chambers, and as noted in this and in a previous plate, the chambers communicate with the subarachnoid space between the second and third meninges.

Within the **cerebrum (A)** are the two paired **lateral ventricles (B)**. The lateral view shows the right ventricle entirely, and it displays a shadow of the left ventricle. The anterior view shows both ventricles, and the frontal section shows how they flare to the lateral aspects. These ventricles were once termed the first and second ventricles, but they have been renamed the lateral ventricles.

The lateral ventricles lead to the **third ventricle (C)** found in the midline at the diencephalon. This ventricle is prominent in the lateral view, and its location is obvious in the front anterior view and frontal section.

The **fourth ventricle (D)** is located dorsal to the **pons (N)** and is seen best in the frontal section, where its width can be evaluated. Note that the fourth ventricle communicates with the **third ventricle (C)** and continues as the **central canal of the spinal cord (K)**. The arrow leading to the central canal may be colored in a dark color at this point.

The CSF contributes mechanical protection to the CNS as a shock-absorbing medium. It also establishes the correct chemical environment for nerve impulse passage, and it is the medium for exchange of gases, nutrients, and waste products.

The walls of the ventricles contain networks of capillaries called choroid plexuses. A **choroid plexus (E)** is indicated in the frontal section, and a spot of color may be used to point out its location. Capillaries of the plexus are covered by epeindymal cells, which formulate CSF from the plasma of the blood. The highly selective epeindymal cells allow only selected substances to pass into the CSF. Once formed, the CSF flows into the lateral ventricles, then passes through a pair of narrow openings called the **interventricular foramina (F)**. A spot of color is recommended here. The openings are also called the foramina of Monro.

We now consider the formation and flow of cerebrospinal fluid (CSF) through the brain and spinal cord. This flow will involve the ventricles and the connections between them as well as spaces between the arachnoid and pia mater. A brief review of the previous plate may be helpful in recalling the meninges. As you read below, color the appropriate titles, then locate and color the structures in any of the three views where they are found.

More CSF enters at the roof of the third ventricle, and the fluid then passes through the **cerebral aqueduct (G)**, also called the aqueduct of Silvius, to enter the fourth ventricle. A choroid plexus near the fourth ventricle contributes additional fluid, and the CSF enters the **subarachnoid space (J)** through three openings at the roof of the fourth ventricle. The openings are the **single median aperture (H)**, and the two **lateral apertures (I)**. Spots of dark color are recommended for these openings.

Once in the subarachnoid space, the CSF is free to enter the **central canal (K)** of the spinal cord. As noted, it also enters the subarachnoid space surrounding the brain and spinal cord and located between the second and third meninges. The fluid is absorbed back into the bloodstream through the arachnoid villi located in the **superior sagittal sinus (L)**. A spot of color is recommended to denote this area. Additional insights into the reabsorption process are presented in the previous plate.

Other areas of the brain are seen in this plate, and you may wish to review their names and locations. These include the **cerebellum (M)**, the **pons (N)**, and the **medulla oblongata (O)**. The **spinal cord (P)** continues with the medulla and is an extension of the brain.

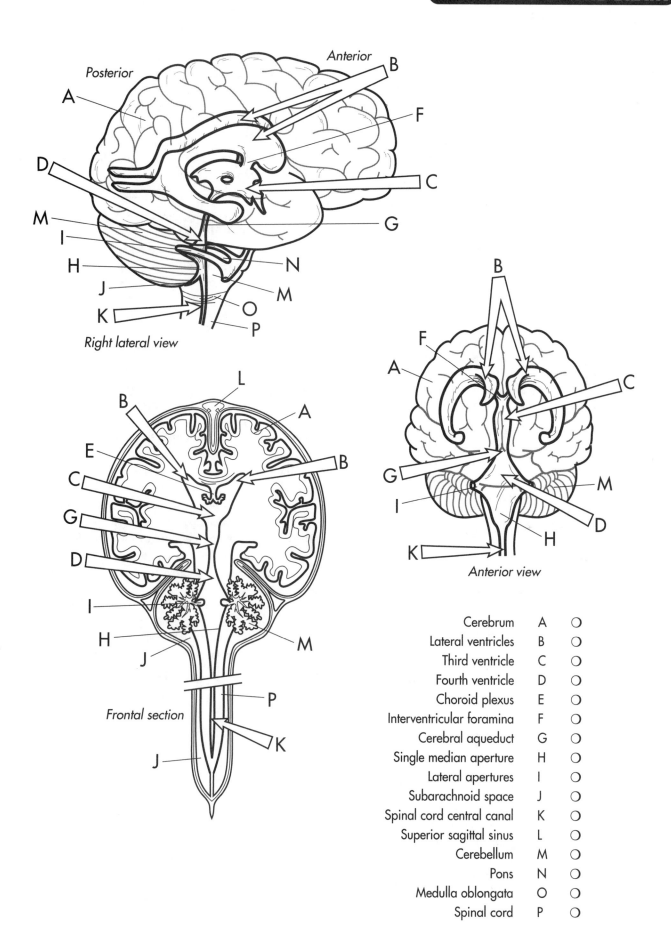

Posterior

Anterior

B

A

F

D

C

M

I

G

H

N

J

M

K

O

P

Right lateral view

B

F

A

C

G

I

M

D

K

H

Anterior view

L

B

A

E

B

C

G

D

I

H

M

J

P

Frontal section

J

K

Cerebrum	A	○
Lateral ventricles	B	○
Third ventricle	C	○
Fourth ventricle	D	○
Choroid plexus	E	○
Interventricular foramina	F	○
Cerebral aqueduct	G	○
Single median aperture	H	○
Lateral apertures	I	○
Subarachnoid space	J	○
Spinal cord central canal	K	○
Superior sagittal sinus	L	○
Cerebellum	M	○
Pons	N	○
Medulla oblongata	O	○
Spinal cord	P	○

the CEREBRUM

As the brain's largest region, the cerebrum processes sensory, somatic, and motor information and is responsible for conscious thought processes and intellectual functions. Two hemispheres make up the cerebrum, and the specific functional areas are distributed among lobes of the cerebrum.

This plate examines some of the anatomic features at the surface of the cerebrum and briefly reviews the tracts of white matter within the tissue. These tracts are found within the white matter of the brain, rather than in the gray matter, where the cell bodies of neurons are located. Additional details of the cerebrum are discussed in the plates to follow.

> Begin your work by coloring the main title The Cerebrum. Then note that the plate contains views of the cerebrum from above and from the lateral aspect. The cerebrum should be colored in four light colors according to the lobes visible. The main emphasis is on the folds and grooves at the surface, and these are pointed out by arrows, which can be colored in bold colors. We begin with a brief review of the gray and white matter.

At its surface, the cerebrum has a surface mantle composed of **gray matter (A)**. This may be seen in the sectional view of the cerebrum at the beginning of the plate. A dark color may be used to denote its presence. This part of the brain is the cerebral cortex, a layer of about 50 billion neurons.

Below the gray matter is a mass of **white matter (B)**, which may be colored in a light color to distinguish it from the gray matter. A series of ridges and grooves increases the surface area of the cerebral cortex many times. A **gyrus (C)** is indicated by the arrow as a fold of the cortex. A deep groove is a **fissure (D)**, also indicated by an arrow, and a shallow groove is a **sulcus (E)**.

> We now examine some of the major gyri, sulci, and fissures of the cerebrum. We also point out the visible lobes of the cerebrum. Bolder colors may be used for the arrows, and pale shades should be reserved for the lobes. You should refer to the superior view from above and from the lateral region in your work.

Several folds and grooves constitute anatomical landmarks of the cerebrum. The **precentral gyrus (C_1)** is the location of a primary motor area of the cerebral cortex. The **postcentral gyrus (C_2)** contains a somatic sensory area for the cerebral cortex.

An important fissure of the cerebrum is the longitudinal **fissure (D_1)**. The longitudinal fissure separates the right and left hemispheres. The hemispheres remain connected by a mass of white matter called the corpus callosum, which we discuss shortly. The second important fissure is the **transverse fissure (D_2)**,

seen in the lateral view. This deep groove separates the cerebellum from the cerebrum.

Three important sulci and the five lobes of the cerebrum are important landmarks of the cerebrum. The **central sulcus (E_1)** separates the **frontal lobe (F)** from the **parietal lobe (G)**. The **lateral cerebral sulcus (E_2)** is seen in the lateral view separating the **frontal lobe (F)** from the **temporal lobe (I)**. The **parieto-occipital sulcus (E_3)** separates the **parietal lobe (G)** from the **occipital lobe (H)**.

At this point, you have identified four of the five lobes of the cerebrum. The fifth lobe is the insula. It is not shown on the plate because it lies deep within the **lateral cerebral fissure (E_2)**.

> In the final portion of this plate, we examine the white matter fiber tracts located within the cerebrum. You should refer to the final two diagrams, and color the gray matter (A) in the same color used above. Variations of the color used for the white matter (B) should be used for the white matter tracts. As you read about the following tracts, color their titles, then locate and color them in the plate.

The thick layer of white matter below the cerebral cortex contains interconnecting groups of axons projecting in several directions. These axon groups are organized into fiber tracts extending in three directions and having three names. The lateral view shows the location of the **association fibers (B_1)**. These fiber tracts link one area of the cortex to another area within the same hemisphere. The second type of tracts are the **commisural fibers (B_2)**. These fibers project from one hemisphere to a corresponding area of the other area. An example is the corpus callosum seen in the frontal section extending from the left to right hemispheres.

The final types of fibers are **projection fibers (B_3)**. The projection fibers ascend and descend to and from the cerebral cortex to other parts of the brain such as the brain stem and spinal cord. The plate shows the corticospinal tract extending toward the spinal cord from the cortex. These fibers of myelinated axons provide the communication networks between the cell bodies of the brain's cortex and the cell bodies of the spinal cord. The peripheral nerves then carry the impulse to the muscles or glands.

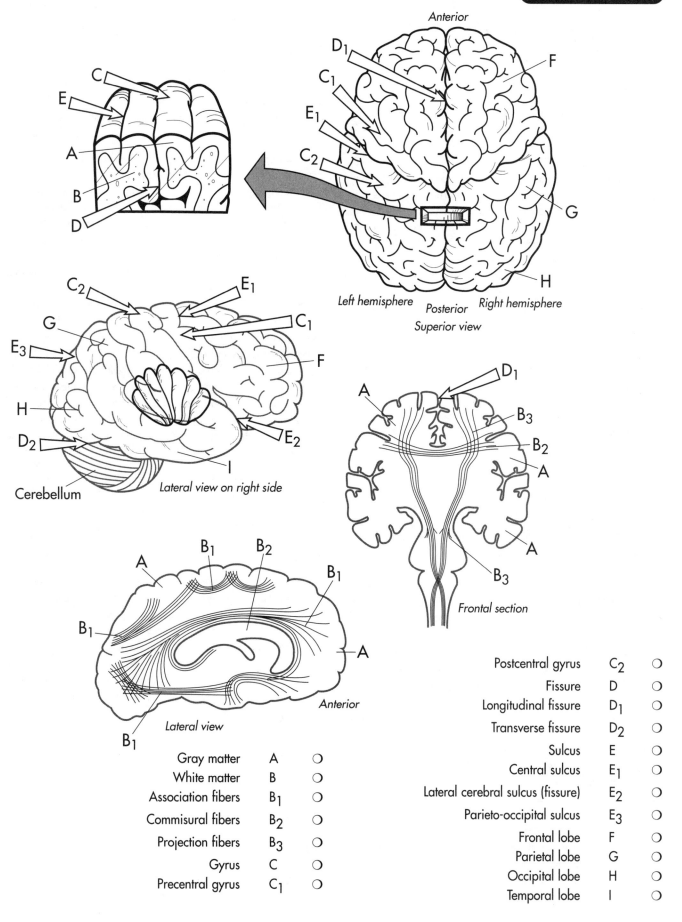

Anterior

D₁
C₁
E₁
C₂
F
G
H

Left hemisphere   Posterior   Right hemisphere

Superior view

C
E
A
B
D

C₂
E₁
G
C₁
E₃
F
H
D₂
E₂
I

Cerebellum   Lateral view on right side

A
D₁
B₃
B₂
A
A
B₃

Frontal section

A
B₁
B₂
B₁
B₁
A

Anterior

Lateral view
B₁

Gray matter	A	○
White matter	B	○
Association fibers	B₁	○
Commisural fibers	B₂	○
Projection fibers	B₃	○
Gyrus	C	○
Precentral gyrus	C₁	○

Postcentral gyrus	C₂	○
Fissure	D	○
Longitudinal fissure	D₁	○
Transverse fissure	D₂	○
Sulcus	E	○
Central sulcus	E₁	○
Lateral cerebral sulcus (fissure)	E₂	○
Parieto-occipital sulcus	E₃	○
Frontal lobe	F	○
Parietal lobe	G	○
Occipital lobe	H	○
Temporal lobe	I	○

the LIMBIC SYSTEM

The limbic system responds to sensory stimuli detected at the body surface. It is also associated with pain and pleasure, as well as many emotional aspects of behavior. The system is not a separate system, but a collection of structures from the cerebrum, diencephalon, and midbrain. It basically consists of a ring of cortex at the medial surface of each cerebral hemisphere surrounding the core of the cerebrum. Some anatomists consider the area a lobe of the cerebrum, but this view is not universally accepted, and we recognize five lobes of the cerebrum in this book, as the previous plate indicates.

The diagram in this plate explores the structures of the limbic system. You will note a variety of structures associated with other brain parts as the system is surveyed. The structures are generally located deep within the brain, and the plate shows the shadow of the "transparent" cerebrum.

> The plate shows the limbic system in an orientation view and in a close detailed view. The structures should be colored in both views as they are located in the terms list. Spots of color are recommended for many of the structures, since the latter tend to be small. You may color the cerebrum in a pale color, being careful to retain its finer details. You should begin by coloring the main title The Limbic System.

The limbic system works with the hypothalamus to receive and send nerve impulses from various portions of the body surface and from the internal environment. Pathways from the system project to the hypothalamus, and the hypothalamus exerts its influence through the autonomic system and endocrine system. Here, the regulation of homeostasis takes place through neurological as well as endocrine functions.

In structural terms, the limbic system consists of several structures, the first of which is **parahippocampal gyrus (A)**. This portion of the cerebrum is indicated with an arrow, which may be colored boldly. Another portion of the system is the limbic "lobe," the **singulate gyrus (B)**, which is also noted with an arrow. These gyri make up a portion of the ring of cortex of the system; however, they have specialized functions in the limbic system.

Part of the hippocampal gyrus extending into the cerebrum is the **hippocampus (C)**. Shaped somewhat like a seahorse, this structure lies at the floor of the lateral ventricle, which is an enlarged fluid-filled area within the cerebrum. The hippocampus is involved with memory of recent events. A third important gyrus is the **dentate gyrus (D)**. It is found between the hippocampus and the parahippocampal gyrus.

> We continue with the examination of the limbic system by noting several structures on both the orientation and detailed views. The hippocampus has previously appeared on the orientation view, and it and others are now presented. We have labeled the thalamus and corpus callosum for reference purposes. Since many of the structures blend with one another, a series of light complementary colors may be selected for this section.

The caudate nucleus is a series of cell bodies and one of the basal nuclei in the diencephalon discussed in the next plate. At its tail end is a collection of neuron groups called the **amygdala (E)**. This structure is alternately known as the amygdaloid nucleus and the amygdaloid body. It is also seen on the plate on the brain stem. Experiments by neurophysiologists indicate that the amygdala is associated with the limbic system.

Near the corpus callosum are the **septal nuclei (F)**, another portion of the limbic system. Still another structure is the **mammillary bodies (G)**, which are part of the hypothalamus and two round masses near the midline. They are also seen in the plate on the brain stem. Associated with both the thalamus and the limbic system is the **anterior nucleus (H)**.

The **olfactory bulb (I)** is associated with the sense of smell, which is part of the limbic system. This is because the smell of an object, such as a good meal cooking, often evokes a sense of pleasure. The olfactory lobe is a flat body located along the cribiform plate of the ethmoid bone. Experimental stimulation of the bulb initiates expressions associated with the system.

> We conclude with a brief examination of the nerve tracts and axons linking various components of the system. As you locate the terms in the reading below, color the appropriate portions of the diagram.

Various components of the limbic system are connected by nerve tracts containing myelinated axons. Among these are the **fornix (J)**, seen in both the overview and complete and detailed diagram. Other tracts are the **stria terminalis (K)**, the **stria medullaris (L)**, and the **mammilothalamic tract (M)**. With these tracts, the structures of the limbic system are involved in visceral and behavioral responses associated with memory and emotion. The system constitutes the affective portion of the brain.

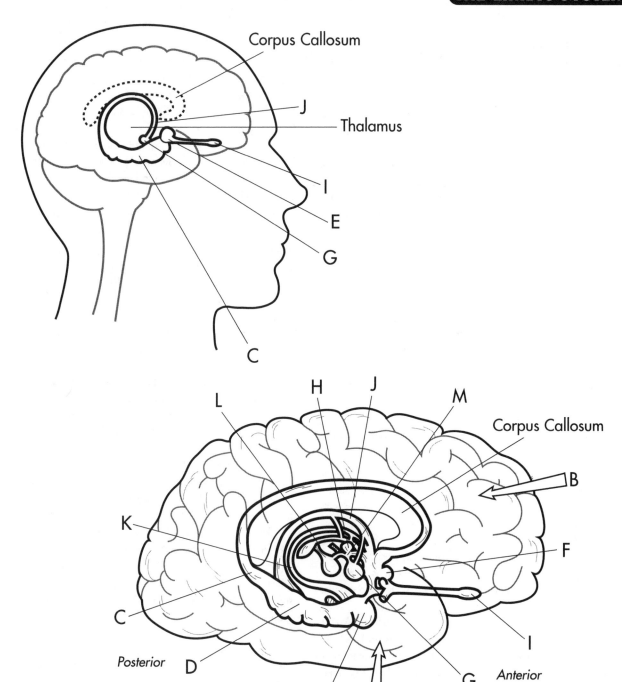

Corpus Callosum

J

Thalamus

I

E

G

C

L   H   J   M

Corpus Callosum

B

K

F

C

I

Posterior   D

E   A

G   Anterior

Parahippocampal gyrus	A	○	Anterior nucleus	H	○
Singulate gyrus	B	○	Olfactory bulb	I	○
Hippocampus	C	○	Fornix	J	○
Dentate gyrus	D	○	Stria terminalis	K	○
Amygdala	E	○	Stria medullaris	L	○
Septal nuclei	F	○	Mammilothalamic tract	M	○
Mammillary bodies	G	○			

the DIENCEPHALON

The diencephalon is the region of the brain surrounding the third ventricle and adjacent to the midbrain. It consists of the epithalamus, which forms the roof of the third ventricle, and it includes the pineal gland at the midline as well as the thalamus and hypothalamus. The thalamus has two lobes, which form the superior portion of the lateral walls of the third ventricle. The inferior portion of the walls are formed by the paired right and left hypothalamus.

Looking over the plate, note that it features the two largest regions of the diencephalon: the thalamus and hypothalamus. Both of these regions are delineated in overall views of the brain, then presented in detail to indicate their important parts. You may use bold colors such as reds, greens, blues, and purples, because the structures are fairly large in the "exploded" views. A pale color may be used to indicate the region under discussion in the view of the brain. Begin your work by coloring the main title The Diencephalon.

Regions of the diencephalon function as relay centers integrating sensory and motor pathways. The roof of the diencephalon, the epithalamus, has an extensive choroid plexus discussed in the meninges plate. The pineal gland, discussed with the endocrine system, is located here.

Much of the neural tissue of the diencephalon is found in the **thalamus (A)**. A light color may be used. This region contains paired oval masses of gray matter, one of which is shown in detail. The oval mass contains tracts of white matter and masses of gray matter organized into nuclei.

One nucleus of the thalamus is the **anterior nucleus (A_1)**. A bold color may be used to color this structure. This nucleus is in the floor of the lateral ventricle and is concerned with emotions, memory, and the limbic system. The **medial nucleus (A_2)** integrates sensory information and projects it to the frontal lobes of the cerebrum.

There are three ventral nuclei within the thalamus. The **ventral anterior nucleus (A_3)** and the **ventral lateral nucleus (A_4)** participate in the somatic motor system. The **ventral posterior nucleus (A_5)** relays sensory information of taste, touch, pressures, heat, cold, and pain.

At the posterior portion of the thalamus is the **pulvinar nucleus (A_6)**. Its cell bodies integrate sensory information and project impulses to the association portions of the cerebrum. Nearby is the **lateral geniculate body (A_7)**. This is an important visual relay center. The **medial geniculate body (A_8)** is an auditory relay center.

Cell bodies within the thalamic nuclei and bodies sort out information and process it before distributing it to other parts of the brain. They also have some function in emotion and a crude recognition of sensation.

We now concentrate on the second portion of the plate, the hypothalamus. As before, we show the area in a cross section of the brain, then we present a detailed "exploded" view. As you read about the structures, color them in the diagram after locating their titles. We are presenting a schematic to give a sense of the variety of roles played by the hypothalamus and the locations of the cell bodies involved.

Inferior to the thalamus in the diencephalon is the **hypothalamus (B)**. A light color should be used to outline this area of the brain. The hypothalamus contains over 10 nuclei organized into different regions extending from the optic chiasma where the optic nerves cross to the posterior region of the mammillary bodies at the midbrain. The hypothalamus is connected to the **pituitary gland (D)** by the **infundibulum (C)**. Hormones from the hypothalamus are stored in the posterior portion of the pituitary gland before release.

The hypothalamus contains several functionally important nuclei. The first is the **supraoptic nucleus (B_1)** lying near the optic chiasma. It secretes antidiuretic hormone, which is stored in the posterior pituitary gland and released to control water reabsorption in the tubules.

The **paraventricular nucleus (B_2)** is located near the third ventricle as the plate indicates. This nucleus secretes oxytocin, which is stored in the posterior portion and causes contraction of the smooth muscle of the uterus.

The third nucleus is the **preoptic nucleus (B_3)**. This nucleus regulates certain autonomic activities such as body temperature. Another nucleus of the hypothalamus is the **tubural region (B_4)**, which includes several nuclei. Hormones are synthesized here for regulating the secretions from the anterior lobe of the pituitary gland.

Areas of the hypothalamus control the activity of the autonomic nervous system (ANS). One such area is the **sympathetic region (B_5)**. Nerves from this area regulate the sympathetic division of the ANS, which stimulates the visceral organs to a higher state of activity. The **parasympathetic region (B_6)** regulates the parasympathetic division of the ANS and reduces the activity of the visceral organs.

Close to the midbrain is the **mammillary region (B_7)** of the hypothalamus. This area includes the mammillary bodies, which relay impulses concerned with the sense of smell.

The final region to be considered is the **emotional center (B_8)**. This region acts with the limbic system to regulate feelings of aggression, pleasure, pain, and the behavior patterns associated with sexual arousal.

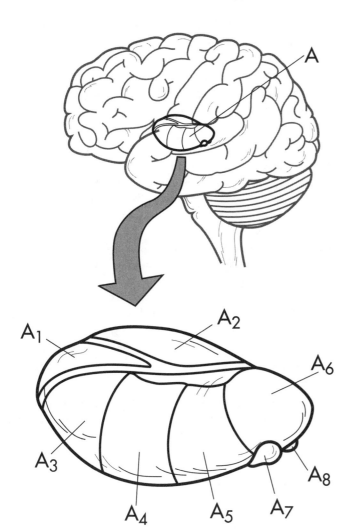

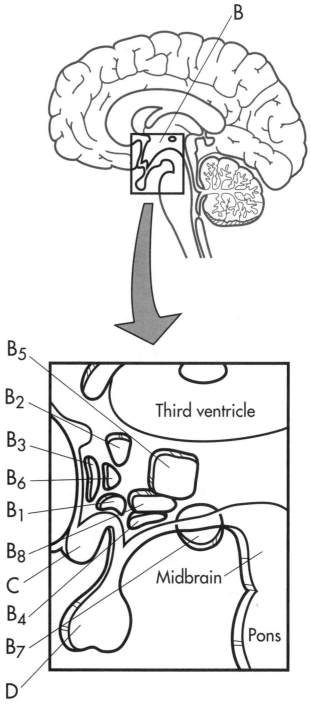

Thalamus	A	○
Anterior nucleus	A₁	○
Medial nucleus	A₂	○
Ventral anterior nucleus	A₃	○
Ventral lateral nucleus	A₄	○
Ventral posterior nucleus	A₅	○
Pulvinar nucleus	A₆	○

Lateral geniculate body	A₇	○
Medial geniculate body	A₈	○
Hypothalamus	B	○
Supraoptic nucleus	B₁	○
Paraventricular nucleus	B₂	○
Preoptic nucleus	B₃	○
Tubural region	B₄	○
Sympathetic region	B₅	○
Parasympathetic region	B₆	○
Mammillary region	B₇	○
Emotional center	B₈	○
Infundibulum	C	○
Pituitary gland	D	○

123

the CEREBELLUM

The cerebellum is shaped somewhat like a cauliflower and is dorsal to the pons and medulla as it protrudes onto the occipital lobes of the cerebral hemispheres. It is separated from these hemispheres by the transverse fissure seen in the cerebrum plate. The cerebellum is supported by the posterior cranial fossa of the skull.

This plate details some of the anatomical features of the cerebellum and indicates some of its functional significances. Most of the structures are relatively large, and bold colors may be used.

> This plate contains two views of the cerebellum. The first is a superior view, as indicated by the orientation diagram. The second is a sagittal section through the cerebral hemisphere, also noted by the orientation view. Begin the plate by coloring the main title The Cerebellum, then read about this region of the brain below. Reds, blues, oranges, and other bold colors may be used, since many of the details are relatively large. When you encounter an arrow, try to use a bold color.

The cerebellum lies apart from the brain stem, which is discussed in the next plate. The cerebellum has a highly convoluted surface composed of neural tissue. As the first diagram indicates, it is composed of a **left cerebellar hemisphere (A_1)** and a **right cerebellar hemisphere (A_2)**. Light colors are recommended here, since the lobes will be pointed out shortly. The two cerebellar hemispheres are connected by a narrow band of tissue called the **vermis (A_3)**.

As the diagram shows, the cerebellum has a complex surface with fine, parallel gyri. In the cerebellum, the gyri are called **folia (A_4)**. The arrows point to the folia, and they may be colored in a purple, orange, or other dark color.

Three lobes make up the cerebellum. The superior view shows the **anterior lobe (A_5)** on both the left and right sides. The **posterior lobe (A_6)** is separated from the anterior lobe by the **primary fissure (A_8)**. Two different colors should be used for the anterior and posterior lobes, and the corresponding areas should be located in the sagittal section. The arrow pointing to the primary fissure should be colored, and the fissure itself may be pointed out by tracing its path with a line of color as it passes across the left and right hemispheres.

The third lobe is the **flocculonodular lobe (A_7)**. This lobe is shaped somewhat like a propeller. It is found below the vermis and posterior lobe and cannot be seen in the surface view. However, it is visible in the sagittal section.

> We now turn to some of the internal structures of the cerebellum and indicate some of the functions it performs. As you read about the structures of the cerebellum, color their titles and location on the diagram. We refer to the sagittal section here.

Deep within the cerebellum are the **cerebellar nuclei (B)**. Cell bodies within these nuclei mediate most of the impulses put out by the cerebellum. Specialized nerve cells called Purkinje cells are found in the **cortex of the cerebellum (C)**. These cells have numerous dendrites throughout the cortex and axons that project toward the cerebellar nuclei. The axons pass through a branching mass of white matter that resembles a tree in the sagittal view. It is, therefore, called the **arbor vitae (D)**, which means "tree of life." After receiving impulses from the spinal cord, the impulses pass through the cortex and arbor vitae and come together at the cerebellar nuclei. Axons then extend from the cerebellar nuclei back to the cortex where the Purkinje cells process them further. Tracks from the Purkinje cells relay motor impulses to nuclei within the brain stem and cerebrum.

> We now examine the connections of the cerebellum to other portions of the brain. Many of these portions are discussed in the next plate on the brain stem. Color the titles below, and indicate the presence of the structures on the sagittal diagram.

The cerebellum is linked by means of nerve tracts to various other portions of the brain. The **superior cerebellar peduncles (E_1)** pass between the cerebellum and nuclei in the diencephalon and cerebrum. The **middle cerebellar peduncles (E_2)** are tracts connecting the pons to the axis of the brain stem and connecting the cerebellum to this area. These peduncles also connect with sensory and motor nuclei in the pons. Finally, the **inferior cerebellar peduncles (E_3)** link the cerebellum with nuclei in the medulla oblongata and carry tracts from the spinal cord to and from the cerebellum. These nerve tracts help the cerebellum adjust the postural muscles of the body and coordinate voluntary and involuntary movements.

As the diagram shows, the cerebellum lies close to the **pons (F)** and the **medulla (G)**. Immediately anterior to it is the **choroid plexus (H)** of the **fourth ventricle (I)**. Much of the fluid supply in the central canal originates in the blood supply of the cerebellum.

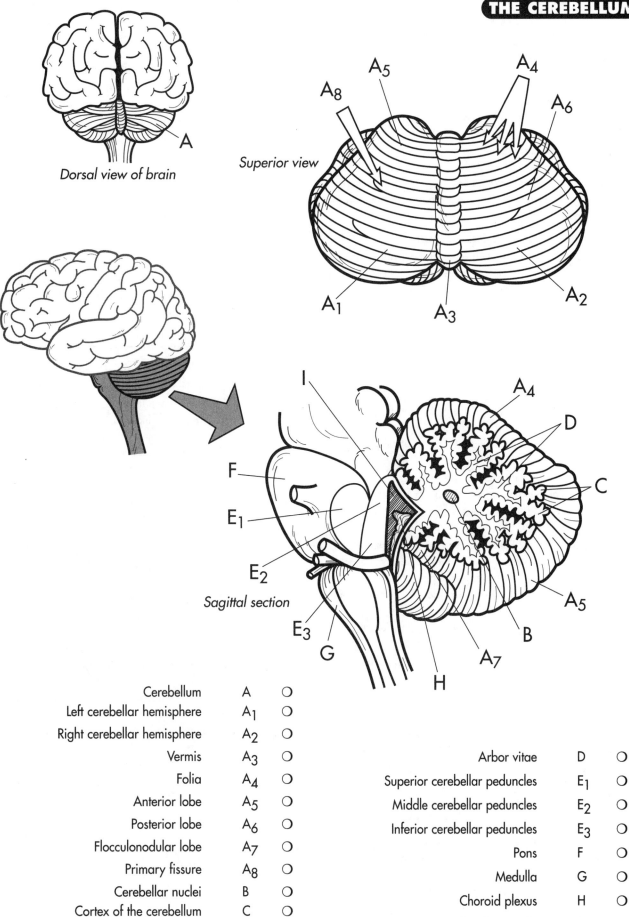

Dorsal view of brain

Superior view

Sagittal section

Cerebellum	A	○
Left cerebellar hemisphere	A_1	○
Right cerebellar hemisphere	A_2	○
Vermis	A_3	○
Folia	A_4	○
Anterior lobe	A_5	○
Posterior lobe	A_6	○
Flocculonodular lobe	A_7	○
Primary fissure	A_8	○
Cerebellar nuclei	B	○
Cortex of the cerebellum	C	○

Arbor vitae	D	○
Superior cerebellar peduncles	E_1	○
Middle cerebellar peduncles	E_2	○
Inferior cerebellar peduncles	E_3	○
Pons	F	○
Medulla	G	○
Choroid plexus	H	○
Fourth ventricle	I	○

the BRAIN STEM

The brain stem lies between the cerebrum and spinal cord. It serves as a passageway for fiber tracts extending between the lower and higher neural centers. In addition, the brain stem contains cell masses called nuclei. Many of the cranial nerves have their nuclei within the brain stem, as the next plate indicates.

This plate examines some of the visible landmarks of the brain stem. The three major regions are described. Each is approximately one inch in length. The regions are the midbrain, pons, and medulla oblongata.

Note that the plate shows two views of the brain stem: An anterolateral view and a posteriolateral view. As you read about the three regions of the brain stem in the following paragraphs, find their locations and structures on the main diagrams and color them in. Light colors would be best, since the regions tend to be detailed.

The first region of the brain stem considered is the midbrain. This area is located between the diencephalon and the pons. The **midbrain (A)** is outlined in a bracket, which may be colored in a bold color. It has two vertical pillars called **cerebral peduncles (A$_1$)** on which the cerebrum appears to rest. The corticospinal tracts pass through these pillars. The midbrain also contains the **superior cerebellar peduncles (A$_2$)**. These are fiber tracts seen best in the posteriolateral view. They connect the midbrain to the cerebellum.

The midbrain is the site of the **corpora quadrigemina (B)**. These are nuclei found within the white matter. Color the bracket that indicates their location. The superior pair of nuclei are the **superior colliculi (B$_1$)**, which function in vision. The **inferior colliculi (B$_2$)** function in hearing.

As the plate shows, there are many **cranial nerves (C)** that arise from the brain stem. Ten pairs of nerves arise here. A single dark color may be used to indicate their position in the brain stem.

The next midbrain structure is the pons. This portion of the brain stem is found between the midbrain and medulla oblongata. It forms part of the fourth ventricle and is discussed below. Then we discuss the medulla. Continue your coloring as before, being sure to color the titles as you proceed.

The **pons (D)** consists primarily of nerve tracts. Color the bracket and structure in the same color. It is a bulging region whose projection fibers run longitudinally and connect the brain centers with the spinal cord. An anatomical feature of the pons is the **middle cerebellar peduncles (D$_1$)**. Transverse fibers in this region connect the cerebellum and pons.

The third region of the brain stem is the **medulla oblongata (E)**. The medulla is the continuation point of the brain with the spinal cord. Its central canal connects to the fourth ventricle and central canal of the spinal cord.

Located on the medulla are two longitudinal bulges called **pyramids (E$_1$)**. Corticospinal tracts are found here. At a point called the **decussation (E$_2$)**, the fibers cross over to opposite sides of the nervous system. For this reason, the cerebral hemisphere on one side of the brain controls movements on the opposite side of the body.

The medulla also contains the **inferior cerebellar peduncles (E$_3$)**, where the medulla connects to the cerebellum. Lateral to the pyramids and seen in both views are the **olives (E$_4$)**. These oval swellings contain nuclei related to sensory input from the muscles for conveyance to the cerebellum.

The plate ends with a brief examination of some of the other visible structures. Although not part of the brain stem itself, these structures serve essential neurologic functions.

Part of the cerebellum is a cluster of nerve cell bodies called the basal nuclei, also known as basal ganglia. (A nucleus is a collection of nerve cell bodies within the central nervous system.) The main mass of the basal nuclei is the **caudate nucleus (F)**, which appears in the shape of a comma. The caudate nucleus arches over the diencephalon which contains the **thalamus (J)**, as the diagram indicates. With the other basal ganglia, the caudate nucleus receives input from the cerebral cortex and other structures of the diencephalon for relay to the spinal cord and provides output to the cerebral cortex. Automatic skeletal movements appear to be controlled by the basal nuclei.

Another basal nucleus is the **lentiform nucleus (G)**. This structure has the shape of a lens, as the plate indicates. Its functions are similar to those of the caudate nucleus. The final structure of the basal nuclei is the **amygdala (H)**. Lying at the tail of the caudate nucleus, this structure belongs functionally with the limbic system.

To complete the work on this plate, we note several other visible structures. At the upper limit of the brain stem are found a number of projection fibers called the **corona radiata (I)**. These are nerve fiber tracts. The **thalamus (J)** has been noted as part of the diencephalon. The **pineal gland (K)** is also located in this brain region. The anterolateral view shows the **mammary body (L)**, which functions as a relay station for olfactory impulses. Nearby is the **infundibulum (M)**, which is the stalk from which the pituitary gland hangs.

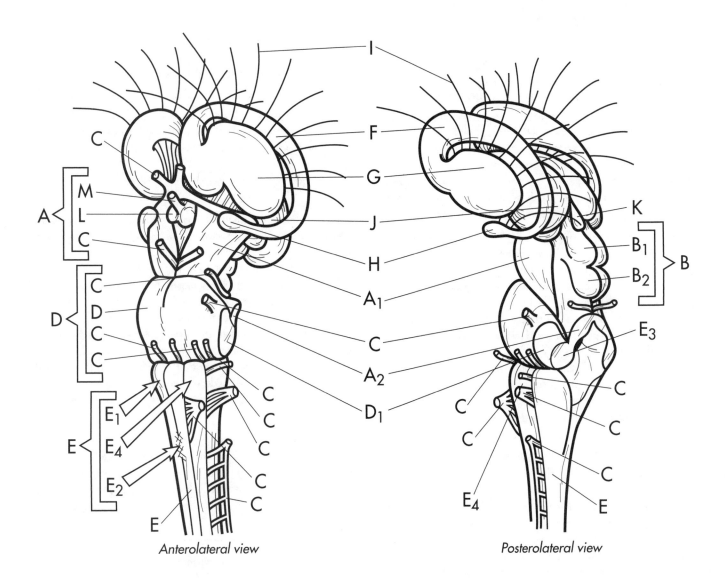

Anterolateral view

Posterolateral view

Midbrain A ○
Cerebral peduncles A_1 ○
Superior cerebellar peduncles A_2 ○
Corpora quadrigemina B ○
Superior colliculi B_1 ○
Inferior colliculi B_2 ○
Cranial nerves C ○
Pons D ○
Middle cerebellar peduncles D_1 ○
Medulla oblongata E ○
Pyramids E_1 ○

Decussation E_2 ○
Inferior cerebellar peduncles E_3 ○
Olives E_4 ○
Caudate nucleus F ○
Lentiform nucleus G ○
Amygdala H ○
Corona radiata I ○
Thalamus J ○
Pineal gland K ○
Mammary body L ○
Infundibulum M ○

the CRANIAL NERVES

Together with the 31 pairs of spinal nerves, the 12 pairs of cranial nerves make up the peripheral nervous system. Two pairs of cranial nerves originate at the cerebrum and 10 pairs originate at the brain stem. All the nerves pass through the skull foramina to their destinations or from the organs they service. Both names and Roman numerals are used to designate the cranial nerves, with the Roman numerals used to designate the nerves that arise from the brain beginning at the anterior and proceeding to the posterior. Distribution or function of the nerve is indicated by its name.

Looking over the plate, you will note that we only show one nerve of the pair in order to simplify the diagram. In some cases the nerve is coming from the left side of the brain, while in others it originates from the right side. However, you should realize that each nerve is accompanied by its partner nerve. To complete this plate, use a bold color to color the nerve itself. The brain may be colored in a light color, but be careful to avoid obscuring the sources of the nerves. Light colors may also be used for the destination of the nerves in the body tissues, and you may label these tissues as you recognize them. Begin by coloring the main title The Cranial Nerves.

Some of the cranial nerves contain only sensory fibers and carry impulses toward the brain. Other cranial nerves are mixed nerves because they contain both sensory and motor fibers. The nuclei within the brain contain the cell bodies of motor neurons, while the cell bodies of sensory neurons are located outside the brain.

The first cranial nerve is cranial nerve I, the **olfactory nerve (A)**. This sensory nerve originates in the mucous membrane of the nose, as the plate shows, and terminates at the olfactory bulb of the cerebrum.

Cranial nerve II is the **optic nerve (B)**. This sensory nerve conveys impulses that result in vision and originates at the retina of the eye. It terminates in the lateral geniculate body of the thalamus and the superior colliculus of the midbrain. It and the olfactory nerve are the two cranial nerves of the cerebrum.

Cranial nerve III is the **oculomotor nerve (C)**. As the plate indicates, this nerve originates at the midbrain and is distributed to the extrinsic muscles of the eyeball, where it controls movement of the eyeball and focusing of the lens. It is a motor nerve.

Cranial nerve IV is the **trochlear nerve (D)**. This motor nerve originates at the midbrain and, like the previous nerve, innervates muscles of the eye to control eye movements.

We have begun the discussion of the cranial nerves with surveys of the first four nerves. We now continue with the next few nerves, indicating their origin, distribution, and function. Continue your coloring as before, and select bold colors to color over the nerves. Next, we consider a complex nerve.

Cranial nerve V is the **trigeminal nerve (E)**. The nerve is both sensory and mixed. It originates at the pons and is distributed to areas of the forehead, maxillary region, and mandibular region. Different colors may be used for these regions to indicate their distributions.

Cranial nerve VI is the **abducens nerve (F)**, seen on the right side of the plate. This nerve carries impulses from the pons to the lateral rectus muscle of the eye and effects lateral movement of the eye.

We now move to the left side of the plate and examine other cranial nerves servicing areas of the face. Continue your coloring as before and locate the nerves as you read about them.

The **facial nerve (G)** is cranial nerve VII. This nerve has both sensory and motor functions. It originates at the pons and is distributed to the tastebuds and muscles that control facial expression. It also has a role in the control of salivation.

The next nerve is cranial nerve VIII, the **vestibulocochlear nerve (H)**. This is a sensory nerve originating at the medulla and having distribution at the cochlea of the inner ear. This is the snail-like structure. It also carries impulses from the semicircular canals shown as projections from the cochlea. The nerve is also known as the auditory nerve and functions in hearing and maintaining equilibrium.

The **glossopharyngeal nerve (I)** is cranial nerve IX. A mixed nerve, it arises from the medulla and is distributed to the tongue, pharynx, and parotid gland. Taste sensations and saliva secretions are associated with it.

We conclude with three cranial nerves originating in the medulla and being of the mixed or motor variety. These nerves innervate areas of the lower jaw, neck, and viscera. Continue your reading, and continue your coloring pattern.

Cranial nerve X is the **vagus nerve (J)**. This mixed nerve arises at the medulla and is distributed to numerous organs as the plate shows. It carries sensations from and to the soft palate, heart muscle, stomach, kidney, and intestine. The nerve is associated with blood pressure, numerous visceral activities, and swallowing.

Cranial nerve XI is the **spinal accessory (K)**. Arising at the medulla, this motor nerve is distributed through muscles of the larynx, neck, and shoulder. It functions in movement of the shoulders, head, and in the production of sound.

The final cranial nerve, XII, is the **hypoglossal nerve (L)**. The last nerve to emerge from the brain, it arises at the medulla. It is a motor nerve distributed through muscles of the tongue, where it plays a role in speech, swallowing, and other movements of the tongue.

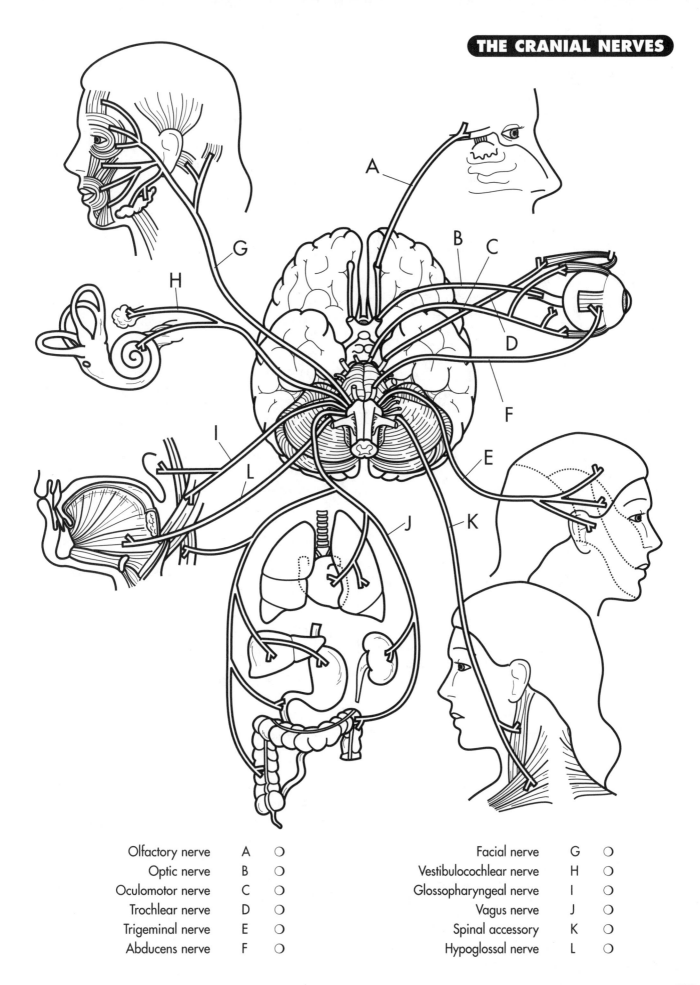

Olfactory nerve	A	○		Facial nerve	G	○
Optic nerve	B	○		Vestibulocochlear nerve	H	○
Oculomotor nerve	C	○		Glossopharyngeal nerve	I	○
Trochlear nerve	D	○		Vagus nerve	J	○
Trigeminal nerve	E	○		Spinal accessory	K	○
Abducens nerve	F	○		Hypoglossal nerve	L	○

the AUTONOMIC NERVOUS SYSTEM (SYMPATHETIC)

The nervous system has two principal divisions: the central nervous system (CNS) consisting of the brain and spinal cord, and the peripheral nervous system (PNS) composed of the peripheral and cranial spinal nerves. The PNS is further divided into a somatic nervous system (SNS), which conveys impulses to and from cutaneous and special senses (especially in the head) and the brain, and the autonomic nervous system (ANS), which conveys impulses to and from the visceral organs. The responses to the SNS are under voluntary control, while those to the ANS are involuntary.

The motor portion of the ANS consists of two branches, the sympathetic division and the parasympathetic division. Visceral organs receive impulses from the CNS via both divisions. Usually the two divisions have opposing actions. For instance, neurons in the sympathetic division increase the heart rate, while neurons from the parasympathetic division slow it down. This plate features the anatomy of the sympathetic division.

> At first glance, the plate may appear somewhat complex because many organs are represented. However, close inspection shows that it consists of the CNS (brain and spinal cord) connected to several organs by a system of nerves constituting the sympathetic division of the ANS. As you read about this division, color the appropriate titles and the structures. In this plate, we have not listed the organs in the titles list, but you may color them as you identify them.

The basic function of the sympathetic division is to regulate visceral functions not usually subject to our conscious control. The system begins at the **spinal cord (a)**, which may be colored a single light color. Arising from the spinal cord is a set of **preganglionic nerve fibers (A)** seen on both the right and left sides of the spinal cord. These fibers arise from the thoracic and spinal nerves (the cranial and sacral nerves supply the parasympathetic division in the next plate).

Axons in the preganglionic fibers move to a set of autonomic ganglia lying along both sides of the spinal cord like a chain of beads. These ganglia are called **sympathetic (vertebral) ganglia (B)**. A single color should be used for both ganglionic chains. The cell bodies of preganglionic neurons are in the spinal cord, and their axons end at the sympathetic ganglia. Here they

synapse with another set of neurons in the **postganglionic nerve fibers (C).** The postganglionic neurons have their cell bodies in the sympathetic ganglia. Their axons then extend out to the organs shown on the right.

> We have now discussed the basic makeup of the sympathetic division including the preganglionic nerve fibers, sympathetic ganglia, and postganglionic nerve fibers. We now continue the discussion with more details of the system.

When a preganglionic nerve fiber arrives at a sympathetic ganglion, it may follow any of three patterns. In some cases, the axons run up or down the chain of ganglia before emerging toward the organs. For example, axons may arise from the thoracic region, then emerge at the cervical ganglia. The **superior cervical (B_1)**, the **middle cervical (B_2)**, and the **inferior cervical (B_3)** ganglia are points where postganglionic fibers emerge. The diagram shows the fibers moving out to the eye, heart, and lungs.

In some cases, a preganglionic fiber passes through the sympathetic ganglia without synapsing. Instead, it extends out to a **collateral (prevertebral) ganglion (D)**, which is out in the tissues. One such collateral ganglion is the **celiac ganglion (D_1)** near the celiac artery. Here a synapse with the postganglionic nerve fiber takes place. Another possibility is the **superior mesenteric ganglion (D_2)**, and a third is the **inferior mesenteric ganglion (D_3)**. Light colors should be used to highlight these ganglia.

Preganglionic fibers passing through the sympathetic ganglia without terminating are called **splanchnic nerves (C_1)**. An arrow points to an example of these. Splanchnic nerves extend to the celiac and other collateral ganglia. The greater splanchnic nerve passes to the celiac ganglion, and the lesser splanchnic nerve passes to the superior mesenteric.

> Many nerve fibers form networks similar to those formed by the arteries and veins. Some of these networks are mentioned in the next paragraph, and a brief view is given of a less complex part of the system. Continue your coloring in the plate.

After passing through the sympathetic ganglia, nerve fibers may pass directly to their target organs, or they may enter a network called a plexus for redistribution. Four of these plexuses are seen in the plate, including the **cardiopulmonary plexus (E_1)**, the **celiac plexus (E_2)**, the **superior mesenteric plexus (E_3)**, and the **inferior mesenteric plexus (E_4)**. Light colors may be used to highlight these networks.

As noted above, many nerve fibers pass through the sympathetic ganglia, then move to terminate directly at the effector organ. In the example shown, nerve fibers are arriving at the skin to bring about a sympathetic response, such as fright, to a situation. The nerve fibers innervate the blood vessels of the **skin (F_1)** to make the skin pale, and the **arrector pili muscles (F_2)** receive impulses to pull the hairs upright. These are typical responses mediated by the sympathetic division.

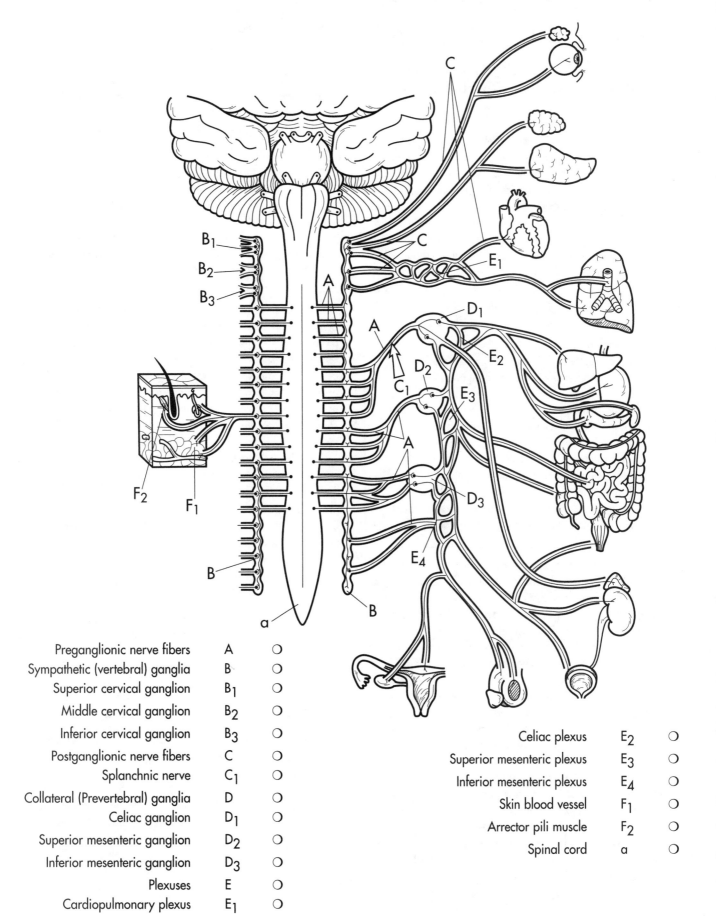

Preganglionic nerve fibers	A	○		
Sympathetic (vertebral) ganglia	B	○		
Superior cervical ganglion	B_1	○		
Middle cervical ganglion	B_2	○		
Inferior cervical ganglion	B_3	○		
Postganglionic nerve fibers	C	○		
Splanchnic nerve	C_1	○		
Collateral (Prevertebral) ganglia	D	○		
Celiac ganglion	D_1	○		
Superior mesenteric ganglion	D_2	○	Celiac plexus	E_2	○
Inferior mesenteric ganglion	D_3	○	Superior mesenteric plexus	E_3	○
Plexuses	E	○	Inferior mesenteric plexus	E_4	○
Cardiopulmonary plexus	E_1	○	Skin blood vessel	F_1	○
			Arrector pili muscle	F_2	○
			Spinal cord	a	○

the AUTONOMIC NERVOUS SYSTEM (PARASYMPATHETIC)

The peripheral nervous system (PNS) contains somatic and autonomic divisions. The somatic nervous system (SNS) receives impulses and delivers them to the body surface, while the autonomic nervous system (ANS) services the visceral organs. There are two divisions of the ANS: the sympathetic division, which is discussed in the previous plate, and the parasympathetic division, discussed in this plate. Visceral organs generally receive impulses from both divisions, but while the sympathetic division increases the activity of visceral organs, the parasympathetic neurons slow them down. Both the sympathetic and parasympathetic divisions generally operate without conscious control.

As you look over the plate, note that it shows the central nervous system of the spinal cord together with a system of nerves extending to the right and moving out to various organs of the body. A similar system occurs on the opposite side of the body. As you read about the parasympathetic division in the following paragraphs, you may color the appropriate nerves and structures. Be sure to contrast this division with the sympathetic division in the previous plate, and note the differences in the anatomical construction. We have not labeled the organs in this plate, but you should recognize them, and you may color them in using appropriate colors.

Both the sympathetic and parasympathetic divisions of the ANS arise from the **spinal cord (a)**. A single light color may be used here. The parasympathetic division is composed of fibers emerging from the brain stem and sacral portion of the spinal cord. The sympathetic division has thoracic and lumbar origins. Like the sympathetic division, there is a preganglionic nerve fiber, a ganglion, and a postganglionic nerve fiber. In the parasympathetic division, however, the preganglionic nerve fibers are extremely long, and the terminal ganglia are small collections of cells close to or in the organs innervated. The postganglionic fibers are equally short and within the organs. For that reason, the terminal ganglia and postganglionic fibers are not seen in this plate, with some exceptions.

We begin with the cranial portion of the parasympathetic division, and note that four cranial nerves supply the preganglionic nerve fibers. Fibers from the cranial nerves are shown on the right side. The root of the fiber is shown on the left side of the plate. The four nerves involved are the third cranial nerve, the **oculomotor (A_1)**, the seventh cranial nerve, the **facial (A_2)**, the **glossopharyngeal (A_3)**, and the **vagus nerve (A_4)**.

As the diagram shows, the first three nerves extend to termi-

nal ganglia (B) near the organs innervated. The **ciliary ganglion (B_1)** lies near the orbit of the eye. A **postganglionic nerve fiber (E)** extends to the smooth muscles of the eyeball. The **pterygopalatine ganglion (B_2)** is near a foramen in the skull. It receives a preganglionic nerve fiber from the facial nerve and sends a postganglionic nerve fiber to the lacrimal glands to control tearing.

The third ganglion is the **submandibular ganglion (B_3)**, located near the duct from the submandibular salivary gland. Finally, the **otic ganglion (B_4)** is found near the foramen ovale. Its postganglionic fiber extends to the parotid salivary gland, as shown.

We now concentrate on the outflow from the vagus nerve as it participates in the parasympathetic division. Here we note several plexuses. Continue as before, but plan to use light colors to indicate the plexuses. The organs may also be colored as you proceed, and they may be identified from the reading as well as from your knowledge from other plates.

Impulses carried over the vagus nerve extend through the preganglionic fibers to numerous portions of the viscera. As the plate indicates, there are many interlaced networks involved before the nerves reach the terminal ganglia in the visceral organs. These networks are called **autonomic plexuses (C)**. For example, the vagus nerve extends to the **cardiopulmonary plexus (C_1)**, which may be colored in a light color. The fibers then continue to the heart and lungs as shown and reduce their activity at the end of the flight-fright phenomenon.

Another important plexus is the **celiac plexus (C_2)**. This is also called the solar plexus. It is the largest mass of nerve cells outside the CNS. Lying outside the aorta, it is the network from which preganglionic fibers pass to the liver, stomach, pancreas, gallbladder, and other abdominal organs. A connection is also made to the **hypogastric plexus (C_3)**. Here, a branching network extends out to the terminal ganglia in the small and large intestines, and a branch is also made with the splanchnic nerves that follow.

We close the plate by examining the sacral flow of nerves to the lower visceral organs. Continue reading about these nerves, and color the appropriate sections in the plate. Try to identify the visceral organs involved, and color them also.

The **second, third,** and **fourth sacral nerves (S_2–S_4)** form the **pelvic splanchnic nerves (D)**. As the plate shows, these nerves extend to the hypogastric plexus, then their branches course to such organs as the rectum, kidney, urinary bladder, and reproductive organs. The terminal ganglia are located within the walls of these organs, with the result that the preganglionic nerve fibers tend to be very long. The postganglionic nerve fibers, by contrast, are extremely short.

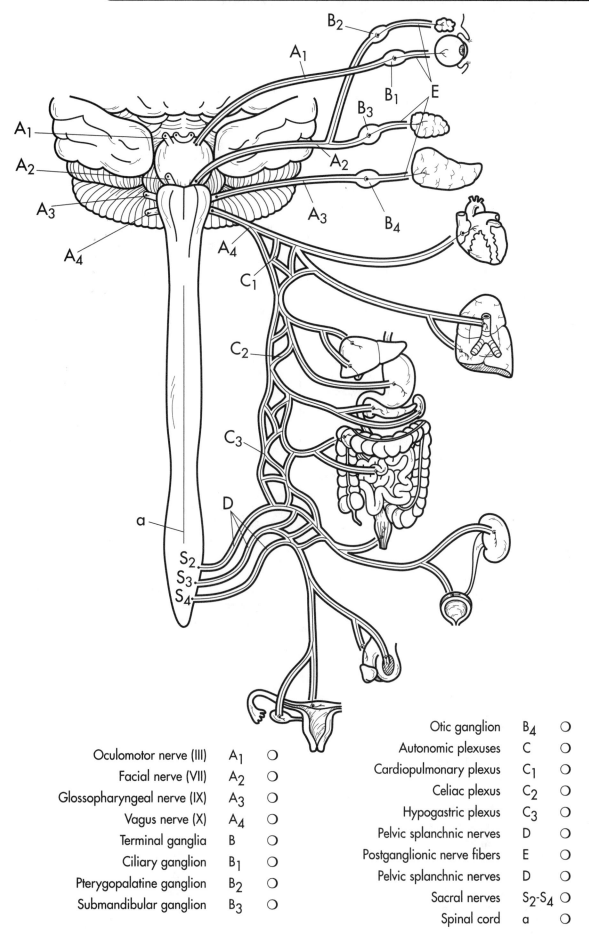

B₂

A₁

B₁

E

B₃

A₁

A₂

A₃

A₄

A₂

A₃

B₄

A₄

C₁

C₂

C₃

D

a

S₂
S₃
S₄

Oculomotor nerve (III)	A₁	○
Facial nerve (VII)	A₂	○
Glossopharyngeal nerve (IX)	A₃	○
Vagus nerve (X)	A₄	○
Terminal ganglia	B	○
Ciliary ganglion	B₁	○
Pterygopalatine ganglion	B₂	○
Submandibular ganglion	B₃	○

Otic ganglion	B₄	○
Autonomic plexuses	C	○
Cardiopulmonary plexus	C₁	○
Celiac plexus	C₂	○
Hypogastric plexus	C₃	○
Pelvic splanchnic nerves	D	○
Postganglionic nerve fibers	E	○
Pelvic splanchnic nerves	D	○
Sacral nerves	S₂-S₄	○
Spinal cord	a	○

the SENSE of TOUCH (SKIN RECEPTORS)

The sense of touch is intimately involved with nerve receptors in the skin. The somatic sensory branch of the peripheral nervous system includes these receptors. The receptors detect changes in temperature, pressure, tension, chemical substances, and other factors in the environment. Within the skin, the receptors include a number of tactile (touch) receptors that send information via the sensory nerves to the central nervous system for interpretation and possible response. Various regions within the cerebrum then respond to the sensation and deliver an appropriate response or make an interpretation. This plate examines six tactile receptors.

Looking over the plate, you will note that we are presenting a view of the deep skin layers in order to point out some of the skin receptors located here. The six types of receptors are found in the orientation view, and detailed presentations are given in the six smaller views. As you continue your study of the nervous system, complete this plate by reading the text below and coloring the structures in the diagram. Bold colors may be used for the skin receptors, but light pale colors should be reserved for the skin layers. The skin layers may be colored in both the overall and detailed views.

The tactile receptors in the skin detect stimuli interpreted by the brain as light touch, heavy touch, and other sensations such as heat and cold. The skin consists of an upper layer called **epidermis (A)**. The bracket indicating this layer may be colored, and the entire layer should be colored in a pale color. The epidermis is the thinner skin layer. Beneath it is the thicker layer called the **dermis (B)**, which may also be colored in a light color together with its bracket. Beneath the dermis is a loose, subcutaneous layer known as the **hypodermis (C)**. This layer contains much fat tissue, also known as **adipose tissue (C_1)**.

One type of skin receptors is the **free nerve ending (D)**. These should be located in the section of the skin as well as in the detailed view. The detailed view also shows the epidermis and dermis, which may be colored in the same colors as used previously. Free nerve endings are the most widely distributed touch (tactile) receptors. They are involved with light touch as well as pain and heat. Note that they have little structural detail and extend through the dermis into the epidermis.

Free nerve endings are attached to modified epidermal cells known as **Merkel's corpuscles (E)**, also known as Merkel's disks. These cells are shown in the detailed diagram together with their nerve endings. Especially prevalent in the palms of the hands and soles of the feet, they are sensitive to light touch and pressure.

This is one reason why the palms and soles are extremely sensitive to touch.

Having surveyed two types of skin receptors, we now continue the discussion with more complex skin receptors. Many of these receptors are found elsewhere in the body such as at the tip of the tongue and at the lips. They function in the same way to detect environmental changes and relay that information to the central nervous system for interpretation. A response is also possible by means of a reflex reaction involving the glands or muscles.

Egg-shaped, encapsulated skin receptors are **Meissner's corpuscles (F)**. Dendrites in these nerve cells are highly coiled and surrounded by Schwann cells, with a capsule enclosing the complex. This construction is shown in the detailed view, and the receptors are seen in the dermis projecting into the epidermis. Meissner's corpuscles detect light touch in the palms of the hand, soles of the feet, lips, and external genitalia.

Ruffini's corpuscles (G) are found in the dermis and are sensitive to pressure and skin distortion. A capsule encloses a set of dendrites, which are interwoven around fibers of collagen. The collagen serves a supportive function.

A number of concentric cellular layers with a distinctive capsule make up the **Pacinian corpuscles (H)**. Also found within the dermis, the Pacinian corpuscles are sensitive to vibration, especially in the fingers, external genitalia, and walls of the urinary bladder.

The final type of tactile skin receptor is the **root hair plexus (I)**. Found deep within the dermis and close to the hypodermis, the root hair plexus is a set of nerve endings associated with the roots of **surface hairs (J)**. When the hair moves, the follicle and root also move, and the movement creates sensations in the nerve endings. The nerve endings thus detect movement as well as touch. Impulses are generated and pass to the **sensory nerve fibers (K)**, which also carry impulses from the other five types of skin receptors. The sensory fiber leaves the skin area through the hypodermis and carries information for interpretation by the central nervous system.

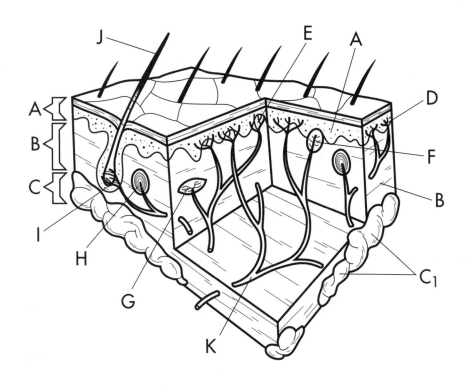

Epidermis	A	○
Dermis	B	○
Hypodermis	C	○
Adipose tissue	C_1	○
Free nerve ending	D	○
Merkel's corpuscles	E	○
Meissner's corpuscles	F	○
Ruffini's corpuscles	G	○
Pacinian corpuscles	H	○
Root hair plexus	I	○
Surface hair	J	○
Sensory nerve fiber	K	○

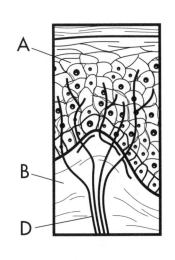

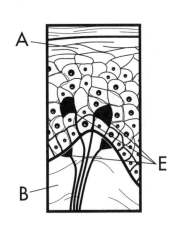

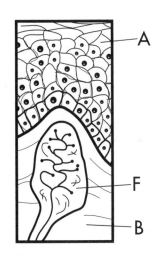

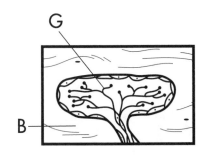

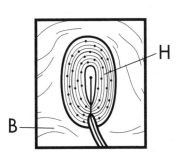

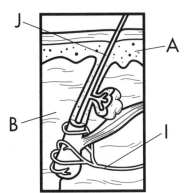

the SENSE of TASTE (GUSTATORY RECEPTORS)

The sense of taste is known as gustation, and the receptors that provide taste are the gustatory receptors. Taste is a chemical sense requiring that food substance be dissolved in fluid and brought into contact with the specialized gustatory cells. The gustatory cells then receive the chemical molecules and develop nerve impulses for relay to the central nervous system.

This plate will examine some details of the gustatory receptors found in the tongue. We shall note four basic tastes and note some anatomical details of the taste buds. You will note that the basic pathways of detection and transmission are similar among all the senses examined in these plates.

> The main title The Sense of Taste (Gustatory Receptors) should be colored to begin work on the plate. Then, as you examine the plate, you will note that we show detailed views of three different types of papillae of the tongue. Also presented is a detailed view of an individual taste bud, where the gustatory sense takes place. As you read about the structures below, color their titles, then locate and color them in the plate.

Receptors for gustation are distributed in approximately 10,000 taste buds, mainly on the tongue, but also on the pharynx, soft palate, and larynx.

The taste buds are found on elevations of the **tongue (A)**, an organ that is attached to several structures including the **epiglottis (a)**, which may be seen in the plate. The taste buds are the centers of gustatory receptors for four different tastes at different regions of the tongue. After coloring the tongue in a light color, you should color the arrows pointing to the different taste areas in bold colors. Note the location of taste buds for the **bitter taste (A_1)** at the back of the tongue. The **sour taste (A_2)** is sensed at the lateral portions of the tongue; the **salty taste (A_3)** near the apex, front, and sides of the tongue; and the **sweet taste (A_4)** at the apex of the tongue.

> In the next part of this plate, we examine three different types of papillae located on the dorsal surface of the tongue. The papillae are presented in detailed view, and the sensory portion is at the center. A single light color can be used to color the sensory portion and a second light color should be used for the remainder of the tissue of the papilla.

The gustatory cells are located in taste buds on elevations of the tongue called papillae. These projections of epithelium occur in three types. The first type includes the **circumvallate papilla (B)**. This large papilla is circular, and the papillae occur in a V-shaped row at the posterior portion of the tongue, as the plate indicates. Bitter taste occurs here. As many as 100 taste buds per papilla may be present. They are indicated in the clefts of the epithelial tissue.

The second type of papilla is the **fungiform papilla (C)**, which resembles a mushroom. Only about five taste buds occur per fungiform papilla, so the sense of taste is not acute here. They occur over the entire surface of the tongue.

The third type is the **filiform papilla (D)**, which is pointed and threadlike. Like the fungiform papilla, few taste buds are found here.

> We now focus on some of the detailed structure of the taste bud. For this purpose, detailed view of a section of the circumvalate papilla is shown. As you read about the details of the taste buds below, color the titles and the structures on the plate.

In order for taste to occur, dissolved materials must contact the oval taste bud within the papilla of the tongue. Chemically dissolved substances enter the **pore (E_1)** of the taste bud and come in contact with the essential receptor cell, the **gustatory cell (F)**. Hairlike extensions called **microvilli (F_1)** occupy the space within the pore and make contact with the chemical. The **nucleus** of the gustatory cell (F_2) may be seen in the plate. The gustatory cells are supported by **supporting cells (G)**, whose **nuclei (G_1)** are also visible. At their base, the gustatory cells synapse with dendrites of neurons. The neurons then come together to form the **cranial nerve (H)**. There are many dendrites present for many gustatory receptors.

The sensation of taste utilizes three cranial nerves arising from the taste buds. These include the facial nerve (cranial nerve VII), the glossopharyngeal nerve (IX), and the vagus nerve (X). Sensations over these nerves pass through the medulla and thalamus, and are projected to the sensory cortex of the cerebrum where an interpretation is made.

The taste bud sits within the **epithelium (I)** of the tongue tissue. Underlying the epithelium and supporting the taste bud is a layer of **connective tissue (J)**. This tissue may be colored in a light color in the plate.

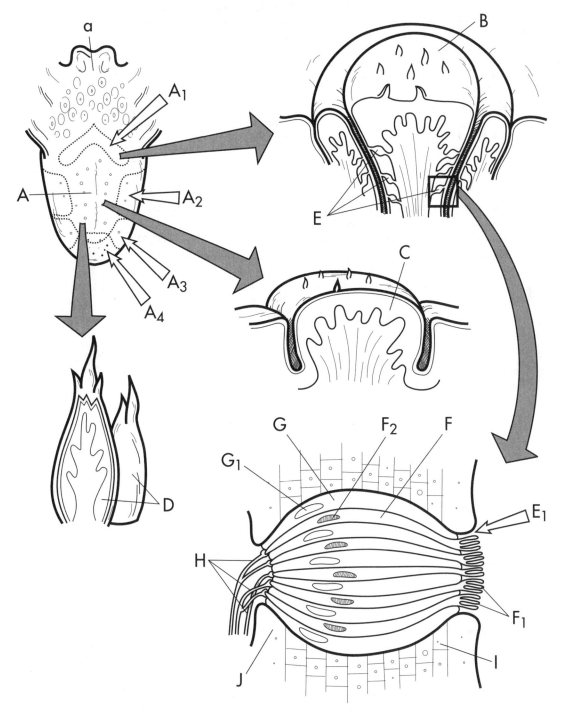

Tongue	A	○	Pore	E₁	○
Bitter taste	A₁	○	Gustatory cell	F	○
Sour taste	A₂	○	Microvilli	F₁	○
Salty taste	A₃	○	Nucleus	F₂	○
Sweet taste	A₄	○	Supporting cell	G	○
Circumvallate papilla	B	○	Supporting cell nucleus	G₁	○
Fungiform papilla	C	○	Cranial nerve	H	○
Filiform papilla	D	○	Epithelium	I	○
Taste bud	E	○	Connective tissue	J	○
			Epiglottis	a	○

the SENSE of SMELL (OLFACTORY RECEPTORS)

The sense of smell is centered in a series of olfactory receptors. These receptors are thousands of times more sensitive than receptors in the taste buds, which are discussed in the previous plate. High in the roof of the nasal cavity, the nasal receptors permit a range of smells that are difficult to classify, but it is believed that humans can distinguish thousands of different chemical substances.

This plate examines some of the anatomical details of the sense of smell centered in the olfactory region of the nose. We note the primary cells for smell and the surrounding tissues that contribute to their efficient function. As you approach this plate, plan to use light colors because most of the structures seen will be relatively small.

> You will note that the plate contains a detailed view of the roof of the nose, where the sense of smell is located. We also include a sagittal section of the nasal area so you may orient yourself. As you read about the individual structures below, color their titles, then locate and color them in the orientation diagrams.

The sense of smell in humans is closely associated with the **olfactory bulb (A)** in which the key nerve tracts are found. This mass of nerve tissue rests on the cribiform plate of the **ethmoid bone (a)** indicated by a bracket and found at the floor of the skull. It is close by the **nasal conchae (b)**, which are shelves of bony tissue where air circulates. We have used small letters for the structures not directly associated with the sense of smell. The **olfactory epithelium (B)** is found at the roof of the nose, high above the nasal conchae. The epithelium may be colored in the orientation view, and its bracket may be colored in the detailed view.

> We now examine some details of the olfactory epithelium and note the position of the significant olfactory receptors that contribute to smell. Note the route of air into the nose both in orientation and detailed views, and visualize how it rushes by the receptor cells. Chemicals dissolved in the air impinge upon the nerve cells and are responsible for the odors we perceive.

Within the **olfactory epithelium (B)**, the olfactory receptors are the olfactory **receptor cells (C)**. These nucleated cells are distributed throughout the epithelium. They are supported by **sustentacular cells (D)** which lie alongside the receptors cells and are plentiful in the epithelium. A third type of cell are the **basal cells (E)**. Only a few of these cells are seen. Lying at the deep portion of the epithelium, they will replace the olfactory receptors cells as the latter are damaged or destroyed during their exposure to the external environment, and as the receptor cells grow old. Scientists believe that approximately 25 million receptors cells exist in the olfactory epithelium.

Where the olfactory receptor cell meets the environment at the air passageway, it forms a thin dendrite terminating in an **olfactory knob (F)**. The fine detailed view shows this structure. The knob contains long cilia, referred to as **olfactory hairs (G)**. These hairs are covered by a thin layer of **mucus (H)**. The mucus layer is also seen in the detailed view. Mucus is formed by **olfactory glands (I)** located within the epithelium.

When air passes through the nose, the chemical molecules of odor dissolve in the mucus and stimulate the olfactory hairs. The hairs are extensions of dendrites. On stimulation, the hairs transmit their impulse to the olfactory receptor cells, which are bipolar neurons. These bipolar neurons are noted in an earlier plate on nerve tissue. Extending from the opposite side of the cell body is an **axon (J)**. The axons of receptor cells pass through a layer of **connective tissue (c)** and conduct the impulses away from the environment.

> Once the olfactory cells have been stimulated and impulses formed, they will be carried to the central nervous system. The final portion of this plate will briefly overview the passageways taken by the impulses. Continue your coloring as before, and be aware of synapses taking place between adjacent cells. The titles should be colored and the structures located in the plate.

The axons of olfactory receptor cells pass through the connective tissue called **basal lamina (c)** and join other axons to form **fiber bundles (K)**. The fibers are unmyelinated. They pass through foramina in the cribiform plate, as shown in the diagram, and emerge in the **olfactory bulb (A)**.

In the olfactory bulb, the fiber bundles synapse with **mitral cells (L)**. The synapse occurs at a tuftlike area called a **glomerulus (M)**, which is outlined by a bracket since it is highly detailed. Thousands of axons merge at the glomerulus, and the impulses are transferred to the mitral cells, which go to form the **olfactory tract (N)**. This tract delivers impulses to the cerebral cortex without passing through the thalamus. In the cortex, an interpretation of the smell is made.

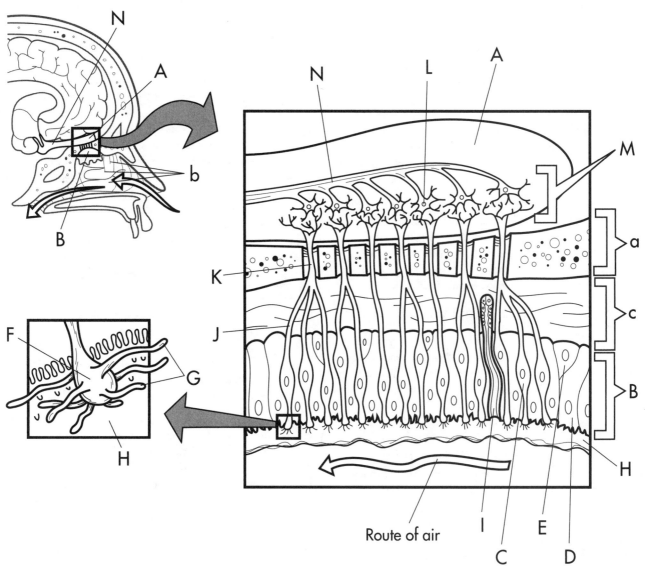

Route of air

Olfactory bulb	A	○	
Olfactory epithelium	B	○	
Olfactory receptor cells	C	○	
Sustentacular cells	D	○	
Basal cells	E	○	
Olfactory knob	F	○	
Olfactory hairs	G	○	
Mucus layer	H	○	
Olfactory glands	I	○	
Axons	J	○	
Fiber bundles	K	○	
Mitral cell	L	○	
Glomerulus	M	○	
Olfactory tract	N	○	

Ethmoid bone	a	○
Nasal conchae	b	○
Connective tissue (basal lamina)	c	○

ANATOMY of the EYE

Sight is the most dominant of the human senses. Over 70% of the body's receptors are the specialized photosensitive cells of the eyes. It has been estimated that a third of all the fibers bringing impulses to the central nervous system come from the eye.

We study the anatomy of the eye in this plate, and use it as a prelude to more detailed studies in the following plates. The structures noted in this plate contribute to vision directly or serve accessory purposes.

To begin the plate, color the main title Anatomy of the Eye. Then note that we are presenting a sagittal section through the eye with an emphasis on the main structures. As you encounter these structures in the reading below, color the titles, then locate and color them in the plate.

The human eye is somewhat like a camera that captures light and focuses it on a light-sensitive area. The wall of the eyeball consists of three layers often referred to as tunics. The first tunic is the fibrous tunic. This layer (or coat of tissue) contains the **sclera (A_1)** known as the "white of the eye." The sclera gives the eyeball its shape, and can be seen around most of the eyeball's surface. A continuation of the sclera and the anterior segment of the fibrous tunic is the **cornea (A_2)**. A similar color can be used for the sclera and cornea to show the continuity of the tissue layer. The cornea is a transparent structure that bulges and has no blood vessels. The cornea helps focus light on the retina of the eye. Where it meets the sclera, there is an area called the **limbus (A_3)**.

The middle layer of the eyeball is the **vascular tunic**. This layer contains many blood vessels. At its most posterior aspect, the vascular tunic includes the **iris (B_1)**, the colored part of the eye seen through the cornea. Muscular movements within the iris cause the iris to open and close. This action increases and decreases the opening to the eye called the **pupil (C)**. The arrow may be colored indicating this opening.

Another portion of the vascular tunic is the **ciliary body (B_2)**. This structure is continuous with the iris, and the same color or a close variation can be used. The ciliary body contains the ciliary muscle, which controls eye movements. At the posterior portion of the ciliary body is the **ora serrator (E)**, a saw-toothed junction where the ciliary body is continuous with the choroid. The **choroid (B_3)** has an extensive capillary network supplying blood to the retina. It can be seen surrounding the eyeball. The **suspensory ligaments (F)** attach to the ciliary processes of the epithelium of the ciliary body. They hold the **lens (J)** in its proper location.

We now examine the chambers of the eyeball and note their location. We also see the nerve layer of the eye as it relates to the other structures. Continue your coloring as you read about these structures below, and color the titles in the titles list and their corresponding structures in the plate.

The eye has three chambers of importance. The first is the **anterior chamber (D)**. This is the fluid-filled space between the iris and the cornea. It contains a fluid material called aqueous humor. Between the suspensory ligaments and the iris is the **posterior chamber (G)**, which also contains aqueous humor.

Posterior to the lens and suspensory ligaments is the large **vitreous chamber (H)**. This cavity contains a clear, gelatinous mass known as the vitreous body. Aqueous humor services the cells in its environment, while the vitreous body appears to help maintain the shape of the eye and give support to the retina. The vitreous body is sometimes called the vitreous humor. The vitreous chamber is sometimes called the posterior cavity, while the anterior and posterior chambers constitute the anterior cavity.

We close this plate with a brief examination of the pathway of light occurring when an image is formed and a brief review of some other structures of the eye. More detailed descriptions of these topics are presented in succeeding plates.

When light enters the eye, it passes through the pupil, cornea, and lens, and is focused on the third tunic of the eye, called the neural tunic. This layer contains an outer pigmented layer and the **outer retina (I)**. The visual receptors are located here. The area of sharpest vision is a region of the retina called the **macula lutea (K_1)**. Within this region, the sharpest point of vision is the **fovea (K_2)**. Photoreceptors are concentrated here. The photoreceptor cells of the retina form a network that comes together at the **optic disk (L)**. This is a blind spot since there are no photoreceptors here. The optic disk penetrates the wall of the eye and forms the **optic nerve (M)**, which carries impulses to the brain. At its outer surface, the eyeball is covered by a thin membrane called the conjunctiva. This mucus membrane covers the outer surface of the eye as the **ocular conjunctiva (N_1)**. As the plate shows, it loops at an area called the **fornix (O)** and continues on the inner side of the eyelid as the **palpebral conjunctiva (N_2)**.

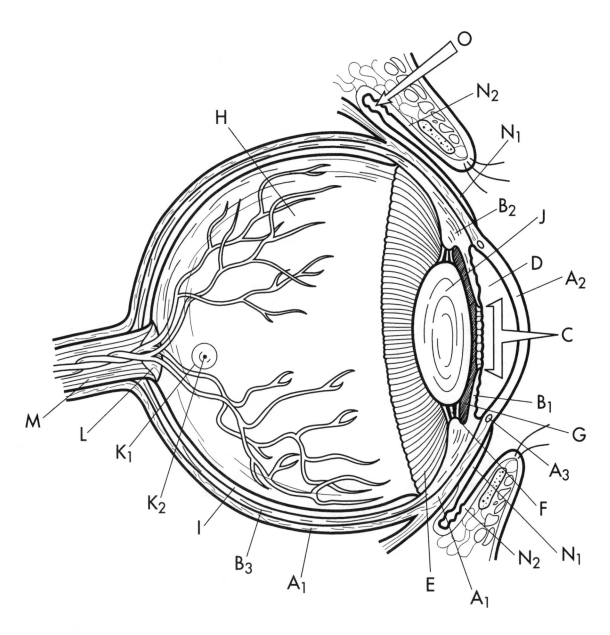

Sclera	A₁	○		Retina	I	○
Cornea	A₂	○		Lens	J	○
Limbus	A₃	○		Macula lutea	K₁	○
Iris	B₁	○		Fovea	K₂	○
Ciliary body	B₂	○		Optic disk	L	○
Choroid	B₃	○		Optic nerve	M	○
Pupil	C	○		Ocular conjunctiva	N₁	○
Anterior chamber	D	○		Palpebral conjunctiva	N₂	○
Ora serrata	E	○		Fornix	O	○
Suspensory ligaments	F	○		Fibrous tunic	A	○
Posterior chamber	G	○				
Vitreous chamber	H	○				

DETAILS of the EYE

In order to see something, an object must emit light or be illuminated by light rays in the receptive range. The receptive range for humans is the "visible light" range. Infrared and ultraviolet light are outside that range.

During vision, light passes through the transparent cornea and is focused by the lens on the retina. The general structures of the eye are considered in the previous plate, while some of the details, including the visual centers, are discussed in this plate.

As you look over the plate, note that we are presenting three views from the posterior portion of the eye. One view shows the three layers of the eyeball, another shows details of the photosensitive area, and the third shows the region where the optic nerve arises. Begin by coloring the main title Details of the Eye and read below and color the appropriate portions of the diagram as they are discussed.

The outer layer of the eye is the **fibrous tunic (A)** which includes the cornea and the sclera. The view here shows the fibers of the sclera, sometimes called the "white" of the eye. Collagen and elastin are contained in the connective tissue of this layer, and small blood vessels may be found here.

The second layer is the **vascular tunic (B)**, also known as the uvea. The intrinsic eye muscles that move the lens, the blood vessels, and the lymphatic passageways are found within this blood-rich layer. Intrinsic muscles within this layer regulate the shape of the lens and the size of the iris (extrinsic eye muscles discussed in another plate rotate and move the eyeball).

The innermost layer is the **neural tunic (C)**, where the photosensitive cells are found and where vision takes place. The construction of this layer is considerably different from the other two tunics.

We now focus on the last part of the plate, showing details where the optic nerve arises. Here the structures are presented in more detail. We use this part as a prelude to the next part. Continue your reading below as you color.

In the most posterior portion of the retina, the fibrous and vascular tunics may be seen, but the emphasis is on the neural tunic. This tunic consists of two layers. There is an outer layer of epithelium containing **pigment (D)**. This is shown as a single layer of cells. The pigmented layer absorbs stray light and prevents reflection from the retina. The remainder of the neural tunic is the **retina (G)**. A light color may be used to prevent obscuring its details.

Note in the diagram how the fibers come together from above and below to form the optic nerve. The point where the fibers converge is the **optic disk (E$_1$)**. The optic nerve will carry impulses from the photosensitive retinal area onto the brain for interpretation. Vision at the optic disk is poorest since there are few photosensitive cells.

Within the optic disk are a number of arteries and veins, the collection of **blood vessels (F)** that supply the eyeball. Note how they pass through the tissue of the optic nerve to emerge and supply the tissues of the posterior portion of the eyeball. The photosensitive cells receive their nourishment and excrete their waste products into these vessels.

We now concentrate on the retina and the photosensitive cells that allow vision. Since there are several different types of cells, we recommend different colors to indicate their presence and relationship to one another. Contrasting colors should be used for the rods and cones. Continue your reading as you continue the coloring.

The main neural area of the eye is the **retina (G)**, indicated by a bracket. The pigmented layer of epithelium lies posterior to the retina and in contact with the vascular layer.

Within the retina, there are two types of **photoreceptors (H)**, and the bracket should be colored. The first type of photoreceptors are the **rods (H$_1$)**. Identify them by their unique structure in the diagram and color them. Rods are sensitive to light and permit vision in dim light. The outer segment is composed of thousands of disks containing light-absorbing cells that initiate the generation of a nerve impulse. These disks may be seen in the cells at the upper end. They contain the pigment rhodopsin.

The second type of photoreceptors are the **cones (H$_2$)**. Cones provide color vision and require intense light. They also have thousands of disks containing the light-sensitive photopigments.

In addition to the rods and cones, the retina contains several other types of neurons. These include the **bipolar neurons (I)**, which should be located and colored a contrasting color. Note that the cell body lies between the single dendrite and axons. Bipolar neurons synapse with the rods and cones and receive impulses generated by them. At this level, there is also a set of **horizontal neurons (J)** regulating the communication between the photoreceptors and the bipolar cells. The bipolar cells synapse with **ganglionic neurons (K)**, at the innermost portion of the retina. The ganglionic neurons contain axons that leave the eye and form the optic nerve. The activity between bipolar cells and ganglion cells is regulated by a horizontal layer of cells called the **amicron neurons (L)**. The complex arrangement of cells is responsible for impulses arriving at the visual centers of the brain, where the vision is interpreted.

Fibrous tunic	A	○
Vascular tunic	B	○
Neural tunic	C	○
Pigmented layer	D	○
Optic nerve	E	○
Optic disk	E_1	○
Blood vessels	F	○
Retina	G	○
Photoreceptors	H	○
Rods	H_1	○
Cones	H_2	○
Bipolar neurons	I	○
Horizontal neurons	J	○
Ganglionic neurons	K	○
Amicron neurons	L	○

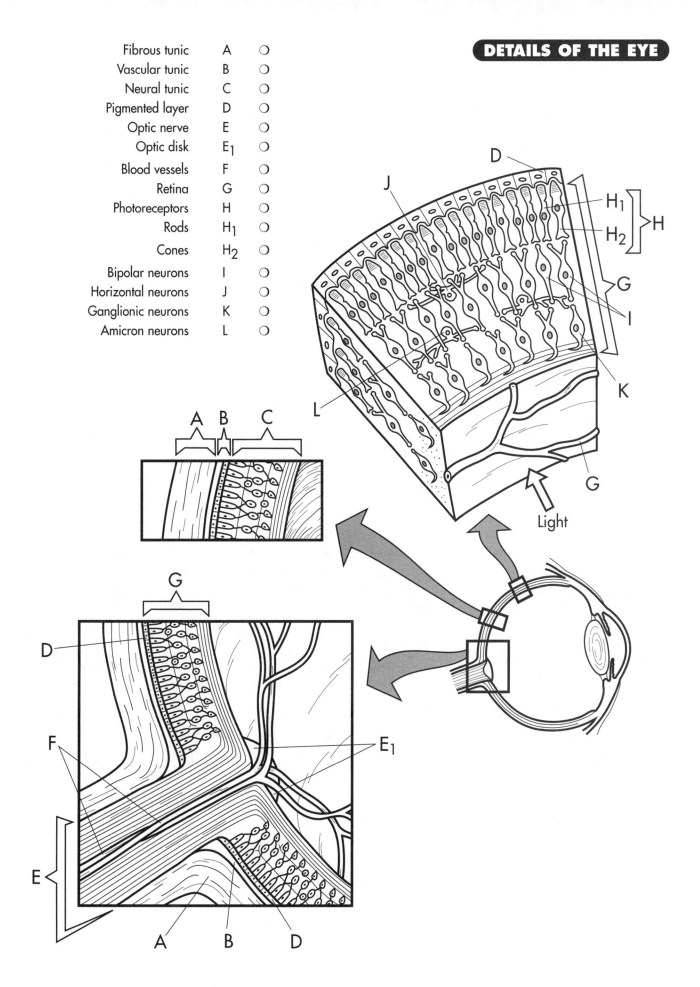

ACCESSORY STRUCTURES of the EYE

The eye has a number of accessory structures involved in protecting it or in its movement. An example is its socket, also called the bony orbit. This structure encloses the eye and protects the eye from sharp blows from outside the body. The maxilla, zygomatic, and palatine bones contribute to the orbit as we have noted on earlier plates.

Other accessory structures are surveyed in this plate. These accessory structures contribute to the efficient functioning of the eye and help it accomplish its visual functions. We present details of the neural function in the previous plate and the general anatomy of the eye two plates previously.

Two views are presented in this plate to indicate some of the eye's accessory structures. We see a lateral and frontal view. As you read about the lateral perspective, color the appropriate titles, then locate and color the structures in the diagram. Lowercase letters are used to indicate structures not directly associated with the eye and uppercase letters indicate those structures of immediate concern to us.

One of the accessory eye structures is the eyebrows. The **eyebrows (A)** consist of thickened ridges of skin that cover the protruding frontal bone. They protect the eye from salt-containing perspiration dripping down the forehead, and they guard against excessive sunlight and foreign matter entering the eye. Deep to the eyebrows are portions of the **orbicularis oculi (a)**, one of the muscles involved in movement of the eyelid. This muscle circles the eye.

The familiar eyelids are anatomically known as palpebrae. These structures, like the eyebrows, are folds of skin that contribute to the opening around the eyeball. The opening is the **palpebral fissure (B_1)**. The bracket pointing to this area may be colored in a bold color. Where the upper and lower eyelids meet, the two areas are called canthi, an area containing oil and sweat glands. Eyelids protect the eyeball from dust and other external substances. When they sweep across the cornea they distribute tears.

Supporting the eyelids are sheets of flat connective tissue called **tarsal plates (C)**. The tarsal plates provide anchorage for the levator palpebrae superioris, a muscle that raises the upper eyelid during blinking.

The edges of the eyelids contain **eyelashes (D),** which are short, thick hairs continually shed and replaced. They act as strainers to trap foreign materials before they contact the eye. Located near the eyelids are the **Meibomian glands (E)**, which

are modified sebaceous glands secreting sebum, an oily material to lubricate the eyelid.

The thin transparent mucous membrane that lines the eyelids is the conjunctiva. The membrane bends back over the surface of the eyeball and terminates at the cornea. The portion covering the cornea is the **palpebral cornea (F_1)**, while the portion covering the cornea is the **ocular**, or **bulbar conjunctiva (F_2)**. Enhancing the membrane with a line of color is best. Between the palpebral and ocular conjunctiva is a space called the **conjunctival sac** or **fornix (G)**. The cornea is shown in the plate as well. A very light color is recommended for this transparent covering.

We now concentrate on the frontal view of the right eye and study the lacrimal apparatus. This gland and series of ducts are responsible for the tearing mechanism. As you read about the mechanism below, color the appropriate titles and their location in the plate. Lighter colors are recommended since many connecting ducts are involved. Where an arrow is used, it may be colored boldly.

The human lacrimal apparatus is responsible for producing tears and delivering them to the eye. When an excess is produced, the tears flow into the nasal cavities, as this portion of the plate illustrates.

The lacrimal apparatus begins with the **lacrimal gland (I)**, seen under the upper lateral eyelid and extending inward from the outer canthus of the eye. Blinking stimulates the lacrimal gland to secrete lacrimal fluid (tears) that washes the eye. It also contains substances that destroy the cell walls of bacteria, and it moistens the surface of the eye. The fluid passes through a series of **excretory ducts (J)** and enters the superior conjunctival sac of the upper eyelid.

The eyelid distributes the tears across the eyeball. The excess fluid then enters the medial canthus where it passes through a tiny orifice called the **lacrimal punctum (K)**. A spot of color can be used to indicate this opening. The tears then enter the **lacrimal canal (L)**. There is an upper and a lower lacrimal canal. They drain into the **lacrimal sac (M)**, which is prominent in the diagram.

As the arrow shows, the excess tears move from the lacrimal sac into the **nasolacrimal duct (N)** and pass through an opening called the **inferior meatus (O)**. The tears then drip out the **external nasal meatus (P)**. This is the reason one sniffles when crying.

Eyebrows	A	○
Palpebral fissure	B_1	○
Tarsal plates	C	○
Eyelashes	D	○
Meibomian glands	E	○
Palpebral cornea	F_1	○
Ocular conjunctiva	F_2	○
Conjunctival sac (fornix)	G	○
Cornea	H	○
Lacrimal gland	I	○
Excretory ducts	J	○
Lacrimal punctum	K	○
Lacrimal canal	L	○
Lacrimal sac	M	○
Nasolacrimal duct	N	○
Inferior meatus	O	○
External nasal meatus	P	○
Orbicularis oculi	a	○
Levator palpebrae superioris	b	○

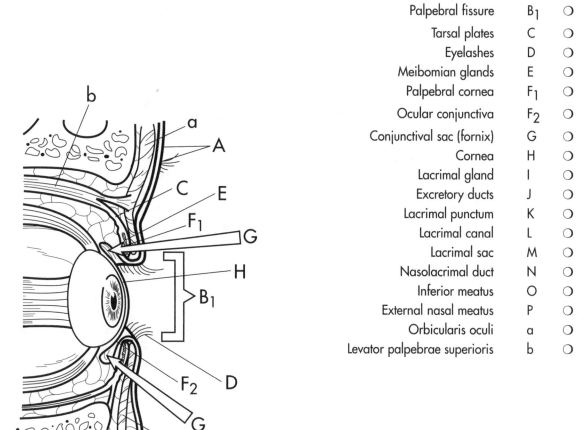

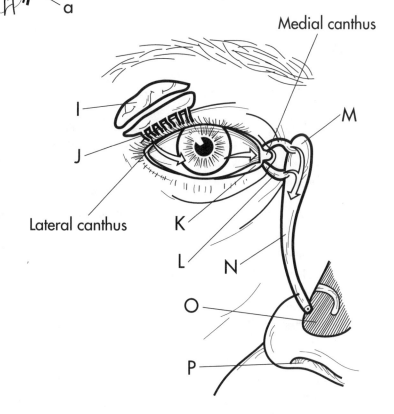

Medial canthus

Lateral canthus

ANATOMY of the EAR

The ear is the organ of hearing and balance in the body. The structures of the ear translate vibrations of the air into fluid vibrations, and then sensory impulses. The sensory impulses are interpreted at the cerebral cortex of the brain and hearing takes place. The ear also contains receptors for equilibrium. These are located at a different site than the receptors for hearing.

This plate discusses the general anatomy of the ear. Both internal as well as external structures are surveyed. Many of the structures are considered in detail in the next plate, and you are referred there for additional discussions.

This plate contains a single diagram of a cut away section of the ear. Located within pockets of the temporal bone, the ear and its structures represent a complex organ. As you read about the structures below, locate and color them in the diagram. We are using subscript numbers to indicate relationships between various main structures. Color the main title Anatomy of the Ear to begin the plate.

The anatomy of the ear is generally discussed according to its three main regions: the **external ear (A)**; the **middle ear (B)**; and the **internal ear (C)**. The brackets indicating these regions should be colored in a bold red, green, or blue.

The outer ear consists of the visible portion known as the **pinna (D)**, also called the auricle. A single light color should be used for the pinna. The deep depression of the pinna is the **concha (D$_1$)**. At this point, the **external auditory canal (D$_2$)** leads away toward the middle ear. A light color is recommended for the canal.

Among the anatomical landmarks of the pinna is a prominent ridge at the uppermost rim known as the **helix (D$_3$)**. The arrow indicating this structure may be colored in a dark tone. A second ridge is the **antihelix (D$_4$)** running parallel to the helix. A furrow called the **scapha (D$_5$)** separates the two ridges. At the lowermost portion of the pinna is the familiar **earlobe (D$_6$)** known as the lobule. Its fatty tissue may be seen within it.

We now move to the middle ear and examine some of the structures where sound vibrations are passed along to the inner ear. Continue your coloring below as you read, and locate the structures in the plate as they are encountered in the reading.

The partition between the external ear and the inner ear is the **tympanic membrane (E)**, also known as the eardrum. The tympanic membrane marks the opening to an air-filled space within the **temporal bone (F)**. A pale color may be used for this bone. The space within the middle ear is the **tympanic cavity (F$_1$)**. It is the site of the **Eustachian tube (G)**. The Eustachian tube leads to the nasopharynx and permits equal air pressures to exist on opposite sides of the tympanic membrane. The tube is alternately called the auditory tube and the pharyngotympanic tube.

Three important landmarks of the middle ear are the **auditory ossicles (H)**, outlined by a bracket. They include the **malleus (H$_1$)**, the **incus (H$_2$)**, and the **stapes (H$_3$)**. These bones are popularly known as the hammer, anvil, and stirrup, respectively. They vibrate in unison with the tympanic membrane and transmit sound vibrations to the inner ear. At the far end they are attached to the membrane at the opening of the inner ear.

The study of the ear is continued and completed in the final portion of this plate discussing the inner ear. Vibrations are converted to sensory impulses here, and the sense of equilibrium takes place as well. Continue your coloring below, and locate the appropriate structures in the plate as you proceed.

The inner ear contains an intricate network of interconnecting chambers and passages. Its two main parts are the **bony labyrinth (I)**, outlined by a bracket, and the membranous labyrinth inside it. Between the bony and membranous labyrinths, there is a fluid called perilymph.

The bony labyrinth consists of three main parts: the first is the **vestibule (I$_1$)**, the central chamber containing fluid-filled sacs associated with the sense of equilibrium. The following plate discusses this area in detail. The second includes the three **semicircular canals (I$_2$)**, also associated with equilibrium.

The third structure is the spiral, coiled **cochlea (I$_3$)**. The cochlea is firmly connected to the stapes by a membranous partition called the **oval window (I$_4$)**. When the three auditory ossicles vibrate, the vibrations are transferred to the perilymph within the cochlea, and as this fluid moves about, nerve fibers are stimulated. Sensory impulses now arise. The **round window (I$_5$)** relieves the pressure exerted at the oval window. The sensory impulses are transferred over the **vestibulocochlear nerve (J)** to the brain for interpretation. Note that this nerve has a branch from the equilibrium area called the **vestibular branch (J$_1$)** and a branch from the cochlea called the **cochlear branch (J$_2$)**. The nerve thus detects sensations for both equilibrium and hearing.

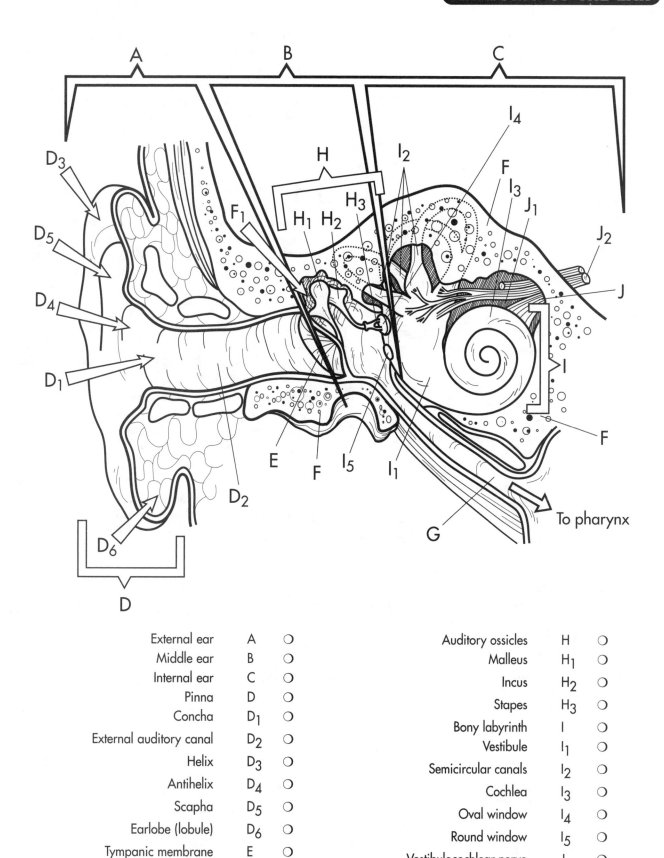

External ear	A	○		Auditory ossicles	H	○
Middle ear	B	○		Malleus	H₁	○
Internal ear	C	○		Incus	H₂	○
Pinna	D	○		Stapes	H₃	○
Concha	D₁	○		Bony labyrinth	I	○
External auditory canal	D₂	○		Vestibule	I₁	○
Helix	D₃	○		Semicircular canals	I₂	○
Antihelix	D₄	○		Cochlea	I₃	○
Scapha	D₅	○		Oval window	I₄	○
Earlobe (lobule)	D₆	○		Round window	I₅	○
Tympanic membrane	E	○		Vestibulocochlear nerve	J	○
Temporal bone	F	○		Vestibular branch	J₁	○
Tympanic cavity	F₁	○		Cochlear branch	J₂	○
Eustachian tube	G	○				

DETAILS of the INNER EAR

The functions of the external and middle ear are to transport air vibrations to organs of the inner ear where the receptors of hearing are located. Also in the inner ear are the organs that contribute to the sense of equilibrium. Hearing and equilibrium are the main topics of this plate.

Begin your work on the plate by coloring the main title Details of the Inner Ear. Then note that we are presenting anterior and posterior views of structures of the inner ear concerned with the senses of hearing and equilibrium. We will treat both senses in turn in this plate. You may use dark greens, reds, blues, and other bold colors, since the structures are of considerable size. Reference to the previous plate is suggested to place the inner ear in perspective.

The inner ear consists of two main divisions: an outer bony labyrinth, which is a shell of bone, and an inner membranous labyrinth, composed of membranes and fluid. A fluid called perilymph lies between the bony and membranous labyrinths, while a fluid called endolymph lies within the membranous labyrinth.

The bony labyrinth is divided into three regions shown in the plate. The first region is the **semicircular canals (A)**, indicated by the bracket. The three canals are the **anterior canal (A_1)**, the **posterior canal (A_2)**, and the **lateral canal (A_3)**. The region at the base of the canals is the **vestibule (B)**, also indicated with a bracket. The semicircular canals function together with the vestibule in the sensation of equilibrium. The combination is referred to as the vestibular complex.

The third area of the inner ear is the **cochlea (C)**. This spiral organ contains the senses for hearing. It may be colored in the anterior view with a light color, except for the central cochlear duct, which we consider next.

We now focus on the functions taking place in the cochlea. Two main structures are considered here, and they may be colored in light colors. As you color, continue your reading below.

As the plate shows, the **cochlea (C)** resembles a snail's shell as it makes almost three turns around a central core of bone. The cochlea contains a slender portion of the membranous labyrinth called the **cochlear duct (C_1)**. This duct is filled with endolymph. It lies between two ducts containing perilymph not shown on the plate. The cochlear duct is also called scala media.

Surrounding the cochlear duct is the **basilar membrane (C_2)**, which is indicated by the arrow. Immediately above the basilar membrane is the **organ of Corti (C_3)**, which should be colored

with a light color. This is a sensory structure containing hair cells and constituting the organ of hearing. The hair cells are sensory neurons acting as receptors for auditory sensations. Vibrations at the **oval window (D)** set up pressure waves within the endolymph of the cochlear duct. Pressure fluctuations of the endolymph move the basilar membrane, and as it vibrates, the attached hair cells of the organ of Corti move against the adjacent tectorial membrane. The basal end of the hair cells synapse with sensory neurons in the tectorial membrane, and impulses are generated for transmission. The pressure causes the **round window (E)** to bulge out as the oval window pushes in.

We now move to the sense of equilibrium and note how organs of the vestibular apparatus are involved in this sense. As you continue reading below, color the titles of the structures, then locate and color them in the diagrams where they are presented. Concentration on the posterior view is recommended for this portion of the plate.

Movement in three rotational planes is analyzed in the semicircular canals. Shaking the head "no" in the horizontal plane stimulates the **lateral canal (A_3)**; shaking the head "yes" activates the **anterior canal (A_1)**; and tilting the head to the side activates the receptors in the **posterior canal (A_2)**.

The receptors within the three canals are located within a swollen region at the base known as the **ampulla (H)**. The arrows may be colored to indicate this area. Within the ampullae are raised structures known as **cristae (H_1)**. An arrow points to a crista in each ampulla. Within the cristae are hair cells attached at the wall. Movement of the endolymph caused by head movement stimulates the hair cells, and they dispatch impulses over the vestibular branch of the vestibulocochlear nerve to the brain. Appropriate movements are made to coordinate the head's activity.

The **vestibule (B)** is continuous with the semicircular canals. It contains two sacs known as the **saccule (F)** and the **utricle (G)**. The anterior view shows them best. At the posterior surfaces are thickened regions called maculae. A **macula (J)** is seen on both saccule and utricle. Fluid within the saccule and utricle passes freely among the sacs and the excess fluid flows to the **endolymph sac (I)** through the endolymph duct for return to the circulation.

Receptors on the saccule and utricle function in equilibrium by generating sensations of acceleration and gravity. The hair cells cluster in the macula in a gelatinous mass covered by a layer of mineral crystals called otoconia, also called otoliths. When the head tilts, gravity pulls the otoconia to one side and the sensory hair cells become distorted. The distortion results in signals to the brain indicating that the head has tilted.

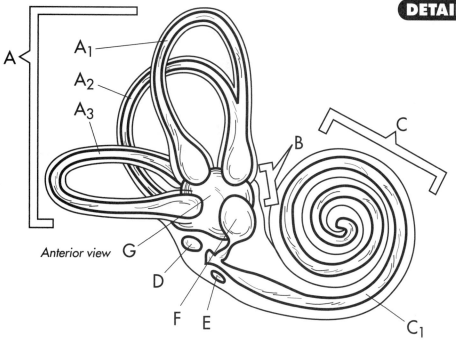

A
A₁
A₂
A₃
B
C
G
D
F
E
C₁

Anterior view

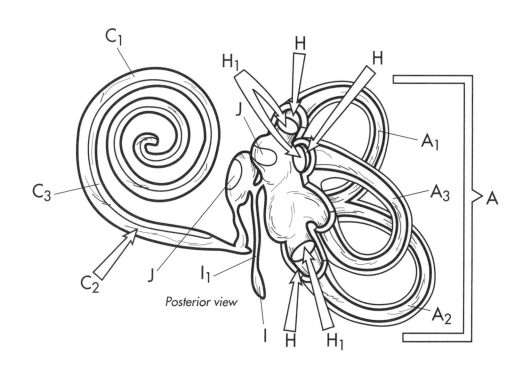

C₁
H₁
H
H
J
A₁
A₃
A
C₃
C₂
J
I₁
A₂
I
H
H₁

Posterior view

Semicircular canals	A	○	Organ of corti	C₃	○
Anterior canal	A₁	○	Oval window	D	○
Posterior canal	A₂	○	Round window	E	○
Lateral canal	A₃	○	Saccule	F	○
Vestibule	B	○	Utricle	G	○
Cochlea	C	○	Ampulla	H	○
Cochlear duct	C₁	○	Cristae	H₁	○
Basilar membrane	C₂	○	Endolymph sac	I	○
			Endolymph duct	I₁	○
			Macula	J	○

CHAPTER SIX:

the ENDOCRINE SYSTEM

the ENDOCRINE GLANDS

The endocrine glands secrete substances called hormones into the fluids of the body. (By comparison, exocrine glands secrete their products into tubes or ducts leading to an internal or external body surface.) As a general group, glands of the endocrine system help regulate metabolic processes such as the rates of chemical reactions, the transport of substances through membranes, and the regulation of water concentrations in the body. They also function in developmental and growth processes. In general terms, a hormone is a substance secreted by a cell that has an effect on another metabolic cell or tissue. Two mechanisms for its action were reviewed in the previous plate.

In this plate, the objective is to briefly survey the major endocrine glands of the body. More detailed descriptions of the glands and the activity of their hormones are given in successive plates, and you are referred to those plates for further study.

> Begin by looking over the plate and noting that the leaders point to various locations of endocrine glands of the body. Most of the glands are large enough to be distinct, and we recommend darker colors. For the smaller glands, such as the first few, lighter colors are preferred. The accessory body structures may be colored in, but we suggest pale or gray colors to avoid obscuring the important endocrine glands. Color the main title, The Endocrine Glands, then read about the glands below. As you encounter the glands in the reading, color their titles, then locate and color the glands in the plate. Our general pattern is to start in the head portion of the body and work down.

We shall begin the study of the endocrine glands with a brief examination of a pea-sized gland called the **pituitary gland (A)**. This gland lies within a depression of the sphenoid bone. The pituitary gland has anterior and posterior divisions, and each division secretes a number of hormones. Lying above the pituitary gland and connected to it by a stalk is the **hypothalamus (B)**. Neurons of the hypothalamus constitute an endocrine gland, because the neurons synthesize and secrete hormones stored in the posterior pituitary gland.

The third endocrine gland of this area is the **pineal gland (C)**. This is a small, oval structure deep within the cerebral hemisphere, and, therefore, it cannot be seen clearly in the plate. We suggest a spot of light color to indicate its general location. The pineal gland secretes melatonin. Varying light conditions outside the body appear to regulate its activity.

> We now move to the neck and thorax region and briefly examine four endocrine glands of this area. Continue as before locating the titles and structures in the plate and coloring them. Be careful when you come to the thyroid and parathyroid gland because they are superimposed on one another.

Located just below the larynx on either side and in front of the trachea is the **thyroid gland (D)**. As the plate shows, this gland consists of two large lobes connected by a broad isthmus. It secretes a number of hormones that have marked effects on the metabolic rates of body cells. The four tiny **parathyroid glands (E)** are located on the dorsal surface of the thyroid gland, but we show them here on the lateral surface to indicate their general location. Hormones of these glands regulate calcium metabolism in the body.

The plate shows a rather large and prominent **thymus gland (F)**. In the mature adult, the gland shown in the plate has atrophied. However, in the very young individual, the thymus gland is quite large. Hormones called thymosins are believed to be synthesized by this gland.

The function of the **heart (G)** in blood circulation is well known, but the endocrine function is less appreciated. Fibers of the cardiac muscle in the right atrium of the heart produce a hormone called atrial natriuretic peptide. This hormone controls the release of a hormone from the posterior pituitary gland and, thereby, helps regulate water balance in the body.

> In the final portion of this plate, we move below the diaphragm and examine the endocrine glands of the abdominal and pelvic cavity. In some cases, the organs have other functions beside their endocrine function. The endocrine function is carried out by specialized cells and tissues of the organ. Continue your coloring as before, as we complete our survey of the endocrine glands.

Many of the digestive processes are controlled by hormones released by the cells along the digestive tract by the **digestive organs (H)**. Such hormones as gastrin and secretin control digestive functions studied in other sections of this book. One digestive organ has an endocrine function. That organ is the **pancreas (I)**, which has specialized cells to produce the hormones insulin and glucagon. Both regulate the amount of glucose in the blood.

Lying atop the kidneys are the **adrenal glands (J)**. These pyramid-shaped glands are also known as suprarenal glands. Each gland has distinctive cortex and medulla regions, and numerous hormones are produced in each region. Cells of the **kidney (K)**, have a urinary function as well as an endocrine function. The endocrine cells produce the hormones erythropoietin and renin, which are part of the angiotensin system that regulates water balance in the body.

The reproductive organs produce sex cells as well as numerous hormones. The **testis (L)** produces hormones that regulate sperm production and the secondary male characteristics. Testosterone is one such hormone. The **ovary (M)** produces hormones that support maturation of the eggs and growth of the reproductive structures. These hormones are called estrogens. Other hormones are also produced by these organs as the appropriate plates indicate.

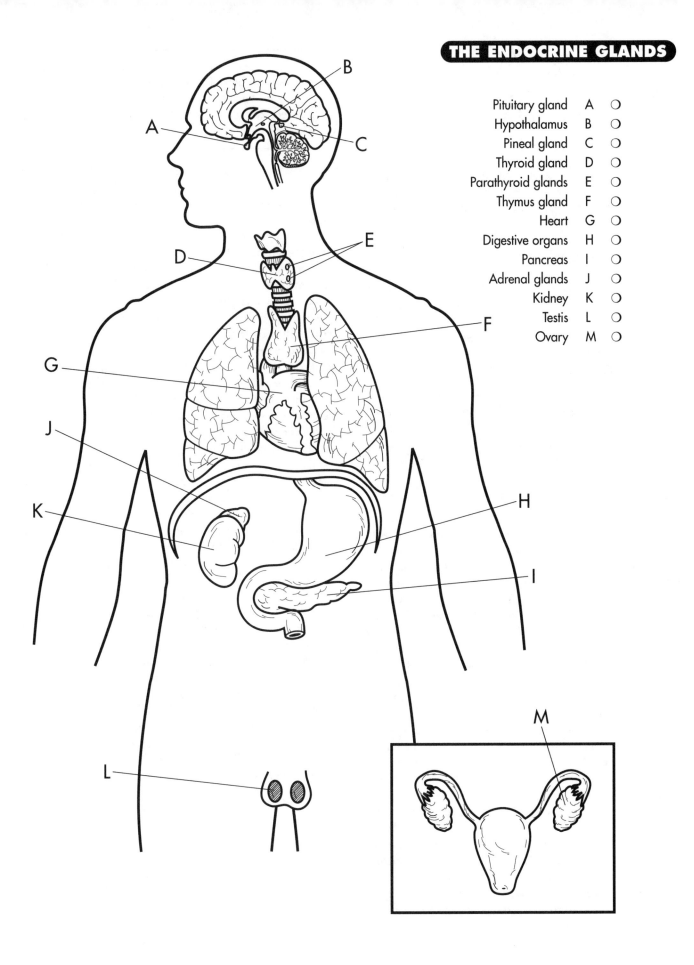

THE ENDOCRINE GLANDS

Pituitary gland   A   ○
Hypothalamus   B   ○
Pineal gland   C   ○
Thyroid gland   D   ○
Parathyroid glands   E   ○
Thymus gland   F   ○
Heart   G   ○
Digestive organs   H   ○
Pancreas   I   ○
Adrenal glands   J   ○
Kidney   K   ○
Testis   L   ○
Ovary   M   ○

HORMONE ACTIVITY

Hormones bring about chemical changes by modifying the physiological activities of their target cells and tissues. Although much is still to be learned about the mechanisms of hormone activity, scientists have discovered that different kinds of hormones act in different ways. Steroid hormones are lipid-soluble and dissolve easily in the cytoplasm of the target cell. Here they bind to receiving molecules called receptors. Protein and amine hormones are water-soluble and cannot diffuse through the cell membrane. They begin the physiological response by combining with receptors in the membrane at the surface of the target cells.

In this plate, we examine mechanisms and study the methods of hormone action. Bold colors such as reds, greens, and blues may be used throughout the plate.

Begin by coloring the main title Hormone Activity. Then look over the plate and the two diagrams reflecting the two known mechanisms of hormonal activity. Color the titles of the mechanisms then locate the appropriate structures on the diagram.

Steroid hormones act on their target cells by a mechanism currently known as the Mobil Receptor Mechanism (in older books the process is called the gene-activated mechanism). This mechanism is so-named because the receptor for the hormone molecule becomes mobile after a hormone-receptor reaction has taken place. The mechanism begins when a **steroid hormone (A)** leaves the bloodstream and approaches the **membrane (B)** of the target cell. The hormone passes through the membrane because steroids are lipids, and the cell membrane is composed primarily of lipids. Now the hormone enters the **cytoplasm (C)** of the cell, where it combines with the **receptor (D)**. This molecule is composed of protein. The union of hormone and receptor forms the **hormone-receptor complex (E)**.

Once the hormone-receptor complex has formed, it enters the **nucleus (F)** of the cell. Here the complex binds to a **DNA molecule (G)** in the nucleus and activates one or more genes into action. (The gene activation is the reason for the alternate name of the mechanism.) This activation induces the DNA molecule to encode a molecule of **messenger RNA (H)**. As normally occurs in cellular metabolism, the mRNA molecule migrates to the **endoplasmic reticulum (I)** of the cell where it provides the biochemical codes for the chemical synthesis of a **protein (J)**. The protein brings about the altered cell response responsible for the activity of the target cell. For example, the protein may act as an enzyme and alter the rate of cellular processes, or it may act as part of a membrane transport system.

We now move to the second mechanism for hormone activity in the body. This mechanism is called the Fixed-Membrane Receptor Mechanism. Color its title and as you read about it, color the titles and structures associated with the process.

Many protein and amine hormones act by combining with specific receptors present on the outer surfaces of target cell membranes. After the union has occurred the receptors remain in the membrane. For this reason the mechanism is called the fixed-receptor mechanism. As the mechanism begins, a **protein hormone (K)** is released from the bloodstream and approaches the **cell membrane (L)**. Here it unites with a **specific receptor (M)** in the membrane. The union of hormone and receptor has an effect on the enzyme adenylate cyclase bound to the other side of the membrane. Normally, this substance exists as **inactive adenylate cyclase (N)**. However, the union changes it into **activated adenylate cyclase (O)**. The activated adenylate cyclase catalyzes the breakdown of an **ATP molecule (P)** into a nucleotide called **cyclic AMP (Q)**, or cAMP. Cyclic AMP has been called the "second messenger" in this biochemical system. (The hormone is considered the "first messenger.") It delivers biochemical information to the **cellular cytoplasm (R)**, and it triggers the changes leading to the cellular response.

The mechanism continues with the cAMP. This nucleotide activates a cellular enzyme called **protein kinase (S)**. Protein kinase causes the target cell to respond to the hormone activation by inciting a distinctive physiological function. For example, it activates liver enzymes to alter glucose metabolism; it reduces the tension of smooth muscles; it increases contractions in cardiac muscle; and it encourages the secretion of thyroid hormone from the thyroid gland. The responses illustrate how hormones serve as chemical messengers in the body.

If AMP remains too long in the cell, the chemical changes could be deleterious. Therefore, the cAMP must be changed to an **inactive cAMP molecule (T)**. This change is brought about by **phosphodiesterase enzymes (U)**. The inactive cAMP then passes out of the target cell and into the **bloodstream (V)**. Now the receptors at the membrane become available for a new reaction to take place, and the process repeats itself. Hormones whose actions involves the fixed-membrane receptor mechanism include TSH, ACTH, FSH, LH, ADH, norepinephrine and epinephrine, and glucagon. A substance called cyclic guanosine monophosphate (GMP) is also thought to function as a second messenger.

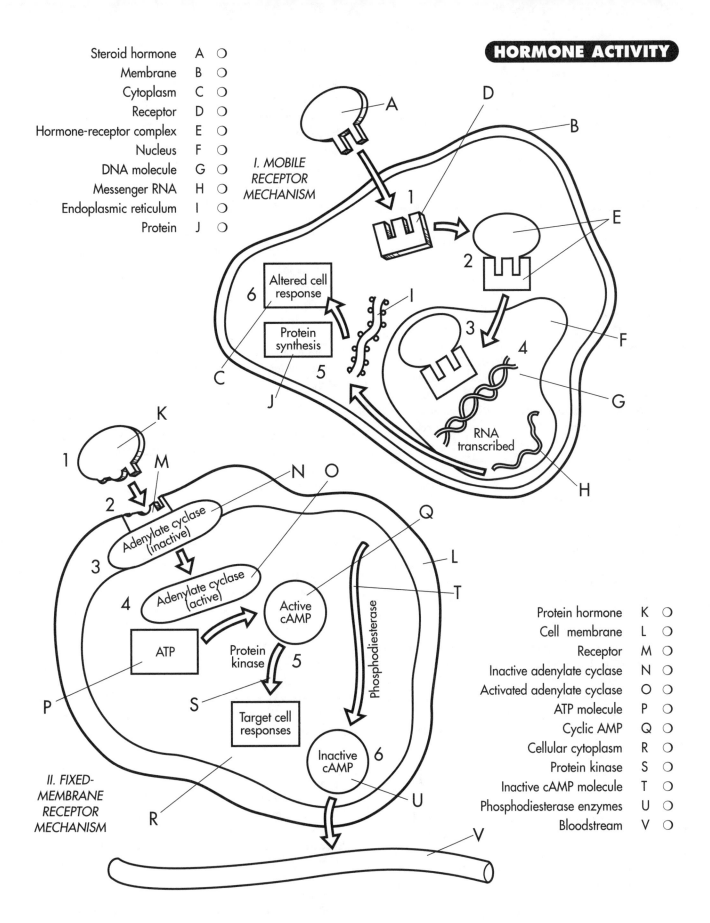

Steroid hormone A ○
Membrane B ○
Cytoplasm C ○
Receptor D ○
Hormone-receptor complex E ○
Nucleus F ○
DNA molecule G ○
Messenger RNA H ○
Endoplasmic reticulum I ○
Protein J ○

I. MOBILE RECEPTOR MECHANISM

A

D

B

1

E

2

6 Altered cell response

Protein synthesis

I

3

4

F

G

5

C

J

RNA transcribed

H

K

1

M

2

N   O

Adenylate cyclase (inactive)

Q

L

3

4   Adenylate cyclase (active)

T

Active cAMP

ATP

Protein kinase   5

Phosphodiesterase

S

P

Target cell responses

Inactive cAMP   6

U

II. FIXED-MEMBRANE RECEPTOR MECHANISM

R

V

Protein hormone K ○
Cell membrane L ○
Receptor M ○
Inactive adenylate cyclase N ○
Activated adenylate cyclase O ○
ATP molecule P ○
Cyclic AMP Q ○
Cellular cytoplasm R ○
Protein kinase S ○
Inactive cAMP molecule T ○
Phosphodiesterase enzymes U ○
Bloodstream V ○

the PITUITARY GLAND

The pituitary gland is found at the base of the brain. It resembles a pea hanging from a stalk connected to the hypothalamus of the brain. The gland is about one centimeter in diameter and has two distinct regions, or lobes, as we shall see in this plate. In the anterior lobe, hormones are synthesized and secreted, but the posterior lobe is only a storage depot for hormones synthesized in the hypothalamus.

Begin by coloring the main title The Pituitary Gland. There are three parts to the plate. In the first part we show the pituitary gland in place, then we explore the hormones from the pituitary gland, and, finally, we focus in on the interconnection between the posterior lobe and the brain. The text will follow this pattern. Many of the structures occur in two or more of the plates, but it would be better to refrain from coloring them until you read about that portion of the plate.

The pituitary gland is also known as the hypophysis. As noted above, it has an **anterior lobe (A)**, which is also called the adenohypophysis. In the posterior aspect is the **posterior lobe (B)**, also called the neurohypophysis. Both the anterior and posterior lobes are in the first part of the plate. The gland sits in a hollowed-out saddle called the **sella turcica (C)** of the **sphenoid bone (F)**. A light color should be used for the sphenoid bone and a dark color such as blue or green may be used to indicate the rim of the sella turcica. Also visible is the rather large **sphenoidal sinus (G)**, which connects to the nasal cavity for air circulation.

The pituitary gland is connected to the brain by a stalk called the **infundibulum (E)**. At the superior aspect of the infundibulum is a portion of the brain called the **hypothalamus (D)**. The posterior lobe of the pituitary gland is composed of neural tissue continuous with the hypothalamus, as we shall see shortly. The **optic chiasma (H)** is closed to the region of the hypothalamus, and the **basilar artery (I)** can be seen supplying the general region of the hypothalamus.

Having located the pituitary gland, we now move to a brief explanation of the hormones it secretes and the regions of the body affected by those hormones. The hormones have been lettered according to the lobe from which they are secreted and numbered in succession. On the plate, you should color in the bubble representing the hormone and note its target. The complete anterior and posterior lobes and other structures can be colored in using the same colors as in the first part.

The anterior lobe produces a number of hormones conveniently divided into six hormones or groups. The first hormone shown in the plate is the **adrenocorticotropic hormone**, abbreviated as **ACTH (A_1)**. This hormone acts on the cortex of the adrenal gland and regulates the secretion of glucocorticoids. The next hormone is **growth hormone** abbreviated as **GH (A_2)**. Also called somatotropin (STH), this hormone affects all cells of the body and contributes to protein synthesis and growth.

The third hormone is **thyroid stimulating hormone**, or **TSH (A_3)**. The target organ of this hormone is the thyroid gland. The hormone stimulates the secretion of thyroid hormones. The fourth hormone from the anterior pituitary gland is a group of hormones collectively called **gonadotropins (A_4)**. These hormones influence the reproductive process and include the follicle stimulating hormones, the interstitial cell stimulating hormone, and the luteinizing hormone.

The next hormone is **prolactin (A_5)**. In the female, the mammary glands are stimulated by this hormone, and the production of milk is regulated. The final hormone is the **melanocyte stimulating hormone**, abbreviated as **MSH (A_6)**. Acting on the skin, this hormone causes the melanocytes to produce melanin, which increases skin pigmentation.

The posterior lobe of the pituitary is a storage location for hormones produced by the hypothalamus. The first hormone is **antidiuretic hormone**, also called **ADH (B_1)**. This hormone acts on the kidneys, as this plate shows, and regulates the reabsorption of water from the kidney tubules. The second hormone is **oxytocin (B_2)**. This hormone acts on the uterus in females and contracts its smooth muscles.

The final portion of this plate briefly explores the relationship between the posterior lobe and the hypothalamus. Light colors are recommended because of the complexity of some of the structures. Use the same colors here that you used in the previous portion.

The posterior pituitary is considered part of the brain. As the plate shows, the cells of the **posterior lobe (B)** are a series of expanded sacs connected to the hypothalamus above a nerve bundle called the **hypothalamic tract (J)**. Following the tract into the brain, we see that the tract arises from neurons in the hypothalamus, which are centered in the supraoptic nucleus and paraventricular nucleus. These **hypothalamic neurons (K)** are collected together and a single color should be used for the encircled groups. Neurons in the nuclei synthesize the posterior lobe hormones and transport them to the storage terminals.

In the anterior lobe, there is an interconnection of the blood systems. Ventral neurons of the **hypothalamus (O)** secrete certain substances that flow into the **primary capillary plexus (L)**, which lead to a series of veins. These veins are the **hypophyseal portal veins (M)**. They transfer their secretions to veins of the **secondary capillary plexus (N)**, which can be seen surrounding the secretory cells of the **anterior lobe (A)**. In this way some control over the anterior lobe can be exerted by neurons of the hypothalamus.

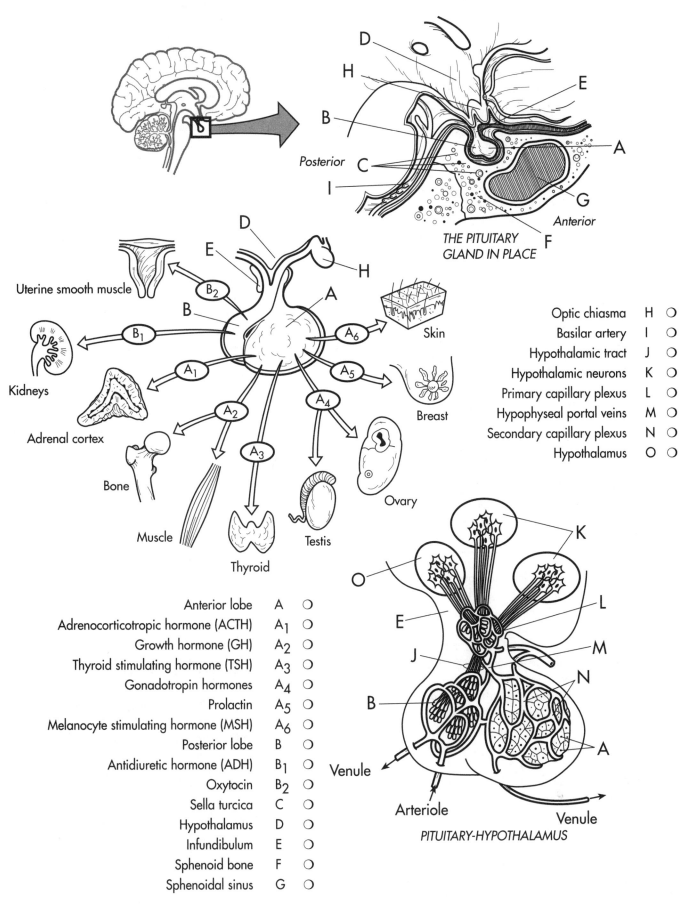

D
H
B
Posterior
C
I
E
A
G
F
Anterior

THE PITUITARY
GLAND IN PLACE

D
E
B₂
B
A
H

Uterine smooth muscle

B₁
Kidneys
A₁
Adrenal cortex
A₂
Bone
A₃
Muscle
Thyroid
A₄
Testis
A₅
Breast
A₆
Skin
Ovary

Optic chiasma	H	○
Basilar artery	I	○
Hypothalamic tract	J	○
Hypothalamic neurons	K	○
Primary capillary plexus	L	○
Hypophyseal portal veins	M	○
Secondary capillary plexus	N	○
Hypothalamus	O	○

Anterior lobe	A	○
Adrenocorticotropic hormone (ACTH)	A₁	○
Growth hormone (GH)	A₂	○
Thyroid stimulating hormone (TSH)	A₃	○
Gonadotropin hormones	A₄	○
Prolactin	A₅	○
Melanocyte stimulating hormone (MSH)	A₆	○
Posterior lobe	B	○
Antidiuretic hormone (ADH)	B₁	○
Oxytocin	B₂	○
Sella turcica	C	○
Hypothalamus	D	○
Infundibulum	E	○
Sphenoid bone	F	○
Sphenoidal sinus	G	○

K
O
L
E
J
M
B
N
A
Venule
Arteriole
Venule

PITUITARY-HYPOTHALAMUS

the THYROID and PARATHYROID GLANDS

The thyroid gland is shaped somewhat like a shield. It is found in the neck anterior to the trachea and inferior to the larynx. The gland consists of two lateral lobes, each about 5 centimeters long and connected to the other by a branch of tissue.

On the dorsal surface of the thyroid are the four parathyroid glands. The parathyroids are found in the connective tissue surrounding the posterior surface of the thyroid gland lobes. Each parathyroid gland is about a half centimeter in diameter. The glands are the second major topic of this plate.

Start your work on the plate by coloring the main title The Thyroid and Parathyroid Glands. As you look over the plate, note that we have concentrated on the thyroid gland and have shown the structures in its region in detail. The parathyroid glands, in contrast, are shown briefly. As you read about the thyroid gland and its accessory structures below, color the titles, then color the structures in the plate. An anterior view of the neck region is presented. Where left and right complementary structures exist, you should color them in the same color. We have numbered them with subscript numbers to denote their location.

The thyroid gland has two lobes, designated the **left lateral lobe (A_1)** and the **right lateral lobe (A_2)**. The shieldlike structure of the gland can be seen in the plate. A bridge of tissue connecting the two lobes is known as the **isthmus (A_3)**.

Internally, the thyroid gland is composed of hollow, spherical follicles, whose cells produce precursors to the thyroid hormones. Externally, the gland lies close to the laryngeal cartilages. The gland is inferior to the large **thyroid cartilage (B_1)** and the smaller **cricoid cartilage (B_2)**. These cartilages may be colored the same color to note their relationship to one another.

A thyroid gland receives its blood from two arteries: the first is the **superior thyroid artery (C)**, seen in the plate arising from the **external carotid artery (D)**. The left and right arteries should be colored in the same darker color. The second artery supplying blood to the thyroid gland is the **inferior thyroid artery (E)**. On each side of the neck, this artery arises from the **thyrocervical trunk (F)**.

Eight important veins carry the blood from the thyroid and carry its hormones to the circulatory system. The first vein is the **superior thyroid vein (G)**, which can be seen on both sides of the

neck. The second vein is the **middle thyroid vein (H)**, which is somewhat inferior to the first. Both of the latter veins empty their contents into the **internal jugular vein (I)**. The third vein draining the thyroid gland is the **inferior thyroid vein (J)**, which is seen overlying the trachea. The veins enter the **brachiocephalic vein (K)**.

Having examined the thyroid region, we now discuss the two thyroid hormones. Examine the structure of the **hormone thyroxin (L)** and read the following paragraph. The entire box may be shaded with a pale color or with a gray as you focus your attention on the structure of the hormone.

The cells of the thyroid gland follicles produce a protein called thyroglobulin. This protein is the basis for thyroxin, an important thyroid hormone. Four iodine atoms are added to thyroglobulin to form thyroxin. The plate shows the structure of thyroxin and indicates the location of the four iodine atoms associated with the molecule. Another thyroid hormone is triiodothyronine; it has only three iodine atoms.

Thyroid hormones stimulate the metabolic rate in cells and promote growth. They are believed to increase the efficiency with which the mitochondria produce ATP. Hormones promote protein synthesis, increase the rate of carbohydrate absorption in the digestive tract, promote lipid metabolism, and encourage the uptake of glucose by the cells for energy metabolism. Other cells of the thyroid gland produce the hormone calcitonin, which assists the regulation of the calcium levels in body fluids.

We now turn to the parathyroid glands and show their anatomy relative to the thyroid glands. Darker colors may be used because we are dealing with structures that are relatively large.

The **parathyroid glands (M)** are about the size of peas. Usually, there are four. They are found along the posterior surface of the thyroid gland, as the plate indicates. A connective tissue capsule covers them, and lobules are found within them. In the plate, the lobes of the thyroid gland may be colored using the same colors as above. The same arteries and veins that supply the thyroid gland also bring blood to and remove it from the parathyroid glands.

The main hormone of the parathyroid glands is called parathormone, also known as parathyroid hormone (PTH). Parathormone raises the level of calcium in the body fluids (calcitonin lowers the level). Acting primarily in the kidney tubules, bone, and intestine, PTH stimulates the release of calcium from the bones and encourages the reabsorption of calcium by the kidney tubules. Calcium is essential for muscle function, nerve activity, bone metabolism, and the general well being of the cells.

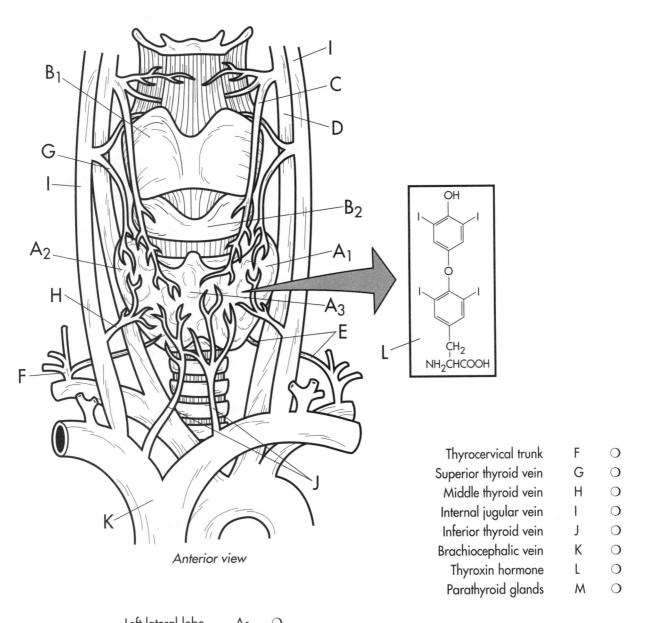

Anterior view

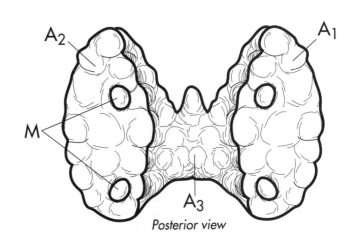

Posterior view

Thyrocervical trunk	F	○
Superior thyroid vein	G	○
Middle thyroid vein	H	○
Internal jugular vein	I	○
Inferior thyroid vein	J	○
Brachiocephalic vein	K	○
Thyroxin hormone	L	○
Parathyroid glands	M	○

Left lateral lobe	A_1	○
Right lateral lobe	A_2	○
Isthmus	A_3	○
Thyroid cartilage	B_1	○
Cricoid cartilage	B_2	○
Superior thyroid artery	C	○
External carotid artery	D	○
Inferior thyroid artery	E	○

159

the PANCREAS (ENDOCRINE FUNCTION)

The pancreas is a unique organ because it contains cells having both exocrine and endocrine functions. In this plate, we are concerned with the endocrine function. The two principal hormones of the pancreas are insulin and glucagon. Initially, we shall study the anatomy of the organ and note some of the important structures associated with it.

> Note in the plate that the main structure is the elongated pancreas in place near the stomach. Superimposed on the pancreas is a large portion of the stomach. This should be colored lightly since the other structures are of more importance to this particular discussion. Begin by coloring the main title The Pancreas (Endocrine Function).

Lying in back of the stomach and behind the parietal peritoneum is the soft, somewhat triangular organ, the **pancreas (A)**. The three main regions of this gland are the **body (A₁)**, the **head (A₂)**, and the **tail (A₃)**. When coloring these portions of the pancreas, you should try to select variations of a light color to show the continuity of the three regions and not obscure the main arteries and veins. As the plate indicates, much of the body of the pancreas lies behind the **stomach (B)**. A very light gray is recommended for the stomach so that the structures beneath it may be seen. The stomach unites with the small intestine, and the first portion, the **duodenum (C)**, is shown.

> We now concentrate on the blood supply to the pancreas. Because the pancreas is a gland, its secretions are plentiful, and its rich blood supply carries them from the endocrine cells. The blood vessels also supply nutrients and oxygen to the cells and bring the components used for the synthesis of hormones. We recommend darker colors for the larger veins, and lighter colors for their smaller branches. In many cases the arteries come together (anastomose). In some cases the arteries lie along the dorsal region or in the pancreas. We have indicated them with broken lines.

Running along the dorsal aspect near the vertebral column is the main thoracic and abdominal artery, the **aorta (D)**. A small portion of this main arterial thoroughfare is shown. Branching from the aorta is the **large celiac trunk (E)** also called the celiac artery. Branching from this artery is the **splenic artery (F)**. The splenic artery runs along the surface of the pancreas on its way to the spleen. Branching from the splenic artery is the **great pan-**

creatic artery (G). As the plate indicates, this artery carries blood to the body and tail of the pancreas.

Another branch of the splenic artery is the **superior pancreatic artery (H)**, seen as a large artery in the plate. This artery branches within the pancreas, and the right branch (the visual left) anastomoses with other arteries. The left branch (the visual right) continues as the **inferior pancreatic artery (I)**, which supplies the inferior aspect of the pancreas.

As the aorta continues along the abdominal wall, it gives rise to the **superior mesenteric artery (J)**. A subdivision of this artery enters the pancreatic tissue, then divides to form the **anterior pancreatoduodenal artery (K)**. The other branch becomes the **posterior pancreatoduodenal artery (L)**. From the superior aspect, the **gastroduodenal artery (M)** arises from the celiac trunk. It enters the head of the pancreas as the **superior pancreatoduodenal artery (N)**, then anastomoses with other arteries.

> Having studied the surface anatomy of the pancreas, we briefly examine the microscopic anatomy of the pancreatic tissue. The pancreas contains both exocrine and endocrine cells, and their relationship is shown in this plate. The arrows indicate how a section of the pancreas has been expanded for this view.

The pancreas is attached to the duodenum by a duct called the **pancreatic duct (O)**. This duct sits deep within the tissue and can be seen running through the pancreas in broken lines. The pancreatic duct receives enzymes and other secretions from **exocrine cells (P)** of the pancreas. These cells should be colored in a dark color such as blue. Note the arrows indicating secretions entering the **pancreatic duct (O)** for transport to the duodenum.

The endocrine cells of the pancreas are arranged in groups closely associated with blood vessels. These groups of cells are called the islets of Langerhans. Alpha cells, beta cells, and delta cells are the **endocrine cells (Q)** of the pancreas. These clusters of cells should be colored in a dark color such as red (to contrast with the exocrine cells). There are no ducts leading from the endocrine cells. Rather, the plate shows **cross sections of two blood vessels (R)**. The secretions of the endocrine cells are liberated into these blood vessels, which are part of the circulatory system of the pancreas.

The hormone produced by the alpha cells of the islets of Langerhans is glucagon. This protein hormone stimulates the liver to convert glycogen into glucose and to form carbohydrates from other noncarbohydrate substances. The hormone of the beta cells is insulin. Also a protein, this hormone stimulates the formation of glycogen from glucose and facilitates the passage of glucose molecules into the tissue cells, which use the glucose in their energy metabolism.

The third hormone, a product of the delta cell, is called somatostatin. This hormone is not as well known as the other two. It is believed to inhibit the production and secretion of glucagon and insulin, thereby controlling their levels in the bloodstream.

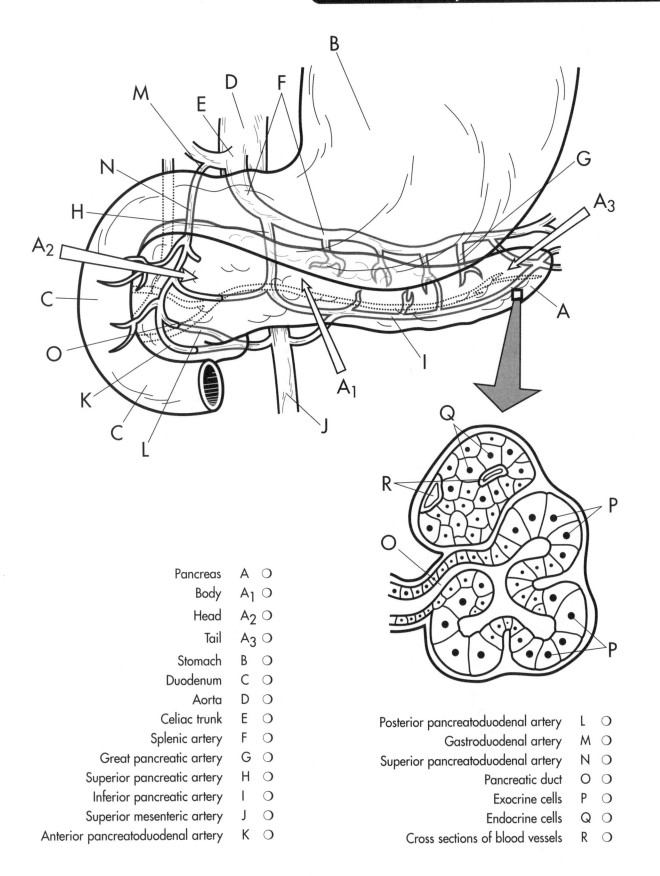

Pancreas	A	○
Body	A₁	○
Head	A₂	○
Tail	A₃	○
Stomach	B	○
Duodenum	C	○
Aorta	D	○
Celiac trunk	E	○
Splenic artery	F	○
Great pancreatic artery	G	○
Superior pancreatic artery	H	○
Inferior pancreatic artery	I	○
Superior mesenteric artery	J	○
Anterior pancreatoduodenal artery	K	○

Posterior pancreatoduodenal artery	L	○
Gastroduodenal artery	M	○
Superior pancreatoduodenal artery	N	○
Pancreatic duct	O	○
Exocrine cells	P	○
Endocrine cells	Q	○
Cross sections of blood vessels	R	○

the ADRENAL GLANDS

The adrenal glands are paired glands, also known as suprarenal glands. One gland sits atop each kidney and is embedded in the fat enclosing the kidney.

The adrenal glands consist of two separate endocrine glands. At the outer region is the cortex, which forms the bulk of the gland and is composed of typical gland tissue. Deep to the cortex is a medulla, arranged in groups around blood vessels. Cells of the medulla are intimately associated with the sympathetic division of the autonomic nervous system. They are modified postganglionic cells.

This plate examines the anatomy of the adrenal glands and their blood supply, then it will focus on the endocrine functions associated with various parts of the gland.

We present in the plate the adrenal glands in position atop the kidneys, together with their accompanying blood supply. We then present an "exploded" view of a portion of the gland to show the various regions of the gland. Start by coloring the main title The Adrenal Glands, then focus your attention on the glands in place as you read about them. Color the glands and titles below, using light colors since the arteries and veins supplying the glands are rather small in the diagram.

The adrenal glands have the shape of a pyramid as they sit at the superior border of each kidney within a fatty layer. The **adrenal glands (A_1 and A_2)** are located at the level of the twelfth rib and are attached to the kidney by a dense capsule. The **kidneys (B_1 and B_2)** may be colored in a dark color, but a light color should be used for the adrenal glands.

The main blood vessel, the **aorta (C)**, is seen as the abdominal aorta in this plate. Arising from it are two **middle suprarenal arteries (D_1 and D_2)**. These large blood vessels supply blood to the adrenal glands. The aorta also supplies blood via the **inferior phrenic arteries (E_1 and E_2)**. The phrenic arteries lead to the **superior suprarenal arteries (F_1 and F_2)**, which carry blood to the superior region of the adrenal gland.

Blood is also carried to the adrenal glands by the **large renal arteries (G_1 and G_2)**, which supply the kidneys. Branches of the renal arteries are the **inferior suprarenal arteries (H_1 and H_2)**, which supply inferior regions of the adrenal glands.

Blood leaves the adrenal glands by two paths. The **left suprarenal vein (I)** drains blood from the gland and carries it to the **left renal vein (J)**, which carries blood from the kidney. On the right side, the **right suprarenal vein (K)** leaves the adrenal

gland and extends toward the inferior vena cava. The vena cava, however, has been cut in this plate, and we do not show the vein entering the vena cava. We do, however, show its position. The **coeliac trunk (a)** and **superior mesenteric artery (b)** are visible but not related to the glands.

Having studied the blood supply to and from the adrenal glands, we now turn to its endocrine function. Your focus should be on the section entitled Endocrine Function. Dark colors may be used for these sections. The brackets we show enclosing the area should be colored darkly, and different colors should be used for different parts of that area. Also, color the titles as you encounter them in the reading below.

In this plate, we show a close-up of the cells of the adrenal gland. A sagittal section has been made through a single gland. The adrenal gland has three main parts. At the surface of the gland is a thick **capsule (N)**, which binds the gland to the kidney surface and protects its glandular tissue below. The capsule is shown in the sagittal section, and a dark color such as a blue or green may be used to indicate it.

Below the capsule, the adrenal gland contains an outer layer called the **cortex (L)**. The cortex may be colored with a dark color in the sagittal section, and the bracket should be colored in the histological view next to it. We shall return to the cortex momentarily. Deep to the cortex is the inner mass called the **medulla (M)**. A third color may be used for the medulla in the sagittal section, and the bracket should be colored.

Returning to the histological section of the adrenal gland, we note the extensive fibrous capsule at its surface. The capsule is seen radiating into the underlying tissue. Beneath it, the cortex has three identifiable layers: the first layer is the **zona glomerulosa (L_1)**. Cells of this region produce mineralocorticoids, such as aldosterone. These steroid hormones control the reabsorption of sodium ions and water from the urine in the kidney.

The second layer is the **zona fasciculata (L_2)**. Steroid hormones, glucocorticoids, from this layer, affect glucose, protein, and fatty acid metabolism in various tissues. The third layer is the **zona reticularis (L_3)**, which produces androgens. These "male hormones" are believed to stimulate early development of the reproductive organs.

The third major layer, the medulla, has a rich blood supply and is composed of nerve cells, as previously noted. The cells produce epinephrine and norepinephrine, which function during stress-related situations such as the "fight-flight" complex of actions. The hormones are catecholamines.

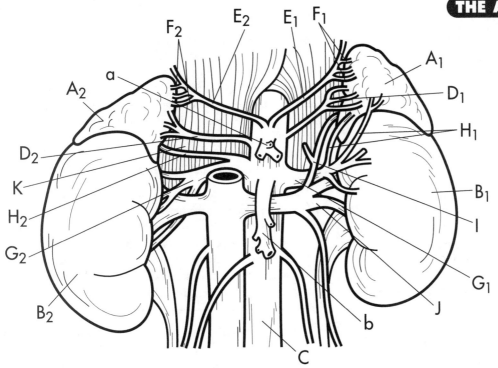

Endocrine Function

Surface of adrenal gland

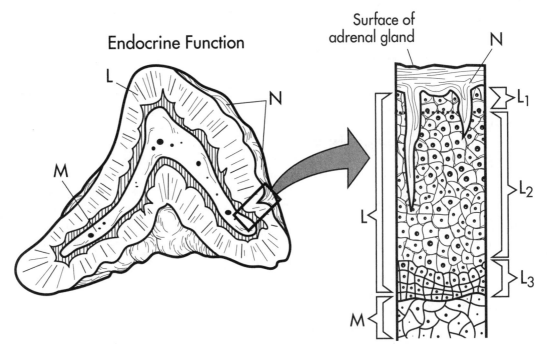

Left adrenal gland	A₁	○	Right inferior phrenic artery	E₂	○	Right suprarenal vein	K	○
Right adrenal gland	A₂	○	Left superior suprarenal artery	F₁	○	Cortex	L	○
Left kidney	B₁	○	Right superior suprarenal artery	F₂	○	Zona glomerulosa	L₁	○
Right kidney	B₂	○	Left renal artery	G₁	○	Zona fasciculata	L₂	○
Aorta	C	○	Right renal artery	G₂	○	Zona reticularis	L₃	○
Left middle suprarenal artery	D₁	○	Left inferior suprarenal artery	H₁	○	Medulla	M	○
Right middle suprarenal artery	D₂	○	Right inferior suprarenal artery	H₂	○	Capsule	N	○
Left inferior phrenic artery	E₁	○	Left suprarenal vein	I	○	Celiac trunk	a	○
			Left renal vein	J	○	Superior mesenteric artery	b	○

the THYMUS and PINEAL GLANDS

The pituitary, thyroid, and adrenal glands are among the better known endocrine glands of the body. There are, however, many other glands that bear mention because their hormones have significance in the body. Among these glands are the kidney, which secretes erythropoietin, a hormone that encourages the bone marrow to increase its production of red blood cells; the heart, which produces in its atrial cells the hormone atrial natriuretic factor, which controls the production of salty urine in the kidney; the gastrointestinal tract whose endocrine cells regulate the blood flow through the digestive organs, the gallbladder's release of bile, and other functions; and the placenta, which secretes hormones affecting the course of pregnancy.

In this plate, we review the activity of the thymus gland and the pineal gland. Because little has been known about these glands in the past, they have attracted the attention of contemporary scientists, and knowledge about these glands continues to grow.

Begin by coloring the main title The Thymus and Pineal Glands. We present the anatomical location of both glands, and a brief description of some of the hormones they produce. You may select dark colors for this plate, because the structures are of substantial size. Some of the accessory structures may be colored in lighter colors so as not to obscure the thymus or pineal glands. We begin with the thymus gland.

The **thymus gland (A)** is located in the mediastinum deep to the sternum and between the lungs. The important feature of the plate is a demonstration of the location of the thymus and its relative size before and after puberty. The thymus is large and conspicuous in infancy and the prepubic years. This is shown in the left portion of the plate. After puberty, the thymus gland diminishes in size and has the relative size shown on the right. The gland continues to diminish, until the gland is composed largely of fibrous connective tissue and adipose tissue by the time an individual is fifty years of age.

In the plate, we show the thymus relative to other organs of the thoracic cavity and neck. These other organs include the **heart (a)**, the **lungs (b)**, the **trachea (c)**, the **thyroid gland (d)**, and the **larynx (e)**. We use lowercase letters because these structures are not part of the gland. These structures may be colored in using dark colors, but be careful to avoid coloring over the thymus gland.

The thymus gland produces a series of hormones, which are peptides. These hormones are called thymopoietins and thymosins. The hormones are essential for the development of the T-lymphocytes, an important cell of the immune system. T-lymphocytes originate in the bone marrow, then pass through the thymus, where they become mature T-lymphocytes. Mature T-lymphocytes then move to the lymphoid tissues of the lymph nodes, spleen, tonsils, adenoids, and other areas of the body. Here they function in cell-mediated immunity, a type of immunity directed at complex microorganisms, tumor cells, and transplanted cells. This immunity is the topic of another plate in this book.

We now focus on the pineal gland and briefly mention its hormone secretions. The plate shows the anatomical location of the pineal gland, and the text considers some of its important derivatives. As you read about the gland in the text, color it in the plate as well as some of the nearby structures in the brain.

The **pineal gland (B)** is derived from the neural tissue of the brain. As the plate shows, the pineal gland protrudes from the roof of the third ventricle of the brain and lies between the hemispheres of the cerebrum. This area of the brain is the diencephalon. As the plate shows, the nearby regions are the **pons (f)**, the **cerebellum (g)**, and the **cerebrum (h)**. These structures are discussed in much more detail in other plates. Our purpose here is to show their relative position to the pineal gland. Dark colors may be used in these structures, and you may test yourself on any other structures you may recognize in the plate.

The pineal gland secretes the hormone melatonin, as well as other hormones. Melatonin is believed to inhibit the secretion of gonadotropins from the anterior pituitary gland. The release of melatonin is apparently controlled by varying light conditions outside the body as impulses reach the gland from the retina of the eye over the optic tracts. As the amount of light decreases, the secretion of melatonin increases, and scientists believe that melatonin is involved in circadian rhythms, the patterns of repeated behavior associated with day and night. The gland is also known to secrete serotonin, a neurotransmitter.

The Thymus Gland

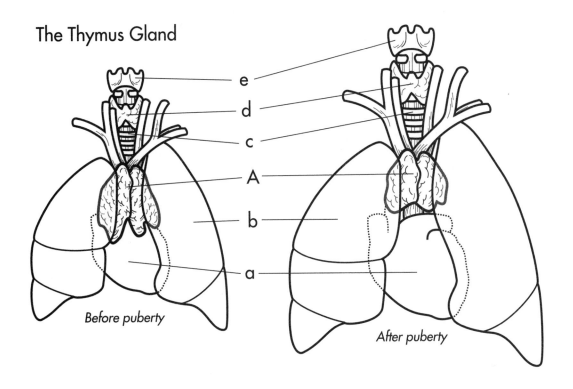

e
d
c
A
b
a

Before puberty

After puberty

Thymus gland	A	○
Pineal gland	B	○
Heart	a	○
Lungs	b	○
Trachea	c	○
Thyroid gland	d	○
Larynx	e	○
Pons	f	○
Cerebellum	g	○
Cerebrum	h	○

The Pineal Gland

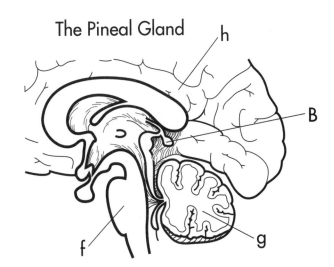

h
B
g
f

CHAPTER SEVEN:

the CIRCULATORY SYSTEM

SCHEMATIC of the CIRCULATORY SYSTEM

The circulatory system of the human body is actually two systems: a pulmonary circulation extending from the heart to the lungs and back to the heart; and a systemic circulation, extending from the heart to all other parts of the body then back to the heart. Successive plates in this part of the book will deal with individual blood vessels to individual portions of the body. Before becoming detailed, however, we shall examine the entire circulatory system by exploring a schematic diagram of the system. The objective is to make note of the two circuits that comprise the system and to see how they relate to one another. In addition, we shall examine the general pattern of circulation in the body.

> Begin your work in the plate by coloring the main title Schematic of the Circulatory System. Then, as you look over the plate you will see that the schematic diagram resembles the blueprint of a building or house. No organs are shown on the plate, except for a vague outline of the heart. As the plate develops, you will see there are two circuits comprising the circulatory system. For the plate, you might consider using three colors: red for arteries (carrying oxygen-rich blood); green for capillaries in the body organs and tissues; and blue for veins (carrying oxygen-poor blood). Dark shades may be used because there is little overlap of the structures. The flow of blood is indicated in the plate by arrows near the tubes. You will also note that we have used a broken line (- - - - -) to show where an artery or vein begins or ends. Since many blood vessels flow into other blood vessels, it is important to know where one begins and another ends. As you encounter the structures of the circulatory system in the reading below, color the titles, then locate them in the diagram and color them using the suggested three colors.

We shall begin the flow of blood through the circulatory system by focusing on the **right atrium (A)** of the heart. Wait to color this structure for a moment. (As the diagram shows, two blood vessels carry blood into the atrium.) Then the blood flows to the **right ventricle (B)**. Note that the anatomical right is your visual left. Blood then flows up and out of the right ventricle into the **pulmonary trunk (C)**. The right atrium and ventricle carry oxygen-poor blood and should be colored blue. (This is an exception to the red color we suggested before.) The pulmonary trunk is also carrying oxygen-poor blood so it should be colored blue.

The pulmonary trunk splits to form the **left pulmonary artery (C_1)** and the **right pulmonary artery (C_2)**. Both of these arteries carry oxygen-poor blood so they should be blue. The arteries lead to the capillaries of the **right lung (D)** and capillaries of the **left lung (E)**. Both of these capillary beds should be colored green. Emerging from the right and left lung, the blood is oxygen-rich. It enters the **left pulmonary vein (F_1)** and the **right pulmonary vein (F_2)**. Both of these veins should be colored red, because

the blood is oxygen-rich. (This is an exception to the blue color we suggested above.) The veins carry blood back to the **left atrium of the heart (G)**. Before we leave the right and left pulmonary vein, we should point out that these are the only veins of the body that carry oxygen-rich blood. As a general rule, arteries carry oxygen-rich blood.

> We have examined the pulmonary circuit of the circulatory system. In this circuit blood is carried from the right ventricle out to the lungs where it receives a supply of oxygen, then returns to the left atrium. We shall now examine the systemic circuit. In this circuit, blood flows from the heart to the organs of the body (except the lungs). It flows through the capillaries of the organs, then returns to the right side of the heart. Be prepared to use reds for the blood carried in arteries leading away from the heart. Green should be used for the capillary beds, and blue for blood in the veins. As you read about the blood vessels below, color their titles and locate them on the diagram.

Having returned from the lungs, oxygen-rich blood enters the left atrium, as noted above. It then flows into the **left ventricle (H)**, which should be colored red. When the muscles of the ventricle contract, oxygen-rich blood flows out of the main artery, the **aorta (I)**. The aorta passes up toward the head, bends to the right, then completes the turn and becomes the **thoracic aorta (I_1)**. The thoracic aorta will continue inferiorly along the spinal column until it passes through the diaphragm. We shall return to the thoracic aorta presently.

Just before the aorta becomes the thoracic aorta, a major set of blood vessels branches off. These vessels are the **carotid arteries (J)**. They carry blood to the capillaries of the head and **upper extremities (K)**. The capillaries should be colored green. After blood has supplied oxygen to these organs, it emerges and returns toward the heart through the **superior vena cava (L)**. This large vein contains oxygen-poor blood and should be colored blue. The vein leads back to the right atrium.

Returning to the thoracic aorta, note that a branch of the aorta leads to the capillaries of the **thoracic organs (M)** such as muscles and glands. After servicing these organs, the blood emerges oxygen-poor and is carried back toward the heart through the **azygous veins (N)**. These veins should be colored blue. They will join the superior vena cava just before it enters the right atrium.

> We have now seen much of the systemic circulation in the area above the diaphragm. We shall complete the plate by briefly mentioning the areas in the systemic circulation below the diaphragm. As before, continue coloring the oxygen-rich arteries in red, and the oxygen-poor blood in the veins blue.

Passing through the diaphragm, the aorta is now referred to as the **abdominal aorta (I_2)**. Major branches of the aorta supply blood to the visceral organs. The capillaries of the **visceral organs (O)** are shown schematically. The abdominal aorta continues and supplies the capillaries of the pelvis and **lower extremities (P)**. From both of these regions, veins emerge and unite to form the **inferior vena cava (Q)**. The dotted line shows the beginning of the inferior vena cava. This important vein flows toward the heart. It enters the right atrium near the point where the superior vena cava also enters. Thus, the systemic circuit is completed from the region above the heart as well as the region below the heart.

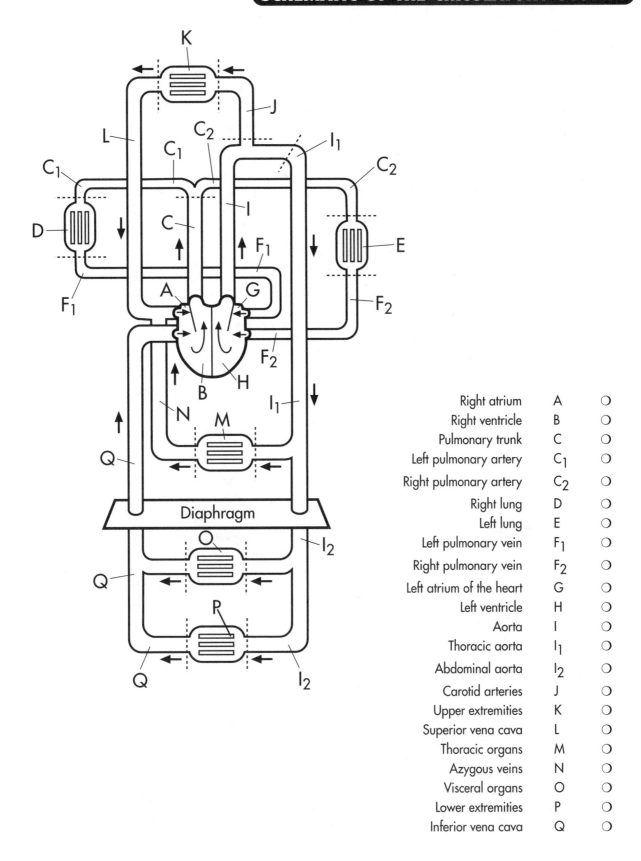

Right atrium	A	○
Right ventricle	B	○
Pulmonary trunk	C	○
Left pulmonary artery	C_1	○
Right pulmonary artery	C_2	○
Right lung	D	○
Left lung	E	○
Left pulmonary vein	F_1	○
Right pulmonary vein	F_2	○
Left atrium of the heart	G	○
Left ventricle	H	○
Aorta	I	○
Thoracic aorta	I_1	○
Abdominal aorta	I_2	○
Carotid arteries	J	○
Upper extremities	K	○
Superior vena cava	L	○
Thoracic organs	M	○
Azygous veins	N	○
Visceral organs	O	○
Lower extremities	P	○
Inferior vena cava	Q	○

the HEART (EXTERNAL ANATOMY)

The heart is the pump of the circulatory system. It uses arteries to deliver blood to the cells and tissues and the veins to receive it back. It also pumps to the lungs where the blood is oxygenated and receives blood back from the lungs after oxygenation has taken place.

In the previous plate, we examined the general plan of the circulatory system, and we focus here on the heart. Enclosed within the mediastinum, the heart is anterior to the vertebral column and posterior to the sternum. Its external anatomy is examined from anterior and posterior views in this plate, and its internal anatomy is discussed in the following plate.

> We present here two views of the heart, the major vessels leading to and from the heart, and the vessels supplying the muscle of the heart. As you encounter the structures in the reading, you should color them in both anterior and posterior views. The coronary circulation is discussed last. Begin by coloring the main title The Heart (External Anatomy).

The heart is about the size of a fist. It is a hollow, cone-shaped organ with its apex at the bottom pointing to the anatomical left, and its broad base at the top, pointing toward the right shoulder. The apex of the heart rests on the diaphragm.

The main blood vessels returning blood to the heart are the **superior vena cava (A$_1$)** and the **inferior vena cava (A$_2$)**. Both vessels may be seen in the posterior view as they join at the **right auricle (B)**. The auricle is a flaplike extension of the atrium, which is the receiving chamber of the heart. The auricle is seen as a flat structure because it contains no blood.

After passing through the right auricle and accumulating in the right atrium, the blood passes to the **right ventricle (C)**. Although prominent in the diagram, the right ventricle is the less muscular of the two ventricles.

Blood exits the right ventricle and enters the **pulmonary trunk (D)**. The trunk has been cut in the anterior view to show the pulmonary veins behind it. The pulmonary trunk immediately divides to form the **left pulmonary artery (E)** and the **right pulmonary artery (F)**. The posterior view shows this division best. The left and right pulmonary arteries lead to the left and right lungs, respectively, where carbon dioxide leaves the blood and oxygen enters. The blood then returns through a series of **pulmonary veins (G)**.

> We have examined how the blood is received by the heart then sent for oxygenation. We now continue to examine the external anatomy of the heart, noting what happens after the blood returns from the lungs. Continue your coloring as before, and locate the titles and structures as you proceed.

On returning to the heart, blood enters the **left auricle (H)**, which is an extension of the left atrium. The blood then enters the **left ventricle (I)**, which is seen prominently in the posterior view. When the heart contracts, the left ventricle pumps blood out through the **aorta (J)**. This is the largest and strongest body artery. The aorta turns at the **arch of the aorta (J$_1$)** and numerous blood vessels arise to the neck, head, and right limb. Further details on these trunks and the arteries to the body are presented in succeeding plates.

Three anatomical landmarks are seen in the external anatomy of the heart. The first is a deep groove called the **coronary sulcus (K)**, pointed out by an arrow. The sulcus indicates the border between the ventricles and the atria. The second depression is the **anterior ventricular sulcus (L)**, where the left and right ventricles meet. On the posterior aspect is the **posterior ventricular sulcus (M)**. Much fat is usually accumulated in this sulcus as the posterior view shows. In the anterior view, the fat has been removed to reveal the coronary blood vessels, which are discussed next.

> Continuing with the external anatomy of the heart, we discuss the coronary arteries that supply the muscle of the heart. This blood supply is essential for continued health of the muscle. Continue your reading, and color the titles and vessels as they are encountered.

The cardiac muscle fibers receive oxygen for their metabolism and release waste products into coronary vessels. The **right coronary artery (N$_1$)** is found in the coronary sulcus. It carries blood to the right atrium and portions of both ventricles. The **left coronary artery (N$_2$)** carries blood to the wall of the left ventricle. Arising from the right coronary artery are the **marginal branches (O)** that extend across the wall of the right ventricle. The left coronary artery gives rise to the **circumflex branch (P)**. The **anterior interventricular branch (Q)** moves near the pulmonary trunk, which has been cut in the anterior view, and descends along the heart's anterior surface within the septum.

Blood returns from the heart wall through a series of coronary veins. The **great cardiac vein (R)** is seen on the anterior surface carrying blood from the apex of the heart within the anterior ventricular sulcus. The **middle cardiac vein (S)** is observed in the posterior view within the posterior ventricular sulcus. Both veins lead to the **coronary sinus (T)**, a large vein found within the coronary sulcus at the posterior portion of the heart. The sinus accumulates blood and returns it into the right atrium for recirculation to the body.

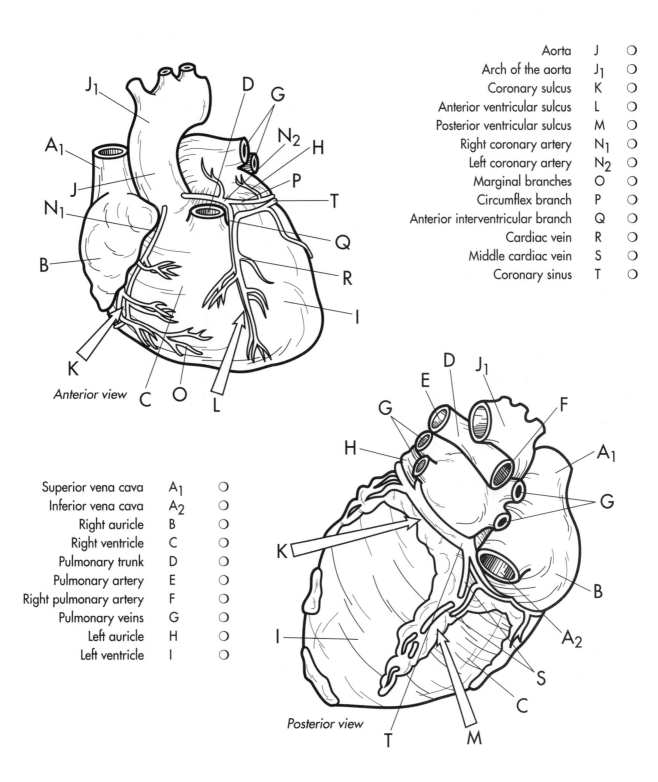

Aorta · J · ○
Arch of the aorta · J_1 · ○
Coronary sulcus · K · ○
Anterior ventricular sulcus · L · ○
Posterior ventricular sulcus · M · ○
Right coronary artery · N_1 · ○
Left coronary artery · N_2 · ○
Marginal branches · O · ○
Circumflex branch · P · ○
Anterior interventricular branch · Q · ○
Cardiac vein · R · ○
Middle cardiac vein · S · ○
Coronary sinus · T · ○

Anterior view

Superior vena cava · A_1 · ○
Inferior vena cava · A_2 · ○
Right auricle · B · ○
Right ventricle · C · ○
Pulmonary trunk · D · ○
Pulmonary artery · E · ○
Right pulmonary artery · F · ○
Pulmonary veins · G · ○
Left auricle · H · ○
Left ventricle · I · ○

Posterior view

the HEART (INTERNAL ANATOMY)

The functions of the cardiovascular system depend on the activity of the heart, as it pumps blood to the lungs and body systems and receives blood back for recirculation. Each day, the heart beats about 100,000 times at a rate of approximately 70 beats per minute. In this plate, we present a view of the internal anatomy of the heart as an extension of the external anatomy surveyed in the previous plate.

> As this plate indicates, cuts have been made in various directions through the muscle, vessels, and other sections of the heart to expose its internal anatomy. To follow the pathway of blood through the heart, the plate contains a number of arrows, which you may color as you move along. Begin your work by coloring the main title The Heart (Internal Anatomy).

The heart pumps blood into two closed circuits: the systemic circulation, which supplies the body cells, tissues, and organs; and the pulmonary circulation, which carries blood to the lungs. After completing these circuits, all blood returns to the heart through the two main veins, the **superior vena cava (A_1)** and the **inferior vena cava (A_2)**.

The vena cavae meet at the **right atrium (B)**. The flaplike sac extending from this cavity is called the auricle, seen in the previous plate. The superior and posterior portion of the right atrium receives blood from the superior vena cava, while the posterior and inferior portions of the right atrium receive blood from the inferior vena cava. Within the right atrium are a number of muscular ridges, the **pectinate muscles (B_1)**. In the wall of the right atrium is a depression called the **fossa ovalis (B_2)**. This area marks the location of the foramen ovale, an opening in the embryonic and fetal stage between the right and left atria.

> We now follow the flow of blood from the right atrium into the right ventricle and out to the lungs. Continue your coloring as before, and locate the titles as they occur in the reading. The structures should also be colored as they are encountered.

From the right atrium, the blood flows through the right atrioventricular valve, also called the tricuspid valve. The arrow shows this blood flow, and a blue color is best. This valve has three flaps or cusps. One **cusp (C_1)** is indicated. Strands of connective tissues called **chordae tendinae (C_2)** support the valve and prevent the cusps from flapping back into the right atrium. The **papillary muscles (C_3)** hold the chordae tendinae in firm position.

On entering the **right ventricle (D)**, the blood enters the smaller of the two heart chambers. Note that its muscle wall is thinner than the opposite ventricle. Walls of the right ventricle contain many folds called **trabecular carneae (D_1)**. Blood flows into the ventricle, and when the ventricle contracts, it is forced upward, as the arrow shows. Note the substantial size of the **interventricular septum (E)** separating the right and left ventricles. The blood is forced out through the **pulmonary semilunar valve (F)**, then into the pulmonary trunk. The valve prevents the blood from flowing back into the ventricle.

The **pulmonary trunk (G)** now divides to form the **left pulmonary arteries (G_1)** and the **right pulmonary arteries (G_2)**, which lead to the two lungs. This begins the pulmonary circuit. Note the direction of the arrows and color them in blue.

> Blood is circulated out to the lungs for oxygenation then returns to the heart for distribution to the body. In the next section we trace the flow of blood through the left side of the heart.

Blood returns to the heart by means of the **pulmonary veins (H)**. Since the blood is oxygenated, the arrows may be colored in red. We show the pulmonary veins only on the left side of the heart because they are hidden on the right side.

Blood now enters the **left atrium (I)** of the heart, the second receiving chamber. The atrium is separated from the right atrium by the **intraatrial septum (J)**.

Blood is now ready to enter the ventricle and it flows through the left atrioventricular valve, also called the mitral valve. A **cusp of the valve (K_1)** is shown. This valve has two cusps and is often called bicuspid valve. The left valve also has **chordae tendinae (K_2)** and **papillary muscles (K_3)**, which support it and prevent it from flapping backward into the atrium.

The blood then enters the **left ventricle (L)**, which is the larger of the two. Note the arrows entering through the valve and following the course of blood through the ventricle. When the ventricle undergoes contraction, the blood is forced up to the aorta. It passes through the **aortic semilunar valve (M)**, which cannot be seen because it lies behind the pulmonary trunk.

On passing through the valve, oxygenated blood enters the **arch of the aorta (N)**. The aorta turns, and several branches emerge, as the succeeding plates discuss. The aorta turns to the posterior region and flows behind the heart. It can be seen emerging as the **descending aorta (O)**. Arteries arising from the aorta reach to all parts of the thorax, abdomen, pelvic cavity, and lower extremities. The blood then nourishes the tissues and returns to the heart to complete the circulation.

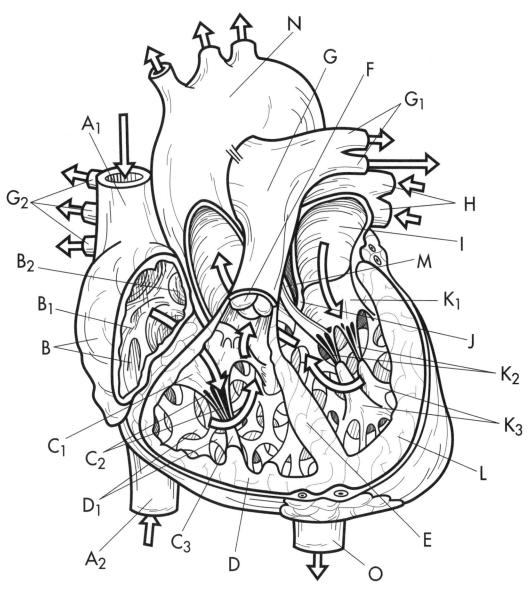

Superior vena cava	A₁	○	Left pulmonary arteries	G₁	○
Inferior vena cava	A₂	○	Right pulmonary arteries	G₂	○
Right atrium	B	○	Pulmonary veins	H	○
Pectinate muscles	B₁	○	Left atrium	I	○
Fossa ovalis	B₂	○	Intraatrial septum	J	○
Cusp	C₁	○	Cusp of the valve	K₁	○
Chordae tendinae	C₂	○	Chordae tendinae	K₂	○
Papillary muscles	C₃	○	Papillary muscles	K₃	○
Right ventricle	D	○	Left ventricle	L	○
Trabecular carneae	D₁	○	Aortic semilunar valve	M	○
Interventricular septum	E	○	Arch of the aorta	N	○
Pulmonary semilunar valve	F	○	Descending aorta	O	○
Pulmonary trunk	G	○			

PRINCIPAL ARTERIES of the BODY

The arteries of the systemic circulation transport blood away from the heart. Their main purpose is to carry oxygen and nutrients to body tissues, but they also carry hormones and elements of the body's immune system. All the systemic arteries of the body branch from the aorta. This major vessel is the source of the principal arteries of the body, as we shall see in this plate.

Begin this plate by coloring the title Principal Arteries of the Body. As you look over the plate, you will note that the emphasis is on the major arterial routes leading away from the heart. Note that many letters carry a subscript 1 or 2. Arteries indicated with a 1 lie on the anatomical left side of the body (your visual right), while those arteries labeled with a number 2 lie on the anatomical right side (your visual left). When considering the arteries, the same name is used for both the right and left artery. Another characteristic of arteries is that they flow into one another, much as one river flows into another. In many cases, a single major artery will give rise to many minor arteries leading to various places in the body. It is often difficult to distinguish where one artery begins and another ends, so we have marked the boundaries (i.e., the beginning and end of the artery) with markers for your use. The area between the markers is the boundary point for a particular artery. When coloring the arteries, darker colors may be used for the large arteries, but as you reach the smaller ones, a lighter color is recommended. Do not be concerned with the smaller, unnamed arteries at this point, since they will be covered in successive plates.

Arising from the left ventricle of the heart is the largest artery of the body, the **aorta (A)**. In the plate, this artery is seen making a curve to the left, at which point the aorta becomes the **thoracic aorta (A_1)**. The thoracic aorta passes near the spine and through the diaphragm. It then becomes the **abdominal aorta (A_2)**, which splits to become the common iliac arteries that we shall encounter presently.

A major branch of the aorta at its arch area is the **brachiocephalic trunk (B)**, also called the innominate artery. It branches into the common carotid artery, which then branches into the **left common carotid (C_1)** and the **right common carotid artery (C_2)**. The right common carotid artery then divides to form the **right external carotid artery (C_3)**. The **right internal carotid artery (C_4)** also arises here. It may be difficult to see on the diagram, because it runs close to the right external carotid. The carotid arteries supply the neck and head with blood.

The third branch from the brachiocephalic trunk is the **right subclavian artery (E_2)**. This pattern is seen only on the right side of the body. On the left side, the **left subclavian artery (E_1)** arises from the arch of the aorta. The subclavian arteries supply the upper limbs with blood. Arising from the right subclavian artery is the **vertebral artery (D)** to the vertebrae, deep muscles of the neck, and spinal cord.

Also arising from the subclavian arteries are the **left and right axillary arteries (F_1 and F_2)**. Axillary arteries supply the muscles of the shoulder and thoracic muscles. They give rise to the **brachial arteries (G_1 and G_2)**, which service the arm. The **radial arteries (H_1 and H_2)** arise from the brachial and carry blood to muscles of the forearm, as do the **ulnar arteries (I_1 and I_2)**.

To this point we have briefly surveyed the principal arteries to the head, neck, and upper extremity. These arteries are explored in more detail in a future plate. For the time being, we shall return to the thoracic and abdominal regions, and locate the principal branches from the aorta. Continue your coloring as you read below, and continue to locate the arteries on the left and right sides. Watch for the beginning and ending of the artery, and try to make your colors blend as one artery becomes another.

The **coronary arteries (J)** are so-named because they "crown" the heart. Arising from the aorta just as it leaves the left ventricle, the arteries pass into the heart muscle, and they supply the muscle of this organ with oxygen and nutrients. After the aorta has passed through the diaphragm, a major trunk emerges. This is an unpaired artery called the **celiac trunk (K)**. Arteries from the celiac trunk branch to the liver, stomach, spleen, and other regions of the upper abdomen. The **hepatic artery (L)** branches from the celiac trunk and extends to the liver. From the abdominal aorta, the **gastric artery (M)** supplies the stomach, while the **splenic artery (N)** moves in the direction of the spleen.

Inferior to the celiac trunk is the origin of the paired renal arteries. The **left renal artery (O_1)** supplies the left kidney, while the **right renal artery (O_2)** extends to the right kidney. Next is the unpaired **superior mesenteric artery (P)**. This artery carries blood to the small intestine, pancreas, and portions of the large intestine. The **gonadal artery (Q)** leads to arteries supplying the ovaries in females and testes in males. Beyond the gonadal artery is the **inferior mesenteric artery (R)**. The plate shows its numerous branches as it services portions of the transverse colon, descending colon, sigmoid colon, and rectum.

At the level of the fourth lumbar vertebra, the abdominal aorta divides and the two major arteries that arise are the **common iliac arteries (S_1 and S_2)**. They soon split to form the internal and external iliac arteries. Only the external iliac arteries are shown (**T_1, T_2**). These arteries lead to the **left and right femoral arteries (U_1, U_2)**. Blood from these arteries will service muscles at the floor of the body cavity and near the femur. More detailed descriptions of arteries in this area are given in a future plate.

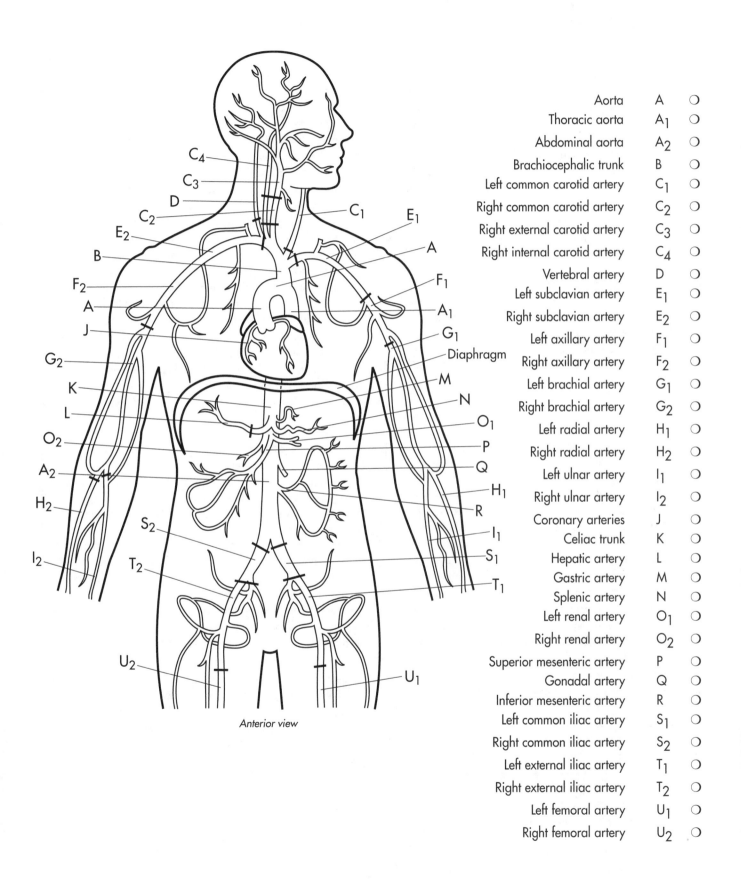

Anterior view

Aorta	A	○
Thoracic aorta	A_1	○
Abdominal aorta	A_2	○
Brachiocephalic trunk	B	○
Left common carotid artery	C_1	○
Right common carotid artery	C_2	○
Right external carotid artery	C_3	○
Right internal carotid artery	C_4	○
Vertebral artery	D	○
Left subclavian artery	E_1	○
Right subclavian artery	E_2	○
Left axillary artery	F_1	○
Right axillary artery	F_2	○
Left brachial artery	G_1	○
Right brachial artery	G_2	○
Left radial artery	H_1	○
Right radial artery	H_2	○
Left ulnar artery	I_1	○
Right ulnar artery	I_2	○
Coronary arteries	J	○
Celiac trunk	K	○
Hepatic artery	L	○
Gastric artery	M	○
Splenic artery	N	○
Left renal artery	O_1	○
Right renal artery	O_2	○
Superior mesenteric artery	P	○
Gonadal artery	Q	○
Inferior mesenteric artery	R	○
Left common iliac artery	S_1	○
Right common iliac artery	S_2	○
Left external iliac artery	T_1	○
Right external iliac artery	T_2	○
Left femoral artery	U_1	○
Right femoral artery	U_2	○

ARTERIES of the HEAD and NECK

The head and neck are supplied with blood by four pairs of arteries, the major considerations of this plate. The plate also contains an arterial flowchart permitting you to follow the course of blood from the aorta to the arteries at the base of the brain at the circle of Willis. Many of the arteries seen in this plate have been encountered in the previous plate, and many will also be encountered in the next plate exploring the arteries of the upper extremity. Because the brain uses the major proportion of oxygen available in the body (approximately 90%), the arteries carrying blood to the brain are among the most important ones in the body.

> Begin the plate by coloring in the main title Arteries of the Head and Neck. Note that we are presenting a view from the right lateral aspect of the head and neck, and we shall be focusing on the arteries of this aspect. The arterial flowchart should also be considered as you read the text below. This chart will show you how blood reaches the brain from the aorta. As you read about the arteries, color their titles, then locate them in the diagram and color them in. Darker colors may be used for the larger arteries, but pale colors should be employed for the smaller ones. In most cases, the origin of the artery will be clear because it is a tributary of a main artery.

As the **aorta (A)** emerges from the heart, it subdivides to form the main trunk called the **brachiocephalic trunk (B)**. The brachiocephalic trunk splits and forms the **common carotid artery (C)** and the **subclavian artery (D)**. The subclavian artery supplies blood to the shoulders, chest wall, arms, back, and central nervous system. (The following plate explores arteries of the upper extremity that arise from it.) In this diagram, we observe the **internal thoracic artery (E)**. The internal thoracic artery is also known as the mammary artery. It supplies blood to the wall of the interior thorax and mammary gland in the female.

Superior and slightly lateral to the internal thoracic artery is the **thyrocervical trunk (F)**. Some scapula muscles and the thyroid gland are supplied by branches of this artery. Further along is the **costocervical trunk (G)**. Muscles of the deep neck region are supplied with blood by this artery, and the superior intercostal muscles receive blood from it also.

> We have noted several important branches from the subclavian artery just before it enters the arm. We shall now move up the neck and encounter the arteries that enter the head and brain region. Many of these arteries will lead to the circle of Willis, and you should color in the arterial flowchart as you proceed. As you encounter the titles of the arteries, color them in also.

Another major branch from the subclavian artery is the **vertebral artery (H)**. This artery carries blood to the brain and spinal cord. Ascending through the foramina of the transverse processes of the vertebrae, the vertebral artery enters the skull through the foramen magnum. Branches extend from the vertebral artery into the spinal cord of the cervical area and into deep structures of the neck. Within the cranium, the left vertebral artery joins with the right vertebral artery to form the **basilar artery (I)**. Descending along the brain stem, this artery has branches extending to the pons, cerebellum, and inner ear.

We shall leave the basilar artery for a moment and return to the **common carotid artery (C)**. The common carotid extends from the brachiocephalic trunk, passes close to the trachea, then swells slightly to form the carotid sinus. Receptors that help control blood pressure are located here. The common carotid artery then divides to form the **external carotid artery (K)** and the **internal carotid artery (L)**. The **occipital artery (O)** arises from the internal carotid artery and supplies blood to the posterior region of the scalp.

The external carotid artery supplies many tissues of the head through its numerous branches. These branches include the **superior thyroid artery (R)**, which extends to the larynx and thyroid gland. The **lingual artery (M)** carries blood to the tongue from the external carotid, and the **facial artery (N)** brings blood to the muscles and skin of the anterior aspect of the face. Further along, the **maxillary artery (P)** brings blood to the lower and upper jaws as well as the chewing muscles of the jaw area. The final vessel we shall consider is the **superficial temporal artery (Q)**. The parotid gland and much of the superficial part of the temporal area receive blood from this artery.

> We shall conclude the plate by examining the region where many blood vessels come together in the brain. This region is found within the cranium at the base of the brain. Therefore it is presented in subdued lines in the diagram. Light colors should be used to highlight the arteries involved.

The basilar artery joins with the left and right internal carotid arteries to form an arrangement of blood vessels called the cerebroarterial circle, or the circle of Willis. Most of the arteries supplying the brain tissue emerge from this circle of arteries. Several arteries are used to form the circle of Willis. They include the **posterior cerebral artery (J_1)**, a **communicating artery (J_2)**, the **middle cerebral artery (J_3)**, and the **anterior cerebral artery (J_4)**. They form a circle as this helps equalize the blood pressure to various parts of the brain while providing alternative routes for blood to enter the brain. Alternative routes are important if any of the arteries are damaged. The circle of Willis is seen in more detail in the plate concerning the arteries of the brain. The flowchart also shows the three arteries contributing to the circle of Willis.

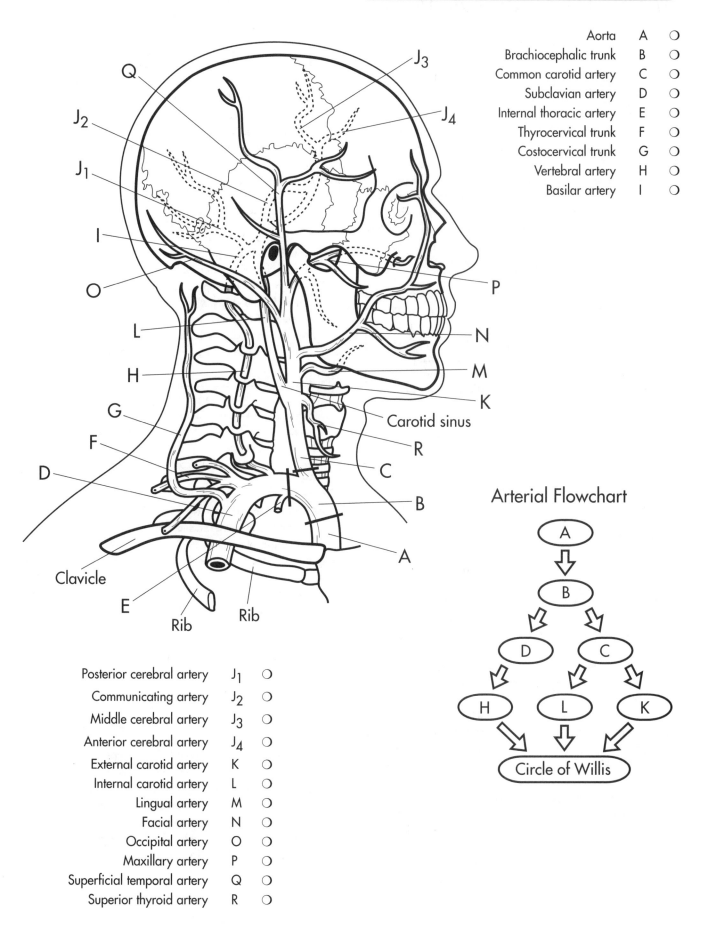

Aorta A ○
Brachiocephalic trunk B ○
Common carotid artery C ○
Subclavian artery D ○
Internal thoracic artery E ○
Thyrocervical trunk F ○
Costocervical trunk G ○
Vertebral artery H ○
Basilar artery I ○

Carotid sinus

Clavicle

Rib

Rib

Arterial Flowchart

A
B
D   C
H   L   K
Circle of Willis

Posterior cerebral artery J₁ ○
Communicating artery J₂ ○
Middle cerebral artery J₃ ○
Anterior cerebral artery J₄ ○
External carotid artery K ○
Internal carotid artery L ○
Lingual artery M ○
Facial artery N ○
Occipital artery O ○
Maxillary artery P ○
Superficial temporal artery Q ○
Superior thyroid artery R ○

ARTERIES of the UPPER EXTREMITY

The tissues of the left and right upper limbs are supplied by arteries arising from the left and right subclavian arteries. The emphasis in this plate will be the right upper extremity (anterior view), but the arteries of the left upper extremity present a mirror image. In this plate, we also present an arterial flowchart showing how a drop of blood would pass from the aorta to the most distal phalanx of the finger. This flowchart will show how the blood vessels are continuous, even though they are known by different names in different parts of the body. The plate is related to the previous plate concerning arteries of the head and neck.

As you look over the plate, note that there are two parts: first we present a diagram of the right upper limb from the anterior view. An arterial flowchart is also presented so that you can follow the course of blood from the heart to the fingertips. You should begin by coloring the main title Arteries of the Upper Extremity. Then as you read about the arteries, color their titles, then locate them in the diagram and flowchart. Not all arteries will be present on the flowchart since many are tributaries of the main arterial network. Where one artery becomes another, we have used marks to indicate the beginning or end of an artery. If possible, you should use variations of the same color to show that the artery is continuous with the next artery.

Emerging from the left ventricle, the aorta is the main artery of the arterial system. In the adult, it is about one inch in diameter, and has the thickest wall of any artery. The **aorta (A)** may be seen arching as it leaves the heart.

Arising from the ascending aorta are three main arteries. The first is the **brachiocephalic trunk (B)**, also called the innominate artery. Next arising from the ascending aorta is the **left subclavian artery (C)**, which will extend toward the left upper extremity. The third artery arising at the aortic arch is the **left common carotid artery (D)**. This artery will branch into the external and internal carotid arteries, as the previous plate shows.

The brachiocephalic trunk has two main branches. After ascending a short distance, it forms the **right common carotid artery (E)**, which extends into the head as the previous plate shows. The second branch is the **right subclavian artery (I)**. The right subclavian artery is the major thoroughfare into the right upper extremity.

The left subclavian artery carries blood to the shoulders, arms, back, and central nervous system. While it is still in the thoracic cavity, the subclavian artery gives rise to the **right vertebral artery (F)**, which carries blood to the brain and spinal cord. Shortly thereafter, the subclavian gives rise to the **thyrocervical trunk (G)**, which carries blood to the neck, shoulder, and upper back muscles and tissues. Arising from the thyrocervical trunk is the **suprascapular artery (H)**. This artery extends toward the scapula and passes near its superior border.

Thus far, we have discussed the major branches from the left ventricle of the heart. We shall now concentrate on the upper extremity and shoulder area. As you look over the plate, notice the single main tube beginning with the subclavian and passing into the forearm, then down to the wrist. Note how other arteries branch off this major thoroughfare. Many of these arteries will be encountered and they should be colored with darker colors if the area is uncluttered. Lighter colors may be used if the area is congested. The bones may be colored using pale shades and grays. This will not obscure the arteries in the area. Where a branch from a main artery has occurred you may assume that the origin of the artery is at that main artery.

The subclavian artery passes under the clavicle and at the region of the first rib, it becomes the **axillary artery (J)**. This artery is shown in the flowchart, and it should also be colored. An important branch of the axillary artery is the **subscapular artery (K)**. This artery supplies the inferior aspect of the scapula. The axillary artery also gives rise to the **posterior humoral circumflex artery (L)**. This artery wraps around the neck of the humerus to supply the shoulder joint and deltoid muscle with blood. The same function is supplied by the **anterior humoral circumflex artery (M)**.

You may complete your work on the plate by focusing on the lower part of the arm, the forearm. Note how the arteries extend through this area to supply the wrist and hands. As before, color the main arteries with darker colors and watch for continuous arteries. Be careful not to obscure the minor arteries.

As the axillary artery emerges into the arm and runs along the humerus, it is known as the **brachial artery (N)**. This artery is seen on the medial aspect of the humerus. A branch of the brachial called the **deep brachial artery (O)** extends to the triceps brachii muscle at the posterior aspect. Several branches extend from the brachial artery along the way. One is the **nutrient artery of the humerus (P)**. This artery enters the bone tissue of the humerus and supplies nutrients and oxygen.

Immediately past the elbow, the brachial artery divides and becomes the **radial artery (Q)** and the **ulnar artery (R)**. The radial artery supplies muscles of the lateral aspect of the forearm, while the ulnar artery services the medial muscles. A branch of the ulnar artery is the **interosseus artery (S)**. The artery passes through the interosseus membrane between the radius and ulna and supplies oxygen and nutrients to the deep muscles of the forearm.

In the region of the palm, branches of the ulnar and radial arteries come together (anastomose) to form the **superficial palmar arch (T)** and the **deep palmar arch (U)**. These arches are the origin points of arteries servicing the metacarpal bones and phalanges. Chief among these arteries are the **digital arteries (V)**, which extend out to the most distal phalanges. The flowchart shows these arteries extending to smaller arterioles, which then extend to capillaries supplying individual cells of the fingers.

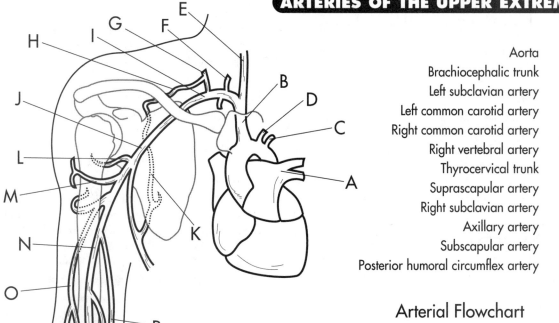

Anterior view

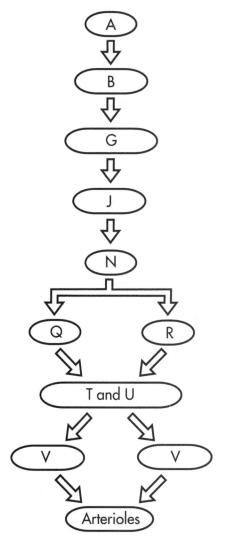

Aorta	A	○
Brachiocephalic trunk	B	○
Left subclavian artery	C	○
Left common carotid artery	D	○
Right common carotid artery	E	○
Right vertebral artery	F	○
Thyrocervical trunk	G	○
Suprascapular artery	H	○
Right subclavian artery	I	○
Axillary artery	J	○
Subscapular artery	K	○
Posterior humoral circumflex artery	L	○

Arterial Flowchart

A → B → G → J → N

N → Q and R → T and U → V and V → Arterioles

Anterior humoral circumflex artery	M	○
Brachial artery	N	○
Deep brachial artery	O	○
Nutrient artery of the humerus	P	○
Radial artery	Q	○
Ulnar artery	R	○
Interosseus artery	S	○

Superficial palmar arch	T	○
Deep palmar arch	U	○
Digital arteries	V	○

ARTERIES to the BRAIN

The brain is supplied with blood arriving by means of the internal carotid arteries and the vertebral arteries. These arteries pass through the skull through foramina and deliver the oxygen and nutrients needed by the brain tissue. In this plate, we discuss the arteries at the floor of the brain. The arterial supply of the nerve tissue extends out from these main passageways.

As you look over the plate, you will note that we are viewing the brain from the inferior position and we present a schematic diagram of the circle of Willis. Many of the arteries we discuss are also explored in a previous plate on arteries to the neck and head. Start the plate by coloring the main title Arteries to the Brain. Then consider using dark colors for the larger blood vessels and lighter ones for the smaller vessels. In addition, some vessels will extend into the brain tissue and may not be as clear as the ones on the surface. These deeper arteries should be colored in pale or light colors, such as grays or yellow. If you wish to color the brain tissue, we recommend choosing a light color.

From the aorta, the common carotid arteries ascend into the neck tissues. They then divide into the external carotid arteries and the internal carotid arteries. The internal carotid arteries pass through the internal carotid foramina of the temporal bone to deliver blood to the brain. The **internal carotid artery (A)** is seen on the right and left side of the brain. It has been cut to allow you to see the underlying tissues.

When the internal carotid artery reaches the level of the optic nerves, it divides to form three important branches. Two of these branches service the tissue of the brain. One branch is the **anterior cerebral artery (B)**. This artery can be seen extending toward the frontal lobe of the brain. It will also reach to the parietal lobe. The other important branch is the **middle cerebral artery (C)**. The diagram shows this artery extending to the right and left lateral surfaces of the brain.

Continuing with the arteries at the base of the brain, we will note the arteries that form the circle of Willis. These arteries are rather large and dark colors may be used to highlight them. As you encounter the artery in the reading below, color its title and the artery in the diagram. In some cases the subscript 1 indicates the left side while the subscript 2 indicates the right side. Both left and right arteries should be colored in the same shade. Also, locate the arteries in the schematic diagram and color them in with the same shade.

Because the brain is an extremely active organ, it must be supplied with nutrients and oxygen without interruption. As we have noted, blood reaches the brain by the internal carotid artery. It also reaches the brain by means of the **right and left vertebral arteries (I_1 and I_2)**. These arteries enter the brain area through the transverse foramina of the cervical vertebrae. They then pass through the foramen magnum and fuse near the medulla oblongata to form the **basilar artery (D)**.

The basilar artery continues along the ventral aspect, with many divisions (to be discussed later). It then divides to form the **posterior cerebral arteries (E_1 and E_2)** and the **posterior communicating arteries (F_1 and F_2)**. Note in the diagram that the posterior communicating arteries lead to the **anterior communicating artery (G)** to form a ring. The ring is called the cerebral arterial ring, also known as the **circle of Willis (H)**.

The circle of Willis encloses the infundibulum, the stalk leading to the pituitary gland. The circle connects the internal carotid arteries and the basilar artery permitting blood to the reach the cerebrum by either artery. Thus, blood is supplied through two major pathways. Should one be blocked, the other will continue to supply the brain.

In the final portion of this plate, some of the other arteries visible at the base of the brain are highlighted. Most of these arteries originate at vessels previously named, and they tend to be smaller vessels in comparison to the internal carotids, cerebral, and vertebral arteries. Light colors are recommended wherever possible.

One of the main arteries supplying the cerebellum is the **superior cerebellar artery (J)**. This artery can be seen originating at the basilar artery just before it divides to form the posterior cerebral arteries. A similar function is served by the **anterior inferior cerebellar artery (K)**, as the plate shows. The anterior inferior cerebellar artery originates at the basilar artery just after it forms.

A third artery of the cerebellum is the **posterior inferior cerebellar artery (L)**. As the name implies, this artery is more posterior than the anterior inferior cerebellar artery. Arising from the vertebral arteries, the left and right portions can be seen extending to the most posterior portions of the cerebellum.

One of the branches of the basilar artery is the **pontine (M)**. This important artery carries blood to the pons area at the base of the brain. The pontine artery is composed of several branches, as the plate shows. Posterior to the pontine is the **labyrinthine artery (N)**. The labyrinthine artery is also a branch of the basilar artery. It extends to the posterior aspect on either side of the basilar artery and supplies the inner reaches of the cerebellum. The cerebellum is intimately involved with muscle coordination, and like the cerebrum, requires an extensive blood supply.

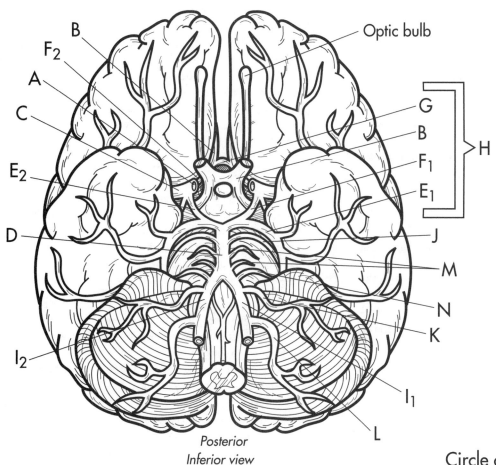

Optic bulb

Posterior
Inferior view

Internal carotid artery   A   ○
Anterior cerebral artery   B   ○
Middle cerebral artery   C   ○
Basilar artery   D   ○
Left posterior cerebral artery E_1 ○
Right posterior cerebral artery E_2 ○
Left posterior communicating artery F_1 ○
Right posterior communicating artery F_2 ○
Anterior communicating artery   G   ○
Circle of Willis   H   ○
Left vertebral artery I_1 ○
Right vertebral artery I_2 ○
Superior cerebellar artery   J   ○
Anterior inferior cerebellar artery   K   ○
Posterior inferior cerebellar artery   L   ○
Pontine   M   ○
Labyrinthine artery   N   ○

Circle of Willis   H

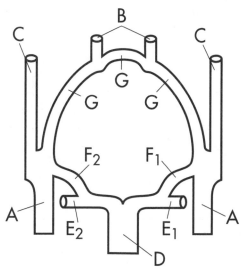

ARTERIES of the THORAX and ABDOMEN

After emerging from the heart, the aorta arches and descends through the thorax and abdomen as the thoracic and abdominal aorta, respectively. Numerous branches from the aorta emerge to supply organs of the abdominal and thoracic cavities. Many of these arteries are surveyed in this plate. An anterior view is presented, and many of the organs have been removed to expose the aorta, which runs along the vertebral column. Some organs are left in place to show their relationship to their arterial blood supply.

> Start by coloring the main title Arteries of the Thorax and Abdomen. Note that the aorta is a very large tube, but that the arteries tend to be small. It would be well, therefore, to use pale colors so that the arteries can be easily distinguished. We have used letters together with the numbers to show left and right. The subscript 1 indicates the left side, while the subscript 2 indicates the right side. Both left and right arteries should be colored with the same shade. The organs and bones may be colored with light colors.

As it leaves the left ventricle of the heart, the **aorta (A)** arches. Three main tubes arise from the aorta, as explained in the plate concerned with the chest and neck. Note that on the left side, the **left subclavian artery (B$_1$)** emerges. The **left common carotid (a)** also emerges and extends to the neck. On the right, the **right subclavian artery (B$_2$)** emerges. Emerging from the right subclavian artery is the **vertebral artery (b)** and the **thyrocervical trunk (c)**. These arteries are noted with lowercase letters because they are incidental to this plate.

Emerging from the subclavian arteries are two important arteries of the thoracic wall: The first is the **internal thoracic artery**, shown on the left and right sides (**C$_1$, C$_2$**). This artery carries blood to the anterior thoracic wall and structures in the mediastinum such as the lymph nodes and diaphragm. The subclavian artery becomes the axillary artery as it continues in the shoulder. Originating in the axial artery are the **lateral thoracic arteries (D$_1$ and D$_2$)**, which provide blood to the muscles of the thoracic wall, the mammary glands in females, and the axillary lymph nodes.

> We shall now turn our attention to many of the arteries emerging from the thoracic aorta and supplying the organs of the thoracic cavity. Note the size of the thoracic aorta in comparison to the much smaller arteries emerging. Lighter colors are recommended for the arteries. Left and right arteries are present.

The thoracic aorta travels along the dorsal thoracic wall slightly to the left of the vertebral column, as the plate shows, in the region between the lungs known as the mediastinum. The so-called visceral arteries emerging from the thoracic aorta supply organs of the thoracic cavity. They include the **bronchial arteries (E)**, which extend to the bronchial tubes, esophagus, and lymph nodes of the region. The **pericardial arteries (F)** carry blood to the membranous pericardium at its posterior aspect. The esophagus is supplied with blood by the **esophageal arteries (G)**. And, a number of **mediastinal arteries (H)** extend to structures at the posterior region of the mediastinum.

Thoracic arteries that supply the chest wall are called parietal arteries. They include the **intercostal arteries (I)** seen running along the ribs. The chest muscles and intercostal muscles receive blood through these arteries. The posterior and superior surfaces of the diaphragm are supplied by the posterior and **superior phrenic arteries (J)**. The diaphragm separates the thoracic and abdominal cavities, and the superior phrenic arteries are the last to emerge from the thoracic aorta.

> We now proceed to the abdominal cavity and note the arteries emerging from the abdominal aorta. Some of these arteries are paired, while others are unpaired arteries. Also, you will note several trunks, which are large arteries leading to smaller arteries. Continue your coloring as before, and take note of the organs supplied by the arteries.

As the thoracic aorta emerges from the diaphragm, it becomes the abdominal aorta. Among the first arteries emerging from the abdominal aorta are the **inferior phrenic arteries (K)**. These arteries carry blood to the inferior portion of the diaphragm.

Also emerging from the abdominal aorta are three unpaired arteries. The first is the **celiac artery (L),** also called the celiac trunk. This main vessel divides into three branches: the **left gastric artery (L$_1$)** extends to the stomach; the **hepatic artery (L$_2$)** extends to the liver; and the **splenic artery (L$_3$)** extends to the spleen. These arteries are studied in depth in the next plate. The second unpaired artery is the **superior mesenteric artery (M)**. It carries blood to the small intestine, pancreas, and large intestine. The third unpaired artery is the **inferior mesenteric artery (N)**. This artery supplies the large intestine and is discussed in the next plate.

The paired arteries emerging from the abdominal aorta include the **suprarenal arteries (O$_1$ and O$_2$)**. These arteries carry blood to the adrenal glands, also called the suprarenal glands. The **renal arteries (P$_1$ and P$_2$)** are shown in place with the kidneys, which receive blood through these arteries. Paired arteries include the **lumbar arteries (Q$_1$ and Q$_2$)**. The abdominal wall and spinal cord receive blood through these arteries. The **gonadal arteries (R$_1$ and R$_2$)** originate at the abdominal aorta and carry blood to the reproductive organs. In the male these include the testes; in the female, the ovaries and fallopian tubes. Therefore, the gonadal arteries are also known as testicular or ovarian arteries, respectively.

Near the level of the fourth lumbar vertebra, the abdominal aorta splits and begins its journey into the pelvis and lower extremities. The main arteries resulting from the division are the **common iliac arteries (S$_1$ and S$_2$)**. These arteries enter the pelvic basin and pass by the sacrum. Then, the arteries become the **external iliac arteries (T$_1$, T$_2$)**. The external iliac arteries pass near the superior iliac spine to enter the thigh as the femoral artery. The further divisions of the external iliac are discussed in the plate on the arteries of the lower leg.

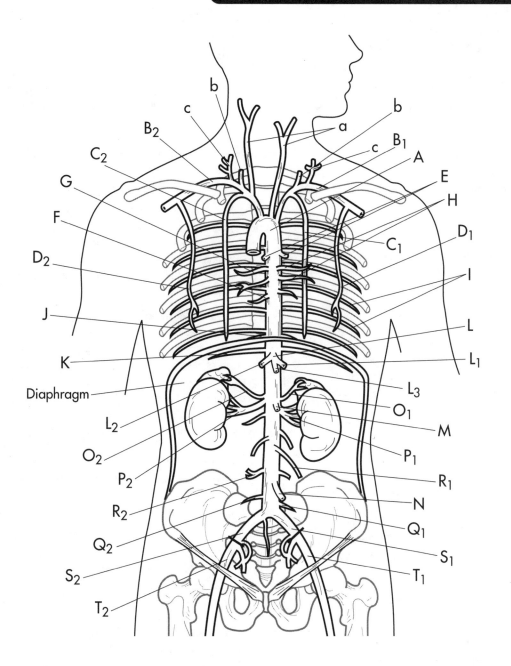

Aorta	A	○	Superior phrenic arteries	J	○	Left lumbar artery	Q_1	○
Left subclavian artery	B_1	○	Inferior phrenic arteries	K	○	Right lumbar artery	Q_2	○
Right subclavian artery	B_2	○	Celiac artery	L	○	Left gonadal artery	R_1	○
Left internal thoracic artery	C_1	○	Left gastric artery	L_1	○	Right gonadal artery	R_2	○
Right internal thoracic artery	C_2	○	Hepatic artery	L_2	○	Left common iliac artery	S_1	○
Left lateral thoracic artery	D_1	○	Splenic artery	L_3	○	Right common iliac artery	S_2	○
Right lateral thoracic artery	D_2	○	Superior mesenteric artery	M	○	Left external iliac artery	T_1	○
Bronchial arteries	E	○	Inferior mesenteric artery	N	○	Right external iliac artery	T_2	○
Pericardial arteries	F	○	Left suprarenal artery	O_1	○	Common carotid arteries	a	○
Esophageal arteries	G	○	Right suprarenal artery	O_2	○	Vertebral artery	b	○
Mediastinal arteries	H	○	Left renal artery	P_1	○	Thyrocervical trunk	c	○
Intercostal arteries	I	○	Right renal artery	P_2	○			

ARTERIES of the GASTRO-INTESTINAL TRACT

The aorta passes through the thoracic cavity, pierces the diaphragm, and enters the abdominopelvic cavity. Then it continues to about the level of the fourth lumbar vertebra, where it divides to become the right and left common iliac arteries.

A number of important arteries branch off the abdominal aorta and service areas of the excretory, reproductive, gastrointestinal, and other systems. The purpose of this plate is to examine these arteries. Many of these arteries arise from unpaired large arteries called trunks. Three major trunks are the celiac, superior mesenteric, and inferior mesenteric trunks.

As you look over the plate, note that there are three diagrams conforming to the celiac, superior mesenteric, and inferior mesenteric trunks (arteries). Each of these arteries will branch off into numerous other arteries supplying regions of the gastrointestinal tract. In most cases, the artery consists of a single long tube with branches. You should start by coloring the main title Arteries of the Gastrointestinal Tract. Then, as you read the paragraphs below, locate the arteries and color them. Light colors are recommended, since many of the arteries are rather small. The organs may be colored in, but use light shades so you do not obscure the arteries. It may be helpful to review the plate of Principal Arteries of the Body in order to orient yourself to the three main trunks (arteries) discussed in this plate.

The **abdominal aorta (A)** is the main thoroughfare of blood through the abdominal and thoracic tract. It lies ventral to the vertebral column and has three main branches discussed in this plate. The first main trunk is the **celiac trunk (B)**, also known as the celiac artery. It is shown very briefly in part A and probably will require only a spot of color. Three branches will arise from this trunk.

The first branch of the celiac artery is the **common hepatic artery (C)**. This artery immediately gives rise to three arteries: the **hepatic artery (D)**, which continues from the common hepatic artery and extends to the liver and gallbladder; the **right gastric artery (E)**, which extends toward the stomach and is seen clearly in the plate (note how it will join with the left gastric artery, which we shall note shortly); and the **gastroduodenal artery (F)**, which carries blood to the stomach, duodenum, and pancreas. In the diagram, three branches of the gastroduodenal artery may be seen extending to the three areas mentioned. The branch to the stomach lining is most apparent.

The second branch of the celiac trunk is the **left gastric artery (G)**. In the diagram, this artery can be seen joining with (anastomosing with) the right gastric artery. A branch of the left gastric artery is the **esophageal artery (H)**. This artery carries blood to the esophagus.

The third branch of the celiac artery is the **splenic artery (I)**. It extends to the spleen and has three branches: the **pancreatic arteries (J)** extending to the pancreas; the left **gastroepiploic artery (K)** extending toward the stomach; and the **short gastric artery (L)** carrying blood to the stomach lining. Also seen briefly in the diagram is the superior mesenteric artery, which is inferior to the celiac trunk. We shall consider it next.

We shall now continue with the second major trunk to the gastrointestinal organs, the superior mesenteric artery. You will note how this artery supplies organs of the intestinal region of the tract. Continue your coloring as you read below, using light colors where the arteries are small in size.

The **superior mesenteric artery (M)** has several branches supplying the intestinal area of the body. The first branch leads to a set of **jejunal arteries (N)**. These arteries supply the region of the jejunum of the small intestine. The next major branch is the **ileal arteries (O)**, which carry blood to the ileum. The ascending colon and the ileum are supplied with blood by the **ileocolic artery (P)**. You will note that this artery joins with its many branches at several locations. The jejunal and ileal arteries do likewise.

The final artery that we shall consider in this group is the **middle colic artery (Q)**. The transverse colon is supplied with blood by this artery, which can be seen extending from the superior mesenteric artery. In part B, the inferior mesenteric artery is briefly seen and you might place a spot of color to denote its position.

The final part of this plate is part C. Here the focus is the inferior mesenteric artery. As with branches of the superior mesenteric, there is much joining of branches of the inferior mesenteric. The anatomical term for this joining is anastomose. Places where the arteries join are called anastomoses (singular, anastomosis). To complete the plate, continue to use light colors for the arteries. A pale shade or a gray may be used for the intestine and other organs shown, but be careful not to obscure the arteries.

The **inferior mesenteric artery (R)** has three main branches that we shall consider. The first branch is the **left colic artery (S)**. This artery carries blood to the transverse and descending colons, and the diagram shows how the branches anastomose. The second branch is the **sigmoid artery (T)**. This is a group of arteries carrying blood to the sigmoid colon and nearby areas.

The third important branch is the **superior rectal artery (U)**. This artery brings blood to the region of the rectum, as the plate shows. Also apparent in the diagram is the **superior mesenteric artery (M)**, which we have seen previously and the **abdominal aorta (A)**, which is ready to branch to the common iliac arteries.

Abdominal aorta	A	○
Celiac trunk	B	○
Common hepatic artery	C	○
Hepatic artery	D	○
Right gastric artery	E	○
Gastroduodenal artery	F	○
Gastric artery	G	○
Esophageal artery	H	○
Splenic artery	I	○
Pancreatic arteries	J	○
Left gastroepiploic artery	K	○
Short gastric artery	L	○
Superior mesenteric artery	M	○
Jejunal arteries	N	○
Ileal arteries	O	○
Ileocolic artery	P	○
Middle colic artery	Q	○
Inferior mesenteric artery	R	○
Left colic artery	S	○
Sigmoid artery	T	○
Superior rectal artery	U	○

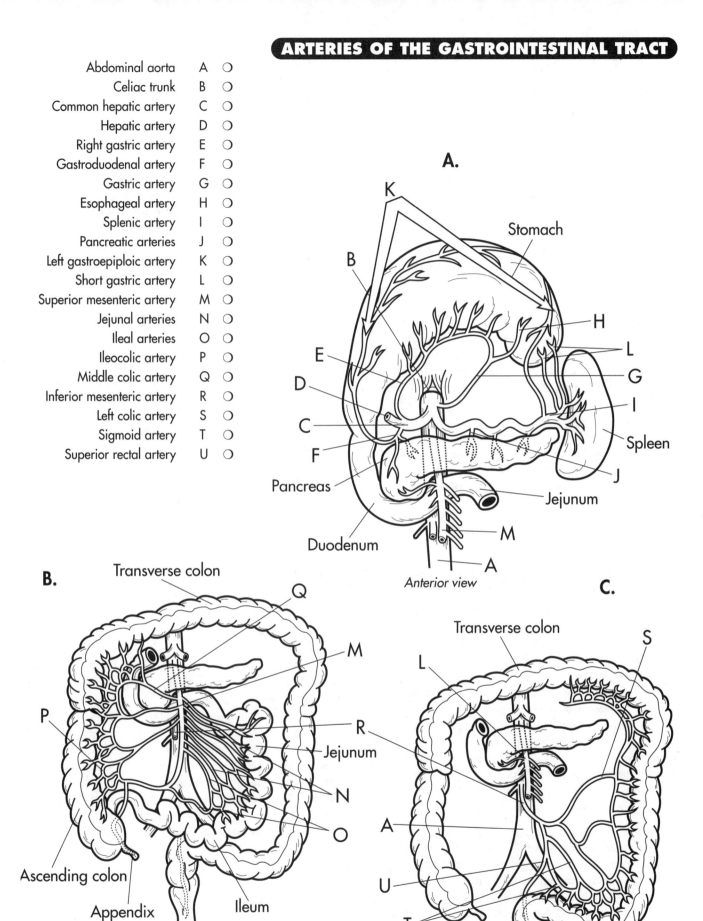

A.

Stomach

Spleen

Pancreas

Jejunum

Duodenum

Anterior view

B.

Transverse colon

Jejunum

Ascending colon

Appendix

Ileum

Anterior view

C.

Transverse colon

Rectum

Descending colon

ARTERIES of the LOWER LIMB

A number of key arteries supply oxygen-rich blood to the lower limb for use in muscle contraction. The blood supply to this region is extensive because of the support and movement functions performed by the lower limb.

In this plate, we explore the arterial system of the lower limb, with a focus on the anterior and posterior views. A flowchart is also presented since many arteries continue and form other arteries.

Start the plate by coloring in the main title Arteries of the Lower Limb. Then note that both anterior and posterior views are presented because the drainage areas for the arteries occur on both anterior and posterior surfaces. Also note that a flowchart is included so that you may follow the course of blood flow from the aorta to the digits of the feet. In the diagram we have used marks to indicate where one artery ends and another begins. You should locate the arteries in anterior, posterior, and flowchart views as you encounter them in the reading below. Also color their titles as you encounter them in the reading. We recommend light colors such as pastels and pale colors since there are many small arteries, especially in the lower leg.

At about the level of the fourth lumbar vertebra, the **aorta (A)** undergoes a splitting, or bifurcation. The two arteries resulting from this division are the **common iliac arteries (B_1, B_2)**. We shall follow the fate of the **right common iliac artery (B_2)**. The common iliac arteries carry blood to the pelvis and the lower extremities. They travel along the inner surface of the ileum, then descend behind the sigmoid colon and divide.

Two arteries result from the division of the common iliac artery: the **internal iliac artery (C)** and the **external iliac artery (D)**. The internal iliac artery is seen only briefly in the plate, but the external iliac artery will continue to the lower limb, as the flowchart shows. The internal iliac artery supplies areas of the urinary bladder, internal and external walls of the pelvis, and external genital organs. In females, the internal iliac also carries blood to the uterus and vagina.

We are now ready to enter the lower limb at the region of the femur. The arteries in the thigh will be rather large, so dark colors may be used for this part. Note the position of the femur relative to the arteries that supply it and the thigh muscles. Continue your coloring, watching for the arteries in the posterior and anterior views and the flow chart.

The external iliac artery passes near the surface of the iliosoas muscle and crosses near the pubic symphysis as it enters the thigh. Then it becomes the **femoral artery (E)**. The femoral artery will pass through most of the area of the thigh, as the anterior and posterior plates show.

At the proximal aspect of the femoral artery emerges the **deep femoral artery (F)**. This artery carries blood to the deep muscles of the thigh and some regions of the skin. Emerging from the deep femoral artery is the **medial femoral circumflex artery (G)**. This artery services the adductor muscles of the thigh and region of the hip joint. Close by is the **lateral femoral circumflex artery (H)**. Also originating at the deep femoral artery, this artery carries blood to the head and neck of the femur as well as the thigh muscles. It is clearly seen in the anterior and posterior views.

Also emerging from the femoral artery is the **descending genicular artery (I)**. The knee joint and neighboring muscles are supplied with blood through this artery.

We now encounter the knee joint and the lower leg (foreleg). The arteries in this area tend to be small and appear close to one another in the diagram. They lead to many divisions, as the flowchart shows, and you should be careful not to obscure them as you color. As you encounter the arteries, color their titles, then locate them in the chart. Some are anterior arteries, while others are posterior arteries, and they will show up on the appropriate view.

As the femoral artery approaches the knee joint, it becomes the **popliteal artery (J)**. This artery can be seen passing the knee joint in both the anterior and posterior view, but it is clearer on the posterior view because it passes on the posterior surface. Emerging from this area, the popliteal artery becomes the **posterior tibial artery (K)**. This artery passes down the posterior surface of the lower leg supplying this general area.

The posterior tibial artery gives rise to the **peroneal artery (L)**. The artery is seen on the posterior surface, and it carries blood to the medial side of the tibia. Also branching off the popliteal tibial artery is the **anterior tibial artery (M)**, as the flowchart indicates. It is seen on the anterior view of the leg. The anterior tibial artery becomes the **dorsalis pedis artery (N)** at the level of the ankle.

Also at the level of the ankle, the **posterior tibial artery (K)** divides to form the **lateral plantar arteries (O)** and the **medial plantar arteries (P)**. These are shown in the flowchart. The dorsalis pedis artery unites with the lateral plantar artery to form the **plantar arch (Q)**. This arch passes across the surface of the foot at the posterior aspect. The **digital arteries (R)** arise from the plantar arch and continue on to supply the phalanges of the toes.

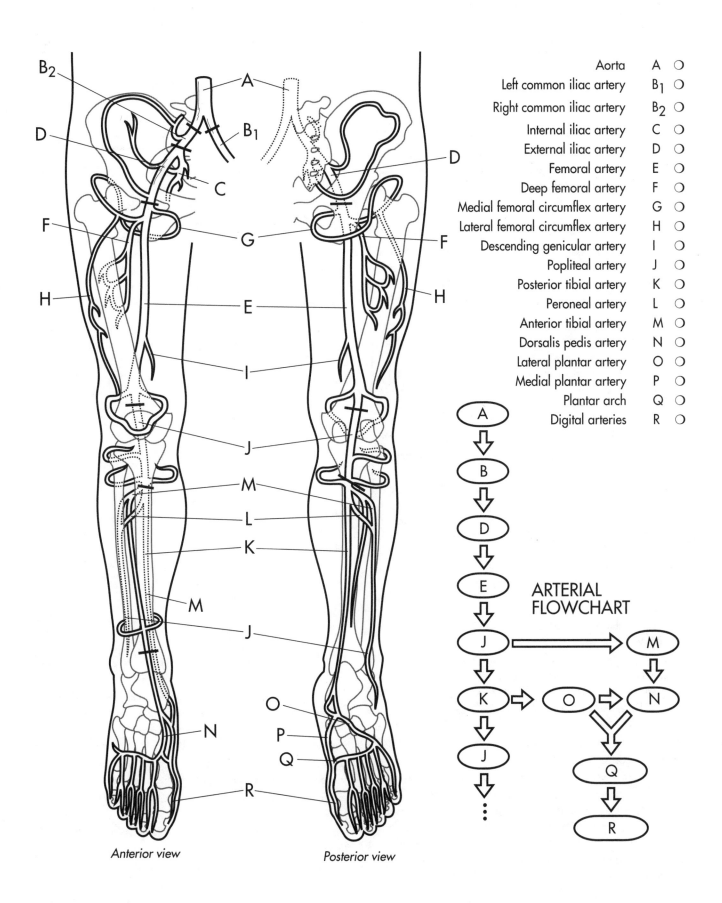

Anterior view

Posterior view

Aorta — A ○
Left common iliac artery — B₁ ○
Right common iliac artery — B₂ ○
Internal iliac artery — C ○
External iliac artery — D ○
Femoral artery — E ○
Deep femoral artery — F ○
Medial femoral circumflex artery — G ○
Lateral femoral circumflex artery — H ○
Descending genicular artery — I ○
Popliteal artery — J ○
Posterior tibial artery — K ○
Peroneal artery — L ○
Anterior tibial artery — M ○
Dorsalis pedis artery — N ○
Lateral plantar artery — O ○
Medial plantar artery — P ○
Plantar arch — Q ○
Digital arteries — R ○

ARTERIAL FLOWCHART

PRINCIPAL VEINS of the BODY

The veins deliver blood back to the right atrium of the heart after oxygen and nutrients have been deposited at the cells and tissues. The blood returning from the veins is oxygen-poor (and rich in carbon dioxide and metabolic waste products). The walls of the veins are generally thinner than those of the arteries because the blood pressure within the veins is lower.

Two great veins receive blood from areas above and below the diaphragm, respectively. These are the superior vena cava and the inferior vena cava. All veins, with one exception, lead to them, as this plate will show. The principal veins are surveyed here, and additional veins are presented when the body areas are discussed in more detail.

> Begin the plate by coloring the main title Principal Veins of the Body. Then look over the plate and note that veins return to the heart from above and below. This plate will show that all veins lead to these two main pathways. Where one vein has flowed into another, we have used crossmarks to indicate where one vein begins and another ends. Darker colors may be used in this plate since the veins are generally large and easy to see. Reds, blues, and greens are advised. Where one vein flows into another, you may use variations of the same color to show that the vein is continuous. As you read the paragraphs below, color the title of the vein as you encounter it in the reading, then color the vein in the plate. We have used the subscripts 1 and 2 to indicate left and right veins, respectively.

All areas of the body superior to the diaphragm are drained by the **superior vena cava (A)**, seen above the heart in the plate. Veins below the diaphragm collect blood and send it to the **inferior vena cava (B)**. We shall begin with the veins leading to the superior vena cava.

The superior vena cava is formed by the union of two veins known as the **left and right brachiocephalic veins (C_1 and C_2)**. You may recall from the plate on arteries that there is only one brachiocephalic artery. To form the brachiocephalic veins, the subclavian veins join with the internal jugular veins. The **subclavian veins (D_1 and D_2)** drain blood from the shoulder area, and they are relatively short in length.

The **internal jugular veins (F_1 and F_2)** receive most of the blood draining from the brain, neck, and head area. As the plate shows, several veins flow into them. One is the **sigmoid sinus (G)**, where the internal jugular vein originates and where blood from the brain collects. Another major vein leading to the internal jugular is the **facial vein (H)**, draining the face area. The subclavian veins receive blood from the **external jugular veins (E_1 and E_2)**, which drain blood from the superficial head and facial areas.

Among the veins leading to the subclavian veins are the **cephalic veins (I_1 and I_2)**. This vein services the area near the radius then travels up the lateral aspect of the arm to the shoulder. Here it empties into the **axillary vein (J_1 and J_2)**, as the plate shows. The axillary vein is formed by the union of the **brachial veins (K_1 and K_2)** and the **basilic veins (L_1 and L_2)**. The basilic vein is more medial than the brachial vein.

> Continue your work by focusing on the veins of the thoracic cavity. Many of these veins will be studied in other plates as well. This plate introduces them to you.

The plate shows a large number of veins in the thoracic cavity. These are the **pulmonary veins (M)**. A single color may be used for the entire grouping. The pulmonary veins return blood from the lung and lead to the left atrium of the heart. You will note that the main pulmonary vein stands next to the superior vena cava because they are entering different atria. Also seen is the **coronary sinus (N)**. This area gathers blood from the coronary veins and leads back to the right atrium. With the superior and inferior vena cavae, the coronary sinus is the third vein returning blood to the right atrium.

> Having briefly surveyed the veins above the diaphragm, we shall now move to the area below the diaphragm and explore the veins leading to the inferior vena cava. It may be more difficult to color these veins because the veins are more numerous. Light colors are suggested. You will note that some of the veins are unpaired veins and are designated by a letter only. Other veins are paired veins, and we continue to use subscripts with the designations.

In the region below the diaphragm, all veins ultimately lead to the **inferior vena cava (B)**. Near the diaphragm, the **hepatic vein (O)** enters the vena cava. This vein returns blood from the liver. The **hepatic portal vein (P)** is an unpaired vein leading from the intestinal veins to the liver. It is a major thoroughfare of the hepatic portal system that carries nutrients to the liver for processing before entering the bloodstream. Close by is the **splenic vein (Q)**, an unpaired vein leading from the spleen.

Moving away from the diaphragm, we encounter the **superior mesentery vein (R)**. This unpaired vein returns blood to the circulation from the area of the small intestine and gastric region. The **renal veins (S_1 and S_2)** are the important veins leading away from the kidneys. In approximately the same area is the **inferior mesenteric vein (T)**. This vein arises from a network of veins draining the intestinal area.

At its most distal portion, the inferior vena cava is formed by the merger of the **common iliac veins (U_1 and U_2)**. This merger occurs at about the level of the fifth lumbar vertebrae. The common iliacs are formed by the merger of the **internal iliac veins (V_1 and V_2)** and the **external iliac veins (W_1 and W_2)**. The internal iliac veins drain the local musculature and numerous organs of the pelvic cavity. The external iliac veins are formed from the femoral veins, which receive blood from the lower limbs. These veins are discussed in a future plate.

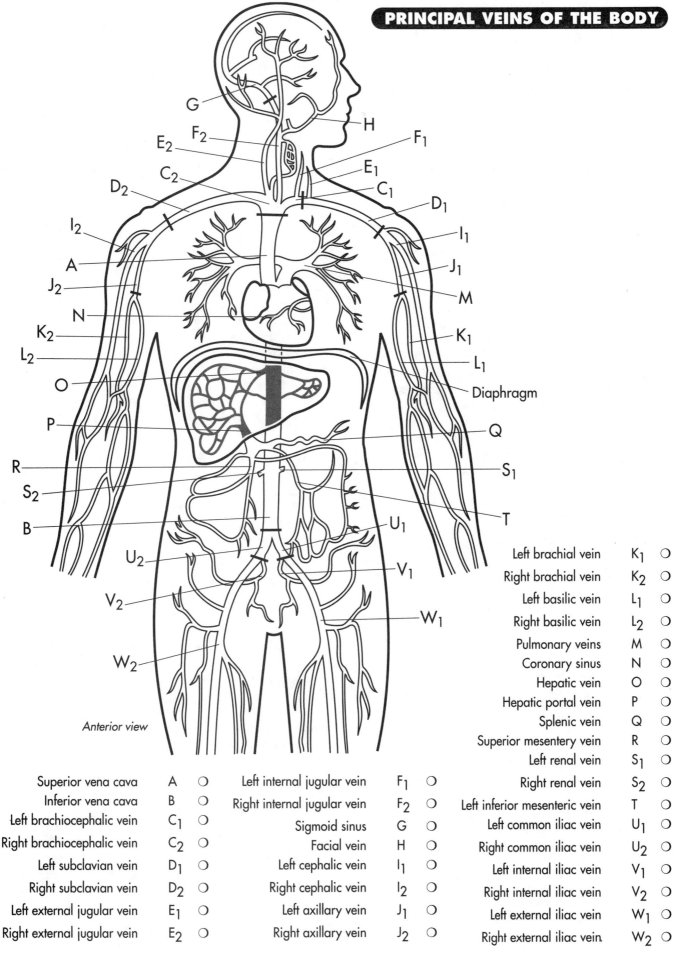

PRINCIPAL VEINS OF THE BODY

G

H

F_2 F_1

E_2 E_1

C_2 C_1

D_2 D_1

I_2 I_1

A

J_2 J_1

N   M

K_2 K_1

L_2 L_1

O   Diaphragm

P   Q

R S_1

S_2

B   T

U_2 U_1

V_2 V_1

W_2 W_1

Anterior view

Left brachial vein	K_1	○
Right brachial vein	K_2	○
Left basilic vein	L_1	○
Right basilic vein	L_2	○
Pulmonary veins	M	○
Coronary sinus	N	○
Hepatic vein	O	○
Hepatic portal vein	P	○
Splenic vein	Q	○
Superior mesentery vein	R	○
Left renal vein	S_1	○
Right renal vein	S_2	○
Left inferior mesenteric vein	T	○
Left common iliac vein	U_1	○
Right common iliac vein	U_2	○
Left internal iliac vein	V_1	○
Right internal iliac vein	V_2	○
Left external iliac vein	W_1	○
Right external iliac vein	W_2	○

Superior vena cava	A	○	Left internal jugular vein	F_1	○
Inferior vena cava	B	○	Right internal jugular vein	F_2	○
Left brachiocephalic vein	C_1	○	Sigmoid sinus	G	○
Right brachiocephalic vein	C_2	○	Facial vein	H	○
Left subclavian vein	D_1	○	Left cephalic vein	I_1	○
Right subclavian vein	D_2	○	Right cephalic vein	I_2	○
Left external jugular vein	E_1	○	Left axillary vein	J_1	○
Right external jugular vein	E_2	○	Right axillary vein	J_2	○

VEINS of the HEAD and NECK

Veins of the head and neck region are drained by three pairs of veins: the internal jugular veins, the external jugular veins, and the vertebral veins. Because the brain receives a plentiful supply of blood, the veins are important thoroughfares. Many of the veins have the same names as arteries leading into the head and neck, although there are some differences. We are providing a schematic in this plate, to allow you to follow a drop of blood from the brain back to the heart. Here we are examining the head from the right side of the body; corresponding veins are found on the left side.

> Start your work on the plate by coloring the main title Veins of the Head and Neck. Then, look over the plate and notice that all veins eventually lead from the head and neck region back down toward the heart. Refer to the schematic flow of blood in the veins as you work and relate the diagram and schematic to one another. As you encounter the veins in the reading below, color in their titles, then locate and color the veins in the head and neck. Some veins will be found within the brain tissue and light colors should be used here. If you wish to color the bones and other structures, we advise light colors so as to avoid obscuring the veins.

The three pairs of veins collecting blood from the head and neck all lead to the **brachiocephalic vein (A)**. In this plate, the left brachiocephalic vein is shown. Technically it ends where the **internal jugular (B)** unites with the subclavian entering from the shoulder. The right brachiocephalic vein shown here unites with the left brachiocephalic vein to form the superior vena cava leading to the right atrium of the heart.

Note that three major veins come together near the brachiocephalic vein. As noted, they include the **internal jugular vein (B)**, the **external jugular vein (C)**, and the **vertebral vein (D)**. We shall examine the drainage areas for each of the three veins in this plate.

> The next section will be concerned with the areas drained by the internal jugular vein. Note how this vein extends into the skull and the brain. As you read about the veins leading to the internal jugular vein, color their titles, then color the veins as you locate them. Some veins will be located in the brain, and light colors such as yellows and pastels should be used here. Where one vein leads to another, try to use colors that blend to show continuity of the vein.

The brain tissue is drained by a set of veins leading to several dural sinuses. Dural sinuses are interconnected enlarged chambers found between the layers of the dura mater. Dural sinuses eventually lead to the **sigmoid sinus (E)**, which leads to the internal jugular vein. In the plate, the sigmoid sinus should be colored with a light color because it is within the brain tissue.

One sinus leading to the sigmoid sinus is the **superior sagittal sinus (E$_1$)**. This sinus is found within the falx cerebri, which is located between the cerebral hemispheres. The **inferior sagittal sinus (E$_2$)** is also found in the falx cerebri. The **straight sinus (E$_3$)** can be seen in the plate, and the transverse sinus extends along the lateral aspect of the **skull (E$_4$)** before joining with the **occipital sinus (E$_5$)** near the occipital bone and occipital lobe. The **cavernous sinus (E$_6$)** lies near the sphenoid bone and drains blood from this area. The **great cerebral vein (E$_7$)** is formed from veins inside the brain tissue. This vein carries blood to the straight sinus, as the plate shows. Another important vein entering the internal jugular vein is the **facial vein (F)**. As the plate shows, this vein drains areas around the maxilla, mandible, and nasal area. Emptying into the facial vein is the **ophthalmic vein (G)**. This vein drains blood from the region of the orbit of the eye. It also leads to the cavernous sinus. The **temporal vein (H)** leads to the internal jugular from the superficial temporal region of the skull.

After collecting blood from the brain, the veins extending from the head pass through the skull through the jugular foramina, then descend through the neck. Branches of the facial and temporal veins enter the neck. The internal jugular vein joins with the subclavian brain to form the brachiocephalic vein as noted previously.

> In the remaining portion of this plate, we shall examine the external jugular vein and vertebral veins. Continue your coloring as before, and watch for numerous small veins in the head area. The small veins should be colored in light colors.

The external jugular vein runs along the inferior surface of the neck outside of the internal jugular veins. The external jugular veins drain the blood from the parotid gland, the muscles of the face and scalp, and other superficial areas.

An important vein entering the external jugular is the **posterior auricular vein (J)**. The vein drains the region of the ear (auricle) as well as cells near the mastoid region, parotid gland, and neck muscles adjacent. One vein leading to it is the **occipital vein (K)**. The vein carries blood from the skin on the side of the head and portions of the external ear. It drains the skin of the scalp and the nearby muscles. As the plate shows, the external jugular vein empties into the subclavian vein just before the subclavian joins with the internal jugular vein to form the brachiocephalic vein.

Branches of the **vertebral vein (D)** carry blood from the cervical area, regions of the spinal cord, and the posterior surface of the skull. The vessels descend through the skull through the transverse foramina of the cervical vertebrae very close to the vertebral arteries. They enter into the brachiocephalic vein close to where the internal jugular also enters. The vertebral arteries carry blood to the brain, but the vertebral veins are not involved in removing excessive amounts of blood from the brain. Instead, the internal jugular vein performs that function. The vertebral veins service the neck muscles.

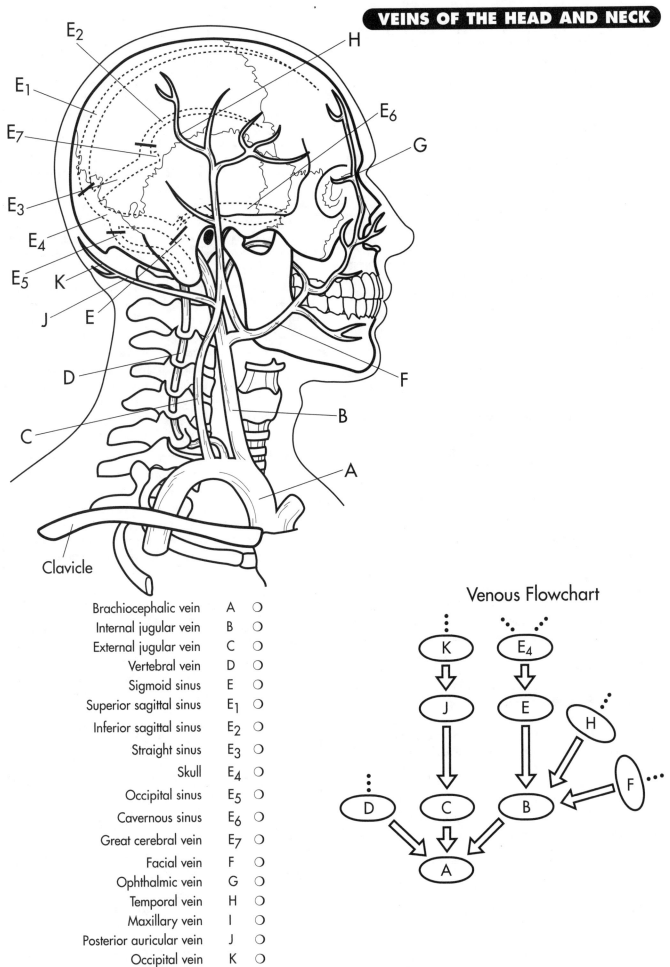

Clavicle

Brachiocephalic vein   A ○
Internal jugular vein   B ○
External jugular vein   C ○
Vertebral vein   D ○
Sigmoid sinus   E ○
Superior sagittal sinus E_1 ○
Inferior sagittal sinus E_2 ○
Straight sinus E_3 ○
Skull E_4 ○
Occipital sinus E_5 ○
Cavernous sinus E_6 ○
Great cerebral vein E_7 ○
Facial vein   F ○
Ophthalmic vein   G ○
Temporal vein   H ○
Maxillary vein   I ○
Posterior auricular vein   J ○
Occipital vein   K ○

Venous Flowchart

VEINS of the UPPER EXTREMITY

Veins of the upper extremity carry blood from the hand, wrist, forearm, and arm up through the shoulder toward the vena cava. There are superficial and deep veins in this group, and the two types anastomose (join) with each other at various locations. The superficial veins are located immediately beneath the skin in the subcutaneous tissues, while the deep veins normally accompany the arteries as they course through the tissues of the extremity. In this plate, we present an anterior view of the right arm. In the upper arm, the arteries are distinct, but in the lower arm (the forearm) they anastomose extensively. We also show a venous flowchart so you may follow the course of a drop of blood from the finger to the heart.

Look over the plate, then color in the main title Veins of the Upper Extremity. In addition to a view of the right arm, note the flowchart of veins from the fingertips. As you read about the veins in the plate, you should locate them in the flowchart as well as the diagram. Light colors are best because the veins join with one another often and are easily obscured by darker colors. If you wish to color the bones of the area, we suggest light colors such as grays and yellows.

The main thoroughfare leading to the right atrium of the heart is the **superior vena cava (A)**. In this plate, the vena cava may be seen to the anatomical right of the pulmonary arteries and the pulmonary veins, which return blood to the heart from the lungs.

The main trunk leading from the right side of the body is the **brachiocephalic vein (B)**. This short vein is formed by the union of the subclavian vein and internal jugular vein. The **internal jugular vein (C)** is the largest vein returning blood from the head and neck.

The **subclavian vein (E)** is a major vein of the shoulder and neck area. The subclavian vein begins at the lateral border of the first rib and extends to the medial end of the clavicle, as the plate indicates. Its origin is a continuation of the axillary vein, which we shall encounter momentarily. Emptying into the subclavian vein is the **external jugular vein (D)**. This vein carries blood from the more superficial areas of the head and neck. The subclavian vein drains the arm, neck, and thoracic wall.

The axillary vein extends from the lower border of the teres major muscle to the lateral border of the first rib, where it is continuous with the subclavian vein. Small veins leading to the axillary vein drain the arm, axilla, and lateral chest wall.

We now move toward the lateral border of the upper arm and encounter the axillary vein. This is the major vein to the upper extremity. Other veins of the thoracic wall flow into it, and we have labeled them with lowercase letters. They are encountered in other plates, but we take brief note of them here. Dark colors may be used for these veins, since the tissue area around them has not been labeled.

Three important veins from the thoracic wall empty their contents to the axillary vein. The first is the **highest thoracic vein (a)**, which drains superior regions of the thorax. The next vein is the **lateral thoracic vein (b)**, located along the lateral thoracic wall, where it drains the chest muscles and mammary glands of females. The third vein is the **subscapular vein (c)**. This vein drains regions inferior to the scapula.

One of the deep veins of the arm is the **brachial vein (G)**. This vein is located near the brachial artery. The brachial vein receives blood from the **radial vein (H)** and the **ulnar vein (I)**. Both of these veins may be difficult to find in the diagram, but if you follow the brachial vein backward, you should be able to locate them. Also, they should be colored on the flowchart together with the other veins encountered.

Both the radial and ulnar veins drain the **palmar venous arch (J)**. This arch is located on the palm surface. It receives blood from the **digital veins (K)**, which drain the fingers. As the plate shows, blood can flow from the fingers into the arch, then to the radial and ulnar arteries, which unite to form the brachial vein at the bend of the elbow.

We have followed the course of blood from the fingers to the superior vena cava and the right atrium of the heart. We shall continue this pattern and examine two other veins leading to the axillary vein, just as the brachial vein does. Continue your coloring as before, and continue to use light colors since the veins tend to be complex and resemble a network. The flowchart should also be completed as you proceed.

In addition to the brachial vein, another vein called the **basilic vein (L)** carries blood from the forearm. The basilic vein proceeds along the posterior surface of the elbow, where it receives blood from the **median cubital vein (M)**. This is the vein used for transfusions and removal of blood samples. The basilic vein merges with the brachial vein to form the axillary vein.

The median cubital vein receives blood from the **median antebrachial vein (N)**. This is a set of veins that drain the palm of the hand and ascend on the anterior forearm to meet the median cubital vein.

The third major vein flowing into the axillary is the **cephalic vein (O)**. The cephalic vein begins in the dorsal arch of the hand, winds upward to the anterior surface of the forearm, and meets the median cubital vein below the elbow. It then ascends up the arm, lateral to the biceps, where it receives the **accessory cephalic vein (P)**, then continues between the deltoid and pectoralis major to enter into the axillary vein just below the level of the clavicle.

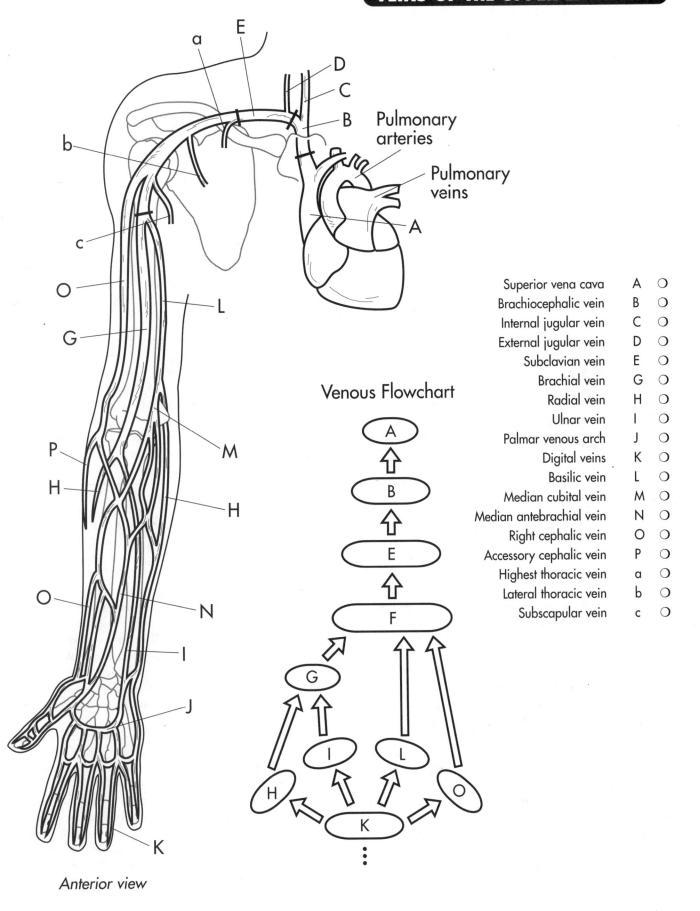

Pulmonary arteries

Pulmonary veins

Venous Flowchart

Anterior view

Superior vena cava	A	○
Brachiocephalic vein	B	○
Internal jugular vein	C	○
External jugular vein	D	○
Subclavian vein	E	○
Brachial vein	G	○
Radial vein	H	○
Ulnar vein	I	○
Palmar venous arch	J	○
Digital veins	K	○
Basilic vein	L	○
Median cubital vein	M	○
Median antebrachial vein	N	○
Right cephalic vein	O	○
Accessory cephalic vein	P	○
Highest thoracic vein	a	○
Lateral thoracic vein	b	○
Subscapular vein	c	○

VEINS of the THORAX and ABDOMEN

An elaborate system of veins collects blood from the tissues of the thorax and abdomen and brings it to the right atrium of the heart through the superior and inferior vena cavae. Complementary arteries and veins often run together in the thorax and abdomen and they usually have similar names. For instance, there are renal arteries and renal veins.

As we study the major veins of the thorax and abdomen in this plate, you will note a difference when you compare the venous and arterial systems: in the venous system, blood draining the digestive organs does not enter the vena cava directly. Instead, it enters a special circulation called the hepatic portal circulation, which is the topic of a future plate in this book.

Look over the plate and notice that we have presented the thorax and abdomen with most organs removed. Many of the veins are shown as trunks at the terminus where they enter a larger vein. Color the main title Veins of the Thorax and Abdomen and begin your work with the veins of the thoracic cavity. As you encounter the veins, color their titles, then locate them and color them in the plate. The veins are separated from one another so that darker colors may be used in most cases. In some instances, we have used lowercase letters to note veins that are visible but are not part of the thorax or abdomen.

The large vein draining blood from the superior aspect of the body is the **superior vena cava (A)**. In this plate, the vein has been cut where it enters the right atrium of the heart so as to expose the nearby veins. Ascending from the inferior portion of the body and draining the area below the heart is the **inferior vena cava (B)**. This vein is also cut where it would otherwise pass near the heart.

Among the important veins entering the superior vena cava are the **mediastinal veins (C)**, which collect blood from the mediastinum area of the thorax. Close by these veins are the **esophageal veins (D)**. The musculature of the esophagus is drained by these veins.

As the plate shows, the aorta is formed by the union of two **brachiocephalic veins (F_1 and F_2)**. Entering the right brachiocephalic vein at the point of union is the **internal thoracic vein (E)**. As the plate indicates, this vein results from an elaborate network of veins draining the lateral musculature of the thoracic cage. Following along the brachiocephalic veins, we see the point where the **internal jugular vein (a)** enters it. This is the point where the brachiocephalic vein is formed by the merger of the internal jugular vein and the **subclavian vein (G)**. The subclavian vein drains the shoulder area and receives two other veins, the **vertebral vein (b)** and the **external jugular vein (c)**. These veins are discussed at length in an earlier plate.

Further to the lateral aspect, the subclavian vein receives blood from the **axillary vein (H)**. Just before the axillary vein empties into the subclavian vein, it receives blood from the **cephalic vein (I)**. These and other veins of the upper extremity are discussed in detail in earlier plates.

Most of the thoracic tissues and wall of the thorax are drained by a complex network of veins collected together as the azygous system. Running alongside the vertebral column is the main vein of the azygous system, the **azygous vein (J)**. It is slightly to the right of the column, and it originates with lumbar veins and intercostal veins, to be discussed presently. Near the fourth thoracic vertebra, the azygous vein empties its blood into the superior vena cava. The azygous vein also receives blood from esophageal veins, mediastinal veins, and pericardial veins.

The next section of the plate concerns veins that drain areas of the thoracic cavity. Continue the plate as before, using darker colors if you wish. The bones of the thoracic cage and vertebral column may be colored, but light colors such as pale yellows and grays are recommended. As you encounter the veins, color the titles and the veins in the plate.

Another vein that empties its blood into the azygous vein is the **hemiazygous vein (K)**, which receives blood from numerous veins including the intercostal veins and mediastinal veins. It joins the azygous vein at the level of the ninth thoracic vertebra, as the plate shows. Tributaries of the azygous vein and the hemiazygous vein are a set of **intercostal veins (L)**, which collect blood from the muscles of the chest.

We now move below the level of the diaphragm and consider the veins of the abdominal cavity. As noted above, many of the veins flow into the hepatic portal system, as discussed in a future plate. Therefore, some of the arteries studied in an earlier plate do not have complementary veins in this plate. Since the veins are quite large, you may choose to use darker colors. If you choose to color the kidneys, adrenal glands, and pelvic bones, a lighter color is recommended.

Immediately below the diaphragm, the inferior vena cava receives numerous branches of the **hepatic veins (M)**, which drain the liver. The latter is the terminus of the hepatic portal system. Proximate to the hepatic vein is the entry point of the **phrenic veins (N)**. These veins drain the inferior surface of the diaphragm and return blood to the circulation.

The suprarenal (adrenal) glands are drained by the **suprarenal (adrenal) veins (O)**. The right suprarenal vein usually enters the inferior vena cava directly, as the plate shows, but the left suprarenal vein enters the left renal vein. The **renal veins (P)** extend from the kidneys and are among the largest veins entering the vena cava. The **gonadal veins (Q)** may be either the ovarian veins in females or the testicular veins in males. They collect blood from the reproductive organs. The right gonadal vein usually enters the inferior vena cava as shown in the plate, while the left gonadal vein brings its contents to the renal veins.

The **lumbar veins (R)** can be seen near the lumbar vertebrae. They drain the lumbar portion of the abdomen and bring their contents either to the inferior vena cava (as the right lumbar vein does), or to the azygous system (as the left lumbar vein does).

At its most inferior location, the inferior vena cava begins at approximately the fourth lumbar vertebra. Here it is formed by the merger of the **common iliac veins (S)**. The **internal iliac veins (T)** drain the muscles of the pelvic region, while the **external iliac veins (U)** carry blood up from the leg. The common iliac veins begin at the merger of the external and internal iliac veins, and we have marked the diagram to show you this location. Different shades of the same color might be suggested for the inferior vena cava and the common iliac veins.

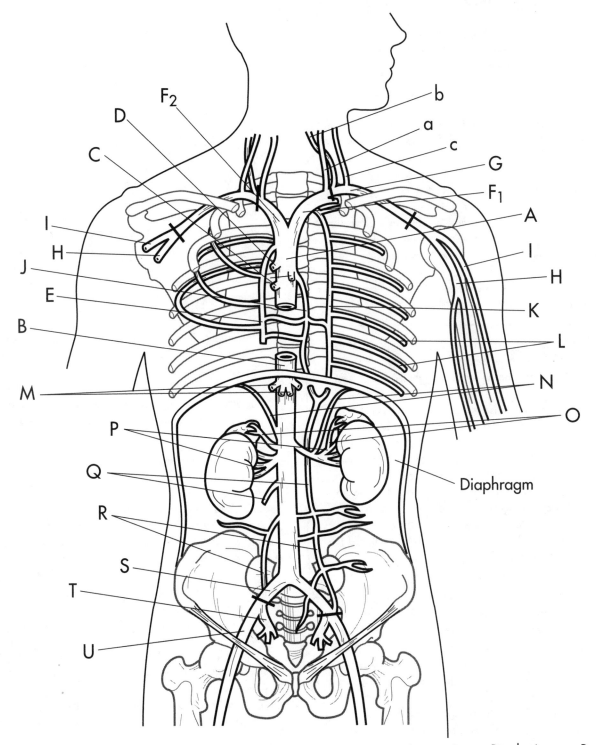

F₂

D

C

b

a

c

G

F₁

I

A

H

I

J

H

E

K

B

L

M

N

P

O

Q

Diaphragm

R

S

T

U

Superior vena cava	A	○		Axillary vein	H	○		Renal veins	P	○
Inferior vena cava	B	○		Cephalic vein	I	○		Gonadal veins	Q	○
Mediastinal veins	C	○		Azygous vein	J	○		Lumbar veins	R	○
Esophageal veins	D	○		Hemiazygous vein	K	○		Common iliac veins	S	○
Internal thoracic vein	E	○		Intercostal veins	L	○		Internal iliac veins	T	○
Left brachiocephalic vein	F₁	○		Hepatic veins	M	○		External iliac veins	U	○
Right brachiocephalic vein	F₂	○		Phrenic veins	N	○		Internal jugular vein	a	○
Subclavian vein	G	○		Suprarenal (adrenal) veins	O	○		Vertebral vein	b	○
								External jugular vein	c	○

VEINS of the LOWER EXTREMITY

A series of superficial and deep veins remove blood from the lower extremity. In many locations, there is an anastomosis between deep and superficial veins, which is why it is sometimes difficult to see the origin of the vein. You will note that many of the veins have names similar to those of arteries and often run in the same general location as their complementary arteries.

In this plate we present an anterior and posterior view of the right lower extremity. Some of the veins are best seen on the anterior view, while others are best seen on the posterior view. We also present a flowchart of the veins leading from the digits of the toes to the inferior vena cava. This should help you to understand how the veins deliver their contents to one another.

Begin by coloring the main title of the plate Veins of the Lower Extremity. Now examine the plate and note that anterior and posterior views of the right leg are presented. A flowchart of the veins is also presented, and it should be colored in as the veins are located on the plate. In some cases, the veins flow into one another, and we have designated where the vein begins and ends. Variations of the same color can be used for these continuing veins to show that they relate to one another. Where the vein is presented in a light shading, the vein has moved deep into the muscle and is not obvious at the body surface. Often it is seen on the posterior side more clearly than on the anterior side. Pale colors should be used for the deep veins.

All blood extending from the veins of the lower extremity eventually comes to the **inferior vena cava (A)**. This major vein to the heart is formed by the union of the **common iliac veins (B$_1$ and B$_2$)**. The vena cava forms at the level of the fourth lumbar vertebra.

The common iliac veins split into two veins. The first is the **internal iliac vein (C)**. As the posterior view indicates, this vein follows the level of the interior iliac artery and drains the gluteal muscles as well as the medial side of the thigh, portions of the pelvic region, and several reproductive organs in both males and females.

The **external iliac vein (D)** receives blood from the lower extremity and a portion of the anterior abdominal wall. The diagram shows a portion of this vein passing at the anterior surface of the pelvic bone where it is continuous with the femoral vein. In the posterior view, the vein is shaded because it is out of view.

Extending on the posterior surface of the knee is the **femoral vein (E)**. This vein is a continuation of the popliteal vein. It begins superior to the knee and ends at the external iliac vein, as noted previously.

With the meeting of the external iliac vein and femoral vein, we enter the thigh region. The major vein draining the thigh is the femoral vein. We shall examine this vein and its tributaries in the paragraph below. As you encounter the veins, color their titles and the vein in both the diagram and flowchart. Dark colors may be used in the thigh region, but light colors should be used in the lower leg and foot region because the veins are small and close together.

Just before the femoral vein continues with the external iliac vein, it receives blood from the **great saphenous vein (F)**. The great saphenous vein is the body's longest vein. It can be seen in the thigh and lower leg, and it receives blood from the **medial plantar vein (G)**. The medial plantar vein receives blood from the **dorsal venous arch (H)**, which can be seen in the anterior view passing across the dorsal surface of the foot. This vein receives blood from the **metatarsal veins (I)**, which service the metatarsal bones, and from the **digital veins (J)**, which receive blood from the phalanges.

The great saphenous vein is one of the superficial veins of the body, while the femoral vein is a deep vein. We shall now examine the veins leading to the femoral vein, as they arise in the lower leg. Continue your coloring as before, coloring the titles and the veins as you read about them. A lighter color is recommended for this section.

The femoral vein also receives blood from the **popliteal vein (K)**. This vein is best seen in the posterior view because it lies posterior to the knee. We have marked the location where the popliteal vein becomes the femoral vein just superior to the knee. The popliteal vein receives blood from the **small saphenous vein (L)**. Beginning on the anterior surface at the dorsal venous arch, this is a superficial vein along the posterior aspect of the leg.

The popliteal vein also receives blood from the **anterior tibial vein (M)**. This vein can be seen on the anterior surface and the posterior surface near the proximal portion of the tibia. It receives blood from the **dorsalis pedis veins (N)**.

A third vein discharging its blood into the popliteal vein is the **posterior tibial vein (O)**. This vein cannot be seen well in the anterior view, but it is clear in the posterior view. The posterior tibial vein receives blood from the **medial plantar vein. (G)** and the **lateral plantar vein (P)**. On the posterior aspect of the leg, it receives blood from the lateral plantar vein. It also receives a large portion of its blood from the **deep venous arch (Q)**.

The posterior tibial vein proceeds along the posterior portion of the leg and receives blood from the **peroneal vein (R)**. The peroneal vein drains a portion of the lateral and posterior leg areas. The posterior tibial vein then unites with the anterior tibial vein to form the popliteal vein, as shown in the posterior view. After the small saphenous vein enters, the popliteal vein continues as the femoral vein.

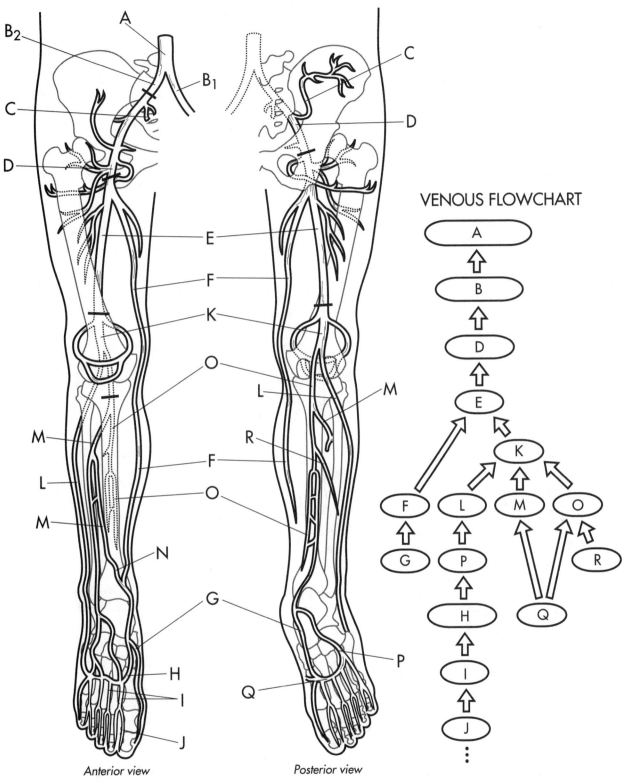

Anterior view

Posterior view

VENOUS FLOWCHART

Inferior vena cava	A	○
Left common iliac vein	B₁	○
Right common iliac vein	B₂	○
Internal iliac vein	C	○
External iliac vein	D	○
Femoral vein	E	○

Great saphenous vein	F	○
Medial plantar vein	G	○
Dorsal venous arch	H	○
Metatarsal veins	I	○
Digital veins	J	○
Popliteal vein	K	○
Small saphenous vein	L	○

Anterior tibial vein	M	○
Dorsalis pedis veins	N	○
Posterior tibial vein	O	○
Lateral plantar vein	P	○
Deep venous arch	Q	○
Peroneal vein	R	○

HEPATIC PORTAL SYSTEM

The liver is the primary organ for processing nutrients in the body. After nutrients have been absorbed into the circulation in the intestinal tract, they are transported to the liver through a system known as the hepatic portal system. This is a system of veins, unique in the body because it carries nutrients, where most other veins of the body carry waste products of metabolism.

In this plate, we shall study the veins of the hepatic portal system. To understand the system, we recommend that you color in the schematic diagram first, then proceed to the main portion of the plate. This will give you a sense of what the hepatic portal system is all about, and then you can locate the veins of the system.

Begin by coloring the main title Hepatic Portal System. As you examine the plate, you will notice that there is the standard plate plus a schematic diagram. If you choose to complete the schematic diagram first, as recommended, you should look over the titles list under Schematic Diagram. Color this title, then notice that the titles have lowercase letters. This is because the schematic includes veins of the hepatic portal system, as well as arteries from the remaining portion of the body circulation. We have therefore reserved the capital letters for the hepatic portal veins. Dark colors are recommended for the schematic since the structures in the schematic are widely separated. As you color the titles, color the structures and learn about the hepatic portal system.

The circulation schematic begins with the **heart (a)**. Blood flows from the heart through the **aorta (b)**. From the aorta, blood enters the **superior mesenteric artery (c)** and the **inferior mesenteric artery (d)**. Both of these arteries are discussed in an earlier plate on the gastrointestinal tract arteries.

The main arteries lead to the smaller arteries of the intestinal tract, which pick up nutrients and other products of digestion. Now, the veins of the intestinal tract unite to form the **hepatic portal vein (e)**. This vein carries the nutrients to the liver, and a multitude of veins distribute the nutrients through the liver tissue, where the nutrients are processed. Blood is also transported into the liver from a branch of the aorta called the **hepatic artery (f)**.

After processing, the nutrients emerge from the liver through a set of **hepatic veins (g)**. The veins come together and empty into the **inferior vena cava (h)**, which carries the blood back to the heart for pumping throughout the body. The salient feature of the schematic diagram is that the vein emerging from the intestinal tract flows to the liver rather than to the inferior vena cava as it does for other organs.

A portal system is one that carries blood between two capillary networks, in this case from the capillary network in the intestine to the capillary network in the liver. We shall begin the network at the intestinal area with the **inferior mesenteric vein (A)**. This vein receives blood from the **left colic vein (B)**. The latter vein takes blood from the descending colon and rectum. Other veins entering the inferior mesenteric are

the **sigmoidal veins (C)**, which drain the area of the sigmoid colon. Still other veins contributing to the inferior mesenteric vein are the **superior rectal veins (D)**. These veins carry blood from the rectal area.

Now we shall turn our attention to the veins of the hepatic portal system. We shall follow the pattern of starting with the smallest arteries, then following their flow into still larger arteries until they finally meet at the hepatic portal vein. Color the titles of the veins as you proceed, then find them on the diagram and use light colors for the first veins we mention, and darker colors for the larger veins. We have labeled the aorta, stomach, and other organs for you. If you wish to color these organs, we recommend a pale color to avoid obscuring the veins.

As the inferior mesenteric courses toward the hepatic portal vein, it meets the **splenic vein (E)**. The splenic vein continues and eventually unites with the **superior mesenteric vein (F)**.

Blood also enters the superior mesenteric vein from the **right colic vein (G)**. This vein collects blood from the ascending colon. Additional blood enters the superior mesenteric vein by the **jejunal and ileal veins (H)**. Blood containing nutrients from the jejunum area and the ileum area enters by this route. Blood also enters the superior mesenteric vein from the **ileocolic vein (I)**. The latter part of the ileum is the site of origin for this vein. The final vein entering the superior mesenteric is the **pancreatoduodenal vein (J)**, which collects blood from the duodenal region and the pancreas.

We have studied the tributaries of the inferior mesenteric and superior mesenteric vein, and we shall now be concerned with the veins entering the splenic vein, which together with the superior mesenteric vein, will form the important hepatic portal vein. Continue your coloring as above, using light colors where possible to avoid obscuring the veins.

We previously noted the **splenic vein (E)** joining the superior mesenteric vein. A vein that empties its blood into the splenic vein is the **gastroepiploic vein (K)**. This vein collects blood from the lesser and greater curvatures of the stomach. The splenic vein also receives numerous tributaries from the spleen, as the plate shows.

After the splenic, inferior mesenteric, superior mesenteric, and other veins have come together, they form the **hepatic portal vein (N)**. The hepatic portal vein reaches in the direction of the liver. Before it reaches the liver, the hepatic portal vein receives blood from the **gastric vein (L)** and the **cystic vein (M)**. The gastric vein drains the region of the lesser curvature of the stomach, while the cystic vein extends from the gallbladder.

Having reached the liver, the hepatic portal vein divides into thousands of smaller veins that distribute nutrients through the liver for processing. After chemical conversions have occurred, the processed nutrients are ready to leave the liver. The vein carrying nutrient-rich blood from the liver is the **hepatic vein (O)**. Just inferior to the diaphragm, this vein will enter the **inferior vena cava (P)**. By this method, chemically-active nutrients and other materials enter the main circulation for transport back to the heart, then through the arteries for distribution to body tissues, cells, and organs.

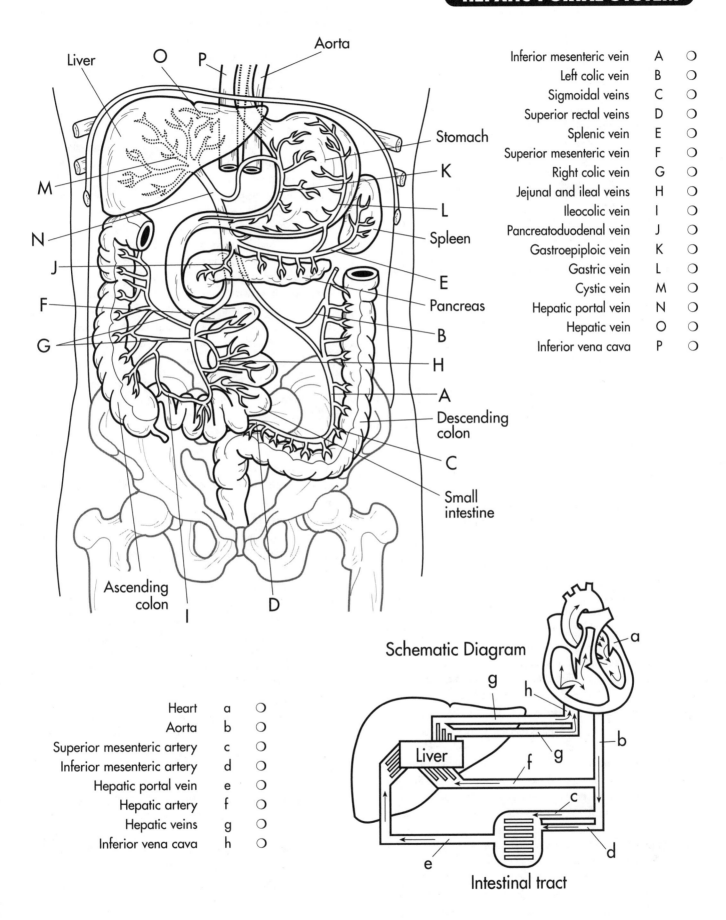

Liver

Aorta

O   P

Stomach

K

L

Spleen

M

E

N

Pancreas

J

B

F

H

G

A

Descending colon

C

Small intestine

Ascending colon

I

D

Inferior mesenteric vein	A	○
Left colic vein	B	○
Sigmoidal veins	C	○
Superior rectal veins	D	○
Splenic vein	E	○
Superior mesenteric vein	F	○
Right colic vein	G	○
Jejunal and ileal veins	H	○
Ileocolic vein	I	○
Pancreatoduodenal vein	J	○
Gastroepiploic vein	K	○
Gastric vein	L	○
Cystic vein	M	○
Hepatic portal vein	N	○
Hepatic vein	O	○
Inferior vena cava	P	○

Schematic Diagram

a

g   h

b

Liver   f   g

c

e   d

Intestinal tract

Heart	a	○
Aorta	b	○
Superior mesenteric artery	c	○
Inferior mesenteric artery	d	○
Hepatic portal vein	e	○
Hepatic artery	f	○
Hepatic veins	g	○
Inferior vena cava	h	○

FETAL CIRCULATION

The circulation of a fetus is a special consideration because blood does not flow to or from the digestive organs, kidneys, or lungs. These organs are not involved because the fetus does not exchange oxygen and carbon dioxide before birth, nor does it consume nutrients for transport to the tissues. In addition, its waste products are cleansed by removal into the mother's circulation. For these reasons, the fetal circulation is different than that of the adult, as we shall see in this plate.

The approach in this plate will be to discuss two aspects of the fetal circulation: first, the general systemic circulation, and second the circulation of blood through the heart. Special changes occur at birth in both aspects to begin the involvement of digestive, excretory, and respiratory organs and change the fetal circulation to the normal postnatal circulation.

Looking over the plate, you will note that we present a display of the circulation of blood in the fetus plus a schematic of the heart and a flowchart of blood thorough the fetal heart. Begin the plate by coloring in the main title Fetal Circulation. Then, as you read about the circulation below, locate the titles of the structures and their location on the plate. The larger arteries and veins may be colored in dark colors, but the umbilical arteries and veins would probably benefit from light colors since they lie close to one another. The placenta on the diagram is the organ of exchange between the maternal and fetal circulation. Also we use subscript numbers to indicate left and right blood vessels.

In the developing fetus, the lungs are collapsed and nonfunctional and the digestive tract is not used. Nutrients are obtained from the mother's blood supply and metabolic waste products are deposited in the maternal circulation.

In the fetus, blood leaves the heart and passes down the dorsal region of the body through the aorta (A), as normal. The aorta splits to become the common iliac arteries (not labeled on the plate). Arising from the common iliac arteries are the internal iliac arteries (B_1 and B_2). These arteries give rise to two umbilical arteries (C_1 and C_2). The plate shows both arteries extending toward the placenta. They carry blood from the fetal circulation to the placenta, where waste products will be deposited and oxygen and nutrients obtained.

The umbilical arteries wind together through the umbilical cord (D). We have circled the cord to indicate its presence, and the circle may be colored to designate the cord. At the placenta, they divide into a multitude of branches that form smaller vessels where exchanges take place. After the exchanges have occurred, the oxygen-rich and nutrient-rich blood emerges from the placenta through a single large umbilical vein (E). This vein extends through the umbilical cord.

As the umbilical vein enters the body of the fetus, it ascends to the level of the liver (F). A light color should be used for this organ.

The umbilical vein branches, and most of the blood flows into a vein called the ductus venosus (G). This vein carries oxygen-rich and nutrient-rich blood into the inferior vena cava (H). The inferior vena cava transports the blood to the heart (I). We recommend a single light color for the entire heart at this point. The heart then pumps the oxygen and nutrients to the body of the fetus by means of the aorta. This completes the fetal circulation.

We have noted how the fetal arteries extend from the fetus to the placenta to gather nutrients and oxygen, then carry them to the fetal liver and heart for pumping to fetal tissues. The fetal heart contains two important modifications to prevent blood from flowing to the lungs. Blood flow to the lungs would not benefit the fetus, because the fetus does not breathe air. Color the titles Heart Schematic and Blood Flowchart, and as you read about the pathway of blood through the heart, color in the titles and the areas. We have used subscript numbers to designate various locations of the heart, and it might be advisable to use variations of the same color to designate that all the structures are areas within or close to the heart. The schematic and flowchart should be colored at the same time, as you continue to read below.

Blood approaches the fetal heart through the inferior vena cava (H). As in the normal circulation, blood enters the right atrium of the heart (I_1). From the right atrium, most blood passes through the valve into the right ventricle (I_2). However, some blood passes through an opening called the foramen ovale (I_3). As the heart schematic shows this is an opening in the septum between the right and left atria. It allows the blood to bypass the right ventricle and flow directly into the left atrium (I_4). In this way, blood is immediately made available for pumping to the fetal body.

As noted above, most blood enters the right ventricle. When the ventricle contracts, it sends blood out the pulmonary artery toward the lungs, however, the passageway to the pulmonary artery is blocked, and blood passes through a short valve called the ductus arteriosus (I_6). This valve leads the blood directly into the aorta at the superior surface of the heart. The valve prevents blood from going to the lungs (the lungs are collapsed in the fetus) and sends it directly to the aorta for distribution to the body. At birth the ductus arteriosus closes and the passageway to the lungs opens so that the newborn baby can receive oxygen through its lungs.

Blood enters the left atrium from the right atrium through the foramen ovale (as discussed above). From the left atrium, the fetal blood enters the left ventricle (I_5). As in the normal postnatal individual, the left ventricle pumps blood through the aorta (A) which then delivers blood to the body tissues. The aorta is shown in the flowchart but not in the heart schematic.

Immediately after birth blood begins flowing through the pulmonary circulation when the ductus arteriosus contracts and closes. In addition, the foramen ovale closes and the right and left atria become completely separated from one another. The umbilical vessels also undergo degeneration, and the digestive and renal arteries and veins begin functioning.

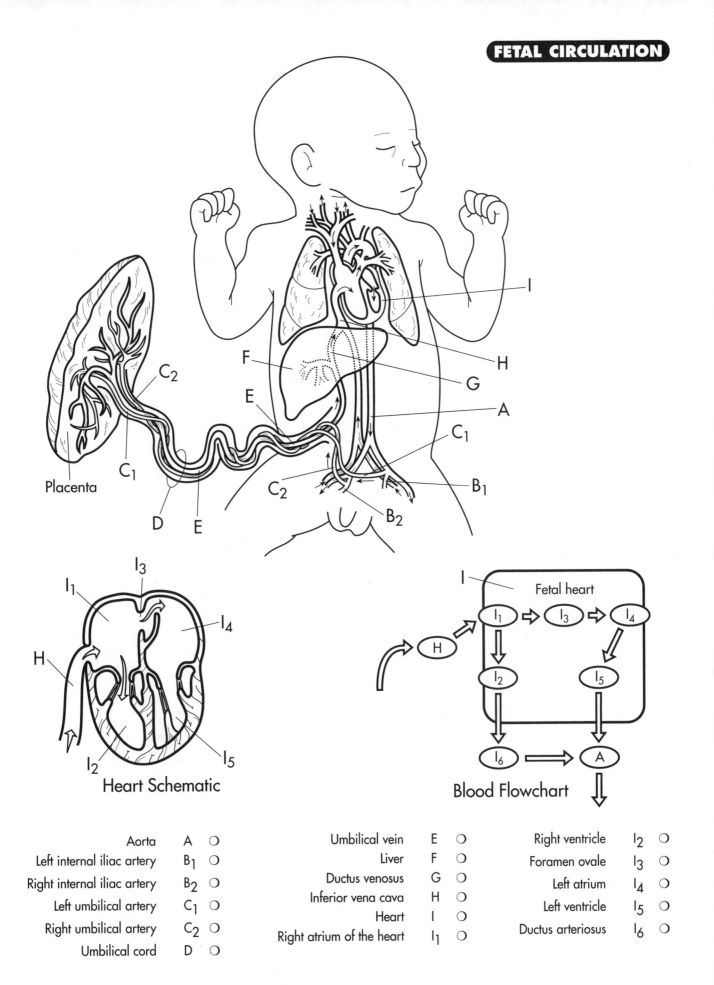

Placenta

C_2
C_1
D
E
Placenta

F
E
C_2
B_2

I
H
G
A
C_1
B_1

Heart Schematic

I_3
I_1
I_4
H
I_2
I_5

Blood Flowchart

Fetal heart
I
H
I_1
I_3
I_4
I_2
I_5
I_6
A

Aorta	A	○
Left internal iliac artery	B_1	○
Right internal iliac artery	B_2	○
Left umbilical artery	C_1	○
Right umbilical artery	C_2	○
Umbilical cord	D	○

Umbilical vein	E	○
Liver	F	○
Ductus venosus	G	○
Inferior vena cava	H	○
Heart	I	○
Right atrium of the heart	I_1	○

Right ventricle	I_2	○
Foramen ovale	I_3	○
Left atrium	I_4	○
Left ventricle	I_5	○
Ductus arteriosus	I_6	○

CHAPTER EIGHT:

the LYMPHATIC SYSTEM

OVERVIEW of the LYMPHATIC SYSTEM

The lymphatic system is a series of vessels, structures, and organs that collect fluid throughout the body and return it to the main circulation for redistribution. The system also contains cells known as lymphocytes, which function in the immune process. In this plate, we examine the anatomy of the lymphatic system and its presence throughout the body. The plate also serves as an introduction to the following plates that detail portions of the system.

This plate is a diagram of the lymphatic system's distribution throughout the body. We point out the major structures and organs of the system, while noting their diverse locations. We also illustrate the two main body regions drained by the two major vessels of the lymphatic system. Spots of color will be most useful, since the lymph nodes are pockets of tissue that make up the bulk of the system. As you encounter anatomical structures in the following paragraphs, locate their titles and locations on the diagram. Use light colors in this plate. Color the main title Overview Of The Lymphatic System.

The fluid draining through the lymphatic system is lymph. It is a clear fluid somewhat similar to the plasma portion of the blood but without many of the larger proteins. The lymphatic system returns lymph to the circulation by means of two major vessels. The first is the left lymphatic duct, also known as the **thoracic duct (A)**. It can be seen near the midline as well as in the mediastinum in the plate. The left lymphatic duct begins as a dilation called the **cisterna chyli (A_1)**, which is close to the second lumbar vertebra.

The left lymphatic (thoracic) duct receives blood from the left side of the head as well as the left portion of the neck and chest, the left upper limb, and the entire body below the level of the ribs. Color this portion in the small diagram to note the area drained.

The second major duct of the lymphatic system is the **right lymphatic duct (B)**. It can be seen on the visual left (anatomical right) of the plate near the **right subclavian vein (b_1)**. The right lymphatic duct empties its contents into the right subclavian vein to return the lymph to the circulation. The left lymphatic duct, by comparison, empties its lymph into the **left subclavian vein (b_2)**.

Having noted the main drainage areas for the two main lymphatic vessels, we now focus on the lymph nodes, which are pockets of lymphatic tissue. Note that these organs are found in numerous areas of the body. Continue your reading, and use spots of color to denote the various lymph nodes. In addition, color the titles as you read about the structures.

The vessels of the lymphatic system pass through small lymphatic structures known as lymph nodes. These oval organs contain the cells of the immune system and have phagocytes for engulfing foreign organisms and debris in the lymph. In the pharyngeal area, the tonsils are considered lymph node. The **palatine tonsil (C)** is shown in the plate. Other tonsils are the lingual tonsils.

Various lymph nodes can be found along lymphatic vessels. The **submandibular lymph nodes (D_1)** are located beneath the mandible. The **cervical lymph nodes (D_2)**, found in the neck region, drain the head area. **Axillary lymph nodes (D_3)** are in the armpit region, and the **mammary lymph nodes (D_4)** are located close to the mammary glands in the female.

Many thoracic lymph nodes are found close to the thoracic duct, and a collection of lymph nodes called **Peyer's patch (D_5)** is located at the surface of the **small intestine (c)**. Also in the abdomen, near the major blood vessels are the **iliac lymph nodes (D_6)**, which drain lymph coming from the legs. The **inguinal lymph nodes (D_7)** are located near the groin area to drain the perineum area, and **intestinal lymph nodes (D_8)** are found near the **large intestine (d)**. These organs receive lymph through the numerous **lymphatic vessels (E)** which are shown in the leg in the plate. Other **lymphatic vessels (E)** are shown in the arm.

There are many other organs of the lymphatic system in addition to those mentioned. These organs all contain the immune system cells and phagocytes. As the organs are mentioned briefly, use color to indicate their presence in the plate. Continue reading as you color.

In the very young individual, the **thymus gland (F)** is prominent in the mediastinum. Within this organ, the T-lymphocytes of the immune system mature before moving to the lymph nodes. The gland atrophies in the teenage years and is quite small in the adult.

Near the stomach and pancreas on the left side of the body is the **spleen (G)**. Also a lymphatic organ, the spleen contains the B-lymphocytes and T-lymphocytes of the immune system discussed in an upcoming plate. The **appendix (H)** is associated with the lymphatic system because many phagocytic white blood cells remain here and engulf debris in the digestive contents. The **bone marrow (I)** is associated with the lymphatic system because lymphocytes originate here before later moving to the lymph nodes.

Thoracic duct A ○
Cisterna chyli A_1 ○
Right lymphatic duct B ○
Palatine tonsil C ○
Submandibular lymph nodes D_1 ○
Cervical lymph nodes D_2 ○
Axillary lymph nodes D_3 ○
Mammary lymph nodes D_4 ○

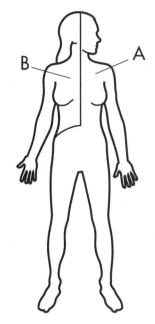

Peyer's patch D_5 ○
Iliac lymph nodes D_6 ○
Inguinal lymph nodes D_7 ○
Intestinal lymph nodes D_8 ○
Lymphatic vessels E ○
Thymus gland F ○
Spleen G ○
Appendix H ○
Bone marrow I ○
Internal jugular vein a ○
Right subclavian vein b_1 ○
Left subclavian vein b_2 ○
Small intestine c ○
Large intestine d ○

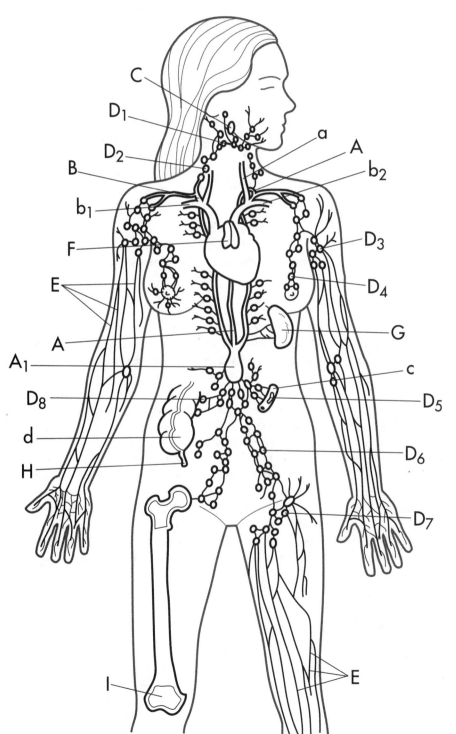

LYMPH NODES

The lymph nodes are oval or bean-shaped organs located along the lymphatic vessels. Usually they occur in groups, at areas such as the groin, maxilla, and mammary glands. The lymph nodes include the single pharyngeal or adenoid tonsil, a pair of palatine tonsils, and a pair of lingual tonsils.

This plate reviews the anatomy of a typical lymph node. We examine the regions of the lymph nodes and the cells located there. The functions of the lymph node are consistent with the cells they contain.

A cross section of a lymph node is presented in this plate. Many structures are large, but others are detailed, and light or pale colors should be used. We follow the flow of lymph through the lymph node, pointing out the cells that the lymph contacts. As you read about the structures of the lymph nodes, color their titles, then color them in the plate.

The lymphatic tissues of the body are clustered in lymphatic nodules and the lymph nodes. Lymphatic nodules are found within the loose connective tissue deep to the epithelia of such systems as the respiratory, digestive, and urinary systems. Occasionally these nodules gather together in aggregates such as Peyer's patch of the intestine. Nodules are also found within the walls of the appendix, and the walls of the pharynx contain nodules called tonsils.

When lymphatic tissue is separated from the surrounding environment by a fibrous connective layer, it is called a lymph node. The spleen and thymus gland are very similar to the lymph nodes, because they also have enclosing fibrous tissue layers.

The covering layer of the lymph node is called the **capsule (A)**. A light color should be used for the capsule to preserve the identity of the nearby structures. The capsule extends into the lymph node as partitions called **trabeculae (B)**. These fibrous extensions may be colored with a medium color to set off the portions of the lymph node. The trabeculae provide support for the lymph nodes and are the sites were blood vessels penetrate into the lymph node.

There are two main regions of the lymph node. The first is the **cortex (C)**, the area indicated by the bracket. Densely packed lymphocytes resembling nodules are known as **follicles (C_1)**. The follicles occupy most of the area of the cortex. The outer cortical area contains B-lymphocytes, while the inner cortical area contains T-lymphocytes, both of which are associated with the immune system. Central areas called **germinal centers (C_2)** are sites where the B-lymphocytes convert into antibody-secreting plasma cells. A set of **cortical reticular fibers (C_3)** provide support for the lobules of the lymph node. The **cortical sinus (C_4)** is an expanded area through which lymph flows on its way into the interior region.

We next focus our attention on the central region of the lymph node and indicate some of the landmark features. This area, like the cortical area, is rich in cells of the immune system, and the immune process goes on here. As you continue to read, color the titles and the structures in the diagram.

At the central portion of the lymph node is the **medulla (D)**, indicated by the bracket. At this location, B-lymphocytes are densely packed in strands of tissue known as **medullary cords (D_1)**. These lymphocytes are stimulated into action by bacteria, viruses, and other pathogens. The **medullary sinus (D_2)** is the region where lymph accumulates as it flows through the lymph node on its way out. A series of **medullary reticular fibers (D_3)** provide a network of support for cells of the medullary area.

Having established the important regions of the lymph node, we follow the flow of lymph through this organ from its entry to its exit. Because the lymph nodes are distributed throughout the body, they are able to filter the lymph fluid from all areas. Continue your coloring as before and complete the plate accordingly.

Two sets of lymphatic vessels are associated with the lymph node. The **afferent lymphatic vessels (E)** deliver lymph to the lymph node, as the arrow indicates at several points. The afferent vessels penetrate the capsule of the lymph node, and bring their lymph into the cortical sinus, then the medullary sinus. Note that the vessels contain valves called **afferent valves (E_1)**. The valves open toward the lymph node, and as they close, the lymph cannot flow backward. Also note that the afferent vessels are entering the lymph node at the visual left side of the plate.

At the visual right side of the plate, lymph leaves the node through the **efferent lymph vessels (F)**. The plate shows the flow of lymph out through these vessels. The efferent vessels exist at an indentation of the lymph node called the **hilus (G)**. The arrow pointing to this area may be colored. The hilus is also the area where nerves enter the lymph nodes. As above, the lymphatic vessels contain valves. In the efferent lymphatic vessels, the valves are **efferent valves (F_1)**. They point away from the lymph node, and close to prevent the lymph from backing up into the lymph node. The presence and activity of valves in the afferent and efferent vessels ensures a one-way flow of lymph as it passes through the lymph node.

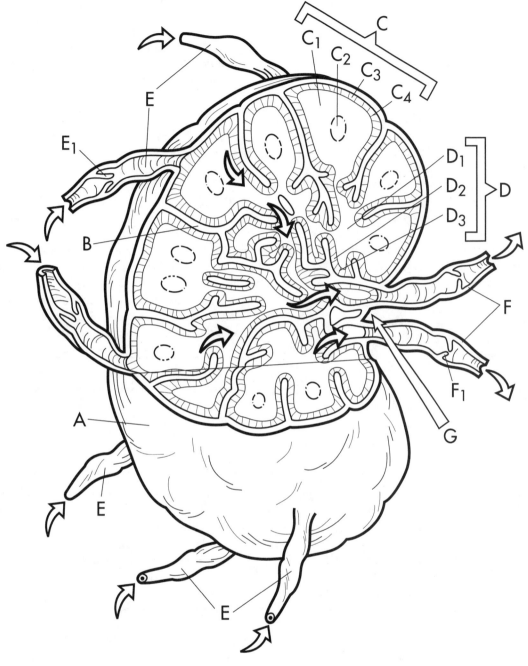

Capsule	A	○		Medullary cords	D₁	○
Trabeculae	B	○		Medullary sinus	D₂	○
Cortex	C	○		Medullary reticular fibers	D₃	○
Follicles	C₁	○		Afferent lymphatic vessels	E	○
Germinal centers	C₂	○		Afferent valves	E₁	○
Cortical reticular fibers	C₃	○		Efferent lymph vessels	F	○
Cortical sinus	C₄	○		Efferent valves	F₁	○
Medulla	D	○		Hilus	G	○

LYMPHATIC DRAINAGE of the HEAD

The lymphatic vessels constitute a one-way system carrying lymph toward the heart. Beginning in microscopic lymph capillaries, the system collects plasmalike lymph and carries it to vessels that pass through the lymph nodes. Here, a cleansing of the lymph takes place, and the body's immune system responds to pathogens.

The anatomical features of an individual lymph node were reviewed in the previous plate. Here we examine the location of the lymph nodes in the head region and, briefly, in the shoulder region of the female. Use spots of color to designate the lymph nodes as they occur in the reading.

> Begin by coloring the main title Lymphatic Drainage of the Head. Then, note the location of the lymph nodes in the region of the head and shoulder of the female. The titles list is primarily composed of the names of lymph nodes. As you study these names in the reading, color their titles, then locate and color them in the plate.

The lymph nodes are clusters of lymphatic cells and supporting tissues, as described in the previous plate. Lymphatic vessels lead into and out from the lymph nodes in numerous places of the body. In the head region, the **infraorbital lymph nodes (A)** are located close to the eye. They occur in the region of the orbicularis oculi muscle, and they drain this area.

The **parotid gland (a)** is found at the angle of the jaw, with the **parotid lymph nodes (B)** found nearby. Much fluid passes through this gland, and the parotid lymph node collects some of the fluid for return to the circulation. The **buccal lymph nodes (C)** are found at the margins of the oral cavity. Spots of dark color should be used to indicate their presence. The **mandibular lymph nodes (D)** are also shown.

Other lymph nodes are located at the floor of the mouth. The **submental lymph nodes (E)** are found near the mental foramen of the mandible. The **submandibular lymph nodes (F)** occur beneath the mandible in the region of the **submandibular gland (b)**. A light color should be used for the gland. Note that we are using lowercase letters to denote structures accessory to the lymph nodes.

> We now proceed to the dorsal portion of the head and survey the lymph nodes of this area. Many of these lymph nodes collect fluid from the skull and brain areas for return to the circulation. Note that the system flows in one direction toward the heart. Continue your coloring as above, and use spots of dark colors to indicate the presence of the lymph nodes. If you wish to identify and color the other organs in the area, feel free to do so.

At the region of the ear, two types of lymph nodes are found. In front of the ear at the margin of the pinna, are the **periauricular lymph nodes (G)**. Lymphatic vessels from the brain are seen in the plate passing through them. The **retroauricular lymph nodes (H)** are found behind the ear. **Occipital lymph nodes (I)** drain areas of the occipital lobe of the brain and occipital bone of the skull.

Fluid extending from the head region normally passes through the cervical lymph nodes for a final cleansing. In the plate, the **superficial cervical lymph nodes (J)** are found close to the body surface, while the **deep cervical lymph nodes (K)** are found in the deeper muscle tissues. The long, straplike muscle of this area is the sternocleidomastoid muscle.

> We now move to the second portion of the plate, and examine the lymph nodes of the shoulder region of the female. The female is used to show the relationship of the lymphatic system to the breast. Continue using spots of color to identify the lymph nodes, and try to identify the muscles as you proceed.

In the shoulder and chest area, several types of lymph nodes have a prominent drainage function. Close to the sternum are the **parasternal lymph nodes (L)**, which are deep in the muscle layers. The **subclavian lymph node (M)** lies close to the subclavian vein and represents a final opportunity for cleansing the lymph before it enters the subclavian vein by the thoracic duct.

The axillary lymph nodes are also prominent in the shoulder area. The **lateral axillary lymph nodes (N)** receive lymph from the shoulder area and upper extremities. The **central axillary lymph nodes (O)** receive blood from this area, as well as from the mammary glands in the breast. Also in the region are the **subscapular lymph nodes (P)**, which lie close to the subscapular artery and vein. The **pectoral lymph nodes (Q)** are found near the pectoral muscles, and are responsible for draining the pectoral area of the thoracic cavity.

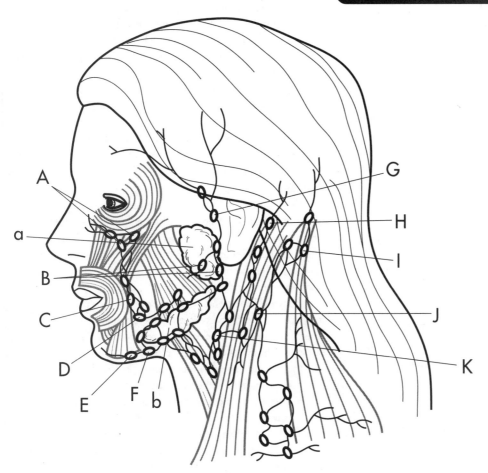

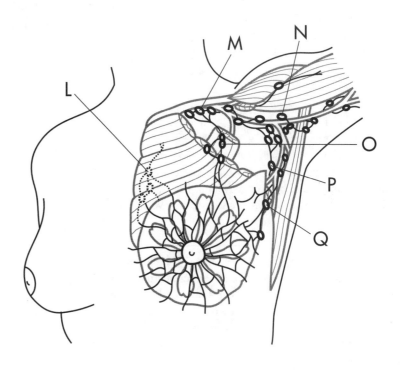

Infraorbital lymph nodes	A	○
Parotid lymph nodes	B	○
Buccal lymph nodes	C	○
Mandibular lymph nodes	D	○
Submental lymph nodes	E	○
Submandibular lymph nodes	F	○
Periauricular lymph nodes	G	○
Retroauricular lymph nodes	H	○
Occipital lymph nodes	I	○
Superficial cervical lymph nodes	J	○
Deep cervical lymph nodes	K	○
Parasternal lymph nodes	L	○
Subclavian lymph nodes	M	○
Lateral axillary lymph nodes	N	○
Central axillary lymph nodes	O	○
Subscapular lymph nodes	P	○
Pectoral lymph nodes	Q	○
Parotid gland	a	○
Submandibular gland	b	○

the SPLEEN

The spleen is the largest mass of lymphatic tissue in the body. It is roughly five inches in length and is found in the left hypochondriac region lateral to the liver. The spleen is similar to a lymph node, but it has no afferent lymph vessels or efferent lymphatic vessels, and it does not filter lymph. We discuss its functions in this plate as we survey its anatomical features and landmarks.

We are presenting in this plate a whole view of the spleen and a cross section of its tissue. These will give you an opportunity to study its functions. A single pale color may be used in the first part of the plate, but darker colors may be suggested for the second part. Color the main title The Spleen then begin reading the following paragraph as you study the plate.

The spleen is found in the body at approximately the level of the ninth to eleventh ribs. It attaches to the stomach at the lateral border of the stomach by the gastrosplenic ligament.

The spleen lies just beneath the diaphragm and is a soft, blood-rich organ. Because it is pliable, the shape of the spleen conforms to the organs it contacts. The **diaphragmatic surface (A)** lies against the diaphragm and the splenic surface is convex as it conforms to the surface of the diaphragm. In the plate, we are viewing the spleen from the lateral aspect and observing the **visceral surface (B)**. The spleen should be colored a single color throughout.

At one point along the surface, the spleen curves to accommodate the stomach. This is the **gastric area (B$_1$)**, indicated by an arrow that should be colored boldly. Another area of the visceral surface contacts the kidney, and the spleen is depressed to accommodate this organ. This is the **renal area (B$_2$)**, also indicated by an arrow.

As noted, the spleen has no afferent or efferent lymphatic vessels, but it is serviced by the splenic artery and vein. These vessels enter and leave the spleen at a region called the **hilus (B$_3$)**. The hilus is a slightly concave anterior region, and the **splenic artery (C)** can be seen entering the spleen, while the **splenic vein (D)** can be seen leaving it. Darker colors may be used for these vessels. Other branches of the vessels are seen nearby.

We focus next on the internal anatomy, the functional area, of the spleen. For this part, we concentrate on the diagram of the interior, and medium or bold colors may be used to designate the different parts. As you continue to read, locate the titles in the titles list and color them, then color the appropriate structures in the plate.

The spleen has several functions related to homeostasis of the body. Phagocytes remove abnormal blood cells from the circulation within the organ. The spleen stores iron removed from aged red blood cells, and the B-lymphocytes and T-lymphocytes within the spleen respond in the immune response to foreign substances detected in the circulation.

The spleen is enclosed in a layer of dense connective tissue known as the **capsule (E)**. This is seen in the section of the spleen. Indentations from this capsule extend partly into the splenic tissue to divide it into lobelike areas. An individual extension is known as a **trabeculum (E$_1$)**. Its arrow may be colored in a dark color, and the trabeculum itself should be colored the same color as the capsule.

The main tissue of the spleen consists of two different kinds of tissue called red pulp and white pulp. The **red pulp (F)** is a dense area consisting of sinuses filled with blood, as the plate indicates. Between the sinuses are plates of tissue called **splenic cords (I)**. The splenic cords contain red blood cells as well as phagocytic cells called macrophages, and B-lymphocytes and T-lymphocytes. The splenic cords contain reticular connective tissue in which the red blood cells and macrophages are found. This is where the spleen recycles aged red blood cells and removes pathogens from the circulating blood.

The second region is the **white pulp (G)**. This white pulp is indicated in the diagram among the areas of red pulp. It contains B-lymphocytes arranged around a series of **trabecular arteries (H)**. Much of the immune function of the spleen occurs in the white pulp. Here the B-lymphocytes respond to the presence of bacteria, viruses, and other pathogens in the blood and revert to plasma cells discussed in the next plate.

After the blood has entered the spleen through the **splenic artery (C)** and passed through the **trabecular arteries (H)**, it enters the extensive **capillary network (K)**. Having been cleansed and the red blood cells removed for disposal, the blood accumulates in a number of **venous sinuses (J)**. It then flows from the sinuses into small venules, which come together to form the main splenic vein. The splenic vein then removes blood from the spleen and returns it to the general circulation.

Diaphragmatic surface   A ○
Visceral surface   B ○
Gastric area B_1 ○
Renal area B_2 ○
Hilus B_3 ○
Splenic artery   C ○
Splenic vein   D ○
Capsule   E ○
Trabeculum E_1 ○
Red pulp   F ○
White pulp   G ○
Trabecular arteries   H ○
Splenic cords   I ○
Venous sinuses   J ○
Capillary network   K ○

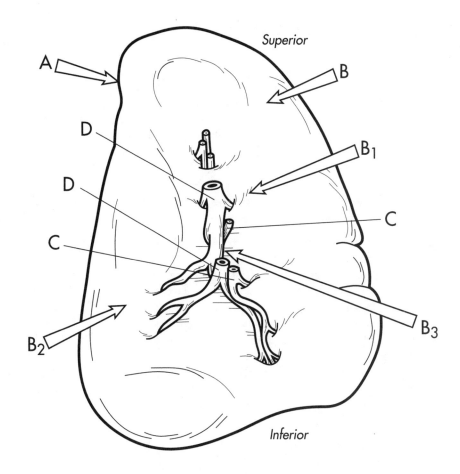

Superior

Inferior

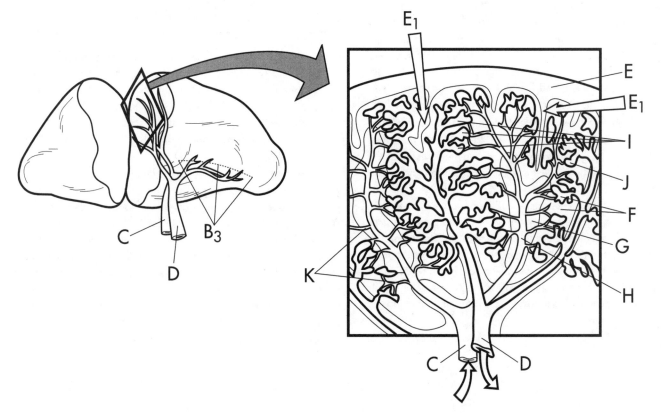

the IMMUNE PROCESS

The immune process is responsible for specific defense in the body and for long-term immunity to disease. It takes place using the cells and factors of the immune system, which are located in the lymphatic system. The two key cells of the system may be found in the lymph nodes, spleen, tonsils, and other lymphatic organs. In this plate, we present a brief overview of the immune process, showing how it relates to the lymphatic system. The process is in the domain of immunology and is more complex than this introductory plate depicts.

We are presenting in this plate a process, that is, a series of events that embody the activities of the immune system. Anatomical features are of lesser consequence than the process itself. Medium colors would be best for most of the cells and structures shown, and the arrows are used to indicate passage from one cell group to another. As you read about the process below, color the appropriate titles, and the structures and other points of interest in the plate. Begin by coloring the main title The Immune Process.

The immune system is a complex series of cells, chemical factors, and organs that contribute to resistance to disease. The cells of the immune system originate in the **bone (A)**. Within the **bone marrow (A_1)**, a series of primitive cells called stem cells emerges during the fetal stage. These stem cells become the cells of the immune system. During the fetal stage, some of the stem cells become **immature T-lymphocytes (B)**. These immature cells migrate to the **thymus gland (C)**, and emerge as **mature T-lymphocytes (D_1)**. Some of the emerging cells become **helper T-lymphocytes (D_2)**. Both types of lymphocytes have at their surfaces a number of chemical complexes called T-lymphocyte receptors. The T-lymphocytes gather together in the lymphatic tissue of the **lymph nodes (a)**. The bracket indicating this tissue may be colored.

Some of the stem cells follow a different route. They mature in the fetal stage in the bone marrow, liver, and other areas of the body and become **mature B-lymphocytes (H)**. The B-lymphocytes also migrate to the lymphatic tissue and replicate to form clusters of cells here. The locations of the cells in the lymph node are shown in the plate on the lymph node. At this point, the T-lymphocytes and B-lymphocytes represent the underpinnings of the immune system.

Having explored the origin of the immune system, we now turn to its activity. Since there are major arms of the system, we shall discuss them in sequence. Our initial focus is the immune process related to the T-lymphocytes. Color the appropriate sections as you read along.

The T-lymphocytes are stimulated by antigens, which are chemical substances not normally found in the body. Such things as virus-infected cells, transplant tissue, cancer cells, and large microorganisms such as fungi and protozoa stimulate the T-lymphocytes. These substances have the antigens for **T-lymphocytes (E)**. Note how the antigen is complementary to the **T-lymphocyte receptors (D_3)**. A reaction takes place on the T-lymphocyte surface, and the **T-lymphocyte is activated (E_1)**. It reverts to a cell called a **cytotoxic T-lymphocyte (F)**. The activation is assisted (G_1) by the **helper T-lymphocyte (D_2)**.

Once the cytotoxic T-lymphocyte has been formed, it enters the **circulation (b)**. Numerous cells will move through the circulation until they locate the foreign object that stimulated their development. Usually an infected cell has been responsible for the stimulation. T-lymphocytes unite with and destroy the cells, thereby providing defense to the body. The process is known as cell-mediated immunity.

In the second part of the plate, we briefly review the second process of immunity, known as antibody-mediated immunity. As you will see, there is no cell-to-cell interaction here, but a slightly different mode of activity involving antibody molecules. Continue coloring as above and locate the titles and structures in the plate.

Antigens from bacteria, viruses, and foreign chemicals enter the body and stimulate the **B-lymphocytes (H)** in the lymphatic tissue to set off this branch of the immune system. The **antigen (I)** selects from a number of different B-lymphocytes and picks the B-lymphocyte with the complementary receptors. Note that the receptor H_3 complements the antigen. The B-lymphocyte is then **activated (I_1)**.

When the B-lymphocytes are activated, they revert into a number of protein-secreting cells called **plasma cells (J)**. Plasma cells secrete enormous numbers of **antibody molecules (K)**. Antibody molecules are strands of protein that enter the **circulation (b)**. They circulate to the site of the virus, bacteria, or other antigen, and their thick strands bind to the antigens, thereby inactivating the microorganism. Soon, large clumps of microorganisms accumulate and phagocytes come along to engulf and destroy those clumps. Specific defense to disease is provided by this process, known as antibody-mediated immunity.

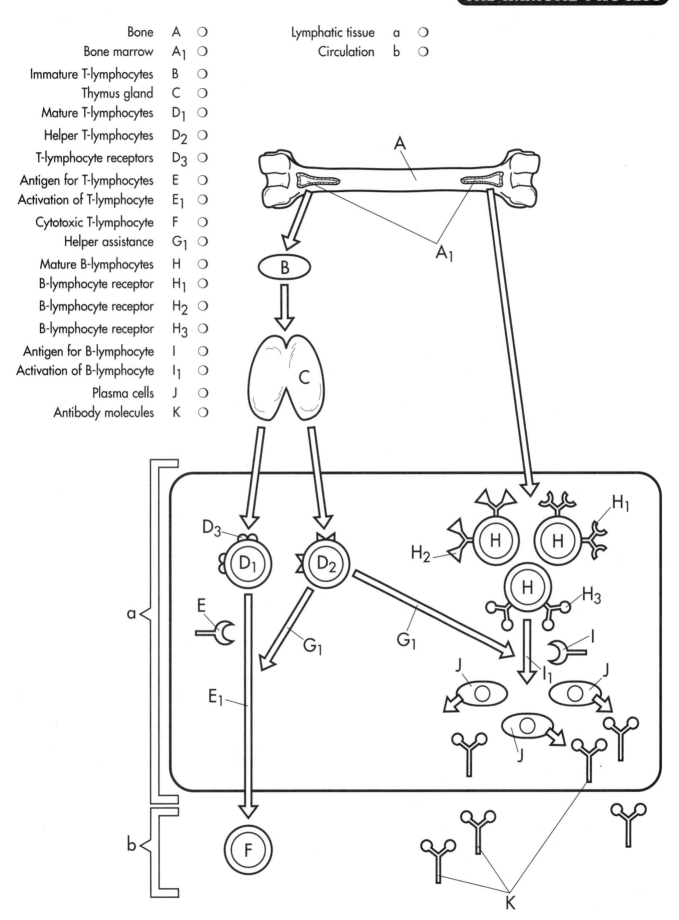

Bone — A — ○
Bone marrow — A_1 — ○
Immature T-lymphocytes — B — ○
Thymus gland — C — ○
Mature T-lymphocytes — D_1 — ○
Helper T-lymphocytes — D_2 — ○
T-lymphocyte receptors — D_3 — ○
Antigen for T-lymphocytes — E — ○
Activation of T-lymphocyte — E_1 — ○
Cytotoxic T-lymphocyte — F — ○
Helper assistance — G_1 — ○
Mature B-lymphocytes — H — ○
B-lymphocyte receptor — H_1 — ○
B-lymphocyte receptor — H_2 — ○
B-lymphocyte receptor — H_3 — ○
Antigen for B-lymphocyte — I — ○
Activation of B-lymphocyte — I_1 — ○
Plasma cells — J — ○
Antibody molecules — K — ○

Lymphatic tissue — a — ○
Circulation — b — ○

CHAPTER NINE:

the DIGESTIVE SYSTEM

OVERVIEW of the DIGESTIVE SYSTEM

The function of the digestive system is to break down large food particles into smaller ones that can pass across the membranes of cells during absorption. Two main groups of organs make up the digestive system. The first group are the organs of the gastrointestinal (GI) tract, also known as the alimentary canal. This is a tube extending from mouth to anus and opened to the exterior at each end. The second group are accessory structures such as the teeth, tongue, and glands lining the GI tract. They aid the mechanical and chemical breakdown of foods.

This plate gives an overview of the digestive system, with a focus on the two groups of organs. We also examine the nine regions of the abdominal cavity, since locating a digestive organ entails reference to one of these regions. Use bold colors in this plate, because the structures and regions are easy to see and separate from nearby structures.

> Begin by coloring the main title Overview of the Digestive System. We are presenting the complete digestive system with organs of the GI tract and accessory organs. Dark colors such as reds, oranges, greens, and blues may be used, as the organs are distinctive. As you read about the organs in the following paragraphs, color their main titles, then locate and color them in the plate.

The process of digestion begins when food enters the first part of the digestive system, the **oral cavity (A)**. Here the food is mechanically processed and moistened with secretions. Food then enters the next part of the GI tract, the **pharynx (B)**, at the rear of the mouth. A color blending with the color used for the oral cavity is advised. No digestion occurs in the pharynx as food passes through it.

The organ for transporting food to the stomach is the muscular **esophagus (C)**. This tube passes through the thoracic cavity, then pierces the diaphragm before entering the pouchlike **stomach (D)**. Here, food mixes with acid and protein-digesting enzymes, then is retained until digested further. Passing from the stomach, food enters the 20-foot-long **small intestine (E)**. A great portion of the abdominal cavity is taken up by the many folds and twists of this organ. The main processes of digestion and absorption occur here.

At the visual lower left portion of the plate (the anatomical right), the small intestine leads into the **large intestine (F)**. This tube can be seen ascending along the anatomical right side, passing along the midline, then turning and descending along the left. A single color should be used for all three sections.

Nondigested material is dehydrated and compacted in this organ. Prior to defecation, indigestible waste is stored in the S-shaped **rectum (G)**. After feces have accumulated, it passes through the **anus (H)**. A spot of color should be used to designate this opening.

> The digestive process is aided by organs lying along the GI tract and by contributing secretions. Three such organs are mentioned briefly in this section, and we recommend dark colors to indicate their location.

Three sets of **salivary glands (I)** supply enzymes for carbohydrate digestion in the oral cavity. The largest organ of the abdominal cavity is the **liver (J)**. This organ secretes bile for fat emulsification, and it processes the products of digestion before sending them to the tissue cells. Beneath the liver, is the **gallbladder (K)**. Bile from the liver is stored here before delivery to the intestine.

An important contributor of enzymes for the digestive process is the **pancreas (L)**. Exocrine cells of this gland deliver their secretions by ducts into the first part of the small intestine.

> In the final portion of this plate, we briefly view the nine regions of the abdominal cavity. These regions are used for convenience in locating digestive and other abdominal organs. We recommend that you use light colors for the nine regions so as to avoid obscuring the organs of the region. Lowercase letters have been used to contrast with the labels used for the structures above.

Examining the abdominal cavity from anatomical right to anatomical left and from superior to inferior, the nine imaginary regions help anatomists locate the organs of this cavity. In the **right hypochondriac region (a)**, the liver and gallbladder are present. The **epigastric region (b)** contains part of the liver and a large portion of the stomach. In the **left hypochondriac region (c)**, a small portion of the stomach, a part of the large intestine, and the spleen are located.

The **right lumbar region (d)** contains a portion of the large intestine and a portion of the small intestine, which has been cut in this diagram. The superficial organs of the **umbilical region (e)** include many loops of the small intestine, also cut in this plate. Portions of the small intestine and large intestine are also seen in the **left lumbar region (f)**.

The **right inguinal region (g)** is at the anatomical lower right. It contains the appendix, cecum, and portion of the small intestine. In the **hypogastric region (h)** are found the urinary bladder and portions of the small intestine and rectum. The **left inguinal region (i)** contains portions of the large intestine.

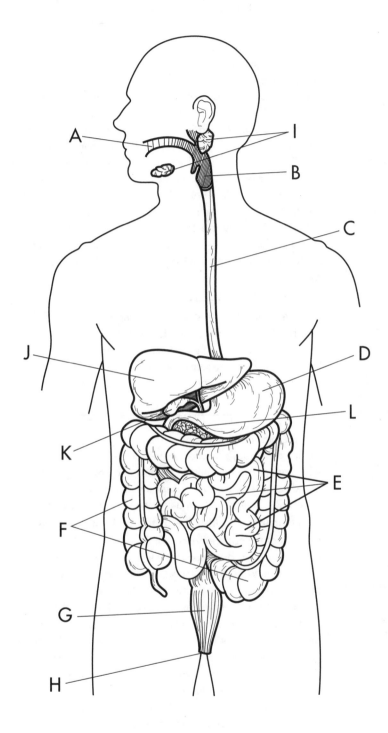

Oral cavity	A	○
Pharynx	B	○
Esophagus	C	○
Stomach	D	○
Small intestine	E	○
Large intestine	F	○
Rectum	G	○
Anus	H	○
Salivary glands	I	○
Liver	J	○
Gallbladder	K	○
Pancreas	L	○
Right hypochondriac region	a	○
Epigastric region	b	○
Left hypochondriac region	c	○
Right lumbar region	d	○
Umbilical region	e	○
Left lumbar region	f	○
Right inguinal region	g	○
Hypogastric region	h	○
Left inguinal region	i	○

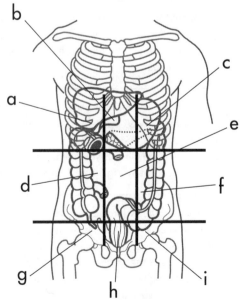

the ORAL CAVITY

The digestive system begins at the mouth, which leads to the oral cavity, the subject of this plate. Food entry to the body takes place here, and mechanical digestion and some chemical digestion occurs.

In this plate, we present a sagittal section of the oral cavity and an anterior view, showing many of the same structures. There is also a focus on the tongue, which is responsible for propulsive processes of swallowing.

Begin by coloring the main title The Oral Cavity. Many of the structures discussed are in both sagittal section and anterior views of the oral cavity, and these structures should be colored in both views as they are studied. In some cases, arrows point to an area, and the arrows should be colored rather than the area. The area can be shaded in with a pale or light gray, tan, or other color to give it detail, but be careful to avoid obscuring the arrows. Color the titles as you encounter the structures in the reading below.

The oral cavity is also known as the buccal cavity. It is outlined by the **cheek (A)**, seen internally in the sagittal section and externally in the anterior view. The arrows should be colored for this structure. The cavity is also defined by the **lips (B)**, also called the labia. The region between the lips and the teeth is the **vestibule (C)**.

The mechanical digestion of food is accomplished by the **teeth (D)**. These structures are examined in more detail in the next plate, but they should be colored here. Note in the sagittal section how the upper and lower teeth are encased in bone. A ridge of oral mucosa, called the gum or **gingiva (E)**, lies at the base of each tooth and surrounds it.

We now turn our attention to portions of the posterior region of the oral cavity. As before, many areas are indicated by arrows, and they may be colored with dark colors. Color the titles as you encounter the structures, then locate them in sagittal and anterior views.

The roof of the mouth is formed by two palates. The **hard palate (F)** is the anterior structure. Its basis is the palatine bones and the palatine processes of the maxillae. More posterior is the **soft palate (G)**. It is composed primarily of skeletal muscle, and no bone is seen in the sagittal section. The last structure of the soft palate is the dangling **uvula (H)**. The uvula helps prevent food from leaving the oral cavity unintentionally. At the lateral aspect, the soft palate joins with the tongue at two pairs of arches. The **palatopharyngeal arch (I)** is the more posterior arch and designates the entry to the pharynx. The **palatoglossal arch (J)** is more anterior and is seen in both sagittal section and anterior view.

We now proceed to an examination of the tongue. This organ can be seen in all three views, and a light color, such as a yellow or tan, is recommended to prevent obscuring its structures. Darker colors can then be used to indicate areas along the surface of the tongue.

Most of the region at the base of the oral cavity is occupied by the **tongue (K)**. This thick, muscular organ is covered by mucous membranes and is anchored in the midline to the floor of the mouth by a fold of membrane called the **lingual frenulum (L)**, as shown in the anterior view. The tongue is anchored partly to the **hyoid bone (M)** and is controlled by several muscles including the hyoglossus and others discussed in a previous plate.

The tongue is divided into two sections, the body and the root. The **body (N)** is outlined by a bracket, and the **root (O)** by a second bracket. The brackets may be colored to indicate these areas. On its superior surface, the tongue contains numerous **papillae (P)**. There are three types of papillae, two of which house the taste buds. At the base of the tongue are the openings of the two **sublingual salivary glands (Q)**, discussed in an upcoming plate.

We conclude with structures related to the oral cavity but not necessarily associated with the digestive system. As you encounter these structures in the reading, color their titles, then locate and color them in the plate. Darker colors may be used for the structures and arrows.

The oral cavity contains elements of other systems that contribute to the body's function. Among these are two sets of tonsils, which are parts of the immune system and are composed of lymphoid tissue. At the posterior aspect of the tongue are the **lingual tonsils (R_1)**. Lateral to them along the wall of the oral cavity are the **palatine tonsils (R_2)**. The **pharyngeal tonsil (R_3)** lies in the pharynx at the posterior aspect of the oral cavity. The function of these tissues was discussed in the lymphoid system chapter.

At its most posterior aspect, the oral cavity continues as the pharynx, beginning at an area called the fauces. The first portion of the pharynx after the fauces is the **oropharynx (T_2)**. Superior to the oropharynx is the continuation of the nasal cavity known as the **nasopharynx (T_1)**. The nasopharynx contains the pharyngeal tonsil noted above, and is the site where the **Eustachian tube (S)** opens. This tube leads to the middle ear and helps equalize the pressure in the middle ear. The **epiglottis (U)**, which is a part of the respiratory system, is also visible. This flap of tissue prevents food from entering the trachea.

Cheek	A	○
Lips	B	○
Vestibule	C	○
Teeth	D	○
Gingiva	E	○
Hard palate	F	○
Soft palate	G	○
Uvula	H	○
Palatopharyngeal arch	I	○
Palatoglossal arch	J	○
Tongue	K	○
Lingual frenulum	L	○
Hyoid bone	M	○
Body	N	○
Root	O	○
Papillae	P	○
Sublingual salivary glands	Q	○
Lingual tonsils	R_1	○
Palatine tonsils	R_2	○
Pharyngeal tonsil	R_3	○
Eustachian tube	S	○
Nasopharynx	T_1	○
Oropharynx	T_2	○
Epiglottis	U	○

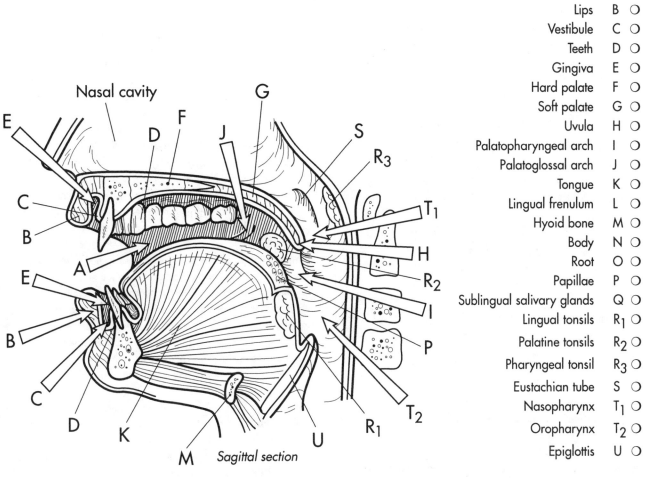

Sagittal section

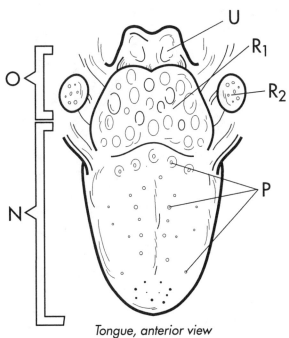

Tongue, anterior view

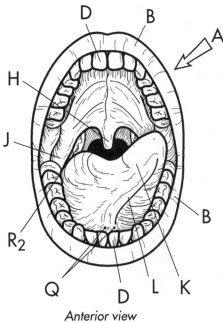

Anterior view

219

the TEETH

The teeth are the organs of mastication, or chewing. They cut, grind, and tear ingested food so it can be mixed with saliva and swallowed. This mechanical digestion increases the surface area of the food and enhances the action of digestive enzymes.

The first teeth to appear in life are the deciduous teeth or "baby" teeth. Generally they are shed between the ages of 6 and 13 years and are replaced by 32 permanent or "adult" teeth. In this plate, we study the permanent teeth, then focus on a single tooth to show some of its important features.

This plate shows an anterior view of the oral cavity with the 32 permanent teeth in place. The individual teeth from half the upper jaw and half the lower jaw are also shown, and details are given on an individual tooth. Color the main title The Teeth and select dark colors for the different types of teeth as you read below. Color their titles also. Reds, greens, purples, and other bold colors may be used here.

Four types of teeth are found in the permanent dentition. The first group are the **incisors (A)**. These teeth are adapted for cutting food and are closest to the midline. The incisors should be colored individually.

Moving posteriorly, the next teeth are the **cuspids (B)**, also known as canines. The pointed surfaces of these teeth help in tearing and shredding food. Next posterior are the **bicuspids (C)**. Both upper and lower surfaces of the jaw have four bicuspids, also known as premolars. They generally have one or two roots. The flattened crown of the bicuspids help crushing and grinding.

The final set of teeth are the **molars (D)**. These teeth act as millstones to crush and grind food. As the plate shows, the upper molars have three roots, while the lower molars have only two.

To assist anatomical location, the teeth of the upper jaw are arranged in an **upper dental arch (E)**. The outline of this arch may be colored in a dark color. The lower jaw contains the **lower dental arch (F)**. Note that the outer surface of the arches are considered the labial surfaces, while the inner surfaces of the upper and lower dental arches are the palatal and lingual surfaces, respectively.

We now turn to a "typical" tooth and describe some of its important features. For some structures, bolder colors can be used, but other structures would probably benefit from pale colors, because they tend to be more detailed. Color the titles as you encounter them and as you locate the structures in the plate.

Although there is no one "typical" tooth, all teeth have some common features and unifying characteristics. A tooth consists of three regions. The visible portion of the tooth above the gums is the **crown (G)**. A dark color may be used to color in the bracket of this region. The next area is the **neck (H)**, the area near the gumline. Here the crown connects to the third region, known as the **root (I)**. As the plate indicates, the root extends to the lower portion of the tooth.

The tooth rests within a bony socket known as the alveolus, which lies in the maxillary bones of the upper jaw and the mandible of the lower jaw. The bony area surrounding the alveolus is the **alveolar bone (J)**. A light color should be used for this area.

Within the alveolus, the root of the tooth forms a strong joint known as a gomphosis. At the top of the joint, is the gum, also called the **gingiva (K)**. Within the joint the root connects to the alveolar bone by fibers from the **periodontal ligament (L)**. A light color should be used here. Covering the root is a protective layer called the **cementum (M)**. The cementum anchors the periodontal ligament to the root.

At the crown of the tooth is a hard chemical substance called **enamel (N)**. Calcium phosphate is a major component of the enamel. Below the enamel and forming the major portion of each tooth is the **dentin (O)**. This material is very similar in substance to bone, but it has no living cells as bone does. The dentin receives materials for growth and deposits its wastes in extensions of cells in the **pulp cavity (P)**. A pale color should be used for the pulp cavity.

The material of the pulp cavity, the pulp of the tooth, is very spongy and highly vascular. The main portion of the pulp receives blood vessels and nerves passing through the **root canal (Q)**, which is indicated by an arrow. Arteries, veins, and nerves enter the root canal through an opening known as the **apical foramen (R)**. This is also indicated with an arrow. The blood vessels and **nerves (S)** pass through the canal on their way to the pulp and supply the tooth with nutrients, carry off its waste products, and supply nerve impulses.

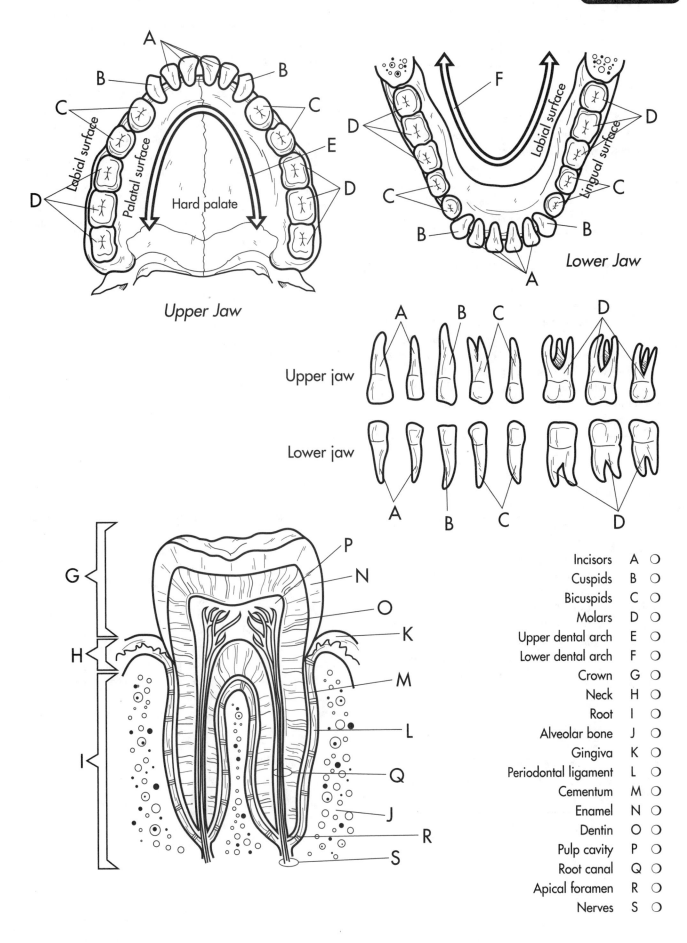

Upper Jaw

Labial surface

Palatal surface

Hard palate

Lower Jaw

Labial surface

Lingual surface

Upper jaw

Lower jaw

Incisors A ○
Cuspids B ○
Bicuspids C ○
Molars D ○
Upper dental arch E ○
Lower dental arch F ○
Crown G ○
Neck H ○
Root I ○
Alveolar bone J ○
Gingiva K ○
Periodontal ligament L ○
Cementum M ○
Enamel N ○
Dentin O ○
Pulp cavity P ○
Root canal Q ○
Apical foramen R ○
Nerves S ○

the SALIVARY GLANDS

The salivary glands are the first organs of chemical digestion within the digestive system. These glands secrete digestive juices containing carbohydrate-digesting enzymes.

The focus in this plate is the three salivary glands located in the tissues of the mouth. We shall note the location of the glands and the means by which they deliver their secretions to the oral cavity. The secretions are collectively known as saliva. Saliva is a watery, tasteless mixture that includes enzymes and mucus. The saliva also contains salts to provide buffering action. Its main enzyme is amylase, an enzyme that acts on starch.

> Begin the plate by coloring the main title The Salivary Glands. We use both capital and lowercase letters. The capital letters refer to the salivary glands and their ducts, while the lowercase letters apply to other structures in the area. Use pale and light colors for the structures to avoid obscuring them. As you read about the first salivary gland, color it and its associated structures in the plate.

Approximately 25 to 35 percent of the daily salivary secretion is produced by the **parotid glands (A)**. As the plate shows, this paired gland lies below the ear at the general region of the **zygomatic arch (a)**. The gland overlies a portion of the **masseter muscle (b)** at its posterior aspect. The parotid gland is a tubuloalveolar gland and the largest of the three salivary glands.

Secretions of the parotid gland are delivered by the parotid duct, also called **Stenson's duct (B)**. This long duct passes forward over the masseter muscle, as the plate shows, and it can be felt as a ridge by moving the tip of the finger up and down over the muscle. The duct ends at a vestibule alongside the **second maxillary molar (c)**. The **opening of the parotid duct (B_1)** is shown in the plate, and a small dot of color may be used to distinguish it. The duct pierces the buccinator muscle on its way to the opening.

> We now move to the second salivary gland and discuss its anatomy and importance. As you encounter this gland in the reading, color its title and locate it in the plate. Bolder colors may be used because this gland is relatively large.

Approximately 60 to 70 percent of the daily secretion of saliva is produced by the **submandibular gland (C)**. This paired gland lies under the **mandible (d)**, and the gland takes its name from this location. The gland is found on the medial side of the mandible and is about the size of a walnut.

The duct leading away from the submandibular gland is called the **submandibular duct (D)**, also known as **Wharton's duct**. The submandibular duct runs along the floor of the oral cavity in the direction of the anterior portion of the cavity. It opens into a papilla on the floor of the mouth just beside the **lingual frenulum (e)**. The opening is not seen on the plate, but the frenulum can be seen, and the openings may be observed in an anterior view of the floor of the mouth in a previous plate. The submandibular gland produces the protein mucin, which is used to form mucus to lubricate food particles so they cling together and slide down the pharynx and esophagus during swallowing.

> We now turn to the third salivary gland and note its location and function. The ducts from this gland are difficult to locate and spots of dark color are useful to identify them.

About 3 to 5 percent of the saliva is produced by the **sublingual glands (E)**. This paired gland lies under the tongue. The sublingual glands are the smallest salivary glands. They lie in front of the submandibular glands, under the mucous membranes covering the floor of the mouth.

Draining the sublingual glands are eight to twenty ducts opening into the floor of the mouth. These ducts are called the **sublingual ducts (F)**, also known as the ducts of Rivinus. Spots of dark color may be used to denote their location at the base of the **tongue (f)**. The tongue has been lifted to show the openings of the ducts.

Saliva produced by the sublingual glands is similar to that produced by the submandibular glands. It cleanses the mouth and teeth of debris while keeping the soft parts of the mouth supple. In addition, the saliva contains bicarbonate ions that help neutralize the acid produced around the teeth by fermenting bacteria. The secretion of saliva by the glands is stimulated by nerves of the parasympathetic system, which terminate at the salivary glands. The smell, taste, or sight of food may also stimulate salivary secretion. The secretion of saliva is entirely controlled by the autonomic nervous system, in contrast to other digestive secretions regulated by nerve as well as hormonal control.

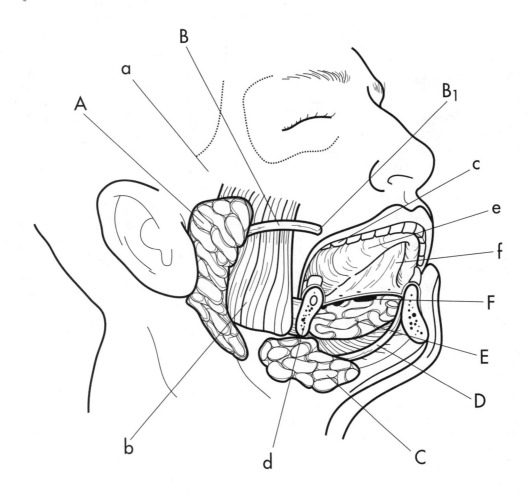

Parotid glands	A	○
Parotid duct (Stenson's duct)	B	○
Opening of the parotid duct	B₁	○
Submandibular gland	C	○
Submandibular duct (Wharton's duct)	D	○
Sublingual glands	E	○
Sublingual ducts	F	○
Zygomatic arch	a	○
Masseter muscle	b	○
Second maxillary molar	c	○
Mandible	d	○
Lingual frenulum	e	○
Tongue	f	○

the STOMACH

Immediately inferior to the diaphragm, the gastrointestinal system elongates and forms the pouchlike stomach. Approximately five-sixths of the stomach is to the left of the median line: the stomach lies in the epigastric and left hypochodriac regions of the abdominal cavity. This plate features the anatomy of the stomach from two viewpoints: the macroscopic anatomy and the microscopic anatomy. We shall proceed from the visible portions of the stomach to those portions having finer detail.

We are moving in the plate from the largest view of the stomach to the most microscopic. In each sequence, a portion is magnified further for your study. Begin by coloring the main title The Stomach. Then as you read about the structures, locate and color their titles. Arrows point to the region of the stomach, and they may be colored with bold colors. Light colors should be used for the other areas.

After passing through the pharynx, the bolus of food is propelled through the esophagus and enters the stomach. On the plate, the inferior portion of the **esophagus (a)** is designated with a lowercase letter, because it is not part of the stomach. At its far end, the stomach empties its contents into the first part of the small intestine, the **duodenum (b)**.

As the plate indicates, the stomach is a J-shaped sac, with a capacity of approximately 1.5 liters. At its medial surface, the stomach has a **lesser curvature (A)** toward the anatomical right and a **greater curvature (B)** toward the anatomical left and its lateral surface. The brackets for these curvatures should be colored with a bold color.

From the esophagus, the bolus of food passes through the **cardiac sphincter (C)**, indicated by an arrow. The bolus then enters the region of the stomach called the **cardia (D_1)**. This general area is indicated by an arrow to be colored in a bold color. The small rounded area above the level of the cardiac sphincter is the **fundus (D_2)**, also noted with an arrow. Then the food enters the large central portion known as the **body (D_3)**. At the far end of the stomach is the **pylorus (D_4)**, after which comes the **duodenum (b)**. The outlet from the stomach is the circular muscle called the **pyloric sphincter (E)**. A portion of the sphincter muscle is shown and may be colored. The outlet itself is the **pyloric outlet (F)**.

We now proceed to the tissues that line the stomach wall and begin a discussion of the microscopic anatomy. Bolder colors can be used for the layers, but be careful to avoid obscuring the direction of the fibers, because they are important identifying characteristics.

When the stomach is empty, the mucous membranes of its inner surface form wrinkles called **rugae (G)**. These should be colored using a light color. The rugae flatten as the stomach fills.

The outer muscle layers of the stomach constitute the **muscularis externa (H)**. The bracket for the muscularis externa may be colored. Three layers of smooth muscle fibers make up this structure. The outermost layer of muscle is the **longitudinal layer (H_1)**, which is continuous with the muscle of the esophagus. Next is the **middle circular layer (H_2)**, which wraps around the body of the stomach and forms the pyloric sphincter. The innermost layer is the **oblique layer (H_3)**, visible in both macroscopic and microscopic views. This layer is prominent in the region of the fundus.

The outermost layer of stomach lining is the **serosa (I)**, a serous membrane having a dense network of arteries and veins supplying the inner reaches of the stomach. Beneath the muscle layers is the **submucosa (J)**. Seen in the microscopic view, the submucosa is a layer of loose connective tissue containing large blood vessels, lymphatic vessels, and a plexus of nerves.

To finish with the plate, we focus on the regions of the mucosa and the digestive functions of the stomach. Our emphasis is on the microscopic anatomy. Lighter colors are recommended, because many structures are involved here. Continue as before, coloring the titles as you encounter them in the list, then locate the structure.

At its inner layer, the stomach contains a lining called the **mucosa (K)**. The bracket outlining this layer may be colored. In the mucosa of the stomach, there are three layers. At the outer portion is a narrow band of smooth muscle and elastic fibers called the **muscularis mucosa (K_1)**. The plate shows this narrow band of two thin layers of muscle. Next toward the inner wall is the **lamina propria (K_2)**. This is an underlying layer of loose connective tissue with blood vessels, sensory nerve endings, smooth muscle fibers, and areas of lymphatic tissue. The innermost layer is **mucosal epithelium (K_3)**, which contains the secreting cells of the stomach. A single light color should be used to color the epithelium.

On closer inspection, we see that the epithelial cells of the stomach open into passageways that lead to the inner stomach wall. The openings of these passageways are called **gastric pits (L)**. There are about 3.5 million gastric pits in the stomach lining. The arrows pointing to them should be colored. Along the walls of the gastric pits, we see many **epithelial cells (K_3)**.

Three other kinds of cells are also visible. The **neck mucous cells (M)** secrete a more neutral mucus than at the surface. Specialized cells called **chief cells (N)** secrete pepsinogen, which is converted to pepsin, a protein-digesting enzyme. The third kind of cell is the **parietal cell (O)**. These cells secrete hydrochloric acid, which assists the conversion of pepsinogen to pepsin for the digestive process. Chief cells and parietal cells are shown in greatest detail in the plate, and different colors should be used to identify them.

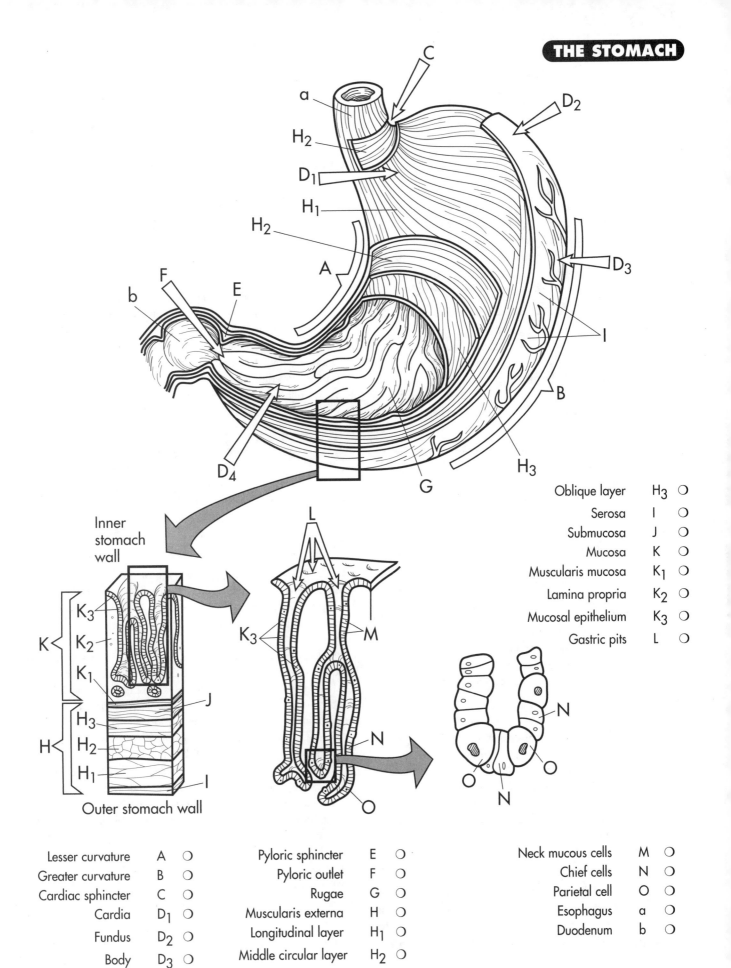

a

C

D₂

H₂

D₁

H₁

H₂

A

F

E

b

D₃

I

B

D₄

G

H₃

Oblique layer	H₃	○
Serosa	I	○
Submucosa	J	○
Mucosa	K	○
Muscularis mucosa	K₁	○
Lamina propria	K₂	○
Mucosal epithelium	K₃	○
Gastric pits	L	○

Inner stomach wall

L

K₃

K₂

K

K₁

J

H₃

H₂

H

H₁

I

Outer stomach wall

K₃

M

N

O

N

N

O

Lesser curvature	A	○
Greater curvature	B	○
Cardiac sphincter	C	○
Cardia	D₁	○
Fundus	D₂	○
Body	D₃	○
Pylorus	D₄	○

Pyloric sphincter	E	○
Pyloric outlet	F	○
Rugae	G	○
Muscularis externa	H	○
Longitudinal layer	H₁	○
Middle circular layer	H₂	○

Neck mucous cells	M	○
Chief cells	N	○
Parietal cell	O	○
Esophagus	a	○
Duodenum	b	○

the SMALL INTESTINE

The small intestine is a long tube filling most of the area of the abdominal cavity. It measures about one inch in diameter and is approximately 20 feet in length. Within the small intestine digestion is completed and most absorption occurs.

This plate reviews the small intestine macroscopically and microscopically. We shall review visible portions of the small intestine, then its finer details. Bold colors can be used for the first part of the plate, but pale colors are best for the remainder.

As you look over the plate, begin by coloring the main title The Small Intestine. Then note how each successive view gives more detail of the structure of the small intestine. Beginning with the macroscopic anatomy, color in the main titles as you encounter them, then locate the regions in the plate. Dark colors are recommended for this early stage.

The small intestine is subdivided into three major portions. The initial segment is the **duodenum (A)**. It extends from the pyloric sphincter of the stomach and is the smallest part of the small intestine, measuring about 10 inches in length. The plate shows a small portion, with the remainder behind the large intestine. We saw the duodenum in more detail in plates on the pancreas and gallbladder. Most digestion of nutrients occurs in the duodenum.

The second portion of the small intestine is the **jejunum (B)**. Extending from the duodenum, this part is about eight feet in length and is the site of digestion and absorption. The third part of the small intestine is the **ileum (C)**. About 12 feet in length, the ileum is continuous with the jejunum and ends at the first part of the large intestine. The absorption of simple nutrients occurs in this organ.

We now focus on the more detailed portions of the small intestine and study its microscopic anatomy. Since the gastrointestinal tract is a continuous tube, many of the structures seen in the stomach in the previous plate are also present in this plate. You should, therefore, watch for similarities in names and structures. Light colors and pale shades are recommended, because the structures are small.

The mucosa of the small intestine is modified to enhance the processes of digestion and absorption taking place in the organ. The small intestine contains permanent circular folds called **plicae circulares (D)**. The bracket outlining one of these folds may be colored in a bold color. Most folds occur in the area of the duodenum and jejunum.

The absorptive area of the mucosa is increased by millions of fingerlike protrusions called **villi (E)**. In the plate, the villi are shown in several areas, and a light shade is recommended for coloring them. At the base of the villi, the mucosa has infoldings of the epithelium known as **intestinal crypts (F)**, also known as the crypts of Lieberkuhn. An arrow points to one of these infoldings in the diagram. The intestinal crypts contain cells that produce digestive enzymes; they also contain endocrine cells that produce hormones such as secretin.

Beneath the tissue of the villus is the **muscularis mucosa (G)**. This layer consists of two thin muscular layers with a nerve plexus. Beneath is the **submucosa (H)**, a vascular layer of connective tissue containing many nerves. Submucosal glands are also present, and the cross section of arteries and veins can be seen.

Beneath the submucosa is the **circular muscle (I)**. This smooth muscle helps move food along the digestive tract by means of wave contractions called peristalsis. Next is the **longitudinal muscle (J)**. The circular and longitudinal muscles constitute the muscularis externa. The most superficial layer is the **serosa (K)**. The portion covering the intestine is the visceral peritoneum. The serosa attaches the intestines to the abdominal wall and it contains blood vessels, nerves, and lymph capillaries.

We now move to a more detailed examination of the villus and note some of the structures it contains. Many of the structures you have encountered previously are seen again, only they are larger and more detailed. Continue using the same colors as before, and use new colors as new structures are introduced.

An expanded view of the villus shows many of the structures encountered previously. We see the **villi (E)** and the **intestinal crypts (F)**. The **muscularis mucosa (G)** and the **submucosa (H)** are also visible. Within the latter, there are traces of submucosal glands.

In this view, we have a detailed view of the **lamina propria (L)**. This structure can be colored using a pale color. The surface of the lamina propria is covered by a layer of **epithelium (M)**. The epithelial cells are the units through which absorption from the small intestine takes place. To increase the absorptive surface area of each epithelial cell, there are thousands of cytoplasmic extensions known as **microvilli (S)**.

Now, note that each villus is supplied with blood by an **artery (N)**. The artery can be seen extending up into the villus where it forms a **capillary network (R)**. Extending down from the villus, blood returns by means of a **vein (O)**. The products of protein and carbohydrate digestion enter the circulation via the villus. A **lymph vessel (P)** carries the products of fat digestion for transport to the rest of the body. A **nerve (Q)** is also part of the villus network.

Duodenum A ○
Jejunum B ○
Ileum C ○
Plicae circulares D ○
Villi E ○
Intestinal crypts F ○
Muscularis mucosa G ○
Submucosa H ○
Circular muscle I ○
Longitudinal muscle J ○
Serosa K ○
Lamina propria L ○
Epithelium M ○
Artery N ○
Vein O ○
Lymph vessel P ○
Nerve Q ○
Capillary network R ○
Microvilli S ○

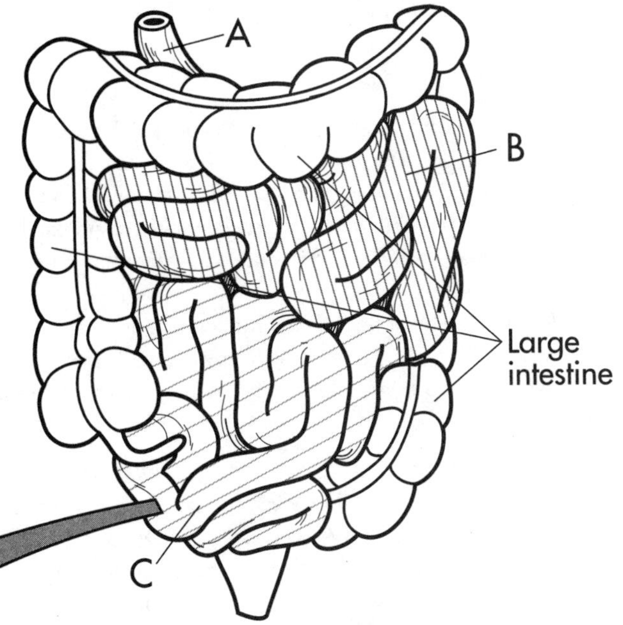

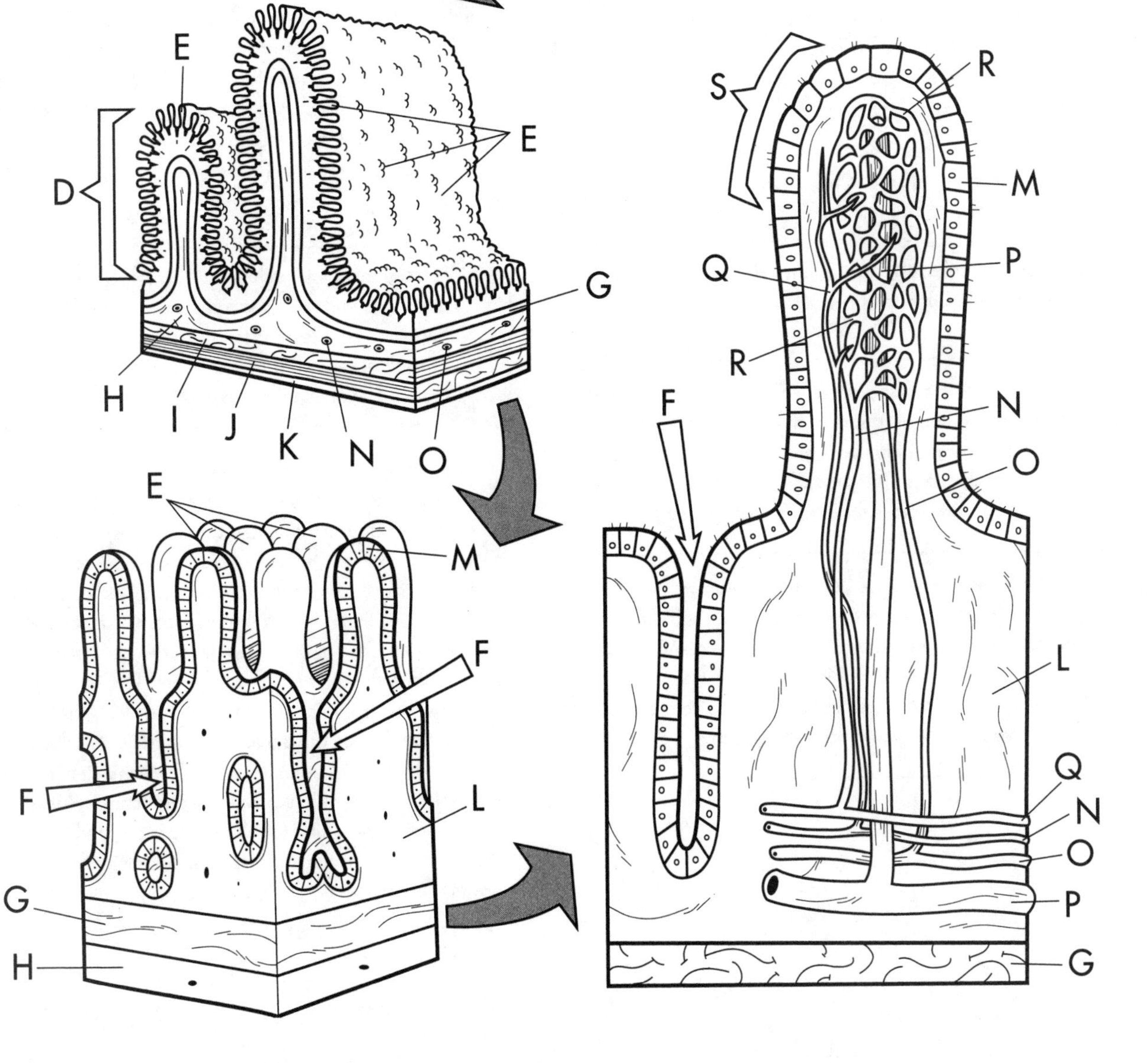

Large intestine

the LARGE INTESTINE

The large intestine extends from the ileum to the anus and is attached to the posterior abdominal wall by a double layer or peritoneum called the mesocolon. The large intestine is between five and six feet in length and is approximately two and one-half inches in diameter, which is noticeably larger than the diameter of the small intestine.

We study the anatomy of the large intestine in this plate by detailing its position in the abdominal cavity and its parts. Most structures are large in this plate, and you may anticipate using bold colors.

We are presenting the large intestine in position, then focusing in on its parts. We use several arrows to detail areas or regions, and bold colors should be used for the arrows. As you encounter the structures in the reading below, color the titles, then locate the structures and color them on the plate. All three portions of the plate may be done simultaneously to develop a clear picture of the overall anatomy of the large intestine.

Visualized in the abdominal cavity, the large intestine has three large regions: the **ascending colon (A)** rises on the right side of the abdomen to approximately the inferior surface of the liver; the large intestine continues across the abdomen to the left as the **transverse colon (B)**; at the level of the spleen the large intestine drops inferiorly to the level of the iliac crest as the **descending colon (C)**.

Other organs of the digestive tract precede the large intestine and are seen in the first diagram. They include the **stomach (a)**, which then leads to the **duodenum (b)**. The duodenum joins with the second portion of the small intestine, the **jejunum (c)**, and the jejunum joins the **ileum (d),** which leads to the large intestine at the visual lower left. This is the anatomical lower right.

Having examined the large intestine in relation to the small intestine, we now turn to some anatomical aspects of the large intestine. Use the same colors used in the first diagram for this part. The ascending, descending, and transverse colons may be colored as before if you have not colored them already.

The **ileum (d)** joins with the large intestine as food passes through the **ileocecal valve (D)**. The arrow pointing to this valve should be colored with a bold color. Hanging from the tissue at this point is a blind pouch of the large intestine called the **cecum (E)**. Color the arrow in a bold color. The cecum is believed to contain bacteria involved in digestion. The cecum is connected to a coiled tube known as the **vermiform appendix (F)**, also a location for bacteria involved in digestion. The appendix is attached to the inferior portion of the ileum by a mesentery called the **mesoappendix (G)**.

As the large intestine proceeds through the abdominal cavity, it abruptly turns twice. The first turn occurs in the right hypochondriac region and is called the **hepatic flexure (H)**. Passing across the epigastric region, the transverse colon makes another turn near the spleen at the **splenic flexure (I)**.

As the large intestine descends toward the iliac crest, it becomes the S-shaped **sigmoid colon (J)**. Color the bracket outlining this area in a bold color. As the tube enters the hypogastric region, the sigmoid colon becomes the **rectum (K)**. The rectum begins at the level of the third sacral vertebra and is the last eight inches of the gastrointestinal tract.

The histology of the large intestine is similar to that of the small intestine except there are no villi or permanent folds in the walls of the large intestine. Absorptive cells function to take water from the lumen of the intestine, and its goblet cells secrete mucus to lubricate the contents of the colon. Longitudinal and circular muscles form bands called **taeniae coli (L)**. Attached to the taeniae coli are small patches of fat and membranes called **epiploic appendages (L_1)**. Contractions of the taeniae coli cause the wall of the colon to form pouches known as **haustra (M)**. An arrow points these out in the diagram.

We close this plate with a brief study of the last portion of the large intestine. The same colors used for the other plates may be used for the third diagram. The focus is on the anal region of the rectum. We have labeled the important levator ani muscle for you.

The terminal inch of the rectum is the anal region of the gastrointestinal tract. The diagram shows the **rectum (K)** leading to this area. No haustra, epiploic appendages, or taeniae coli are found in the rectum. The rectum pierces the pelvic diaphragm and turns sharply downward and backward as the **anal canal (P)**.

Shelves of tissue within the anal canal are known as **plicae transversales (O)**. An arrow points out these shelves of muscular tissue. Within the anal canal are several longitudinal columns of mucus membrane called the **anal columns (Q)**. The opening from the anal canal is the **anus (N)**. Two sphincter muscles and the levator ani control the size of the anus. The sphincters are the **external anal sphincter (R)** and the **internal anal sphincter (S)**. The external sphincter is under voluntary control and is composed of striated muscle, while the internal sphincter is composed of smooth muscle and is not under voluntary control.

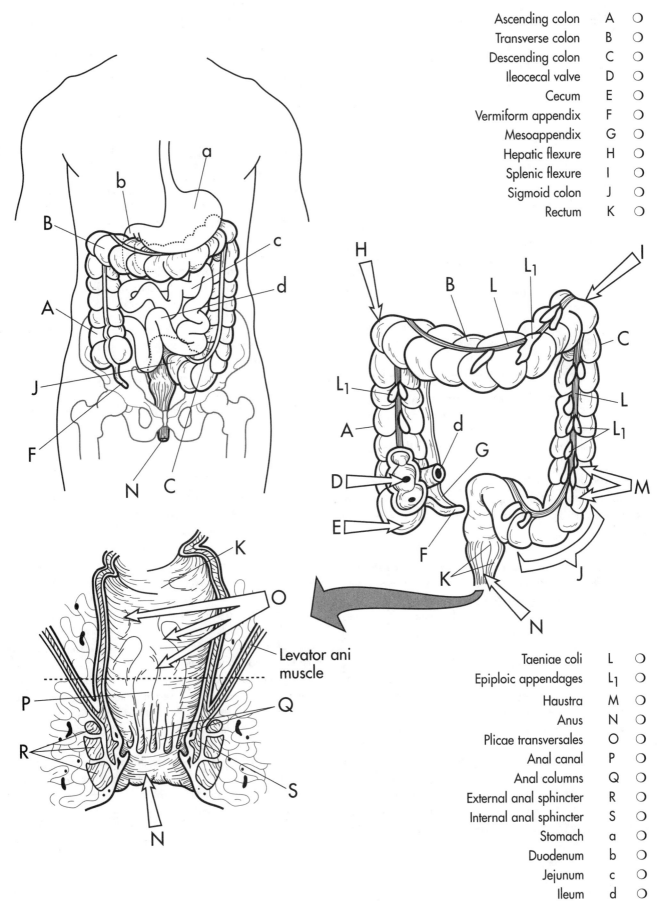

Ascending colon	A	○
Transverse colon	B	○
Descending colon	C	○
Ileocecal valve	D	○
Cecum	E	○
Vermiform appendix	F	○
Mesoappendix	G	○
Hepatic flexure	H	○
Splenic flexure	I	○
Sigmoid colon	J	○
Rectum	K	○

Levator ani muscle

Taeniae coli	L	○
Epiploic appendages	L₁	○
Haustra	M	○
Anus	N	○
Plicae transversales	O	○
Anal canal	P	○
Anal columns	Q	○
External anal sphincter	R	○
Internal anal sphincter	S	○
Stomach	a	○
Duodenum	b	○
Jejunum	c	○
Ileum	d	○

the PANCREAS (EXOCRINE FUNCTION)

The pancreas is a grayish pink gland about six to nine inches in length. It lies in the region of the duodenum, stomach, and spleen and is composed of two types of glandular tissue. In this plate we are concerned with the exocrine tissue, which produces enzymes and other substances essential to the digestive process.

> We present the pancreas in place in the abdominal cavity, then focus on some of the cellular features seen with the microscope. We also use uppercase letters to refer to the pancreas and its parts and lowercase letters for other organs in the area. This plate, therefore, serves as a review of the upper abdominal area. The colors you select should be light ones, since many of the structures overlap.

We begin with an examination of the pancreas in place in the abdominal cavity. The **pancreas (A)** should be colored in a light tone. It vaguely resembles a fish and has three distinct regions. The **head of the pancreas (A_1)** is indicated by an arrow, which may be colored boldly. Note how the head is encircled by the C-shaped **duodenum (d)**. The main portion of the pancreas is the **body (A_2)**, also denoted with an arrow. The **tail of the pancreas (A_3)** touches the spleen in the left hypochondriac region of the abdominal cavity.

Many other organs lie close to the kidney. The **esophagus (a)** is seen piercing the **diaphragm (b)** and uniting with the **stomach (c)**. The outline of the stomach is shown, and we recommend you outline this organ or color it in very lightly.

The stomach is continuous with the **duodenum (d)**, and this organ has been opened to show its inner surface. A light color is recommended. The duodenum continues as the second part of the small intestine, the **jejunum (e)**. Occupying the right hypochondriac and epigastric regions is the very large **liver (f)**. We show the liver pulled back with a forceps to reveal the organs beneath including the **gallbladder (h)**. **Hepatic ducts (g)** drain digestive materials from the liver and unite to form the **common bile duct (i)**. In the left hypochondriac region, we observe the **spleen (j)**. Inferior to the spleen in the left lumbar region is the **left kidney (k)**. The **right kidney (l)** is observed behind the duodenum. Tubes leading from the kidneys are the **left ureter (m)** and **right ureter (n)**. Among the major blood vessels are the **superior mesentery artery (o)** and the **superior mesentery vein (p)**. Bold colors are recommended here.

> Our focus is now on the pancreas and its macroscopic structures. As you encounter these structures in the reading, color their titles, then locate and color them in the plate.

The exocrine products of the pancreas are released into ducts for transport to the duodenum. Centrally located within the pancreas is the main **pancreatic duct (B)**, called the duct of Wirsung. It carries enzymes, ions, and other digestive materials toward the descending portion of the duodenum. Before entering the duodenum, however, it unites with the **common bile duct (i)** leading from the gallbladder and liver. The union of these two ducts forms a reservoir called the **ampulla of Vater (C)**, which empties into the lumen of the duodenum. A spot of dark color is recommended to indicate its location. The reservoir is also called the hepatopancreatic ampulla.

Digestive juices are also brought to the duodenum through the **accessory pancreatic duct (D)**. This duct arises from the main accessory duct and enters the duodenum at a point about two centimeters above the ampulla of Vater.

> We close with a brief examination of the organization of the exocrine cells of the pancreas. Much of this may be related to the discussion of the pancreas as an endocrine gland. As you focus on the microscopic anatomy of the pancreas, read about it, and color the titles as you encounter the structures. Light colors are recommended to avoid obscuring the details of the cells.

Within the tissue of the pancreas, the exocrine cells cluster around tiny ducts passing through the pancreas from head to tail. Each group of exocrine cells is called an **acinus (E)**. An acinus is bracketed in the plate, and the bracket may be colored to indicate its presence. The acinus is composed of **exocrine cells (F)**. A light color should be used for the cells. Note that the cells are clustered around a duct into which they empty their contents. This arrangement is a compound acinar arrangement, which indicates that the ducts have branches. As shown in the plate, the ducts unite with one another to form larger ducts eventually leading to the **main pancreatic duct (B)**.

Embedded within the acini of the pancreas, there are many clusters of endocrine cells called the **islets of Langerhans (G)**. In the plate, we use an arrow to point to one such islet. A bold color may be used for the arrow. Note that the **exocrine cells (H)** are clustered about a **blood vessel (I)**. The hormone secretions of the endocrine cells are released into the bloodstream for transport out of the pancreas and distribution to the body. This endocrine function of the pancreas is explored in more detail in a plate within the endocrine system chapter.

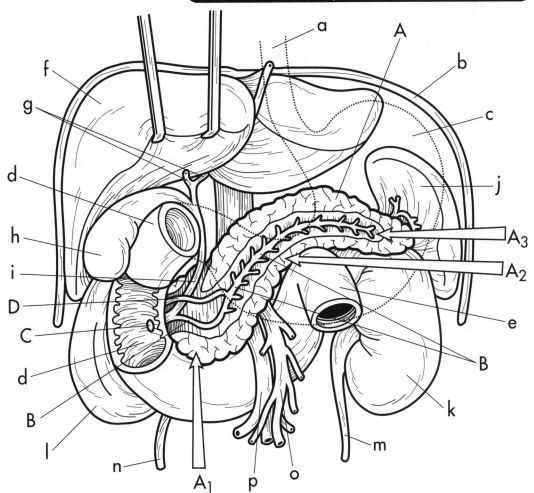

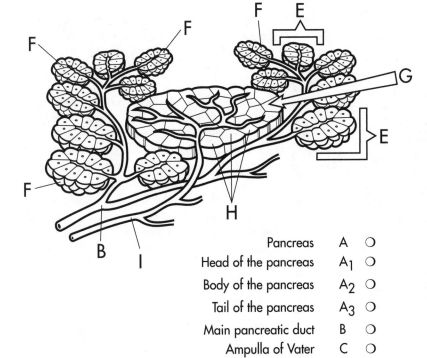

Islets of Langerhans	G	○
Exocrine cells	H	○
Blood vessel	I	○
Esophagus	a	○
Diaphragm	b	○
Stomach	c	○
Duodenum	d	○
Jejunum	e	○
Liver	f	○
Hepatic ducts	g	○
Gallbladder	h	○
Common bile duct	i	○
Spleen	j	○
Left kidney	k	○
Right kidney	l	○
Left ureter	m	○
Right ureter	n	○
Superior mesentery artery	o	○
Superior mesentery vein	p	○

Pancreas	A	○
Head of the pancreas	A_1	○
Body of the pancreas	A_2	○
Tail of the pancreas	A_3	○
Main pancreatic duct	B	○
Ampulla of Vater	C	○
Accessory pancreatic duct	D	○
Acinus	E	○
Exocrine cells	F	○

the LIVER and GALLBLADDER

In an average adult, the liver weighs about three pounds, making it the heaviest gland of the body. Many of the functions performed by liver cells are related to metabolism. For instance, the liver cells maintain the level of glucose in the blood, store certain fats, convert amino acids to energy-yielding compounds, synthesize bile salts, store certain vitamins, and produce bile.

In this plate we study the external anatomy of the liver, noting its position in the abdominal cavity and examining its blood supply. We also focus on the gallbladder, where bile secreted by the liver is stored.

> We view the liver from anterior and posterior views and discuss its blood supply. Most of the structures are of substantial size, and medium colors can be used for the larger structures and bolder colors for the smaller ones. Note that we label many structures with lowercase letters. These structures are not part of the liver itself.

Seen in place in the body, one of the body's largest organs is the **liver (A)**. As the first diagram shows, the liver lies immediately inferior to the **diaphragm (a)** and occupies the right hypochondriac region primarily and part of the epigastric region. It is protected by the ribcage and partly covers the **stomach (b)**.

The liver is encased in dense irregular connective tissue lying deep to the peritoneum. In the anterior view, we see the **left lobe (A$_1$)** and the **right lobe (A$_2$)**. Light colors are recommended for these lobes. In the posterior view, both lobes are seen again. We also view the **caudate lobe (A$_3$)** and the **quadrate lobe (A$_4$)**. There is question as to whether the caudate and quadrate are true lobes of the liver or regions of the left lobe. The **inferior vena cava (c)** marks the division between the right and left lobes.

Three important ligaments are associated with the liver. At its anterior surface, the liver has a ventral mesentery called the **falciform ligament (B)**. This ligament separates the right and left lobes at the anterior surface and is a continuation of the parietal peritoneum. It extends from the inferior surface of the diaphragm. The second important ligament is the **round ligament (C)**, also known as the ligamentum teres. This ligament is a fibrous band extending to the umbilicus region. The third important ligament is the **coronary ligament (D)**, extending from the inferior surface of the diaphragm.

The muscular sac lying at the posterior surface of the liver is the **gallbladder (E)**. The tube leading from the gallbladder meets other important vessels at a region known as the **porta hepatis (F)**.

In this area, we observe the **common bile duct (G)**, as well as the **hepatic portal vein (d)**, and the **hepatic artery (e)**. As previously noted, we see the substantial size of the **inferior vena cava (c)** in the posterior view.

> We now turn to the blood supply of the liver and follow the circulation through this organ. Variations of red are recommended for the arteries, and variations of blue are recommended for the veins. A separate color may be used for the bile duct and portal system.

Focusing your direction on the diagram of the hepatic blood supply, note that the liver receives blood from the **hepatic portal vein (d)**. This vein carries nutrients to the liver for processing before release to the bloodstream. Blood also reaches the liver from the aorta by means of the **hepatic artery (e)**. Within the liver, the hepatic portal vein and hepatic portal artery anastomose and form an extensive **capillary network (f)** that extends to all lobules of the liver. The blood then leaves the liver through the **hepatic vein (g)**, flows into the **inferior vena cava (c)**, and returns to the heart for distribution. In this diagram, we also see the **gallbladder (E)** at the posterior surface. It is drained by the **cystic duct (H)**, which directs bile to the **common bile duct (G)**.

> We complete the plate by examining the gallbladder and the structures leading from it. Your focus should be on the final portion of this plate and as you read about the gallbladder and its structures, color their titles, then locate and color the structures in the plate. Bold colors may be used.

Each day, the liver cells secrete approximately one quart of bile, a liquid made of water, bile salts, acids, and cholesterol. It has a basic pH. The bile is stored in the **gallbladder (E)**, a pear-shaped sac found in a depression of the liver's posterior surface and composed of smooth muscle.

Contractions of the smooth muscle propel bile into the **cystic duct (H)**, which also drains the liver. The cystic duct unites with the **hepatic duct (I)** leading from the liver to form the **common bile duct (G)**. This duct delivers bile to the **duodenum (j)**, the first part of the small intestine. A **sphincter (J)** controls the flow through the common bile duct. At this point, the duodenum also receives secretions from the **pancreas (h)**. The main duct leading from the pancreas is the **pancreatic duct (i)**. It joins with the common bile duct at the ampulla of Vater. The ampulla opens into the lumen of the duodenum, and bile and pancreatic juice enter. The duodenum then becomes the **jejunum (k)**, and the small intestine continues.

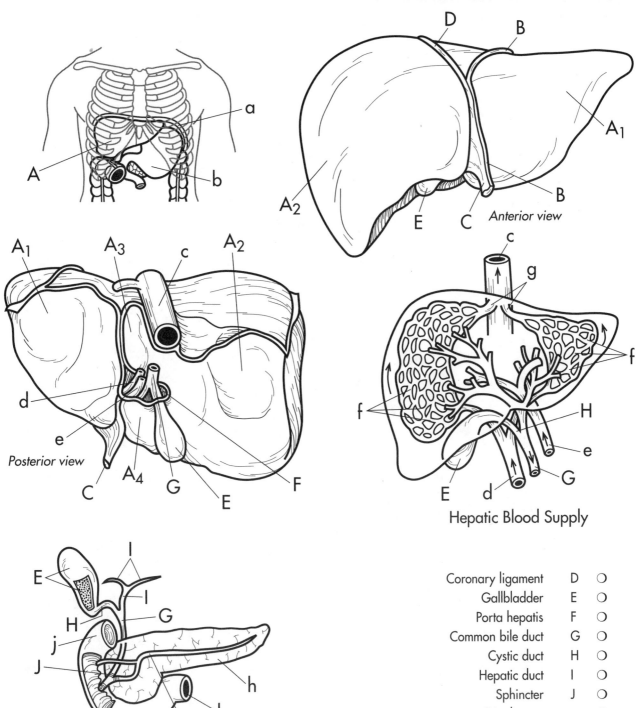

Anterior view

Posterior view

Hepatic Blood Supply

The Gallbladder

Liver	A	○
Left lobe	A₁	○
Right lobe	A₂	○
Caudate lobe	A₃	○
Quadrate lobe	A₄	○
Falciform ligament	B	○
Round ligament	C	○

Coronary ligament	D	○
Gallbladder	E	○
Porta hepatis	F	○
Common bile duct	G	○
Cystic duct	H	○
Hepatic duct	I	○
Sphincter	J	○
Diaphragm	a	○
Stomach	b	○
Inferior vena cava	c	○
Hepatic portal vein	d	○
Hepatic artery	e	○
Capillary network	f	○
Hepatic vein	g	○
Pancreas	h	○
Pancreatic duct	i	○
Duodenum	j	○
Jejunum	k	○

CHAPTER TEN:

the RESPIRATORY SYSTEM

OVERVIEW of the RESPIRATORY SYSTEM

The respiratory system consists of passageways that filter incoming air and carry it into the lungs. Here in the microscopic air sacs, exchanges take place between the external atmospheric air and the internal body environment.

In this and several plates to follow, we review the respiratory system in gross anatomy and detail. This plate presents an overview of the system. Many of the structures seen in this system have been encountered in previous plates, and we review them here and place them in perspective.

> Begin the plate by coloring the main title Overview of the Respiratory System. The plate consists of a single anterior view of the head and thoracic cavity. Certain structures are designated with lowercase letters because they belong to other systems. The uppercase letters are reserved for portions of the respiratory system. As you read about the structures, color their titles and locate and color the structures. Use light and dark colors as we move along.

On entering the body, air passes through the first organ of the upper system, the **nasal passage (A)**. A light color should be used for this passageway. Within the nasal passage, outcroppings of bone from the lateral wall divide the main passageway into smaller passageways. These outcroppings are called **nasal conchae (A_1)**. The arrows pointing to the nasal conchae should be colored in a dark color such as a red, green, or blue.

The upper respiratory system also contains a number of air-filled spaces between the maxillary, frontal, ethmoid, and sphenoid bones of the skull. These spaces are called sinuses. The diagram shows the **frontal sinus (B_1)** and the **sphenoid sinus (B_2)**. Air is "conditioned" in these spaces.

In this section of the head, we also see features of the digestive system. The **tongue (a)** is a large muscular organ filling most of the space of the oral cavity. The oral cavity leads to a major passageway called the **pharynx (C)**, which serves both the respiratory and digestive systems. The **esophagus (b)** leads from the pharynx to the stomach.

> As we enter the neck area we encounter the passageways leading to the lungs. We shall examine these in more detail in upcoming plates. Pale colors should be used for these structures.

Below the pharynx, we encounter the first portion of the passageway leading to the lungs, the **larynx (D)**. The bracket outlining this structure should be colored, and a pale color may be used for the structure itself. The flaplike epiglottis guards the entry to the larynx, and several cartilages make up the walls of the larynx.

Leading from the larynx is the windpipe, more correctly known as the **trachea (E)**. The trachea is continuous with the larynx. The rings that you note in the plate contain cartilage, and you may use a dark color to highlight them.

The trachea extends in front of the esophagus into the thoracic cavity, then splits to form two passageways called bronchi. On the visual right (the anatomical left) is the **left bronchus (F_1)**, and at your visual left (the anatomical right) is the **right bronchus (F_2)**. The same color used for the trachea should be used here to designate the continuity of the tube. The arrow may be colored in a bold color.

Each bronchus continues as the bronchial tree. The left bronchial tree and the right bronchial tree are designated with arrows that may be colored boldly, but the tubes themselves should be colored with a light color continuous with that used for the bronchi. The **left bronchiole tree (G_1)** and the **right bronchiole tree (G_2)** are seen in the plate.

> The main organ of gas exchange in the body is the lung. This paired organ should be outlined with a very light color in the plate. We also show some of the bones surrounding the lungs. It would be best to outline them in bold color without coloring them in to avoid obscuring the lungs. As you read about these structures below, color their titles, then finish coloring the plate.

The right and left bronchial trees lead to the smaller alveolar ducts, then to the air sacs of the lungs. The **left lung (H_1)** and the **right lung (H_2)** occupy most of the space of the thoracic cavity. The lungs are soft, spongy organs in the shape of a cone. They are separated by the heart and mediastinum, and their gross anatomy is reviewed in an upcoming plate.

The expansion of the lungs depends heavily on the activity of intercostal muscles and the large, dome-shaped **diaphragm (I)**. When this muscle contracts, air enters the lungs. Enclosing the lungs are the bones of the thoracic cage. These include the **ribs (c)**, the **sternum (d)**, and the **clavicles (e)**. We suggest you simply outline the margins of these bones to show their proximity to the lungs.

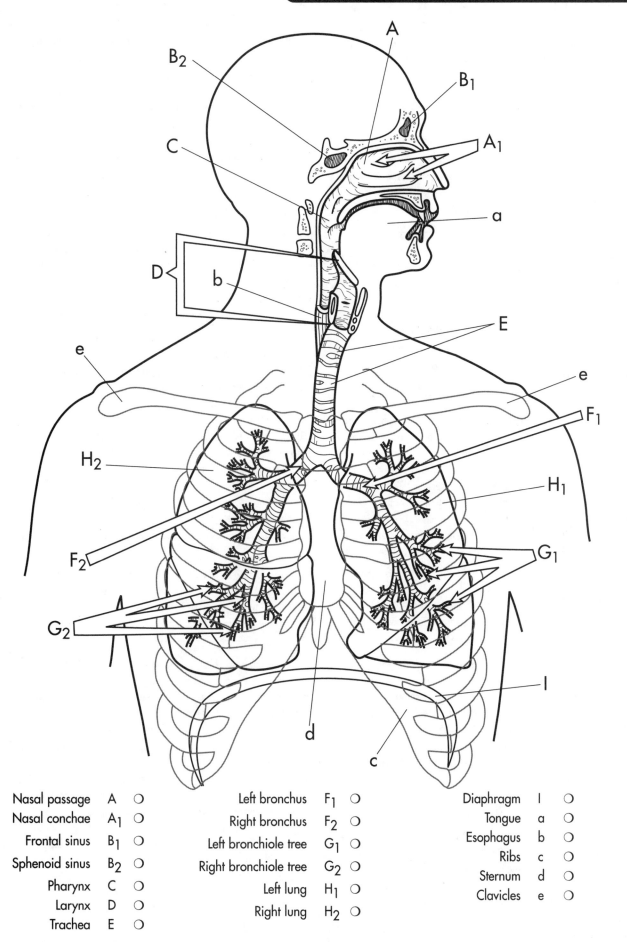

Nasal passage	A	○	Left bronchus	F₁	○	Diaphragm	I	○
Nasal conchae	A₁	○	Right bronchus	F₂	○	Tongue	a	○
Frontal sinus	B₁	○	Left bronchiole tree	G₁	○	Esophagus	b	○
Sphenoid sinus	B₂	○	Right bronchiole tree	G₂	○	Ribs	c	○
Pharynx	C	○	Left lung	H₁	○	Sternum	d	○
Larynx	D	○	Right lung	H₂	○	Clavicles	e	○
Trachea	E	○						

the UPPER RESPIRATORY TRACT

The respiratory organs outside the thorax constitute the upper respiratory tract, the focus of this plate. We examine some of the fine details of the nasal cavity and surrounding passageways, then briefly touch on the respiratory organs of the neck.

> Begin by coloring the main title The Upper Respiratory Tract. Note that we present two diagrams: a sagittal section of the head and neck and a frontal section. The frontal section is shown primarily to indicate the location of the paranasal sinuses. There are many arrows in this plate, and they should be colored in bold colors. Pale colors should be used for other structures. Accessory structures and organs in the area are designated by lowercase letters.

Although air may enter the respiratory tract through the oral cavity, the preferred entrance is the nose. The main passageway of the nose is the **nasal cavity (A)**, and a pale color should be used for this entire region. The nasal cavity is divided into two bilateral halves by the **nasal septum (B)** seen in the frontal section. The septum is formed by the perpendicular plate of the ethmoid bone and the vomer bone.

Air enters the nasal cavity by first passing through the **external nares (A_1)**, also known as the nostrils. The area surrounded by the nostrils is called the **vestibule (A_2)**. Hairs in this region trap large airborne particles. At the superior region of the nasal cavity is the **olfactory region (A_3)**, the location of the olfactory sense organs used in the sense of smell. At the end of the nasal cavity is the **internal nares (A_4)**. Beyond this point, the nasal cavity becomes the pharynx.

> We now study the sinuses and bony projections of the nasal cavity, where air is conditioned and purified before passage into the lower respiratory tract. Reference to both the frontal and sagittal sections should be made, and the arrows should be colored in boldly. Other areas should be colored in lightly, since they are small or are superimposed on other regions.

Air is warmed, moistened, and cleansed within various paranasal sinuses, the blind sacs opening into the nasal cavity. The **maxillary sinus (C_1)** is shown in the frontal section. The **frontal sinus (C_2)** is seen in the sagittal section, and the **ethmoid sinus (C_3)** is shown in the frontal section. The fourth sinus, the sphenoid sinus, is located in the sphenoid bone and is shown in the previous plate.

Extending into the nasal cavity are the turbinate bones, also known as the **nasal conchae (D)**. The three nasal conchae may be colored in boldly. They are the **superior nasal concha (D_1)**, the **middle nasal concha (D_2)**, and the **inferior nasal concha (D_3)**. These bones bear longitudinal ridges covered with vascular mucosa. The blood in the mucous membranes heats the air and the moisture increases its humidity. The folds between the ridges of the conchae are called the **superior nasal meatus (E_1)**, the **middle nasal meatus (E_2)**, and the **inferior nasal meatus (E_3)**.

As the diagram shows, the inferior border of the nasal cavity is formed by the **hard palate (a)** and the **soft palate (b)**. Beneath the structures are the **oral cavity (c)**, the **tongue (d)**, and its attachments.

> We now turn to the structures associated with the pharynx. The pharynx should be colored in a single pale color, and the arrows pointing to the various regions should be colored boldly. Note that the pharynx is continuous with the nasal cavity, and a variation of the color used for the nasal cavity should be used here.

As previously noted, the internal nares mark the beginning of the pharynx. The first portion of the pharynx is the **nasopharynx (F)**. This is the superior portion of the pharynx continuous with the nasal cavity and is the site of the **lingual tonsil (f)**. In this region is the opening to the **Eustachian tube (e)**.

The next important portion of the pharynx is the **oropharynx (G)**. This area is found between the soft palate and the base of the tongue. In this passageway are located the **palatine tonsil (g)** and the **pharyngeal tonsil (h)**. The fauces is the area where the oral cavity opens to the oropharynx.

The third portion of the pharynx is the **laryngopharynx (H)**. This is a small area near the opening to the esophagus and trachea.

> To complete this plate, we focus on structures of the upper respiratory tract that are located in the neck. Most are associated with the respiratory passageway or trachea. A single light color may be used for this tube, and bold colors may be used for the arrows pointing to its regions.

After passing through the three regions of the pharynx, the warmed, moistened, and cleansed air is ready to enter the respiratory passageways. The main passageway is the **trachea (N)**, an open tube extending to the lungs.

The first part of the trachea is the larynx. The opening to the larynx is guarded by a flap of cartilage called the **epiglottis (I)**. This structure prevents food from entering the respiratory passageway and directs it to the **esophagus (i)**. Beneath the epiglottis is the opening to the larynx called the **glottis (J)**. The **vocal cords (K)** are an important component of the larynx used in speaking.

The larynx itself is composed of several cartilages, including the **thyroid cartilage (L)** and the **cricoid cartilage (M)**. These cartilages are studied in upcoming plates, and a spot of color may be used here to denote their presence. The **thyroid gland (j)** is also seen in the neck tissue.

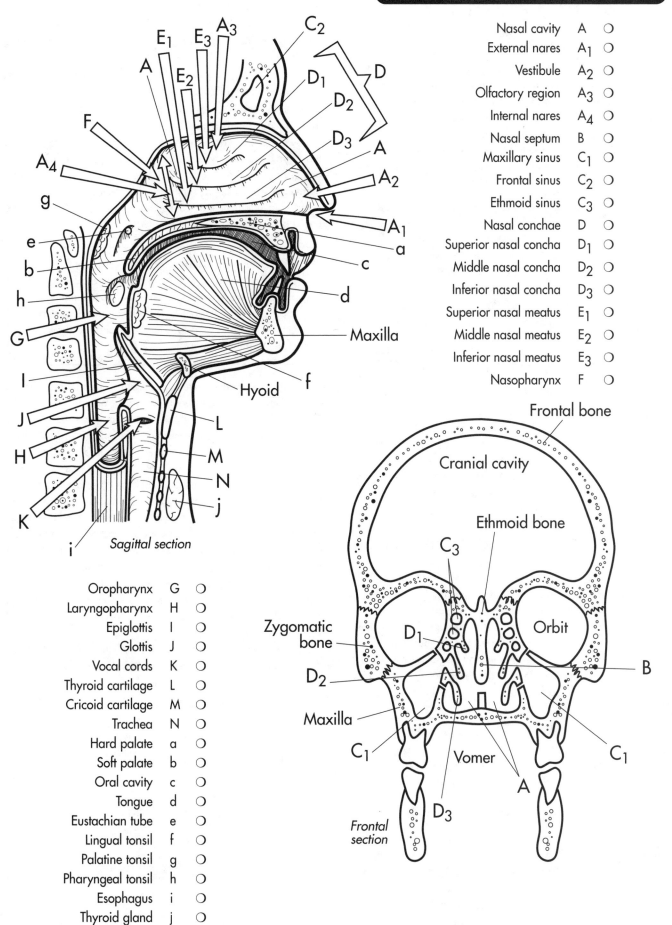

Sagittal section

Frontal section

Nasal cavity	A	○
External nares	A_1	○
Vestibule	A_2	○
Olfactory region	A_3	○
Internal nares	A_4	○
Nasal septum	B	○
Maxillary sinus	C_1	○
Frontal sinus	C_2	○
Ethmoid sinus	C_3	○
Nasal conchae	D	○
Superior nasal concha	D_1	○
Middle nasal concha	D_2	○
Inferior nasal concha	D_3	○
Superior nasal meatus	E_1	○
Middle nasal meatus	E_2	○
Inferior nasal meatus	E_3	○
Nasopharynx	F	○

Oropharynx	G	○
Laryngopharynx	H	○
Epiglottis	I	○
Glottis	J	○
Vocal cords	K	○
Thyroid cartilage	L	○
Cricoid cartilage	M	○
Trachea	N	○
Hard palate	a	○
Soft palate	b	○
Oral cavity	c	○
Tongue	d	○
Eustachian tube	e	○
Lingual tonsil	f	○
Palatine tonsil	g	○
Pharyngeal tonsil	h	○
Esophagus	i	○
Thyroid gland	j	○

Frontal bone

Cranial cavity

Ethmoid bone

Zygomatic bone

Orbit

Maxilla

Vomer

the LARYNX

The larynx is an enlargement in the upper respiratory tract at the top of the trachea and below the pharynx. It is a passageway for air moving in and out of the trachea, and it houses the vocal cords. For this reason, it is often called the voice box.

The larynx is made up of muscles discussed in previous plates and cartilages discussed here. The larynx lies in the midline of the neck anterior to the fourth through sixth cervical vertebrae.

> We present three views of the larynx: an anterior view, a posterior view, and a sagittal view from the left side. As you encounter the structures in the reading below, you should locate them in all three views. We use subscript numbers to indicate right and left side and assist your locating the structures. We also view a small portion of the upper trachea.

The wall of the larynx is composed of nine pieces of cartilage of which three are single cartilages and three are paired. The first single cartilage is the **thyroid cartilage (A)**. In the anterior view, it appears as a shield and is prominent in both the posterior and sagittal views. A bold color may be used here. As the largest cartilage, it forms most of the anterior and lateral walls, and it is sometimes called the Adam's apple. A prominent marking of the thyroid is the **laryngeal prominence (A_1)** where two pieces of cartilage fuse in the fetal stage. The superior horn of the **thyroid cartilage (A_2)** is seen in the sagittal section and is the point of connection with the **hyoid bone (a)**. Ligaments can be seen connecting the cartilage to the hyoid bone in the anterior view.

The second cartilage of the larynx is the **cricoid cartilage (B)**. This ring of cartilage sits below the thyroid cartilage and connects it with the trachea below. It is the lowest portion of the larynx, as indicated by the bracket. The third cartilage is the leaflike **epiglottis (C)**. This flap of tissue projects above the glottis. When one swallows, the larynx elevates and the epiglottis folds over the glottis to prevent entry of food to the respiratory tract. A bold color may be used to color it.

> We now move to the six remaining cartilages of the larynx. As you encounter them in the reading below, color their titles then locate and color them in the appropriate diagram. As before, bold colors may be used, since these cartilages are rather large in size.

The paired cartilages of the larynx are smaller than the unpaired cartilages. The first of the paired cartilages is the pyramid-shaped **arytenoid cartilages (D_1 and D_2)**. They are seen in the posterior view. The triangular pieces of cartilage attach to the vocal folds and support the pharyngeal muscles.

The **corniculate cartilages (E_1 and E_2)** are conelike structures serving as attachments for muscles that regulate the tension on the vocal cords. One of the pair (E_2) is shown in the sagittal section. The cartilage is also present in the final diagram concerning the vocal cords.

The final cartilage pair is the **cuneiform cartilages (F_1 and F_2)**. These small cartilages are found in the mucous membranes between the epiglottis and arytenoid cartilages. They help stiffen the soft tissue in this region.

Two types of ligaments bind the nine cartilages together in the larynx. The first type are the **intrinsic ligaments (G)**, which connect the cricoid, thyroid, and other cartilages. The **extrinsic ligaments (H)** are more superficial ligaments. They include the thyrohyoid ligament that connects the thyroid cartilage to the **hyoid bone (a)**.

> We conclude the plate with an examination of the vocal cords. For this study, you should concentrate on the last portion of the plate and note that we are examining the vocal cords from above. The anterior and posterior regions are indicated to orient you, and we show the location of the tongue.

Within the larynx, there are two pairs of horizontal folds of the mucous membrane extending inward from the lateral walls. The superior pair are called the **ventricular folds (I)**. These are known as the false vocal cords. The inferior pair are called the **vocal folds (J)**. These are also known as the true vocal cords.

The vestibular folds (false vocal cords) help close the larynx during swallowing. The inferior vocal folds (true vocal cords) contain elastic fibers that help produce sound when air is forced between the vocal cords. The sound waves are formed into words by changing the shapes of the pharynx and oral cavity and by using the tongue and lips. The space between the ventricular folds is called the **rima vestibuli (I_1)**. Note in the diagram how the ventricular folds are shown in both open and closed positions. The intrinsic muscles of the larynx attach to the cartilages and vocal folds and contract to vary the position of the vocal folds and vibrate to set up sound waves.

Note how the larynx is continuous with the trachea. The **rings of cartilage (K)** encircling the trachea are shown. They are examined in more detail in the next plate.

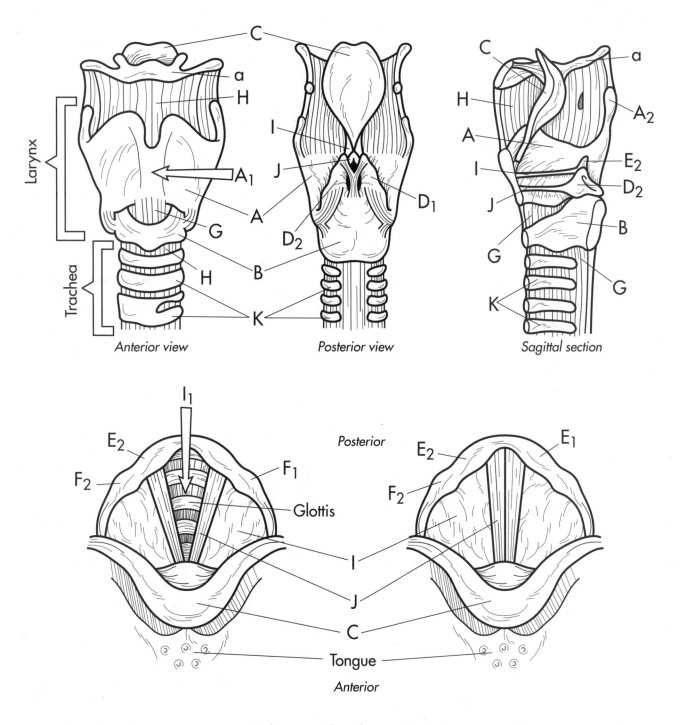

Larynx

Trachea

C
a
H
A₁
A
G
B
H
K

Anterior view

C
I
J
D₂
D₁

Posterior view

C
H
A
I
J
G
a
A₂
E₂
D₂
B
G
K

Sagittal section

I₁
E₂
F₂
F₁
Glottis

Posterior

E₂
F₂
E₁

I
J
C

Tongue

Anterior

Thyroid cartilage	A ○	Right arytenoid cartilage	D₂ ○	Extrinsic ligaments	H ○
Laryngeal prominence	A₁ ○	Left corniculate cartilage	E₁ ○	Ventricular folds	I ○
Thyroid cartilage	A₂ ○	Right corniculate cartilage	E₂ ○	Rima vestibuli	I₁ ○
Cricoid cartilage	B ○	Left cuneiform cartilage	F₁ ○	Vocal folds	J ○
Epiglottis	C ○	Right cuneiform cartilage	F₂ ○	Rings of cartilage	K ○
Left arytenoid cartilage	D₁ ○	Intrinsic ligaments	G ○	Hyoid bone	a ○

the TRACHEA and BRONCHIAL TREE

The trachea is a flexible cylindrical tube about one inch in diameter and approximately four inches in length. It extends downward in front of the esophagus and into the thoracic cavity, where it splits to right and left bronchi and respective bronchial trees. Often called the windpipe, it is the passageway for air to the lungs.

> Begin the plate by coloring the main title The Trachea and Bronchial Tree. As you look over the diagram, note that we are presenting the passageway from the pharynx to the lobules of the lung showing the details of the tubes involved. We also present a cross section of the trachea so you may see the tissue layers of this organ. Bold colors such as purples, oranges, greens, and reds may be used for this plate because the structures are large and separated from each other. We begin with a brief review of the larynx.

At its superior border, the trachea is continuous with the **larynx (A)**. Also known as the voicebox, the larynx was considered in detail in the previous plate. Some notable features are the large, shieldlike **thyroid cartilage (A_1)**, which is more prominent in males than in females. Connected to the thyroid cartilage is the smaller **cricoid cartilage (A_2)**, which connects to the trachea. The **cricothyroid ligament (A_3)** connects these two large cartilages to one another, and the **thyrohyoid ligament (A_4)** connects the thyroid cartilage to the **hyoid bone (A_5)**.

Inferior to the larynx is the **trachea (B)**. Viewed from the anterior aspect, the trachea contains 16 to 20 incomplete rings of **hyaline** or **tracheal cartilage (B_1)**. These cartilages may be colored in dark colors. The cartilages have the shape of a C, where the open portion faces the esophagus. The cartilage rings provide a semirigid support to the wall of the trachea, preventing it from collapsing inward.

The tracheal cartilages are connected to one another by elastic **annular ligaments (B_2)**. A lighter color is recommended for these ligaments. The annular ligament may also be seen in the cross section of the tracheal wall. Note that it also surrounds the cartilage.

> Before moving on to the bronchial tree, we shall examine a cross section of the trachea. Here we see some of the structures mentioned previously as well as other structures important to the integrity of this organ. Dark colors may be used for most structures, since they are fairly clear.

In cross section, one can see the **tracheal cartilage (B_1)** and the **annular ligament (B2)** mentioned previously. The inner layer of the trachea is the **mucosa (J)**. A dark color may be used to indicate the bracket. Within the mucosa, the innermost layer is the **ciliated epithelium (K)**. Cilia along the borders of the cells trap particles in the air. The surface is moistened by mucus secreted by **mucous cells (N)**. The mucus traps airborne particles, which are then carried back to the pharynx.

The second layer of the mucosa is the **lamina propria (L)**. The lamina propria contains elastic and reticular fibers and provides support to the other tissues. Finally, the trachea contains a band of **smooth muscle (M)**. This smooth muscle connects the ends of the tracheal cartilages and provides a flexible surface against which the esophagus can expand.

> We now return to the main passageway and study the divisions of the trachea into smaller tubes entering the lung tissue. Bold colors are recommended as before, and you should note the changing nature of the tissues involved in the passageways. As you encounter the structures, color the titles before locating and coloring them in the diagram.

The bronchial tree consists of the branched airways extending from the trachea to the air sacs of the lungs. It begins with the **left** and **right primary bronchi (C_1 and C_2)**. The openings to these tubes are separated by a ridge of cartilage called the **carina (D)**. Beyond the carina, each bronchus, accompanied by large blood vessels, enters a lung.

Note that the structural organization of the primary bronchus is similar to that of the trachea. There are C-shaped rings of cartilage that support the tissue. Also note that the **right primary bronchus (C_2)** has a slightly larger diameter than the left, and it descends at a steeper angle into the lung.

A short distance from its origin, each primary bronchus subdivides and forms **left and right secondary bronchi (E_1 and E_2)**. The secondary bronchi proceed to the five lobes of the lung. There are two secondary bronchi on the left side of the bronchial tree and three secondary bronchi on the right side. At this point, the cartilage rings become plates of **cartilage (F)**. The same color as that used for the rings may be used. As the secondary bronchi branch into **tertiary bronchi (G)**, the number and size of cartilage plates decreases. The structure of the bronchial tree at this point is composed largely of **smooth muscle (M)** and attending tissue.

Further along, the tertiary bronchi become **bronchioles (H)**. These small branches enter the basic units of the lung, called **lobules (I)**. The lobule contains the terminal bronchioles as well as the alveolar air sacs and capillaries. They are discussed in greater detail in upcoming plates and you are referred there for the details.

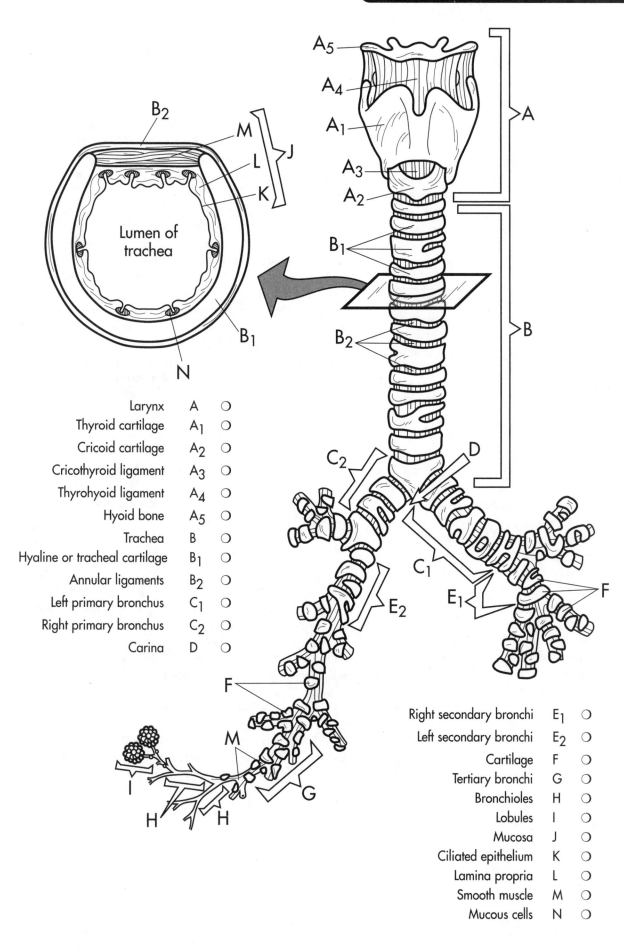

B₂

M
L   J
K

Lumen of
trachea

B₁

N

A₅

A₄

A₁

A₃

A₂

A

B₁

B₂

B

C₂   D

C₁

E₁   F

E₂

F

M

I   G

H   H

Larynx   A   ○
Thyroid cartilage   A₁   ○
Cricoid cartilage   A₂   ○
Cricothyroid ligament   A₃   ○
Thyrohyoid ligament   A₄   ○
Hyoid bone   A₅   ○
Trachea   B   ○
Hyaline or tracheal cartilage   B₁   ○
Annular ligaments   B₂   ○
Left primary bronchus   C₁   ○
Right primary bronchus   C₂   ○
Carina   D   ○

Right secondary bronchi   E₁   ○
Left secondary bronchi   E₂   ○
Cartilage   F   ○
Tertiary bronchi   G   ○
Bronchioles   H   ○
Lobules   I   ○
Mucosa   J   ○
Ciliated epithelium   K   ○
Lamina propria   L   ○
Smooth muscle   M   ○
Mucous cells   N   ○

the LUNGS

In the lower respiratory tract, the trachea, bronchi, and bronchial tree lead to the main organs of gas exchange, the lungs. Separated medially by the heart and mediastinum, the lungs are enclosed by the thoracic cage and diaphragm. A layer of serous membrane, the visceral pleura is firmly attached to each lung. This membrane folds back to become the parietal pleura, which forms part of the mediastinum and lines the inner wall of the cavity. The space between the visceral and parietal pleura contains serous fluid and is called the pleural cavity.

The focus of this plate is the gross anatomy of the lungs. Five main colors are needed for the five lobes, and a number of bold colors may be used for the arrows pointing to regions of these lobes.

> Begin by coloring the main title of this plate The Lungs. Then examine the plate and note that we are describing the anatomy of the five lobes. To avoid obscuring the texture and regions, select tans, pastels, and pale colors for the five main lobes and reserve your bold colors for the arrows. We display the anterior view of the lungs, then present lateral and medial views of both right and left lungs.

The cone-shaped lungs extend from a region slightly superior to the clavicles down to the level of the diaphragm. The right lung consists of three lobes, known as the **right superior lobe (A)**, the **right middle lobe (B)**, and the **right inferior lobe (C)**. Light colors should be used for these lobes.

On the left side, there are only two lobes. They are the **left superior lobe (D)** and the **left inferior lobe (E)**. The superior and middle lobes of the right lung are separated by the **horizontal fissure (F_h)**. Separating the right middle and inferior lobes is the **oblique fissure (F_o)**. On the left side, there is no horizontal fissure.

Air reaches the right and left lung through a series of passageways briefly shown here. They include the **trachea (a)**, which splits to form the **primary bronchus (b)** on the right and left side. As they enter the lungs, the bronchi divide to form smaller passageways called **secondary bronchi (c)**. The right lung has three secondary bronchi corresponding to its three lobes, while the left lung has two secondary bronchi. The secondary bronchi branch to form the **tertiary bronchi (d)**. Ten tertiary bronchi are found in each lung.

> We now turn to the lung's anatomical features. Several arrows point to the individual regions or points of interest. The arrows should be colored with bold colors. The same five colors used in the first diagram should be carried forward in the individual diagrams of the lungs from lateral and medial aspects.

Examining the lungs in the anterior view, we note that each lung has a narrow portion at the superior aspect termed the **cupula** or **apex (G_1 and G_2)**. These regions are seen in both medial and lateral views. At its most inferior aspect, each lung has a **base (H_1 and H_2)**.

The surface of the lung lying along the rib is the **costal surface** designated I_1 and I_2 for left and right. The rounding of this surface matches the curvature of the ribcage. An irregular shape is seen in the **mediastinal surface (J_1 and J_2)**.

In the medial view of the right lung, an **esophageal groove (K)** marks the passage of the esophagus. In the medial view, the left lung displays the cardiac notch, a concave area conforming to the shape of the heart. The impression created by the heart is the **cardiac impression (L_1)**, also seen in the **right lung (L_2)**. At the base of the lung, a concave impression is formed by the diaphragm. It is known as the **diaphragmatic impression (M_1 and M_2)**.

> We shall complete the plate by examining structures at the hilus of the lung. This is the region where the passageways enter and leave the lung. The passageways are seen in cross section and a spot of color will best indicate their presence. As you read about the structures below, color their titles, then add a spot on the diagram.

On the mediastinal surface, each lung has a region called the **hilus (N_1 and N_2)**. These are indicated by arrows. At the hilus, the visceral pleura attached to the lung surface folds back to become the parietal pleura. At the hilus are the three main passageways to the lungs. Two **bronchi (O)** are shown, representing the two secondary bronchi in the left lung. A cross section of the **pulmonary artery (P)** represents the main tube carrying blood to the lungs. Blood emerges from the lungs through the **pulmonary veins (Q)**. Cross sections of two pulmonary veins are seen in both the right and left lung.

A final point of note is the **aortic groove (R)** seen in the medial view of the left lung. It represents the area where the aorta rests against the left lung as the aorta arches and becomes the thoracic aorta.

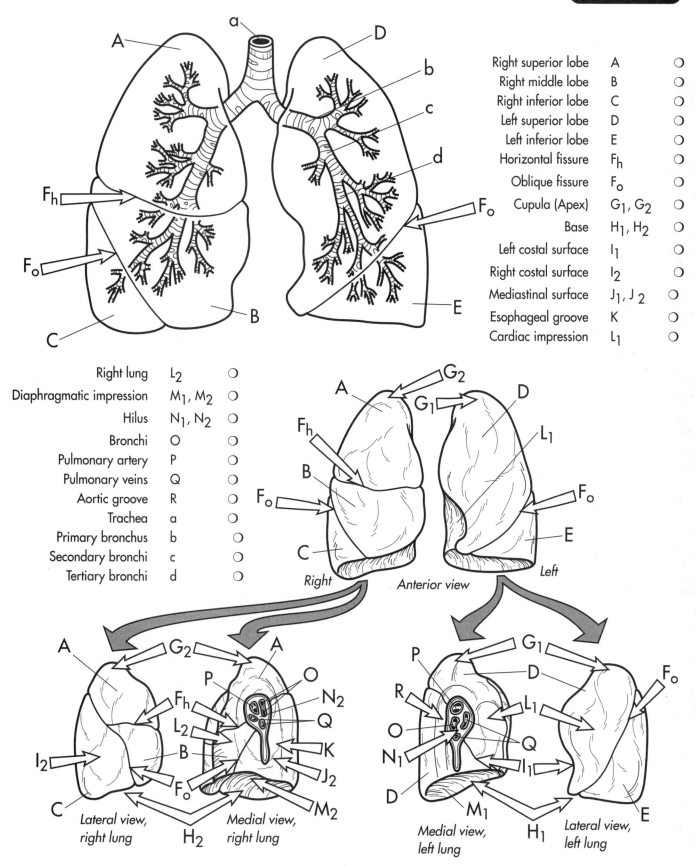

Right superior lobe	A	○
Right middle lobe	B	○
Right inferior lobe	C	○
Left superior lobe	D	○
Left inferior lobe	E	○
Horizontal fissure	F_h	○
Oblique fissure	F_o	○
Cupula (Apex)	G_1, G_2	○
Base	H_1, H_2	○
Left costal surface	I_1	○
Right costal surface	I_2	○
Mediastinal surface	J_1, J_2	○
Esophageal groove	K	○
Cardiac impression	L_1	○

Right lung	L_2	○
Diaphragmatic impression	M_1, M_2	○
Hilus	N_1, N_2	○
Bronchi	O	○
Pulmonary artery	P	○
Pulmonary veins	Q	○
Aortic groove	R	○
Trachea	a	○
Primary bronchus	b	○
Secondary bronchi	c	○
Tertiary bronchi	d	○

Right   *Anterior view*   *Left*

Lateral view, right lung

Medial view, right lung

Medial view, left lung

Lateral view, left lung

CHAPTER ELEVEN:

the URINARY SYSTEM

OVERVIEW of the URINARY SYSTEM

Excretion involves the elimination of the waste products of cellular metabolism. It also encompasses the removal of surplus materials from the body tissues, and it includes regulation of the water and salt content of the body. Regulatory functions such as these are accomplished by the kidneys and their accessory structures in the urinary system. In this plate, we present an overview of the urinary system in anterior, posterior, and inferior views. We indicate the major organs of this system and their location and structure and prepare for a detailed study in the plates ahead.

The plate shows the organs of the urinary system in three views. In anterior and posterior views, the organs are shown relative to each other and to other nearby structures. The major thrust of the third diagram is to indicate the position of the kidneys relative to the peritoneal cavity. You may begin by coloring the main title Overview of the Urinary System. Then, as you read the text below, locate the titles and the structures on the diagrams. The anterior and posterior views should be colored before proceeding to the inferior view.

The main organs of excretion in the body are the **kidneys (A_1 and A_2)**. The same pale color is recommended for both kidneys; the numbers are used to indicate left and right kidneys respectively.

The kidneys are bean-shaped organs roughly about the size of the fist. They are located on each side of the vertebral column and usually extend from the twelfth thoracic vertebra to the third lumbar vertebra. As the posterior view shows, the twelfth rib partially protects them. The upper portion of each kidney is in contact with a part of the diaphragm, and the **left kidney (A_1)** touches the spleen. The **right kidney (A_2)** is near the liver and is slightly lower.

We now turn to the blood supply of the kidney and discuss it briefly. The passageways for blood have been mentioned previously in the discussion of the circulatory system, and we review them here. As you encounter the structures in the reading below, color their titles, then color them in the anterior and posterior views.

Leading from the kidneys are the two tubes, the **ureters (B)**. These tubes carry urine away from the kidney. The ureters lead to the main storage organ, the **urinary bladder (C)**. This hollow muscular sac is located in the midline at the floor of the pelvic cavity. The bladder is discussed in more detail in an upcoming plate.

The tube leading from the bladder to the exterior is the **urethra (D)**. This tube of smooth muscle is about one and a half inches long in the female and about eight inches long in the male as it passes through the penis.

We now turn to the blood supply of the kidney and discuss it briefly. The passageways for blood have been mentioned previously in the discussion of the circulatory system, and we review them here. As you encounter the structures in the reading below, color their titles, then color them in the anterior and posterior views.

The main circulatory vessel transporting blood to the kidney is the **renal artery (E)**, clearly seen in the posterior view. The **renal vein (F)** lies behind the renal artery in the posterior view and, therefore, is difficult to see. A light color is recommended. The renal vein transports blood away from the kidney after it has been cleansed. The renal artery is supplied with blood by the **abdominal aorta (G)**, while the renal vein empties its blood into the **inferior vena cava (H)**. Lying on top of the kidneys are the **suprarenal glands (J)**, discussed with the endocrine system.

We close the plate with a transverse section through the body and a view from the inferior aspect. We are looking down from above at the level of the stomach, transverse colon, pancreas, and other organs of the abdominal cavity. These organs have been removed to reveal an empty peritoneal cavity. A gray color may be used for this cavity. Our objective is to view the organs of the urinary system in position and to indicate some of their coverings.

The view in the plate shows the organs of several systems. For example, we see an outline of the **lumbar vertebra (I)**, and the spinal cord is visible. Sections are also shown through the **kidneys (A_1 and A_2)**. Note the **renal artery (E)** arising on the right and left sides from the **abdominal aorta (G)**. Also note the **renal veins (F)** leading on both sides to the **inferior vena cava (H)**.

The kidney is surrounded by three layers of supportive tissue. Immediately adhering to the kidney surface is the **renal capsule (K)**. A dark color may be used to highlight this layer. The capsule is composed of fibrous tissue providing an impenetrable barrier to infection of the kidney surface. Outside the renal capsule is a middle covering layer of fat. It is called the **adipose capsule (L)**. A pale color is recommended. The fat tissue of the capsule helps cushion the kidney against blows. Outside the adipose capsule is the **renal fascia (M)**. A dark color is also recommended to outline this layer. The fascia is composed of dense fibrous connective tissue. It helps protect the kidney and adrenal glands while anchoring these organs to the nearby tissues.

Like many organs of the digestive system, the kidneys lie outside the peritoneal cavity. This position is called retroperitoneal. As the diagram shows, the peritoneal cavity is bordered by the **peritoneum (N)**. The continuous nature of this membrane can be seen, and you may note that the kidneys are not within the membrane.

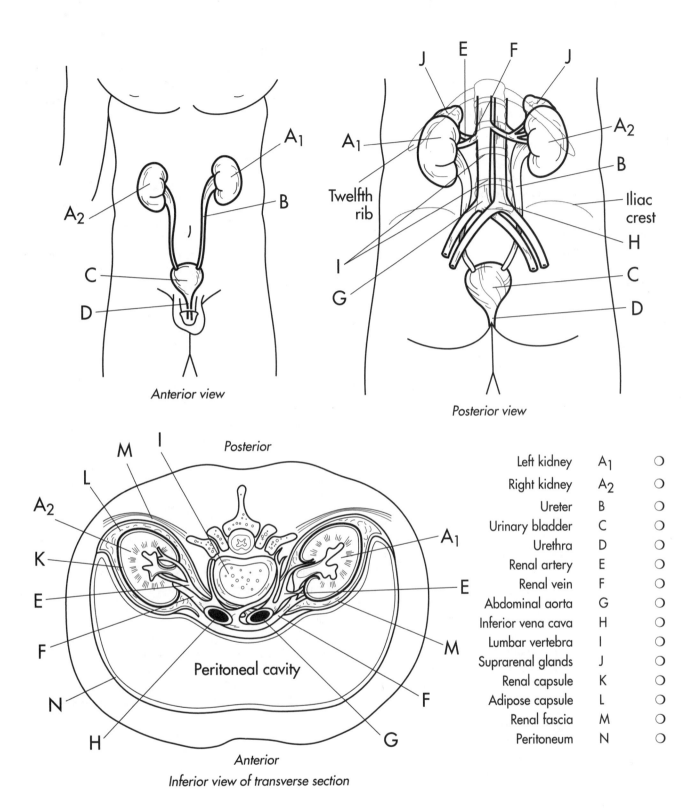

Anterior view

Posterior view

Twelfth rib

Iliac crest

Posterior

Peritoneal cavity

Anterior

Inferior view of transverse section

Left kidney	A₁	○
Right kidney	A₂	○
Ureter	B	○
Urinary bladder	C	○
Urethra	D	○
Renal artery	E	○
Renal vein	F	○
Abdominal aorta	G	○
Inferior vena cava	H	○
Lumbar vertebra	I	○
Suprarenal glands	J	○
Renal capsule	K	○
Adipose capsule	L	○
Renal fascia	M	○
Peritoneum	N	○

the KIDNEY

The two major organs of excretion are the kidneys. Lying between the dorsal body wall and the parietal peritoneum, the kidneys are retroperitoneal. An average adult kidney weighs approximately five ounces and is about the size of the heart.

In this plate, we study the regions and blood supply of the kidney. The plate consists of the two sections. In the first section, a mix of dark and light colors may be used according to the area designated, whereas in the second section, light colors are best because the blood vessels tend to be small.

In this plate, we present frontal sections of the right kidney. The first diagram is used to designate the important areas and regions of the kidney, while the second diagram indicates its blood supply. Beginning with the first diagram, read the following section, and as you encounter the structures, color their titles, then locate them and color them in the plate. Darker greens, reds, and blues are recommended, except where indicated.

At its outer surface, each kidney is surrounded by a fibrous membrane known as the **capsule (A)**. The capsule helps maintain the shape of the kidney.

Within the section of the kidney, there are two distinct regions. The first is the **renal cortex (B),** the more superficial area extending around the rim of the kidney. A pale tan or gray is recommended to color the entire cortex. Deep to the cortex is another major portion of the kidney known as the **renal medulla (C)**. A bracket outlines this area, and a light color is recommended. Similar pale colors may be utilized later.

Within the renal medulla, the kidney has a number of cone-shaped tissue masses called **renal pyramids (D)**. Appearing as brushlike structures in the diagram, there are approximately eight to eighteen pyramids in each kidney. The **base** of the pyramid **(D$_1$)** faces the renal cortex, while the apex or **renal papilla (D$_2$)** points toward the center of the kidney. The pyramids are formed of bundles of tubules that collect urine. Separating the pyramids are masses of cortical tissue extending inward from the cortex and known as **renal columns (L)**. A renal pyramid and the cortical tissue outside it constitute a lobe of the kidney.

We now focus at the area at the center of the kidney and indicate the tubes entering and leaving this area. Continue your reading as before and color the titles of the structures as you encounter them. Then locate them in the section of the kidney and color them in.

As the diagram shows, the lateral surface of the kidney is convex. Its medial surface is concave and has a large cleft known as the **hilus (E)**. The hilus leads to a space within the kidney known as the **renal sinus (F)**. Within the sinus are blood vessels, lymphatic vessels, and nerves. The **renal artery (M)** and the renal vein (N) occupy a portion of the sinus.

Within the renal sinus is a flat, funnel-like tube called the **renal pelvis (J)**. The pelvis is continuous with the **ureter (K)**. Urine is produced in tubules occupying the cortex and medulla in a complex arrangement called the nephron. One such nephron is pointed out in the diagram, and nephrons are discussed in more detail in the next plate. The tube carrying urine from the nephron is the **papillary duct (G)**, indicated by an arrow. The papillary duct leads to a cuplike structure called the **minor calyx (H)**, where urine collects. The minor calyces lead to two or three **major calyces (I)**. The major calyces empty their contents of urine into the renal pelvis, which leads to the ureter.

We now examine the vascular system operating within the kidney. For this purpose, we focus on the second diagram of the plate and the blood flowchart. This circulation through the kidney provides a pathway for the entry and exit of blood. Within the kidney tissues, the blood is cleansed in the nephrons, as explained in the next plate.

As previously noted, blood enters the kidney through the **renal artery (M)** at the hilus. Just beyond the hilus, the renal artery separates to form five **segmental arteries (O)**. A pale shade of red is recommended for this artery, and variations of the red may be used for successive arteries.

Leaving the segmental artery, blood flows into an **interlobar artery (P)**. Note how the blood flows out toward the cortex through this artery. You should search for other interlobar arteries paralleling this one. Near the junction of medulla and cortex tissues, the interlobar artery divides and gives rise to several **arcuate arteries (Q)**. Note how these arteries form arches at the bases of the renal pyramids.

From the arcuate arteries arise the **interlobular arteries (R)**. The cortex tissue is supplied with blood by these arteries. They eventually lead to **afferent arteries (S)**, which are indicated only in the flowchart. The afferent arteries enter a **glomerulus (T)**, also indicated only in the flowchart. The glomerulus is discussed in detail in the next plate. Blood leaves the glomerulus in the **efferent arteriole (U)** and enters a **peritubular capillary (V)**. The **interlobular vein (W)** arises from the peritubular capillary and leads blood to the **arcuate vein (X)**. Arcuate veins lead blood to the **interlobar veins (Y)**, which can be seen extending down toward the sinus. The interlobar veins unite to form **segmental veins (Z)**, which come together to form the **renal vein (N)**. This vein leads blood out of the kidney and completes the circuit.

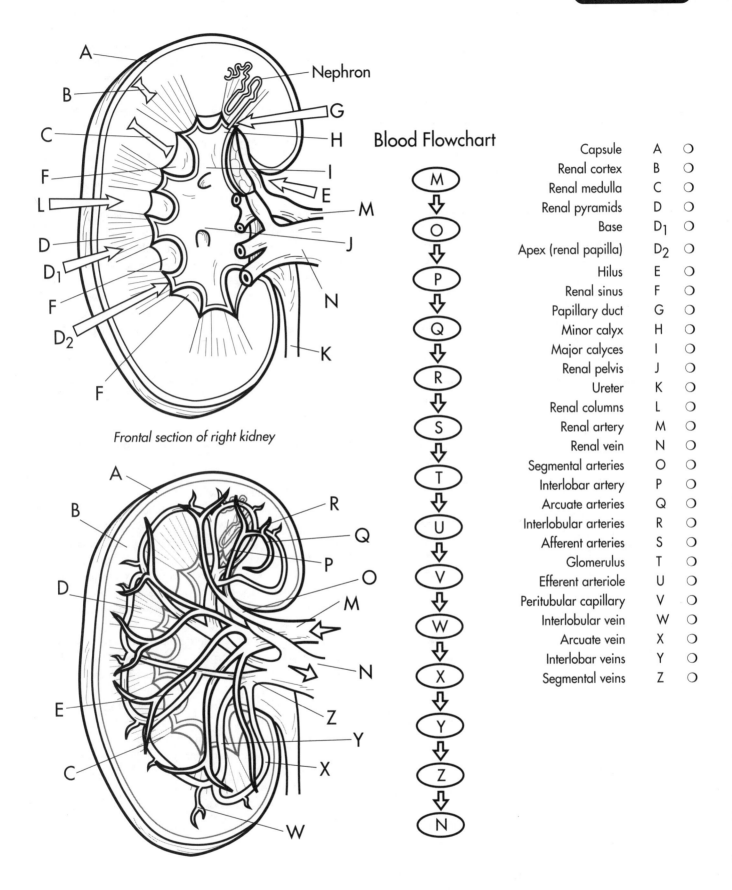

Nephron

A
B
C
F
L
D
D₁
F
D₂
F

G
H
I
E
M
J
N
K

Frontal section of right kidney

A
B
D
E
C

R
Q
P
O
M
N
Z
Y
X
W

Blood Flowchart

M → O → P → Q → R → S → T → U → V → W → X → Y → Z → N

Capsule	A	○
Renal cortex	B	○
Renal medulla	C	○
Renal pyramids	D	○
Base	D₁	○
Apex (renal papilla)	D₂	○
Hilus	E	○
Renal sinus	F	○
Papillary duct	G	○
Minor calyx	H	○
Major calyces	I	○
Renal pelvis	J	○
Ureter	K	○
Renal columns	L	○
Renal artery	M	○
Renal vein	N	○
Segmental arteries	O	○
Interlobar artery	P	○
Arcuate arteries	Q	○
Interlobular arteries	R	○
Afferent arteries	S	○
Glomerulus	T	○
Efferent arteriole	U	○
Peritubular capillary	V	○
Interlobular vein	W	○
Arcuate vein	X	○
Interlobar veins	Y	○
Segmental veins	Z	○

the NEPHRON

The independent unit within the kidney that produces urine is the nephron. There are approximately one million nephrons in each kidney. Nephrons perform the functions of filtration, reabsorption, and secretion. A basic understanding of kidney function can be obtained by understanding the activities at the nephron.

This plate reviews the structures associated with the nephron. We briefly discuss the formation of urine and see how the kidney performs its excretory functions.

Looking over the plate, you will note that it is composed of three diagrams: a diagram of the kidney progressing to a detailed presentation of a microscopic unit of the kidney. Bold colors may be used throughout this diagram, and contrasting colors are recommended as we proceed. Color the main title The Nephron, then read below and color the titles and structures as you discuss them in the reading.

The million or so nephrons of each kidney contain the same basic set of tubular and vascular components. In the first diagram, we see the **kidney (A)**, as seen in previous plates. A dark color may be used. One area of the kidney is shown in detail. This area contains a **nephron (B)**. A pale shading is recommended to highlight it. The **renal artery (C)** delivers blood to the kidney, while the **renal vein (D)** removes it from the kidney, and the **ureter (E)** is responsible for carrying urine away.

We now focus on an exploded view of the kidney, where we see eight nephrons. We briefly review this region before going on to the detailed view of the nephron. As you read about the structures, color them in as recommended.

The second diagram of the plate shows the two main areas of the kidney. The first area is the **cortex (F)**, indicated by a bracket. The bracket should be colored in a bold color, and the general area can be colored in a pale hue. The second area is the **medulla (G)**.

Within the cortex and medulla we present the outlines of eight nephrons. Each of the eight nephrons has a **renal corpuscle (H)**. The renal corpuscles of **cortical nephrons (H_1)** have tubular structures extending to the base of the renal pyramid. By comparison, the renal corpuscles of **juxtamedullary nephrons (H_2)** have tubules extending deep into the renal pyramid, as explained in the previous plate. For each of these nephrons, we recommend that you color in the cuplike renal corpuscle then color in the tubule leading from the corpuscle as it extends toward a collecting duct. The collecting duct receives urine from many nephrons. The tubules associated with the other seven nephrons are not shown in this diagram.

Now we come to the nephron itself. Recall that there are vascular and tubular components. We recommend your using variations of one color for all components of the vascular component, and variations of a contrasting color for all components of the tubular component. Portions of the components blend with one another so that the variations of color should be continuous. Continue reading as you study the nephron, and color the structures as you come upon them.

As noted previously, blood passes through a series of arteries described in the previous plate, including the segmental, interlobar, arcuate, and finally the **interlobular artery (J)**. A branch of this artery is the **afferent arteriole (K)**. Blood flows through this vessel into a tuft of capillaries called the **glomerulus (L)**. Filtration takes place here, then the blood leaves and enters a vessel called the **efferent arteriole (M)**. The efferent arteriole branches into a network of capillaries, the **peritubular capillary network (N)**. We recommend using a single color for these vascular tubes, with variations to show where one passageway ends and another begins.

As blood passes through the glomerulus, it is forced into the wall of the cuplike structure called **Bowman's capsule (O)**. (The combination of glomerulus and Bowman's capsule is the renal corpuscle.) Blood fluid is forced out of the glomerulus into the walls of the Bowman's capsule, then into the remainder of the tubular component. First encountered is the **proximal convoluted tubule (P)**. At this point, useful substances such as water, sodium ions, glucose, and amino acids are reabsorbed back to the blood in the peritubular network.

At this point, note that the proximal tubule descends toward the renal medulla, seen earlier. In the diagram, the descending tubule is called the **descending limb (Q)**. The tubule turns abruptly at the **loop of Henle (R)** and ascends as the **ascending limb (S)**. A variation of the same color used for the proximal tubule should be used for these portions. The peritubular capillaries surround the tubules in this area, and precise amounts of water and salts are reabsorbed back into the blood.

As the tubule ascends, it forms the **distal convoluted tubule (T)**. Again, it winds with capillaries of the **peritubular capillary network (N)**, and selective reabsorption takes place. The capillary network eventually moves back in the direction of the renal corpuscle and forms the **interlobular vein (U)**. This vein leads to the arcuate vein, interlobar vein, and finally to the renal vein to remove the cleansed blood from the kidney.

Following the tubule once again, note that the **distal convoluted tubule (T)** comes to the **collecting duct (I)**. The fluid present in the collecting tubules is urine. The collecting duct receives urine from several tubules and sends it to the renal pelvis for discharge.

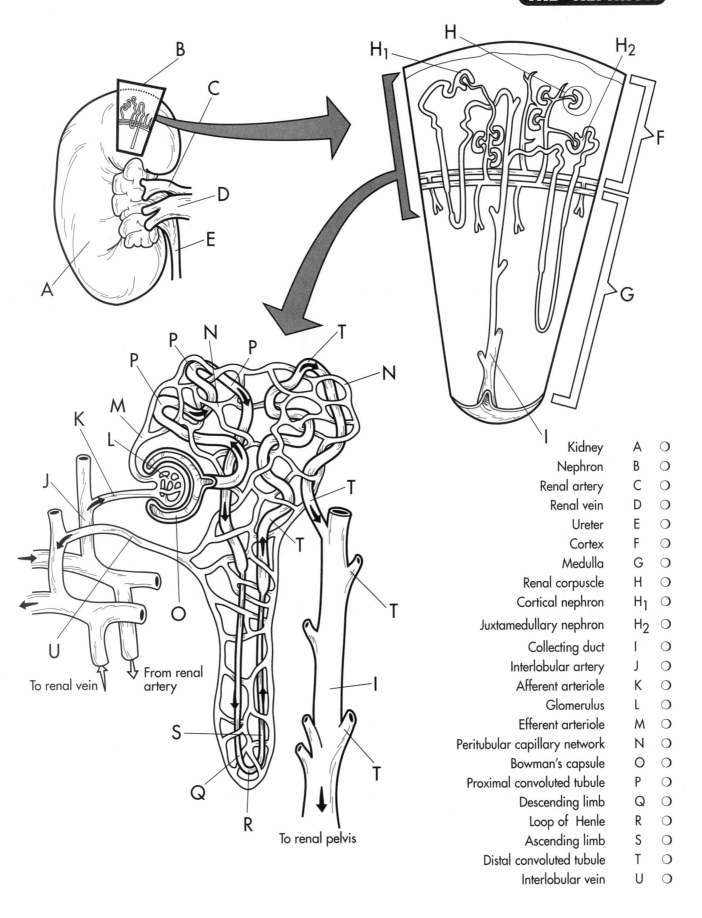

B

C

D

E

A

H₁

H

H₂

F

G

I

P N T

P

N

M

K

L

J

T

T

I

U

O

T

To renal vein

From renal artery

S

Q

R

To renal pelvis

I

Kidney	A	○
Nephron	B	○
Renal artery	C	○
Renal vein	D	○
Ureter	E	○
Cortex	F	○
Medulla	G	○
Renal corpuscle	H	○
Cortical nephron	H₁	○
Juxtamedullary nephron	H₂	○
Collecting duct	I	○
Interlobular artery	J	○
Afferent arteriole	K	○
Glomerulus	L	○
Efferent arteriole	M	○
Peritubular capillary network	N	○
Bowman's capsule	O	○
Proximal convoluted tubule	P	○
Descending limb	Q	○
Loop of Henle	R	○
Ascending limb	S	○
Distal convoluted tubule	T	○
Interlobular vein	U	○

the URINARY BLADDER

At this point, we focus our attention to the point where urine exits the bladder. As you encounter the structures in this area, color their titles, then check their location on the plate and color the plate appropriately. Note the difference in the urethra in the male and female.

As urine is produced in the kidney, it is carried to the urinary bladder for storage until it is removed from the body. Located on the floor of the pelvic cavity, the urinary bladder is anterior to the rectum in males. In females, it is anterior to the uterus and upper vagina.

In this plate, we study the details of the urinary bladder and the urethra, the tube leading to the exterior. We present the anatomical details of both the male and the female as there is considerable difference.

Begin by coloring the main title The Urinary Bladder. The plate presents the male and female bladders in an anterior view. As you read about the details of these organs, color the titles in the titles list, then locate and color the structures in the plate. Both male and female structures may be colored at the same time, and comparisons may be drawn as you proceed.

As the previous plate indicates, urine eventually makes its way to a slender tube leading away from the kidney. This tube is the **ureter (A)**. Each ureter is retroperitoneal and connects the urinary pelvis to the urinary bladder. At the posterior aspect of the urinary bladder, the ureters pass through the wall of the bladder at the **orifices** of the **ureters (A_1)**. There is no valve or sphincter muscle at the orifices.

The urinary bladder is a hollow organ in the pelvic cavity. It is held in place by folds of the peritoneum, but the bladder lies outside the **peritoneum (B)** and is, therefore, retroperitoneal. A pale color should be used to color the parietal peritoneum in the female view and male view. On its anterior surface, a muscular layer lies below the parietal peritoneum. This layer, called the **detrusor muscle (C)**, consists of smooth muscle fibers in longitudinal and circular layers. The muscle layer should be colored in a tan color to avoid obscuring its details.

In the plate, the anterior wall of the bladder has been reflected in the male and removed in the female to reveal the interior surface. The interior surface is the **mucosa (E)**. The walls form folds called **rugae (E_1)** when the bladder contains a small amount or no urine. When the bladder is full, the rugae disappear. The arrows pointing to the rugae may be colored in a bold color. Along the wall of the mucosa, a smooth triangular region is outlined by the openings of the two ureters and urethra. This region is the **trigone (D)**. It is an important anatomical point of reference.

Urine accumulates in the bladder until it is full, then is released in the process of micturition. The urine flows from the bladder at a point of the trigone called the **neck of the bladder (F)**. Here it enters a thin walled muscular tube called the **urethra (H)**. In both the male and female, there is an internal urethral **sphincter (G)** at the neck of the urinary bladder. This thickening of the detrusor muscle is an involuntary sphincter that closes the urethra when urine is not passing through.

The urethra is very short (about one and one half inches) in the female and passes through the **urogenital diaphragm (J)** before terminating at the orifice of the **urethra (H)**. The passageway through the urogenital diaphragm is controlled by a circular muscle called the **external urethral sphincter (I)**. A muscle called the levator ani also constricts the urethra.

In the male, the urethra is considerably longer than in the female and has three regions. Beginning at the neck of the bladder, the first portion of the urethra is called the **prostatic urethra (H_1)**, since it passes through the **prostate gland (a)**. A similar color is advised for the three regions of the urethra in the male. The next portion is the **membranous urethra (H_2)**. At this point, the urethra passes through the male urogenital diaphragm. The external urethral sphincter is located here, as in the female. A spot of color will suffice to point out its presence.

The third portion of the urethra in the male is the **spongy urethra (H_3)**. The spongy urethra passes through the **penis (b)** and terminates at the external orifice of the **urethra (H)**. The arrow should be colored boldly. In the female, the urethra carries only urine, but in the male the urethra conveys semen as well as urine to the exterior. Thus it services both the urinary and reproductive systems. The urethra is also discussed in upcoming plates on the reproductive systems.

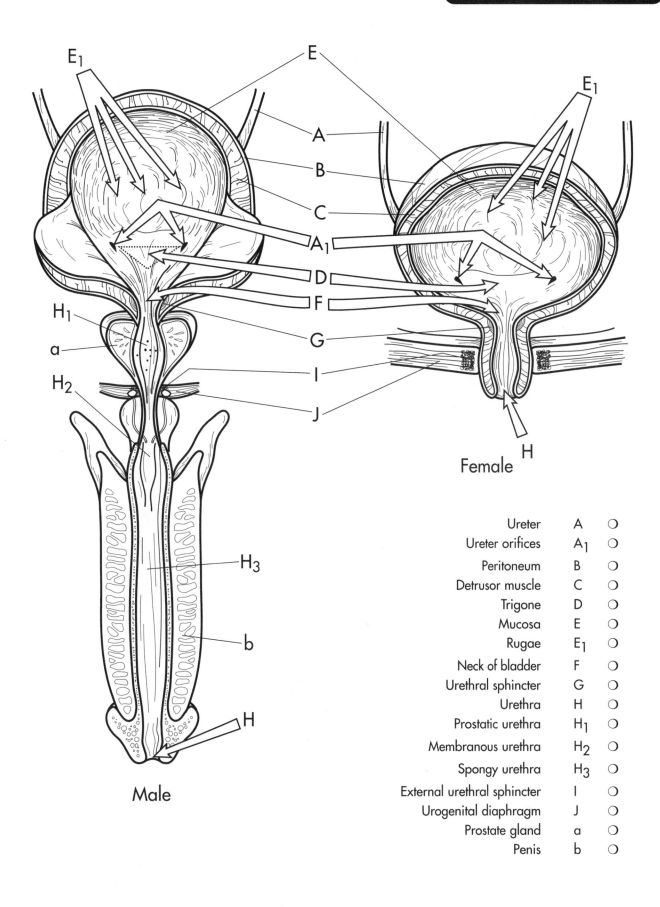

E₁ E E₁

A
B
C
A₁
D
F
G
I
J

H₁
a
H₂

H₃

b

H

Male

Female

H

Ureter	A	○
Ureter orifices	A₁	○
Peritoneum	B	○
Detrusor muscle	C	○
Trigone	D	○
Mucosa	E	○
Rugae	E₁	○
Neck of bladder	F	○
Urethral sphincter	G	○
Urethra	H	○
Prostatic urethra	H₁	○
Membranous urethra	H₂	○
Spongy urethra	H₃	○
External urethral sphincter	I	○
Urogenital diaphragm	J	○
Prostate gland	a	○
Penis	b	○

the REPRODUCTIVE SYSTEM

OVERVIEW of the MALE REPRODUCTIVE SYSTEM

The genetic material is passed from generation to generation and new individuals are produced through the activity of the reproductive system. The primary function of the male reproductive system is to produce sperm cells and deliver them to the female reproductive system for fertilization of the egg cells. In this plate, we present an overview of the male reproductive system. The structures reviewed in this plate are covered in more detail in succeeding plates.

Begin by coloring the main title Overview of the Male Reproductive System. We present a sagittal section through the mid-body plane. We then examine the male system from the left side and note its main structures. Uppercase letters are used for reproductive structures, and lowercase letters are used for accessory structures to show their relationship. In some cases we use subscript numbers to indicate parts of larger structures. Pale and light colors are recommended for this plate, because many of the structures are very small.

The major organs of the male reproductive system are the paired testes, where sperm cells are produced. A single **testis (A)** is noted in the diagram, and a dark color may be used for this large structure. Surrounding the testis is a comma-shaped structure called the **epididymis (B).** Sperm cells mature in the tightly coiled tubules of this organ.

Arising from the epididymis is a long tube that leads sperm cells out of the body. This tube is called the **ductus deferens (C),** also referred to as the vas deferens. Note the long length of this tube as it courses from the epididymis up into the body, curves to the left, passes the **urinary bladder (d),** curves again near the **ureter (e),** and passes downward. At this point, the ductus deferens comes to an enlargement called the **ampulla (C_1).** Here it joins with the duct leading from the **seminal vesicle (J)** and forms the **ejaculatory duct (D).** The ejaculatory duct joins with the urethra from the urinary bladder.

The urethra is a long tube in the male. It is discussed in a previous plate on the urinary system. The first portion of the urethra is the **prostatic urethra (E)** where it passes by the prostate gland. It is approximately one inch in length. The prostatic urethra becomes the **membranous urethra (F),** and it passes through the muscular partition known as the **urogenital diaphragm (f).** On emerging from the urogenital diaphragm, the urethra enters the penis and is now known as the **spongy urethra (G).** The spongy urethra is approximately six to eight inches in length.

We now follow the pathway of sperm cells and urine out of the body. A common tube, the urethra, services both the reproductive and urinary systems at this point. Note that the tube from the reproductive system has entered the body to join with the tube from the urinary bladder. As you continue to read, color the titles as you encounter them in the reading, then locate and color the structures in the diagram.

The course of the urethra takes it through the male organ of copulation, the **penis (H).** The **corona of the penis (H_1)** is the margin of the **glans penis (H_2).** Covering the glans in the uncircumcised penis is a portion of skin tissue called the **prepuce (H_3).** This is removed during circumcision.

The terminus of the urethra is the **orifice of the urethra (H_4),** indicated by an arrow that should be colored. The penis is suspended from the muscle above by a **suspensory ligament (H_5).** The penis is attached to the sac that contains the testis. This sac, the **scrotum (I),** hangs from the root of the penis. A bracket outlining the scrotum may be colored.

We now consider three accessory glands that add secretions to the sperm cells to produce the semen. These glands are quite small, and you should prepare to use light colors. We also note some of the other structures that can be seen in the area.

The first accessory gland is the **seminal vesicle (J).** This paired gland lies near the base of the urinary bladder. Its alkaline fluid is added to the sperm cells as they enter the ejaculatory duct. The second gland is the **prostate gland (K).** This large, single gland is about the size of a walnut. It surrounds the urethra and lies just above the urogenital diaphragm. Its acidic fluid contains several enzymes. The third gland we consider is the **bulbourethral gland (L),** which adds alkaline secretions to the sperm. This paired gland, also known as Cowper's glands, lies close to the membranous urethra within the urogenital diaphragm.

For reference purposes, we have included several accessory structures in the diagram to show their relationships. For example, the **sacrum (a)** and **coccyx (b)** are visible. The location of the **pubic symphysis (c)** shows the position where the urethra enters the body. The **urinary bladder (d)** is quite large in the diagram, and the **ureter (e)** can be seen near the bladder. The last portion of the large intestine is the **rectum (g),** and the terminus of the gastrointestinal tract is the **anus (h).**

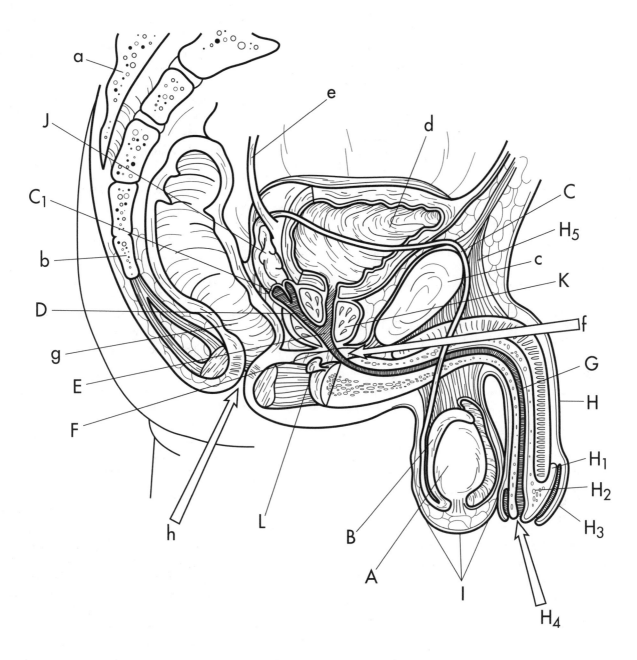

Testis	A	○	Glans penis	H₂	○	Coccyx	b	○
Epididymis	B	○	Prepuce	H₃	○	Pubic symphysis	c	○
Ductus deferens	C	○	Orifice of urethra	H₄	○	Urinary bladder	d	○
Ampulla	C₁	○	Suspensory ligament	H₅	○	Ureter	e	○
Ejaculatory duct	D	○	Scrotum	I	○	Urogenital diaphragm	f	○
Prostatic urethra	E	○	Seminal vesicle	J	○	Rectum	g	○
Membranous urethra	F	○	Prostate gland	K	○	Anus	h	○
Spongy urethra	G	○	Bulbourethral gland	L	○			
Penis	H	○	Sacrum	a	○			
Corona	H₁	○						

the TESTIS

The paired testes produce sperm cells for use in reproduction. Each testis is approximately one inch in diameter and approximately one and one-half inches long. This plate discusses the anatomy of the testis. We present an anterior view and a sagittal section of this organ and show the tubes that supply it with blood and nutrients and remove its sperm cells.

> Start the plate by coloring the main title The Testis. Note the anterior view in which the penis has been sectioned to view the testes within the scrotum. The second part of the plate shows a sagittal view of the testis and its intricate parts. Both views may be colored at the same time with the same colors. As you read about the structures below, color their titles and locate and color them in the two diagrams in the plate.

The testes of the male reproductive system hang outside the body in a sac of skin and fascia called the **scrotum (A)**. The scrotum provides an environment about 3°C below body temperature, the reduced temperature required for the production and survival of sperm cells. A **septum (B)** at the midline divides the scrotum into right and left halves to accommodate the two testes. Superficial muscle makes up the septum together with a layer of smooth muscle called the **dartos (C)**.

The testes are connected to other muscles of the body and elevated by the **cremaster muscle (D)**. This muscle is continuous with the **internal oblique muscle (E)**. Note that the two muscles join one another in the anterior view. During cold periods, the cremaster muscle pulls the testes toward the body.

> We now focus on the gross anatomy of the testis as seen in the anterior view. Several layers cover the testis tissue. We recommend light colors to preserve the margins of these tissue layers. As you read below, color the titles and color the tissue layers in the diagram.

Deep to the dartos, the testis is covered by two layers of **fascia (F)**. The **external spermatic fascia (F_1)** is more superficial, and the **internal spermatic fascia (F_2)** lies within it.

Deep to the internal spermatic fascia is a serous membrane, an extension of the peritoneum known as the **tunica vaginalis (G)**. It is a double membrane shown in the sagittal sections with a **cavity (G_1)** between the two layers. Internal to the tunica vaginalis is a capsule of dense white fibrous material called the **tunica albuginea (H)**.

In the sagittal section of the testis, the tunica albuginea is seen extending inward as a series of separating membranes called septa. A single **septum (I)** is indicated by an arrow, which should be colored in a bold color. The septa divide the testis into internal compartments called **lobules (J)**.

The lobules of the testis contain a series of tightly coiled tubules known as **seminiferous tubules (K)**. This is where sperm cells are produced. A pale color should be used to highlight the tubule series in the diagram. The sperm cells then flow through a series of straight tubules called the tubulus rectus. These straight tubules converge at a tubular network called the **rete testis (L)**. A series of ducts called **efferent ductules (L_1)** lead from the rete testis to the next organ, the epididymis.

> Our attention now turns to the sagittal section for an examination of the internal structure of the testis. As before, pale and tan colors are recommended to highlight the structures. We shall return to the anterior view.

The **epididymis (M)** is shaped somewhat like a comma, as the sagittal section illustrates. It lies at the border of each testis and is seen in the anterior view. Its parts include a **head (M_1)**, a **body (M_2)**, and a **tail (M_3)**. Variations of the same color can be used to highlight these three separate areas. Sperm cells mature in the epididymis.

> We now return to the anterior view to examine some of the drainage structures of the testis. Note how the system is continuous from the tubules of the testis through several of the drainage ducts and on to the exterior.

Returning to the sagittal section, note how the tail of the epididymis is continuous with a long tubule called the **ductus deferens (N)**, or vas deferens. This tube penetrates the inguinal canal and enters the pelvic cavity to loop over the ureter and enter the urethra, as noted in the previous plate. Closely associated with it are a number of **blood vessels (O)**, including arteries, veins, and nerves (including the testicular artery and vein). A bracket is used to indicate these structures collectively. The drainage ducts collectively are known as the **spermatic cord (P)**.

After entering the body, the sperm cells continue out through the urethra, which enters the penis as the **spongy urethra (U)**. A cross section of the penis is presented here. Two important ligaments suspend it from the pelvic muscle. One is the **suspensory ligament (Q)**, and deep to it is the **fundiform ligament (R)**. Two masses of erectile tissue are shown within the penis. The first is the **corpora cavernosa (S)**, which makes up most of the mass of the penis. The second mass is the **corpus spongiosum (T)**. These tissues are studied in more detail in an upcoming plate.

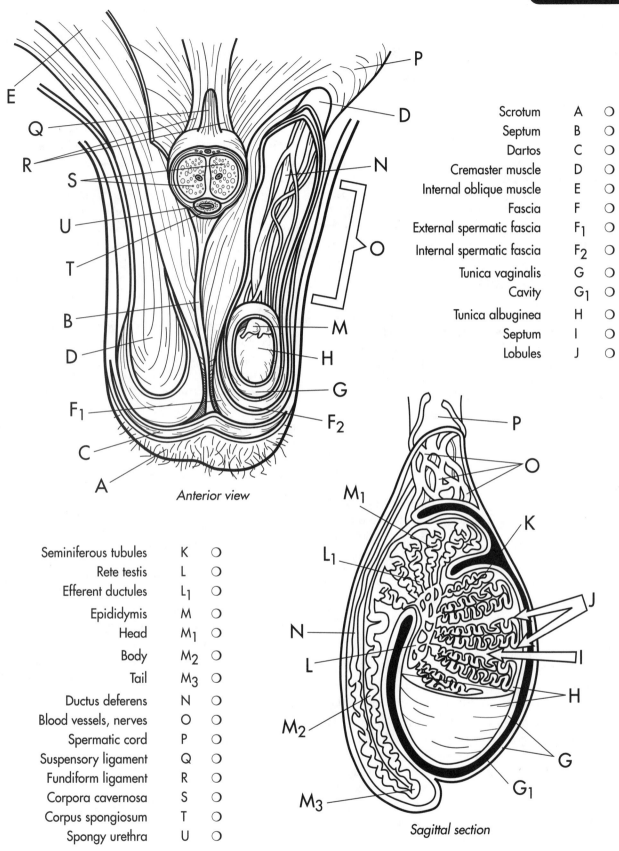

Anterior view

Scrotum	A	○
Septum	B	○
Dartos	C	○
Cremaster muscle	D	○
Internal oblique muscle	E	○
Fascia	F	○
External spermatic fascia	F_1	○
Internal spermatic fascia	F_2	○
Tunica vaginalis	G	○
Cavity	G_1	○
Tunica albuginea	H	○
Septum	I	○
Lobules	J	○

Seminiferous tubules	K	○
Rete testis	L	○
Efferent ductules	L_1	○
Epididymis	M	○
Head	M_1	○
Body	M_2	○
Tail	M_3	○
Ductus deferens	N	○
Blood vessels, nerves	O	○
Spermatic cord	P	○
Suspensory ligament	Q	○
Fundiform ligament	R	○
Corpora cavernosa	S	○
Corpus spongiosum	T	○
Spongy urethra	U	○

Sagittal section

MALE ACCESSORY GLANDS

We now turn to the prostate gland and bulbourethral glands and examine their structure. As you encounter the important parts of the glands, color their titles, then locate and color the structures in the plate. Recall that we are viewing the glands from the posterior aspect in order to see them clearly.

The semen is composed of sperm cells and secretions from three accessory glands of the male reproductive system. The accessory glands provide an acceptable environment for sperm survival in the female reproductive tract.

The accessory glands of the male reproductive tract are the seminal vesicles, the prostate gland, and the bulbourethral glands. In this plate, we examine the structure of these glands and their locations along the tubules to the exterior.

We present in the plate the three accessory glands with details of the seminal vesicle and prostate gland. Locate the structures in the three diagrams, and use the same color throughout. In some cases, we have used subscript numbers to refer to parts of a structure or regions. Light colors are recommended for much of the plate, because the structures are small. Lowercase letters are used for structures belonging to other systems.

The male accessory glands lie close to other organs in the area. The largest organ seen in this plate is the **urinary bladder (a)**. The view here is from the posterior aspect, and the entry of the **ureters (b)** from the kidney can be seen. Looping over the ureters is the main duct for removal of semen, the **ductus deferens (A).** Two ductus deferens can be seen passing along the posterior wall of the urinary bladder and merging at an expanded portion called the **ampulla (B)**. Note that the tissue has been cut away to reveal the **smooth muscle (A_1)** located along its wall. Peristalsis in the smooth muscle propels sperm cells and fluid along.

The first accessory gland is the **seminal vesicle (C)**. The two seminal vesicles are seen in the posterior view and should be colored in the same light color. This gland has many **folds (C_1)** and **outpockets (C_2)**. Bold colors may be used here. The **body (C_3)** of the seminal vesicle is shown, and the **base (C_4)** is apparent. The seminal vesicle lies against the wall of the urinary bladder. It is a tubular gland with many side branches whose secretions constitute about 60 percent of the volume of semen. The seminal vesicle has a **duct (C_5)** joining with the ductus deferens to form the short **ejaculatory ducts (D)**. They penetrate the wall of the prostate gland and empty their contents into the urethra. The posterior view shows this merger.

The **urethra (E)** arises from the urinary bladder and extends to the tip of the penis. A portion of the urethra passes through the prostate gland shown in the posterior view. This region is the prostatic urethra. The **prostate gland (F)** is a small, muscular organ having a diameter of about one and one-half inch. It encircles the urethra immediately as it arises from the urinary bladder. A light color is recommended for the prostate gland. The alkaline secretion of the prostate gland constitutes about 20 to 30 percent of the volume of the semen.

The prostate gland is surrounded by a thin, firm capsule of connective tissue and smooth muscle. The capsule is seen in the cross section, and the color used for the prostate gland may by used here. Smooth muscle fibers lie underneath the capsule and contract to squeeze the prostatic secretions through ducts and openings to the urethra. Three types of glands make up the compound tubuloalveolar glands of the prostate. The innermost glands are the **mucosal glands (F_1)**, which secrete mucus. Next superficially are the **submucosal glands (F_2)**. The **main prostatic glands (F_3)** occupy most of the prostate gland and are distributed throughout the tissue, as the cross section shows. **Ducts (F_4)** from these glands can be seen leading to the **urethra (E)** as it passes through the prostate gland. The two **ejaculatory ducts (D)** are also seen, and they receive secretions from the prostate gland. The ejaculatory ducts then carry the secretions to the urethra, into which they empty their contents. A spot of color may be used to designate the ejaculatory ducts in the cross section of the prostate gland.

The third accessory glands are the **bulbourethral glands (G)**, also called Cowper's glands. The paired glands are about the size of a pea. They lie at the undersurface of the urethra at the base of the penis and are covered by fascia of the urogenital diaphragm. A **duct (G_1)** from each gland travels a short distance next to the spongy urethra, then empties its contents into the lumen of the urethra. The bulbourethral glands secrete a thick, sticky, alkaline mucus to neutralize any acids that might be present.

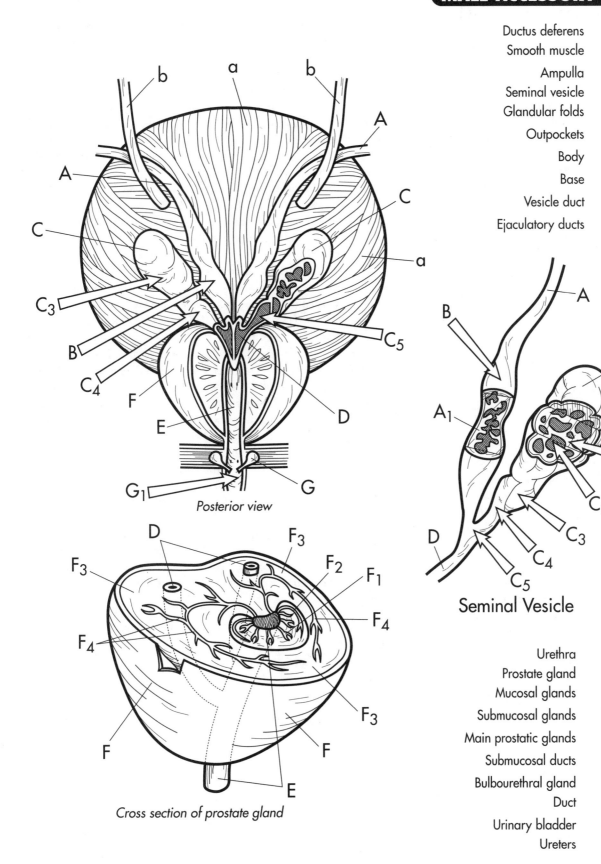

Ductus deferens	A	○
Smooth muscle	A$_1$	○
Ampulla	B	○
Seminal vesicle	C	○
Glandular folds	C$_1$	○
Outpockets	C$_2$	○
Body	C$_3$	○
Base	C$_4$	○
Vesicle duct	C$_5$	○
Ejaculatory ducts	D	○

Posterior view

Seminal Vesicle

Cross section of prostate gland

Urethra	E	○
Prostate gland	F	○
Mucosal glands	F$_1$	○
Submucosal glands	F$_2$	○
Main prostatic glands	F$_3$	○
Submucosal ducts	F$_4$	○
Bulbourethral gland	G	○
Duct	G$_1$	○
Urinary bladder	a	○
Ureters	b	○

the PENIS

The penis has two functions in the male body: it carries urine through the urethra to the external environment during the process of urination, and it transports semen to the vagina during ejaculation. The penis and scrotum constitute the external reproductive structures of the male known as the external genitalia.

This plate reviews the anatomical features of the penis. Many of the structures encountered here have been seen in previous plates, and they are reviewed to place them in perspective. Greens, reds, blues, and purples may be used in this plate, because the structures tend to be relatively large.

> The plate contains a frontal section of the penis as well as some of the nearby organs. A cross section through the penis is also shown to show the relative sizes and positions of some of its structures. As you read about this organ below, color its titles and locate and color the structures in both the frontal and cross sections. In some cases, subscript numbers indicate different regions of the same structure.

We begin the study of the penis by noting its position relative to a nearby structure, the **urinary bladder (a)**. The urinary bladder stores urine and releases it to the **urethra (B)** through the **internal urethral orifice (b)**. The urethra passes through the center of the penis, and it should be colored in a single light color from the **internal urethral orifice (b)** to the **external urethral orifice (R)**. Note that the urethra has three important regions: the **prostatic urethra (B_1)**, which passes through the prostate gland; the **membranous urethra (B_2)**, which is the passageway through the urogenital diaphragm; and the **spongy urethra (B_3),** which is the passageway through the penis. Arrows pointing to these regions should be colored with bold colors.

In the prostatic urethra, we observe the orifices of the **ejaculatory duct (C)**. A spot of color may be used. The ejaculatory duct carries secretions from the seminal vesicle and sperm from the ductus deferens. At this point, both enter the urethra. Note also the tiny pea-sized **bulbourethral gland (D)** at the **urogenital diaphragm (E)**. These glands also send their secretions to the urethra.

> We now focus on the main topic, the penis. Three masses of tissue make up the major portion of this organ. On reading about the tissues, color their titles and then locate and color them both in the frontal and cross section. Darker colors may be used in this section.

The penis is a cylindrical organ consisting of three sections: the root, the shaft, and the glans penis. A bracket in the first diagram indicates the **root of the penis (F)**, and the bracket should be colored. The root is the portion where the penis attaches to the body trunk. It contains a structure called the **bulb (G)**, which attaches to the inferior surface of the urogenital diaphragm, as the plate indicates. The bulb is an expanded portion of the corpus spongiosum, to be discussed presently. The bulbospongiosus muscle encloses the bulb. The root also contains a **crus (H)** on each lateral side. The crura are tapered portions of the corpora cavernosa, that attach to the pubic rami and are enclosed by the ischiocavernosus muscle.

The second major portion of the penis is the **shaft (I)**. The bracket may be colored with a dark color. The shaft contains three cylindrical masses of tissue. Two masses are the **corpora cavernosa (J)** seen on either side of the urethra. The large size is also apparent from the cross section. The corpora cavernosa are enclosed by the **tunica albuginea (L)**, seen in the cross section.

The smaller mass at the midventral area is the **corpus spongiosum (K)**. It is seen surrounding the urethra in the frontal section, and its size is apparent in the cross section. The **spongy urethra (B_3)** passes through corpus spongiosum. The three masses are erectile tissue that contain numerous **blood vessels (M)**. Two major vessels may be seen within the corpora cavernosa. **Smaller blood vessels (N)** are seen in the dorsal aspect. These arteries deliver blood to the erectile tissues when the penis becomes erect during sexual intercourse. When veins remove the blood, the penis returns to its flaccid condition.

The third region of the penis is the **glans penis (O)**. This is an enlarged area of the corpus spongiosum. Both the bracket and anatomical structure may be colored in the same color. At the margin of the glans penis is the **corona (P)**, indicated by an arrow. This is an area of high sensitivity. The fold of tissue enclosing the glans penis is the **prepuce (Q)**. In the circumcised individual, this fold of skin has been removed. The **external urethral orifice (R)** is the terminus of the urethra and the conclusion of both urinary and reproductive tubes in the male.

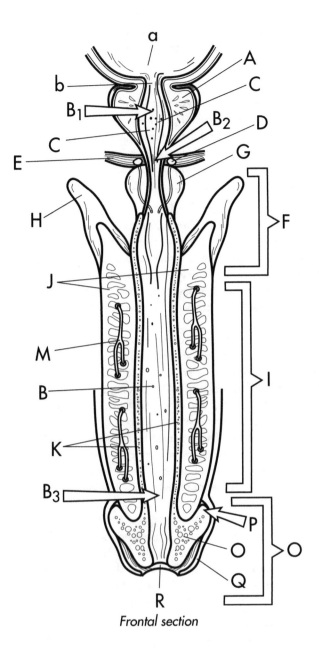

Frontal section

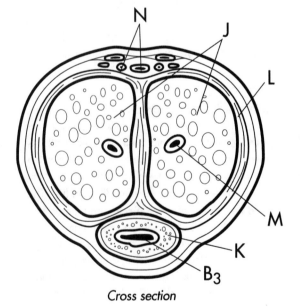

Cross section

Prostate gland	A	○
Urethra	B	○
Prostatic urethra	B₁	○
Membranous urethra	B₂	○
Spongy urethra	B₃	○
Ejaculatory duct	C	○
Bulbourethral gland	D	○
Urogenital diaphragm	E	○
Root of penis	F	○
Bulb	G	○
Crus	H	○
Shaft	I	○
Corpora cavernosa	J	○
Corpus spongiosum	K	○
Tunica albuginea	L	○

Blood vessels	M	○
Smaller blood vessels	N	○
Glans penis	O	○
Corona	P	○
Prepuce	Q	○
External urethral orifice	R	○
Urinary bladder	a	○
Internal urethral orifice	b	○

OVERVIEW of the FEMALE REPRODUCTIVE SYSTEM

The female reproductive system is responsible for producing sex cells for potential union with male sperm cells. In addition, the female system nurtures the developing embryo and fetus for a nine-month period. For this reason, the female system is more complex than the male system.

In this plate, we present an overview of the female reproductive system as a prelude to discussions in the following plates. We present the main structures here to show their relationships to organs of the reproductive system and other organ systems.

The plate contains a single diagram of a sagittal section of the female reproductive tract as seen from the left side. Many of the organs of the reproductive system have been sectioned to expose their interiors. We have used capital letters to indicate organs of the female reproductive system and lowercase letters for organs of nearby systems. As you read about the female reproductive system, color the titles, then locate and color the organs in the plate. Bold colors are good for the arrows, but lighter colors are better for the reproductive structures.

The **ovaries (A)** are the female reproductive organs in which egg cells are formed. These organs also produce female sex hormones. The egg cells are liberated into the **uterine tubes (B)**. As the diagram shows, the end of the uterine tube drapes over the ovary as a structure called the **fimbria (B$_1$)**. The first portion of the tube immediately behind the fimbra is the **infundibulum (B$_2$)**. The uterine tube should be colored in a single color, and the arrows pointing to portions of the tube should be colored boldly.

The uterine tubes lead the egg cell to the **uterus (D)**, a muscular organ found between the **rectum (d)** and **urinary bladder (a)**. The thick muscle of the uterus is apparent, and the most internal layer of muscle is the **endometrium (D$_1$)**. Bands of fibrous tissue called the **round ligament (C)** help maintain the position of the uterus. The area of the round ligament may be colored in gray, because it is indistinguishable from the peritoneum of the area. The entire area surrounding the uterine tubes, uterus, and ovaries should be also be colored in gray. The **uterosacral ligament (E)** helps connect the uterus to the **sacrum (g)**.

On the anterior and posterior surfaces of the uterus, there are two pouches between the uterus and adjacent organs. On the posterior side, the **rectouterine pouch (F)** lies between the uterus

and the anterior surface of the rectum. On the anterior side is the **vesicouterine pouch (G)** between the uterus and posterior wall of the bladder.

We continue with the examination of the female reproductive system by focusing on the passageways leading from the uterus and the external genitalia. Follow the reading and color the titles. Light colors should be used because of the complexity of the areas studied.

The narrow opening leading from the uterus is called the **cervix (J)**. The arrow showing this structure may be colored in a bold color. The next structure encountered in the system is the **vagina (K)**. A light color is recommended for this passageway. Where it attaches to the uterus, a region called a fornix is found. In the reproductive system, there is a **posterior fornix (H)** and an **anterior fornix (I)**. The arrows should be colored prominently for these structures.

The vagina is a tubular organ approximately four inches in length. It serves as a passageway for the egg cell and receives the penis during sexual intercourse. The vagina passes through the **urogenital diaphragm (L)**. At this point, the **greater vestibular gland (M)** is located. Also called Bartholin's gland, this paired gland produces mucus to provide lubrication. The vagina opens at the **vaginal orifice (N)**, indicated by the arrow.

At the region of the vaginal orifice is the vulva, the area encompassing the external genitalia of the female. One component of the vulva is the **mons pubis (O)**. This is an elevation of adipose tissue covered by skin and coarse pubic hair. It cushions the **pubic symphysis (h)**. Another structure of the vulva is the **clitoris (P)**, a small mass of erectile tissue homologous to the penis of the male. The paired labia are also located in this area. The **labium minora (Q)** is the smaller fold of skin tissue of the vulva, and the **labium majora (R)** is the larger fold of tissue. The labia are homologous to the scrotum of the male.

We complete the plate by noting some of the other organs of the area. These organs are discussed in other plates, but we show them here to illustrate their relationship to the female reproductive tract.

In the pelvic region of the abdominal cavity, other organs lie close to the female reproductive system. Among these are the **urinary bladder (a)**, whose muscle can be seen in the plate. The short tube leading from the urinary bladder is the **urethra (b)**, which terminates at the **external urethral meatus (c)**.

Posterior to the uterus is the **rectum (d)** of the gastrointestinal tract. It terminates at the **anus (f)**. Posterior to the rectum, the plate shows the **sacrum (g)** and the **coccyx (e)**, which indicates the terminus of the spinal column.

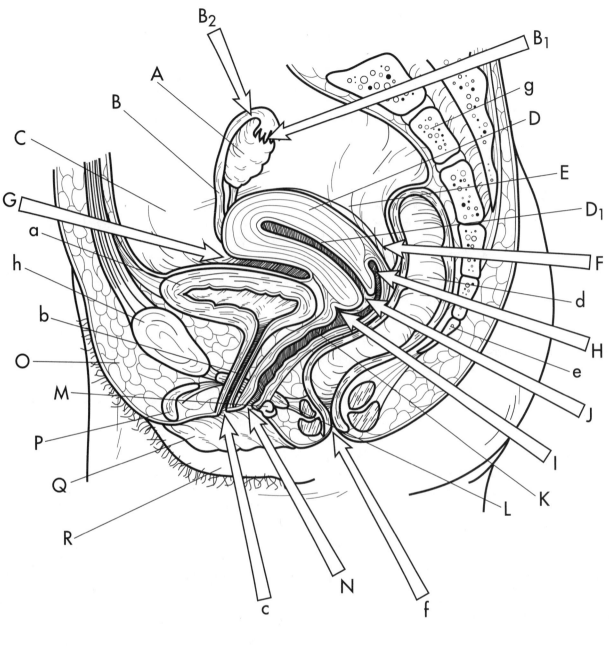

Ovaries	A	○	Posterior fornix	H	○	Urinary bladder	a	○
Uterine tubes	B	○	Anterior fornix	I	○	Urethra	b	○
Fimbria	B_1	○	Cervix	J	○	External urethral meatus	c	○
Infundibulum	B_2	○	Vagina	K	○	Rectum	d	○
Round ligament	C	○	Urogenital diaphragm	L	○	Coccyx	e	○
Uterus	D	○	Greater vestibular gland	M	○	Anus	f	○
Endometrium	D_1	○	Vaginal orifice	N	○	Sacrum	g	○
Uterosacral ligament	E	○	Mons pubis	O	○	Pubic symphysis	h	○
Rectouterine pouch	F	○	Clitoris	P	○			
Vesicouterine pouch	G	○	Labium minora	Q	○			
			Labium majora	R	○			

the OVARY and UTERINE TUBES

The paired ovaries of the female reproductive system produce ova and female hormones. The organs are about the size and shape of an unshelled almond. They are found in the pelvic portion of the abdominopelvic cavity on either side of the uterus. Egg cells from the ovaries enter the uterine tubes, also known as the Fallopian tubes.

We show in this plate the ovaries and uterine tubes in place in the female reproductive system. A subsection of the plate is a cross section of an ovary showing the development of an egg cell. Some structures are found in both views. As you read, locate the structures in the titles list, then find them in the plate. The organs are covered over by membranes and ligaments, which may obscure their view. We suggest you color the organs, then either outline the ligaments or shade them in lightly to show they lie over the organs.

The **ovary (A)** is an elongated, somewhat flattened body. In the plate, the left ovary is covered over by a ligament and the right ovary is open to show the internal contents. A light color is recommended for the organ.

In the right ovary, and in the cross section, the two main parts of the organ are shown with arrows. The **cortex (A_1)** is the peripheral area of the ovary, and the **vascular medulla (A_2)** is the central area. Where the ovary attaches to a thick fold of mesentery, the area is called the **ovarian hilum (A_3)**. The ovarian artery and vein **(h)** travel to and from the ovary at this point. Covering the tissue of the ovary is a layer of dense connective tissue known as the **tunica albuginea (A_4)**.

We now examine the tubes leading from the ovary, the uterine tubes. These tubes are commonly known as Fallopian tubes. They are the site of fertilization, and they transport the fertilized or unfertilized egg cell to the uterus. A single color should be used for the tubes, and the arrows should be colored in bold colors to indicate areas and regions of the tubes.

The **uterine tube (B)** is a hollow, muscular tube about five inches in length. Concentric layers of smooth muscle make up the major mass of the tubes. Where the uterine tube drapes over the ovary, the fingers of tissue are called the **fimbriae (B_1)**. The fimbriae form an expanded funnel called the **infundibulum (B_2)**. Beating cilia move the egg cell through the infundibulum to an enlarged portion of the uterine tube called the **ampulla (B_3)**. The next important area is a small diameter region called the **isthmus**

(B_4), which exists just before the uterine tubes enter the uterus. The area where the tube passes through the wall of the uterus is the **intramural portion of the uterine tube (B_5)**. It is difficult to see the **uterus (C)** in this plate because it is covered by thick membranes and ligaments.

The extensive mesentery enclosing the ovaries, uterine tubes, and uterus is the **broad ligament (D)**. We recommend a light shading or stippling to avoid obscuring the organs below. A thickened fold of the broad ligament is the **mesovarium (E)**. This mesentery supports and stabilizes each ovary.

Two other ligaments support and stabilize the ovaries. The first is the **ovarian ligament (F)** extending from the uterus to the medial surface of the ovary. The **suspensory ligament (G)** extends from the lateral surface of the ovary and inserts at the lateral surface of the pelvic wall, as the diagram illustrates. The ovarian artery and vein travel in association with this ligament.

Also seen in the diagram is the neck of the uterus known as the **cervix (I)**. The **cervical os (I_1)** is the opening to the **vagina (J)**. The muscular composition of the vagina may be seen.

To complete the plate, we focus on the development of the egg cell by examining the cross section of the ovary. The structures seen in this diagram form in a continuous pattern over long periods of time. Subscript numbers are used for various stages of the same structure.

The cross section of the ovary shows the **cortex (A_1)** at the periphery and the **vascular medulla (A_2)** at the center of the organ. Blood vessels such as the ovarian artery and **vein (h)** are seen entering the vascular medulla portion.

The egg cell develops in the ovary within a cluster of cells called the follicle. Follicles develop during fetal development as germ cells develop into primary oocytes surrounded by a single layer of follicle cells. The result is the **primordial follicle (K_1)**. After birth, a primordial follicle forms a primary follicle with several layers of **cells (K_2)**. The primary follicle continues to **grow (K_2)**. As development continues, the follicle becomes a **secondary follicle (K_3)**, and the first appearance of the **egg cell (L)** occurs.

After puberty, hormones stimulate the further development of the secondary follicle resulting in a **mature follicle (K_4)**. The **egg cell (L)** matures further within this follicle, also called the Graafian follicle. At the time of ovulation, the **mature follicle (K_4)** ruptures and releases the mature egg cell. A surrounding layer called the **corona radiata (L_1)** encloses the egg cell.

The remnants of the mature follicle now undergo a reorganization to form an **early corpus luteum (M_1)**. This name translates to yellow body, and the color yellow is recommended for this structure. The corpus luteum develops **veins (h)**, and soon becomes a **mature corpus luteum (M_2)**. This body produces progesterone and other hormones for the two weeks following ovulation and, if fertilization takes place, for several weeks thereafter. It eventually degenerates and becomes a body of fibrous tissue called the **corpus albicans (H)**.

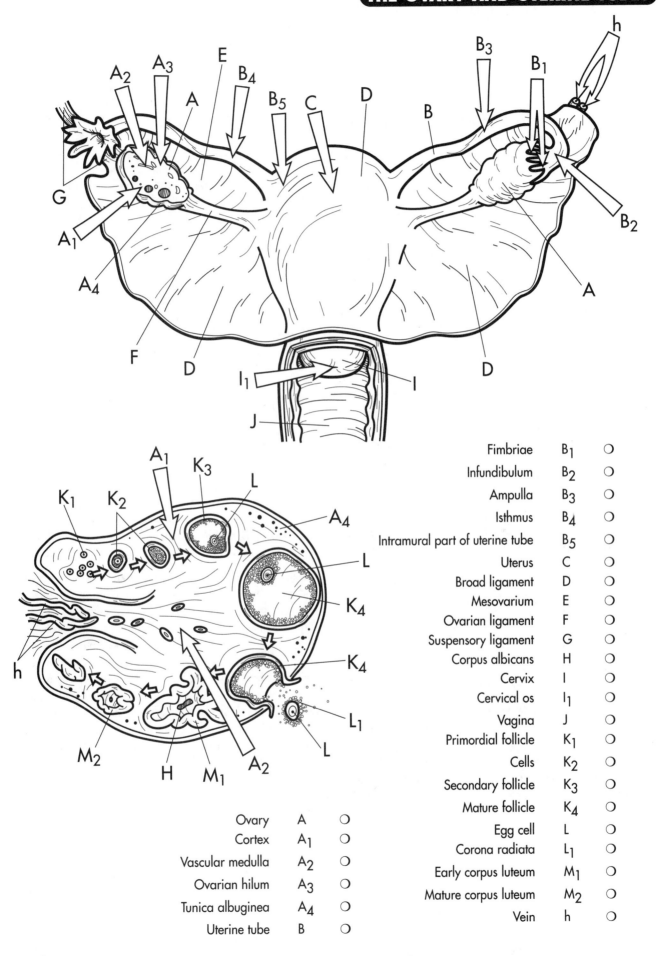

Fimbriae	B₁	○
Infundibulum	B₂	○
Ampulla	B₃	○
Isthmus	B₄	○
Intramural part of uterine tube	B₅	○
Uterus	C	○
Broad ligament	D	○
Mesovarium	E	○
Ovarian ligament	F	○
Suspensory ligament	G	○
Corpus albicans	H	○
Cervix	I	○
Cervical os	I₁	○
Vagina	J	○
Primordial follicle	K₁	○
Cells	K₂	○
Secondary follicle	K₃	○
Mature follicle	K₄	○
Egg cell	L	○
Corona radiata	L₁	○
Early corpus luteum	M₁	○
Mature corpus luteum	M₂	○
Vein	h	○

Ovary	A	○
Cortex	A₁	○
Vascular medulla	A₂	○
Ovarian hilum	A₃	○
Tunica albuginea	A₄	○
Uterine tube	B	○

269

The UTERUS and VAGINA

In the female body, the uterus is the organ through which sperm passes on its way to the uterine tubes. It is also where the fertilized ovum implants and develops during pregnancy. The vagina is the muscular passageway between the uterus and the external environment. It is about four inches in length and is found between the rectum and urinary bladder. In this plate, we study the anatomical features of these two organs.

> We examine in this plate the uterus and vagina from the posterior view. The outline of the body indicates the view. We present a superficial overview of the ovaries, uterine tubes, and uterus, then focus on some of the anatomical details of this organ and the vagina. The organs should be colored in light colors and the arrows in bolder tones. Begin the plate by focusing on the overall view of the reproductive system.

The **uterus (A)** should be colored in a pale gray, tan, or yellow. It is a pear-shaped organ. The opening at the inferior aspect is the cervical os. At the upper end, the uterus at its lateral edges receives the **uterine tubes (B)**. These tubes drape over the left and right **ovaries (C)**. Parts of the uterine tubes have been seen in the previous plate. They include the **fimbriae (B_1)**, the **infundibulum (B_2)**, the **ampulla (B_3)**, and the **intramural portion (B_4)**, which connects with the uterus. This portion can be seen in the detailed diagram to follow. Note how the ovarian ligaments connect the ovary to the lateral wall of the uterus.

> We now focus on the parts of the uterus, and the layers of tissue that make up this organ. The uterus may be colored in the same color as used previously, and the arrows should be colored using a bold tone such as red, green, or blue.

The uterus is about three inches long, two inches wide, and one inch thick. Anatomically, the uterus contains a major central portion called the **body (A_1),** or corpus. The rounded portion of the uterus where the uterine tubes enter is the **fundus (A_2).** At its inferior aspect, the body of the uterus constricts to form the **isthmus (A_3)**. An isthmus also exists in the uterine tube, as noted in the previous plate.

The isthmus of the body of the uterus leads to a narrow portion extending to the vagina. This portion is called the **cervix (A_4).** The opening from the cervix into the vagina is the **cervical os (A_5)**, also known as the external orifice. Sperm cells entering the cervical os pass through the **cervical canal (A_6)** on the pathway toward the ovary. Where the cervical canal enters the body of the uterus, the passageway is called the **internal os (A_7)**, also known as the internal orifice. The sperm cells then pass through the **uterine cavity (A_8)**.

There are several layers that compose the wall of the uterus. The outer layer is the **perimetrium (D)**, also called the serosa. The major aspect of the uterine wall is composed of three layers of smooth muscle fibers collectively called the **myometrium (E)**. A separate color may be used for this layer and for the perimetrium. Contractions of the muscles in this layer encourage expulsion of the fetus during childbirth. The innermost layer of uterus is the **endometrium (F)**, which may be outlined in a bold color. This highly vascular layer builds up in blood and tissue and is shed during menstruation. When a fertilized egg is present, it implants in the endometrium and begins its development.

The blood supply to the uterine wall is considerable. The major artery supplying the uterine wall is the **uterine artery (G)**. The many branches that extend into the myometrium include the arcuate arteries, the radial arteries, and the straight arteries. Blood emerging from the tissues flows away through the **uterine vein (H)**. On the right side of the uterus, these vessels are seen beneath the broad ligament covering the uterine wall.

> The plate concludes with a brief examination of the vagina. This tube receives sperm during sexual intercourse and serves as a passageway during birth and menstruation. As you encounter the structures in the reading, color their titles, then color them in the plate.

The **vagina (I)** is an elastic muscular tube. At the proximal end, the cervix of the uterus projects into the cavity of the vagina known as the **vaginal canal (I_1)**. Surrounding this entryway is a recess known as the **fornix (I_2)**. The anterior and posterior fornices were seen in a previous plate. The two muscle layers of the vagina stretch considerably to receive the penis and during birth. Folds called **rugae (I_3)** are found in the collapsed vagina.

Blood is supplied to the vagina by the **vaginal artery (J)**, which is a branch of the internal iliac artery. Blood is removed by the **vaginal vein (K)**. The other structure seen in this diagram passing close to the uterus and vagina is the **ureter (L)** extending to the urinary bladder in the region.

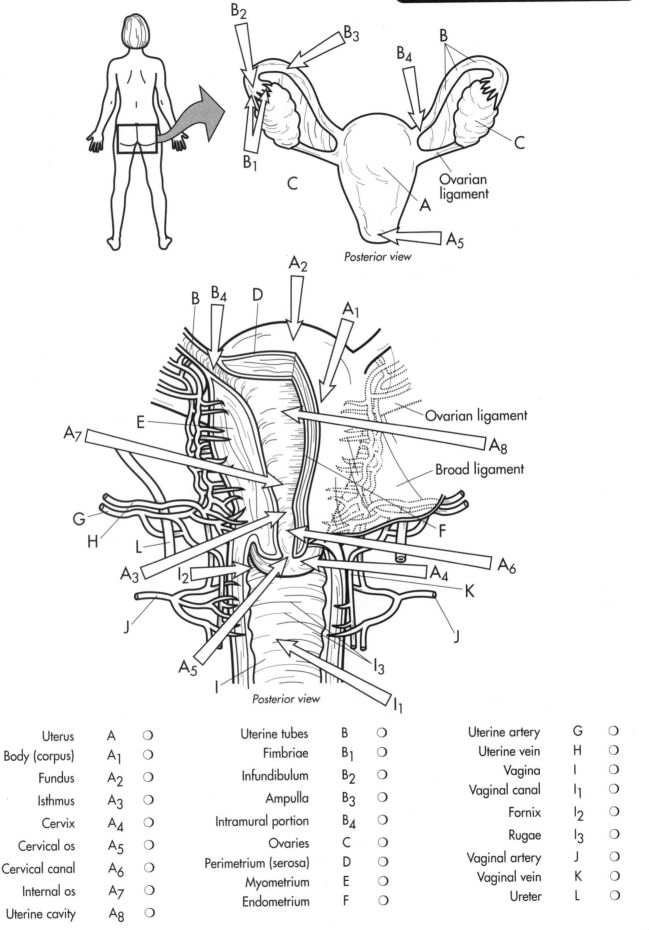

Posterior view

Ovarian ligament

Ovarian ligament

Broad ligament

Posterior view

Uterus	A	○	Uterine tubes	B	○	Uterine artery	G	○
Body (corpus)	A_1	○	Fimbriae	B_1	○	Uterine vein	H	○
Fundus	A_2	○	Infundibulum	B_2	○	Vagina	I	○
Isthmus	A_3	○	Ampulla	B_3	○	Vaginal canal	I_1	○
Cervix	A_4	○	Intramural portion	B_4	○	Fornix	I_2	○
Cervical os	A_5	○	Ovaries	C	○	Rugae	I_3	○
Cervical canal	A_6	○	Perimetrium (serosa)	D	○	Vaginal artery	J	○
Internal os	A_7	○	Myometrium	E	○	Vaginal vein	K	○
Uterine cavity	A_8	○	Endometrium	F	○	Ureter	L	○

the EXTERNAL GENITALIA

The diamond-shaped area medial to the thighs and buttocks is the perineum. The perineum of both females and males contain the anus and external genitalia, which encompass the external reproductive structures. The external reproductive structures are accessory to the major organs of reproduction, the testes and ovaries and their associated ducts and tubules. In the female, the external genitalia is also called the vulva, or pudendum. In this plate, we review its components and structures.

> Begin the plate by coloring the main title The External Genitalia. We are presenting a sectional view of the organs of the internal reproductive organs as they relate to the external structures of the external genitalia. As you read about these structures in the following paragraphs, color their titles, then locate and color them in the plate. Where arrows are used, they should be colored boldly. Other structures can be colored in the plate in gray tones.

The external genitalia, also known as the vulva, is the region where the reproductive tract opens in the female. The system includes the **ovary (A)**, followed by the uterine tubes leading to the **uterus (B)**. The uterus opens to the **vagina (C)** at the **cervical os (D)**. A spot of color may be used for this structure. As the plate indicates, the vagina is about four inches in length and is composed of thick muscle. It passes through the **urogenital diaphragm (E)**, a region discussed in the plate concerning the female perineum. The pubic symphysis, where the pubic bones come together, is located here. The vagina has its opening at the **external genitalia (G)**, indicated by the arrow. The arrow may be colored using a dark color. This general region is the **vestibule (H)**, indicated by the bracket. A bold color may also be used here.

> We continue this study of the female external genitalia with a view of the perineum. In this area of the body, the urinary, reproductive, and digestive tracts have their openings. As you read about the structures involved, color their titles, then locate and color them in the plate. We recommend lighter colors for shading purposes and spots of bold color where systems have their openings.

The reproductive system extends through the vagina, which opens into a central space called the **vestibule (H)**. In the main diagram, the opening at the vagina is indicated and the surrounding area is the vestibule. A pale color is recommended for the vestibule.

The vestibule is surrounded by folds of smooth skin called the **labia minora (I)**. These two folds of skin have few glands, and do not contain fat or hair. Among the glands they do contain are a number of oil glands for lubrication of the area during sexual arousal. The vaginal orifice may be covered by the membrane called the **hymen (F)**. The area of the hymen is seen in the sectional view. It may be absent as a result of injury or tearing resulting from sexual intercourse.

Anterior to the orifice of the vagina is the orifice of the **urethra (J)**. A spot of color is recommended to mark this opening. Anterior to the opening of the urethra is the **clitoris (K)**. This small mass of erectile tissue and nerves is located at the anterior junction of the labia minora. The clitoris is covered by a layer of skin called the **prepuce (L)**, which is analogous to the prepuce of the penis. The clitoris is analogous to the penis of the male.

Close to the opening of the vagina are the **greater vestibular glands**, also called Bartholin's glands. The opening from these glands is indicated **(M)**, and a spot of color is suggested to note their presence. The border of the vulva is established by the mons pubis and the labia majora. The **mons pubis (N)** contains fat tissue and skin. It helps cushion the pubic symphysis against injury and during sexual intercourse. The **labia majora (O)** encircle the structures of the vestibule. Coarse hairs cover both the mons pubis and the labia majora.

Also seen in the plate is the external opening of the digestive system, the **anus (P)**. The anus is contained within the anal triangle of the perineum. The muscles associated with this area were discussed in a previous plate.

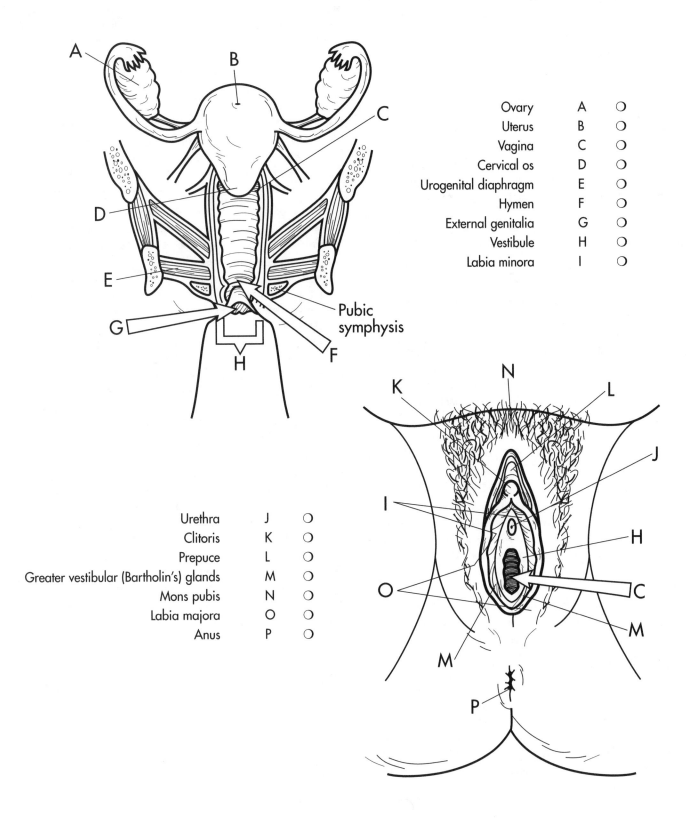

Ovary	A	O
Uterus	B	O
Vagina	C	O
Cervical os	D	O
Urogenital diaphragm	E	O
Hymen	F	O
External genitalia	G	O
Vestibule	H	O
Labia minora	I	O

Pubic symphysis

Urethra	J	O
Clitoris	K	O
Prepuce	L	O
Greater vestibular (Bartholin's) glands	M	O
Mons pubis	N	O
Labia majora	O	O
Anus	P	O

the MAMMARY GLANDS

The mammary glands are modified sweat glands that produce and secrete milk. They are located within the breasts of the woman. Each mammary gland is composed of 15 to 20 lobes composed of compound areolar glands, which resemble bunches of grapes and radiate out from a central location. The secretion of milk is related to the sucking reflex and is regulated by prolactin and other hormones secreted by the anterior lobe of the pituitary gland.

In this plate, we review the anatomy of the mammary glands and the structures associated with them that are used to carry milk to the exterior. Both light and dark colors may be used for the structures, depending upon their size.

We present in the plate three views, two anterior and one sagittal, of the mammary glands within the female breast. The structures and regions apply to all three diagrams, and the same color may be used in all three. In some cases, we have used subscript numbers to indicate that the structures are related to one another in the plate. As you locate the structure in the reading, color its title, then find and color it in the appropriate diagram. Begin your work by coloring the main title The Mammary Glands, then continue.

The mammary glands secrete milk to aid the development of the newborn. The production of milk is called lactation and is a part of the reproductive process involving the woman and the newborn. The mammary glands are found within the breasts. The breasts rest upon the **pectoralis major muscle (A)** on the anterior thoracic wall. Overlying the muscle and in direct contact with the breast is a layer of **deep fascia (C$_1$)**. The muscle is seen in the anterior view, and the layer is prominent in the sagittal section. Bold colors can be used for it and for the layer of associated deep fascia. The breasts also contain an extensive set of **lymph vessels and lymph nodes (B)** seen on the anterior view. Swollen lymph nodes may reflect disease in the breast tissues. The lymph nodes, which contain elements of the immune system, are parts of the lymphatic system reviewed in another plate.

In addition to the deep fascia, the breast also contains a layer of **superficial fascia (C$_2$)**. This layer is closer to the body surface. The openings from the mammary glands come together at the **nipple (D)**. As the plate shows, this structure is surrounded by a circular pigmented area of skin known as the **areola (E)**. The areola contains modified oil glands.

Between the skin and deep fascia, the breast contains strands of connective tissue called **Cooper's ligaments (F)**. These ligaments support the tissues of the breast and mammary glands. They loosen when stress is placed upon them or with age.

We now examine the detailed structure of the mammary glands within the breast. As you read about the detailed structures in the following paragraphs, locate the titles in the title list, then color the appropriate structures in the diagram. Use light colors because many of the structures are of a fine texture or are tubular in nature. This is especially true in the section dealing with the lobes and tubules of the mammary glands.

As noted previously, the mammary glands are modified sweat glands. As such, they are histologically a part of the skin. Within its internal structure, each mammary gland contains about fifteen to twenty **lobes (G)**. A single lobe is shown in one of the anterior views. The lobes radiate around the nipple and send their secretions to this area for release to the exterior. Cooper's ligaments separate the lobes from one another, as previously noted.

Smaller units within the lobes are the **lobules of the mammary gland (H)**. The sagittal section shows several lobules. The lobules contain clusters of milk-secreting glands, which are known as alveoli. The alveoli are embedded in connective tissue. When milk is produced, it is propelled from the alveoli into a series of **secondary tubules (I)**. The secondary tubules carry milk away from the alveoli and converge at the **mammary ducts (J)**. The mammary ducts lead to expanded areas called **the lactiferous sinuses (K)**, where the milk collects. On stimulation by the suckling newborn, milk leaves the lactiferous sinus and enters a **lactiferous duct (L)**. Generally there is one lactiferous duct leading from a lactiferous sinus. The lactiferous duct opens to the exterior at the nipple to complete the process.

It should be noted that the structures described are well developed in nursing women and those in their final months of pregnancy. In nonnursing and nonpregnant women, the system is much less developed. The deposits of fat contribute to the size of the breast.

Pectoralis major muscle	A	○
Lymph vessels and lymph nodes	B	○
Deep fascia	C_1	○
Superficial fascia	C_2	○
Nipple	D	○
Areola	E	○
Cooper's ligaments	F	○
Lobes	G	○
Lobules of mammary gland	H	○
Secondary tubules	I	○
Mammary ducts	J	○
Lactiferous sinus	K	○
Lactiferous duct	L	○

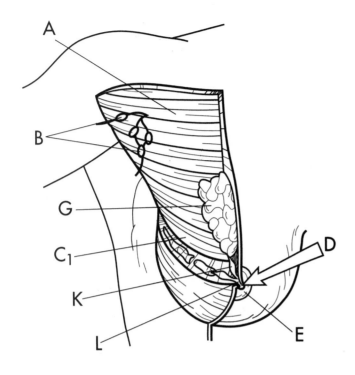

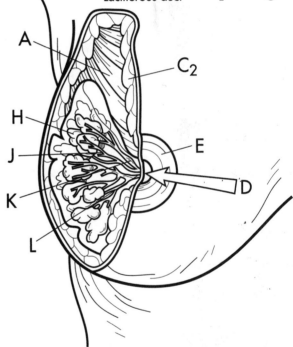

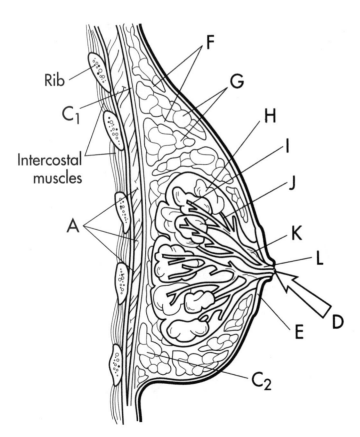

INDEX